Fodor's

VANCOUVER & BRITISH COLUMBIA

5th Edition

**Where to Stay and Eat
for All Budgets**

**Must-See Sights
and Local Secrets**

Ratings You Can Trust

Fodor's Travel Publications   New York, Toronto, London, Sydney, Auckland
www.fodors.com

FODOR'S VANCOUVER & BRITISH COLUMBIA
Editor: Caroline Trefler

Editorial Production: Linda K. Schmidt
Editorial Contributors: Carolyn Heller, Sue Kernaghan, Chris McBeath
Maps: David Lindroth, *cartographer*; Bob Blake and Rebecca Baer, *map editors*
Design: Fabrizio La Rocca, *creative director*; Guido Caroti, *art director*; Moon Sun Kim, *cover designer*; Melanie Marin, *senior picture editor*
Production/Manufacturing: Colleen Ziemba
Cover Photo (West Coast First Nations Native Totem pole and longhouse painting in Victoria, Vancouver Island): Robert Leon/www.robertleon.com

Fifth Edition

ISBN: 1–4000–1601–0

ISBN-13: 978–1–4000–1601–3

ISSN: 1531–3425

SPECIAL SALES
This book is available at special discounts for bulk purchases for sales promotions or premiums. Special editions, including personalized covers, excerpts of existing books, and corporate imprints, can be created in large quantities for special needs. For more information, write to Special Markets/Premium Sales, 1745 Broadway, MD 6-2, New York, New York 10019, or e-mail specialmarkets@randomhouse.com.

AN IMPORTANT TIP & AN INVITATION
Although all prices, opening times, and other details in this book are based on information supplied to us at press time, changes occur all the time in the travel world, and Fodor's cannot accept responsibility for facts that become outdated or for inadvertent errors or omissions. So **always confirm information when it matters,** especially if you're making a detour to visit a specific place. Your experiences—positive and negative—matter to us. If we have missed or misstated something, **please write to us.** We follow up on all suggestions. Contact the Vancouver and British Columbia editor at editors@fodors.com or c/o Fodor's at 1745 Broadway, New York, New York 10019.

PRINTED IN THE UNITED STATES OF AMERICA

10 9 8 7 6 5 4 3 2 1

Be a Fodor's Correspondent

Your opinion matters. It matters to us. It matters to your fellow Fodor's travelers, too. And we'd like to hear it. In fact, we *need* to hear it.

When you share your experiences and opinions, you become an active member of the Fodor's community. That means we'll not only use your feedback to make our books better, but we'll publish your names and comments whenever possible. Throughout our guides, look for "Word of Mouth," excerpts of your unvarnished feedback.

Here's how you can help improve Fodor's for all of us.

Tell us when we're right. We rely on local writers to give you an insider's perspective. But our writers and staff editors—who are the best in the business—depend on you. Your positive feedback is a vote to renew our recommendations for the next edition.

Tell us when we're wrong. We're proud that we update most of our guides every year. But we're not perfect. Things change. Hotels cut services. Museums change hours. Charming cafés lose charm. If our writer didn't quite capture the essence of a place, tell us how you'd do it differently. If any of our descriptions are inaccurate or inadequate, we'll incorporate your changes in the next edition and will correct factual errors at fodors.com *immediately.*

Tell us what to include. You probably have had fantastic travel experiences that aren't yet in Fodor's. Why not share them with a community of like-minded travelers? Maybe you chanced upon a beach or bistro or B&B that you don't want to keep to yourself. Tell us why we should include it. And share your discoveries and experiences with everyone directly at fodors.com. Your input may lead us to add a new listing or highlight a place we cover with a "Highly Recommended" star or with our highest rating, "Fodor's Choice."

Give us your opinion instantly at our feedback center at www.fodors.com/feedback. You may also e-mail editors@fodors.com with the subject line "Vancouver and British Columbia Editor." Or send your nominations, comments, and complaints by mail to Vancouver and British Columbia Editor, Fodor's, 1745 Broadway, New York, NY 10019.

You and travelers like you are the heart of the Fodor's community. Make our community richer by sharing your experiences. Be a Fodor's correspondent.

Happy traveling!

Tim Jarrell, Publisher

CONTENTS

ABOUT THIS BOOK

Our Ratings

Sometimes you find terrific travel experiences and sometimes they just find you. But usually the burden is on you to select the right combination of experiences. That's where our ratings come in.

As travelers we've all discovered a place so wonderful that its worthiness is obvious. And sometimes that place is so unique that superlatives don't do it justice: you just have to be there to know. These sights, properties, and experiences get our highest rating, **Fodor's Choice**, indicated by orange stars throughout this book.

Black stars highlight sights and properties we deem **Highly Recommended**, places that our writers, editors, and readers praise again and again for consistency and excellence.

By default, there's another category: any place we include in this book is by definition worth your time, unless we say otherwise. And we will.

Disagree with any of our choices? Care to nominate a place or suggest that we rate one more highly? Visit our feedback center at www.fodors.com/feedback.

Budget Well

Hotel and restaurant price categories from ¢ to $$$$ are defined in the opening pages of each chapter. For attractions, we always give standard adult admission fees; reductions are usually available for children, students, and senior citizens. Want to pay with plastic? **AE, D, DC, MC, V** following restaurant and hotel listings indicate whether American Express, Discover, Diner's Club, MasterCard, and Visa are accepted.

Restaurants

Unless we state otherwise, restaurants are open for lunch and dinner daily. We mention dress only when there's a specific requirement and reservations only when they're essential or not accepted—it's always best to book ahead.

Hotels

Hotels have private bath, phone, TV, and air-conditioning and operate on the European Plan (aka EP, meaning without meals), unless we specify that they use the Continental Plan (CP, with a continental breakfast), Breakfast Plan (BP, with a full breakfast), or Modified American Plan (MAP, with breakfast and dinner) or are all-inclusive (including all meals and most activities). We always

list facilities but not whether you'll be charged an extra fee to use them, so when pricing accommodations, find out what's included.

Many Listings
★	Fodor's Choice
★	Highly recommended
⊠	Physical address
✢	Directions
⌖	Mailing address
☎	Telephone
🖷	Fax
⊕	On the Web
✍	E-mail
✇	Admission fee
☉	Open/closed times
▶	Start of walk/itinerary
Ⓜ	Metro stations
▭	Credit cards

Hotels & Restaurants
🏨	Hotel
�‹	Number of rooms
♿	Facilities
❑	Meal plans
✕	Restaurant
⌂	Reservations
🏛	Dress code
⟍	Smoking
🍷	BYOB
✕🏨	Hotel with restaurant that warrants a visit

Outdoors
🏌	Golf
⛺	Camping

Other
☺	Family-friendly
🛈	Contact information
⇨	See also
⊠	Branch address
☞	Take note

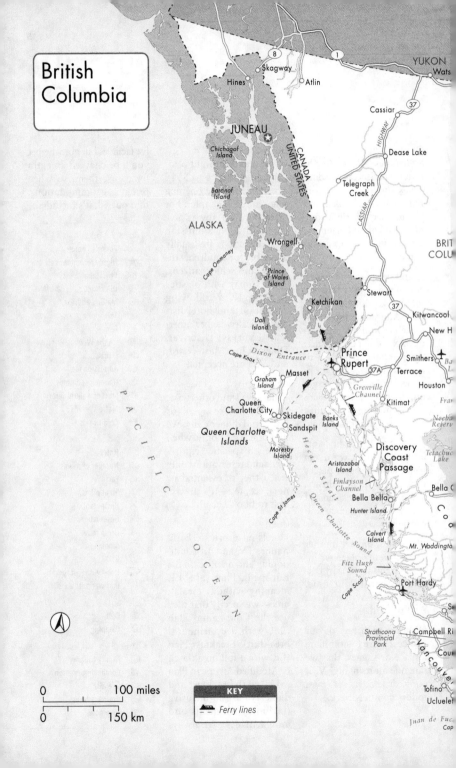

British Columbia

YUKON
Wats

8 Skagway

Hines   Atlin

Cassiar   37

JUNEAU

*Chichagof
Island*

Dease Lake

*Baranof
Island*

Telegraph
Creek

ALASKA

Wrangell

Cape Ommaney

*Prince
of Wales
Island*

Stewart

37   Kitwancool

New H

Ketchikan

*Dall
Island*

Dixon Entrance

Prince
Rupert   37A   Smithers   Ba
L

Terrace   Houston

Cape Knox

Masset   Grenville
Channel   Kitimat   Fra

*Graham
Island*

Queen
Charlotte City   Skidegate
Sandspit   *Banks
Island*   Neobe
Reserv

*Queen Charlotte
Islands*   Discovery
Coast
Passage   *Tetachu
Lake*

*Moresby
Island*   *Aristazabal
Island*   Bella C

*Finlayson
Channel*

Cape St James   Bella Bella

Hunter Island   Co

*Calvert
Island*   Mt. Waddingto

*Fitz Hugh
Sound*

Cape Scott   Port Hardy

P A C I F I C

H e c a t e   S t r a i t

Q u e e n   C h a r l o t t e   S o u n d

Strathcona
Provincial
Park   Campbell Ri

O C E A N   Vancou

Cou

Tofino
Ucluelet

*Juan de Fuca
Cap*

CANADA
UNITED STATES

CASSIAR HIGHWAY

BRIT
COLU

0 —————————— 100 miles
0 —————————— 150 km

KEY
🚢 *Ferry lines*

WHAT'S WHERE

VANCOUVER

One of the most beautifully sited cities in the world, Vancouver is much more than a pretty layover for Alaskan cruises. The Pacific Ocean and the mountains of the North Shore form a dramatic backdrop to the gleaming towers of commerce downtown. Vancouver is a new city when compared to others but one that's rich in culture and diversity. Indeed, it's become a hot destination, so hot, in fact, it's been chosen, with Whistler, to host the 2010 Winter Olympic Games. The arts scene bubbles in summer, when the city stages most of its film, music, and theater festivals. You'll also find opera, ballet, and symphony, as well as plenty of pubs, bars, and nightclubs. The cuisine scene is equally vibrant and diverse. Superb Chinese food and creative Pacific Northwest cooking, long on seafood, are special treats, but other fine ethnic menus also dazzle. For all its culinary and cultural temptations, Vancouver also provides great strolls. One obligatory amble is through **Gastown,** the oldest quarter, now brimming with cafés, shops, and lofts. Adjacent is **Chinatown**—the third largest in North America—site of the Ming Dynasty–style Dr. Sun Yat-Sen Classical Chinese Garden. On **Granville Island,** buskers, art studios, and a bustling public market delight the senses. A half-hour drive west, on the University of British Columbia campus, the Museum of Anthropology serves as a window on civilizations that flourished here long before the British sailed in. A celebrated aquarium and other attractions punctuate nature's work in the trail-laced wilderness of **Stanley Park,** just blocks from the city center. **Kitsilano Beach,** a short hop across English Bay, is as trendy as the neighborhood around it, but nearby are hidden coves where you can contemplate, among other things, how clever you were to vacation in this splendid place.

VICTORIA & VANCOUVER ISLAND

Worth the trip for the ferry ride alone, **Victoria** is a stunner. The capital of British Columbia, it's full of stately Victorian structures such as the Parliament Buildings, outlined at night with thousands of starry lights. Victoria grew up Anglophile but has been reinventing itself as a city of the Pacific Rim, with due regard for its Asian and native heritage. You can still find a proper afternoon tea, but you'll also find the country's oldest and most intact Chinatown and, at the Royal British Columbia Museum, the definitive First Peoples exhibit. Don't miss Beacon Hill Park; it provides spectacular views of the Olympic Mountains and the Strait of Juan de Fuca, as well as a slim chance for baseball fans to get hooked on cricket. North of town, **Butchart Gardens'** 55 glorious acres are a celebration of flowers and garden styles—Japanese, Italian, rose—with summer fireworks and live music. Farther north, the rest of **Vancouver Island** stretches 483 km (300 mi) end to end—North America's largest Pacific coastal island. At **Strathcona Provincial Park,** in the middle of the island, stargazers escape the haze of city lights, as do hikers, canoeists, and campers. Whales and seals are among the sights at the **Pacific Rim National Park Reserve,** but winter storms, symphonic in their grandeur, are the draw for tempest lovers. At the park's northern edge are funky, charming **Tofino** and island-dotted **Clayoquot Sound,** where lodging options include high-end wilderness retreats. What you can't put a price on is the experience, spiritual for many, of the stillness, the clarity of light, the beauty all around.

BRITISH COLUMBIA

British Columbia is clearly a world apart. This sprawling province includes some of the last true wilderness in North America—and the chance to enjoy it from a kayak, sailboat, floatplane, or hiking path before bedding down at a high-style lodge or a back-to-nature campsite. In the Lower Mainland, in and around Vancouver, British Columbia appears to be a brash young province with a population that sees its future on the Pacific Rim. Paradoxically, in the north are ancient rain forests, untamed wilderness, and First Nations peoples who have lived on the land for more than 10,000 years. A short drive from Vancouver is Brackendale Eagles Park, where thousands of bald eagles gather in winter, and the superb runs at Whistler, where residents are preparing to host the 2010 Winter Olympics. At the massive Garibaldi Provincial Park, hiking is just one of a slew of options for outdoors enthusiasts. Eastward lie the vineyards and orchards of the Okanagan Valley, where the tastings can be many and a driver should be designated at breakfast. In the lovely Haida Gwaii, or Queen Charlotte Islands, native Haida culture is undergoing a renaissance. Kayakers love these waterways. If you'd rather not paddle, let a ferry take you through the enchanted Inside Passage to the funky seaport of Prince Rupert. Explore a few of the Gulf Islands (there are hundreds, each with its own personality), or head north to the Cariboo for living history and a Wild West flavor. Those with the time and a taste for adventure could head even farther north, to the wildlife-rich wilderness that stretches to the Yukon border and on to Alaska. Plan well: this is big country. You can't do it all in one go, which gives you a fine reason to return.

GREAT ITINERARIES

THE GOLD RUSH TRAIL & INSIDE PASSAGE
7 TO 15 DAYS

In the mid-19th century, rumors of gold in the province tempted thousands of men and women to risk their lives on an arduous journey north. These days, though the traveling is easier, much of the landscape is unchanged. You also have the option of a return trip by sea along the fjord-cut wilderness of the north coast. This itinerary follows B.C.'s Heritage Discovery Circle Route; watch for blue-and-gold signs along the highways.

Fraser Canyon

1 day. From Vancouver the Trans-Canada Highway follows the route tracked by the early prospectors along the Fraser River and into the deep gorge of the Fraser Canyon. At Hell's Gate, the river's narrowest and deepest point, you can cross the churning waters by cable car. ⇨ *Coast Mountain Circle in Chapter 3.*

The Cariboo

1 to 3 days. From the town of Cache Creek, Highway 97 heads north through the ranchland of the Cariboo region, where more than a few Hollywood westerns have been filmed. You can stop at a dude ranch or spa for a break. ⇨ *The Cariboo-Chilcotin in Chapter 3.*

Barkerville

1 or 2 days. Once the largest town north of San Francisco and west of Chicago, Barkerville was the hub of B.C.'s gold rush. It's now a living museum where stagecoaches roll through town and actors play the townsfolk. ⇨ *The Cariboo-Chilcotin in Chapter 3.*

Yellowhead Highway

2 to 5 days. You can spot eagles, deer, and possibly bears as you follow Highway 16 west of Prince George, through the forest to the coast. Several historic sites make worthwhile detours, including the restored Hudson's Bay trading post at Fort St. James National Historic Site; the 'Ksan Historical Village, a First Nations site near Hazelton; the North Pacific Historic Fishing Village, south of Prince Rupert; and the excellent collection of First Nations artifacts at Prince Rupert's Museum of Northern British Columbia. ⇨ *Northern British Columbia in Chapter 3.*

Inside Passage

1 day. The roadless fjord-cut coast of B.C.'s northwest is among the last true wilderness areas in North America. One of the easiest ways to see it is from the deck of BC Ferries' *Queen of the North,* which hugs the misty coastline from Prince Rupert to Port Hardy, on the northern tip of Vancouver Island. ⇨ *North Coast in Chapter 3.*

LASKA
.S.A.)

Prince Rupert

North Pacific Historic
Fishing Village

Hazelton

Prince
George

Yellowhead
Highway

Quesnel

Barkerville

ALBERTA

Inside
Passage

BRITISH COLUMBIA

The Cariboo
Region

Cache
Creek

Pacific Ocean

Port Hardy

Telegraph
Cove

Campbell River

Hell's Gate

Fraser
Canyon

VANCOUVER
ISLAND

Nanaimo

Vancouver

Victoria

U.S.A.

Vancouver Island

1 to 3 days. Explore the northern reaches of this forested island, visit the stilt village of Telegraph Cove, see the whales in Johnstone Strait, fish for salmon in Campbell River, or hike or canoe in Strathcona Provincial Park. A ferry from Nanaimo or Victoria gets you back to the mainland. ⇨ *Vancouver Island in Chapter 2.*

By Public Transportation

This route can be traveled without a car, using a combination of buses, trains, and ferries. You'll need to contact a private tour company if you want to include a side trip to Barkerville, though. Greyhound Line buses travel from Vancouver to Prince George (consider an overnight stop en route). From Prince George, VIA Rail's Skeena line travels to Prince Rupert, where you can catch the ferry that travels along the Inside Passage (it's a 15-hour trip to Port Hardy). From Port Hardy you can get a bus to Nanaimo or Victoria and another ferry back to Vancouver.

GREAT ITINERARIES

HIGHLIGHTS OF BRITISH COLUMBIA
7 TO 11 DAYS

Larger than many countries, British Columbia can be daunting for its size alone. Fortunately, some of its best mountain, ocean, and island scenery lies within easy driving—and sailing—distance of Vancouver. After a few days of exploring the city, head north into the mountains.

Whistler

1 or 2 days. The Sea to Sky Highway hugs fjordlike Howe Sound before veering into the Coast Mountains toward Whistler, arguably the best ski resort on the continent. In warm weather you can golf, raft, bike, or hike in the surrounding wilds or shop, dine, and celebrity-spot in the pedestrian-only alpine village. ⇨ *Coast Mountain Circle in Chapter 3.*

Pacific Rim National Park Preserve

2 or 3 days. You need a full day to get here from Whistler, including the ferry crossing from Horseshoe Bay to Vancouver Island (arrive at the ferry terminal an hour before sailing time for Nanaimo, even if you have a reservation). It's worth it, though, to see the crashing Pacific surf and old-growth forest on British Columbia's wild west coast. Stay a day or two to go whale-watching, visit Hot Springs Cove, hike in the temperate rain forest, or beachcomb along the 16-km (10-mi) stretch of sand at Long Beach. The villages of Tofino and Ucluelet, which bracket the park, have several of the province's best oceanfront lodges. ⇨ *Vancouver Island in Chapter 2.*

Victoria

2 or 3 days. The British Empire may not have tamed the wilderness, but it certainly made its mark on Victoria, British Columbia's flower-draped 19th-century capital. You can stop in for a formal afternoon tea at the ivy-covered Fairmont Empress Hotel and stroll through Butchart Gardens. Don't miss the excellent historical and First Nations artifacts at the Royal British Columbia Museum. ⇨ *Victoria in Chapter 2.*

Southern Gulf Islands

2 or 3 days. From Swartz Bay, the bucolic islands of Salt Spring, Mayne, Pender, and Galiano are a ferry ride away (35 minutes to Salt Spring, 40 minutes to three hours to the others). Salt Spring is known for its galleries, Saturday market, and artisans' studios, though rustic country inns, seaside pubs, and white-shell beaches are common to all. ⇨ *The Gulf Islands in Chapter 3.*

By Public Transportation

Though it takes some planning, this tour can be done by public transportation. Buses link all the towns and ferry terminals, and floatplanes serve the coastal and island villages. The Gulf Islands don't have public transportation, though they do have taxi service, and Salt Spring also has a ferry shuttle.

WHEN TO GO

°F VANCOUVER °C

Most travelers visit British Columbia between June and September, when the sun shines and the wilderness is at its most accessible. The cities—Vancouver and Victoria—are perhaps most enjoyable in the shoulder seasons: May and June, September and October, when the weather is still mild and the crowds thin. December to April brings snow to the interior ski resorts, but on the coast, the winter months mean rain and dramatic winter storms. Spring brings the wine festival in the Okanagan and the Whale Festival on the west coast of Vancouver Island.

Climate

The following are average daily maximum and minimum temperatures in Vancouver.

Forecasts **Weather Channel Connection** ☎ 900/932-8437 95¢ per minute from a Touch-Tone phone ⊕ www.weather.com.

ON THE CALENDAR

	There's always something going on in Vancouver and British Columbia, but residents look forward to a few with extra anticipation. If you want your visit to coincide with one of these occasions, be sure to plan well in advance.
ONGOING	For festivals in British Columbia, check out ⊕ www.festivalseeker.com.
WINTER Dec.	**Skiing competitions** take place at most alpine ski resorts throughout British Columbia (through February). The **Carol Ships** ⊕ www.carolships.org boats full of carolers and decorated with colored lights, ply Vancouver harbor each night for the first three weeks of December.
Jan.	The annual **Icewine Festival at Sun Peaks** is held in alpine Sun Peaks Resort, near Kamloops. The event showcases British Columbian ice wine, a sweet wine made from grapes frozen on the vine. At the **Polar Bear Swims** on New Year's Day in Vancouver, Victoria, and many smaller communities throughout the province, locals mark the new year by plunging into the icy ocean waters.
Feb.	**Chinese New Year** festivities in Vancouver and Victoria's Chinatown include dragon parades.
Late Feb.– early Mar.	The **Vancouver Playhouse International Wine Festival** ☎ 604/872–6622 ⊕ www.playhousewinefest.com, one of North America's longest-running wine festivals, attracts more than 100 wineries from around the world.
Mar.	The **Pacific Rim Whale Festival** ☎ 250/726–7742 ⊕ www.island.net/~whalef on Vancouver Island celebrates the spring migration of gray whales with whale-watching tours and more than 70 events, from art shows to chowder cook-offs. More than 100 international wineries converge on the capital for the **Victoria Festival of Wine** ⊕ www.victoriafestivalofwine.com.
SPRING May	The **Vancouver International Children's Festival** ☎ 604/708–5655 ⊕ www.vancouverchildrensfestival.com, said to be the largest event of its kind in the world, presents dozens of open-air stage performances in mime, puppetry, music, and theater. **Swiftsure International** draws competitors from around the world to Victoria for the region's leading long-distance yacht race and a shoreside festival. ⊕ www.swiftsure.org.

Late May	**Victoria Day,** on the second-to-last weekend in May, is a holiday throughout Canada, but Victoria celebrates in earnest, with picnics and a parade.
SUMMER June	Vancouver's **Alcan Dragon Boat Festival** ☏ 604/688–2382 ⊕ www. adbf.com hosts races between long, slender boats decorated with huge dragon heads, an event based on a Chinese "awakening the dragons" ritual. The festival also includes community and children's activities, dance performances, and arts exhibits. The **Vancouver International Jazz Festival** ☏ 604/872–5200 ⊕ www.coastaljazz.ca, in late June, celebrates a broad spectrum of jazz, blues, and related improvised music, with more than 200 performances in venues around Vancouver.
June–Sept.	**Bard on the Beach** ☏ 604/739–0559 or 877/739–0559 ⊕ www. bardonthebeach.org is a series of Shakespearean plays performed under two seaside tents at Vancouver's Vanier Park. **Whistler Summer Festivals** present street entertainment and a variety of music at Whistler Resort ☏ 800/944–7853 ⊕ www.mywhistler.com.
July 1	**Canada Day** inspires celebrations around the province in honor of Canada's birthday. In Vancouver, Canada Place and Granville Island both host an entire day of free outdoor entertainment.
July	People travel from all over Canada to attend the **Vancouver Folk Music Festival** ☏ 604/602–9798 or 800/985–8363 ⊕ www.thefestival.bc. ca, held in Vancouver on the third weekend in July. The **Tour de Gastown** ☏ 604/836–9993 ⊕ www.tourdegastown.com brings elite cycle racers to the cobblestone streets of Vancouver's Gastown. The nine-day **ICA Folkfest** ☏ 250/388–4728 ⊕ www.icafolkfest. com, western Canada's largest multicultural event, brings an international celebration of music, dance, food, and art to Victoria's Inner Harbour.
Late July–early Aug.	In Vancouver the **HSBC Celebration of Light** ⊕ www.celebration-of-light.com, an international musical fireworks competition, blasts off over four evenings from a barge in English Bay. The **Vancouver International Comedy Festival** ☏ 604/683–0883 ⊕ www.comedyfest. com presents all manner of silliness in Downtown Vancouver. The **Squamish Days Logger Sports** ☏ 604/892–9244 ⊕ www.squamishdays. org is a five-day event that draws loggers from around the world to compete in tree climbing, ax throwing, speed chopping, and birling (log rolling).

ON THE CALENDAR

Aug.	**Festival Vancouver** ☎ 604/688–1152 ⊕ www.festivalvancouver. bc.ca, one of North America's largest musical events, stages orchestral, chamber, choral, world, and early music as well as opera and jazz performances.
FALL Late Sept.– early Oct.	The **Vancouver International Film Festival** ☎ 604/685–0260 ⊕ www. viff.org showcases lesser-known international filmmakers.
Oct.	The Annual **Okanagan Fall Wine Festival** ☎ 250/861–6654 ⊕ www. thewinefestivals.com takes place over 10 days, with more than 165 events. There's also an annual wine festival in spring and summer. Pop and highbrow authors read, sign books, and speak at the **Vancouver International Writers and Readers Festival** ☎ 604/681–6330 ⊕ www.writersfest.bc.ca.
Nov.	Winemakers, restaurateurs, and food lovers gather for tastings and seminars at **Cornucopia** ☎ 800/944–7853 ⊕ www.whistlercornucopia. com, Whistler's annual food-and-wine celebration.

PLEASURES & PASTIMES

First Nations Culture

Before the arrival of Europeans, the lush landscapes of the Pacific Northwest gave rise to one of the continent's richest and most artistically prolific cultures. Along with numerous museums, attractions and cultural centers—such as the re-created villages at 'Ksan, near Hazelton, at Secwepemc in Kamloops, and at Quw'utsun Cultural Centre on Vancouver Island—share this living culture through music, dance, and food. Although the Museum of Anthropology in Vancouver and the Royal British Columbia Museum in Victoria have renowned collections of Northwest Coast First Nations art, smaller museums in northern and coastal communities are also building world-class collections as artifacts are gradually repatriated to their communities of origin.

Food & Wine

Although British Columbian cuisine is not easily definable, all the ingredients are there: a rich bounty from the land and sea (oysters, salmon, organic produce, game, lamb, and forest-foraged mushrooms); a multicultural population bringing culinary influences from every corner of the world; and such a passion for fresh, local, organic foods that small-scale farming is actually on the increase here. A food-and-wine tour of B.C. could start in Vancouver, with its vast selection of excellent restaurants and refreshingly low prices. Then take in a visit to some small-scale wineries and country inns on southern Vancouver Island and the Gulf Islands, and finish up with a tour of the Okanagan Wine Country, where about 60 wineries produce chardonnay, riesling, gewürztraminer, and more in a scenic lakeside setting.

Skiing

British Columbia has some of the best, and least expensive, skiing in the world. Whistler Resort is not only known internationally for its long runs, wealth of activities, and high-end après scene, but it also will host the 2010 Winter Olympics. Inland, though, such smaller resorts as Big White, Silver Star, and Sun Peaks have all the facilities, with fluffier powder and a more family-friendly, laid-back ambience.

Outdoor Activities

Whether it's kayaking among the transparent waters of the Broken Group Islands, hiking through the old-growth forest of the West Coast Trail, or paddling across a northern lake, British Columbia has plenty of opportunity for outdoor adventure. For a gentler introduction to the wilds, deserted beaches, forest trails, and mountain lakes are easily reached from the cities, and a network of campsites, wilderness lodges, floatplanes, and outdoor outfitters provides access to the untouched corners of the province.

FODOR'S
CHOICE

The sights, restaurants, hotels, and other travel experiences on these pages are our editors' top picks—our Fodor's Choices. They're the best of their type in the area covered by the book—not to be missed and always worth your time. In the destination chapters that follow, you can find all the details.

LODGING $$$$	**The Aerie,** Victoria. Eagle's-eye views over outlying islands are an inspiring draw at this Mediterranean-style villa, north of Victoria. Dinners here rely almost exclusively on local ingredients and make a superb introduction to British Columbian cuisine.
$$$$	**Delta Victoria Queen Pointe Resort and Spa,** Victoria. Romantic waterfront views highlight this property, which also provides a resort's worth of facilities and spacious rooms and suites.
$$$$	**Fairmont Château Whistler Resort,** Whistler. This family-friendly fortress is a self-contained, ski-in, ski-out resort-within-a-resort, with its own shopping arcade, an impressive spa with exotic Asian and ayurvedic treatments, and rooms with mountain views.
$$$$	**Pan Pacific Hotel,** Vancouver. A centerpiece of the Canada Place complex, the luxurious Pan Pacific has a dramatic three-story atrium lobby and expansive views of the harbor and mountains.
$$$$	**Sooke Harbour House,** Sooke. West of Victoria, this airy oceanfront inn looks like the home of a discerning but casual art collector. The restaurant is one of Canada's finest.
$$$$	**Wedgwood Hotel,** Vancouver. This intimate antiques- and art-filled Vancouver boutique hotel is run by an owner who cares fervently about her guests.
$$$$	**The Wickaninnish Inn,** Tofino. On a rocky promontory above Chesterman Beach, sits this cedar-sided inn where every room overlooks the ocean, including the glass-enclosed Pointe Restaurant.
$$–$$$	**Desolation Resort,** Lund. Tree-houselike chalets with large decks and big picture windows perch high above Okeover Arm at this isolated retreat 10 minutes from Lund.
$–$$	**The Victorian Hotel,** Vancouver. This beautiful European-style pension is perfect for those on a budget but looking for some of the finer touches.
RESTAURANTS $$$$	**Hastings House,** Salt Spring Island. Inside this regal Tudor-style manor, five-course prix-fixe dinners are served, which include local lamb, seafood, and herbs and produce from the inn's gardens.

$$$$	**Lumière**, Vancouver. Creative takes on French cuisine, using regionally sourced organic, shine in chef Robert Feenie's multicourse tasting menus.
$$$–$$$$	**C Restaurant**, Vancouver. The name and decor are minimalist, but the innovative seafood and the stunning location overlooking False Creek make this one of Vancouver's most exciting restaurants.
$$$–$$$$	**Empress Room**, Victoria. Inside the Fairmont Empress hotel's flagship restaurant, a French-influenced Pacific Northwest menu is served beneath beneath a carved mahogany ceiling.
$$–$$$$	**Il Terrazzo**, Victoria. With charming redbrick terrace tucked away off Waddington Alley near Market Square and inventive Italian cuisine, this trattoria is a local favorite for romantic alfresco dining.
$$–$$$	**All Seasons Cafe**, Nelson. Tucked into an alley, this former family cottage creates a contemporary, seasonally changing menu that uses fresh, local ingredients.
$$–$$$	**Liliget Feast House**, Vancouver. Near English Bay is one of the few restaurants in the world where you can have original Northwest Coast First Nations cuisine. The longhouse setting is intimate.
$$–$$$	**Mahle House**, Nanaimo. Innovative Pacific Northwest cuisine is served at this cozy 1904 farmhouse.
¢–$	**Bin 941**, Vancouver. Part tapas restaurant, part up-tempo bar, this bustling, vibrant hole-in-the-wall serves some of the best snack-size cuisine in town.
MARKETS	**Granville Island**, Vancouver. This small sandbar was a derelict factory district, but its industrial buildings and tin sheds, painted in primary colors, now house restaurants, a public market, marine activities, and artists' studios.
MUSEUMS	**Haida Gwaii Museum at Qay'llnagaay**, Skidegate. Haida masks, totem poles, works by contemporary Haida artists, carvings of silver and argillite (soft black slate), and other artifacts are on display at this Queen Charlotte Islands longhouse museum overlooking the ocean.
	Museum of Anthropology, Vancouver. The city's most spectacular museum displays aboriginal art from the Pacific Northwest and around the world—dramatic totem poles and canoes; exquisite carvings of gold, silver, and argillite; and masks, tools, and textiles from many cultures.

FODOR'S CHOICE

	Royal British Columbia Museum, Victoria. An authentic longhouse, a simulated submarine ride, a complete frontier town, and one of the province's leading collections of First Nations artifacts help trace several thousand years of British Columbian history at this impressive museum.
PARKS & GARDENS	**Butchart Gardens**, Victoria. The stunning gardens here exhibit more than 700 varieties of flowers.
	Dr. Sun Yat-Sen Classical Chinese Garden, Vancouver. The first authentic Ming Dynasty–style garden outside of China incorporates symbolism and design elements from centuries-old Chinese gardens.
	Pacific Rim National Park Reserve, Vancouver Island. This park on Canada's far west coast has a 16-km- (10-mi-) long white-sand beach, a group of islands, and a demanding hiking trail with panoramic views of the sea and the rain forest.
	Stanley Park, Vancouver. An afternoon in this 1,000-acre wilderness park blocks from downtown can include beaches, the ocean, the harbor, Douglas fir and cedar forests, children's attractions and sculptures, and a good look at the North Shore mountains.
TOWNS & VILLAGES	**Barkerville Historic Town**, Barkerville. Experience a piece of B.C. history at this historic village, composed of original and recreated buildings, where actors in period costume, stagecoach rides, and live musical revues capture the town's heyday.
	Whistler. At the base of the Whistler and Blackcomb mountains, which holds the two longest vertical ski drops on the continent, this ski-in, ski-out village has enough shops, restaurants, nightlife, and other activities that it's easy to fill a vacation without ever hitting the slopes.

SMART TRAVEL TIPS

Finding out about your destination before you leave home means you won't spend time organizing everyday minutiae once you've arrived. You'll be more streetwise when you hit the ground as well, better prepared to explore the aspects of Vancouver and British Columbia that drew you here in the first place. The organizations in this section can provide information to supplement this guide; contact them for up-to-the-minute details, and consult the A to Z sections that end each chapter for facts on the various topics as they relate to Vancouver and British Columbia. Happy landings!

AIR TRAVEL

BOOKING

When you book, look for nonstop flights and remember that "direct" flights stop at least once. Try to avoid connecting flights, which require a change of plane. Two airlines may operate a connecting flight jointly, so ask whether your airline operates every segment of the trip; you may find that the carrier you prefer flies you only part of the way. To find more booking tips and to check prices and make online flight reservations, log on to www.fodors.com.

CARRIERS

When flying internationally, you must usually choose between a domestic carrier, the national flag carrier of the country you are visiting, and a foreign carrier from a third country. National flag carriers have the greatest number of nonstops. Domestic carriers may have better connections to your hometown and serve a greater number of gateway cities. Third-party carriers may have a price advantage.

Of the U.S. airlines, American, Continental, Delta, Northwest, and United fly to Vancouver. Among smaller carriers, Horizon Air (an affiliate of Alaska Airlines) flies to Vancouver and Victoria from many western U.S. cities. From the United Kingdom, Air Canada and British Airways fly to Vancouver. Canadian charter line Air Transat flies to Vancouver, usually at lower rates than the other airlines offer.

Within Canada, regularly scheduled flights to every major city and to most smaller cities are available on Air Canada. Air Canada's regional carrier, Air Canada Jazz, flies to most major towns in B.C. WestJet and CanJet are regional carriers serving most Canadian cities. Within B.C., WestJet flies to Vancouver, Victoria, Abbotsford, Comox, Kelowna, and Prince George.

For more information on flights within British Columbia, *see* the A to Z sections in each chapter.

For regulations and for the locations of air bases that allow private flights, check with regional tourist agencies for carriers and with the Transport Canada Centre in Vancouver. Private pilots should obtain information from Nav Canada, which has the "Canada Flight Supplement" (lists of airports with Canada Customs services) as well as aeronautical charts.

🛪 Major Airlines **Air Canada** ☎ 888/247-2262 ⊕ www.aircanada.ca. **American** ☎ 800/433-7300 ⊕ www.aa.com. **Continental** ☎ 800/525-0280 ⊕ www.continental.com. **Delta** ☎ 800/241-4141 ⊕ www.delta.com. **Northwest** ☎ 800/225-2525 ⊕ www.nwa.com. **United** ☎ 800/241-6522 ⊕ www.united.com.

🛪 Smaller Airlines **Horizon Air** ☎ 800/547-9308 ⊕ http://horizonair.alaskaair.com.

🛪 From Australia & New Zealand **Air Canada** ☎ 8248-5757 in Sydney, 1300/655-767 elsewhere in Australia, 09/969-7470 or 0508/747-767 in New Zealand ⊕ www.aircanada.com.au. **Air New Zealand** ☎ 800/663-5494 in Vancouver, 0800/737-000 in Auckland ⊕ www.airnz.com. **Qantas** ☎ 800/227-4500 in North America, 13-13-13 in Australia ⊕ www.qantas.com.au.

🛪 From the U.K. **Air Canada** ☎ 0871/220-1111 in U.K., 888/247-2262 in Canada ⊕ www.aircanada.com. **Air Transat** ☎ 8705/561-522 in U.K., 877/872-6728 in Canada ⊕ www.airtransat.com. **British Airways** ☎ 0870/850-9850 in U.K., 800/247-9297 in Canada ⊕ www.britishairways.com.

🛪 Within Canada **Air Canada** ☎ 888/247-2262 ⊕ www.aircanada.ca. **Air Canada Jazz** ☎ 888/247-2262 ⊕ www.flyjazz.ca. **CanJet** ☎ 800/809-7777 ⊕ www.canjet.com. **WestJet Airlines** ☎ 800/538-5696 ⊕ www.westjet.com.

🛪 Contacts for Private Pilots **Nav Canada** ✉ 77 Metcalfe St., Box 3411, Station D, Ottawa, ON K1P 5L6

☎ 800/876-4693 ⊕ aero.nrcan.gc.ca. **Transport Canada** ⊕ www.tc.gc.ca.

CHECK-IN & BOARDING

Always **find out your carrier's check-in policy.** Plan to arrive at the airport about two hours before your scheduled departure time for domestic flights and 2½ to 3 hours before international flights. You may need to arrive earlier if you're flying from one of the busier airports or during peak air-traffic times. To avoid delays at airport-security checkpoints, try not to wear any metal. Jewelry, belt and other buckles, steel-toe shoes, barrettes, and underwire bras are among the items that can set off detectors.

Assuming that not everyone with a ticket will show up, airlines routinely overbook planes. When everyone does, airlines ask for volunteers to give up their seats. In return, these volunteers usually get a several-hundred-dollar flight voucher, which can be used toward the purchase of another ticket, and are rebooked on the next available flight out. If there are not enough volunteers, the airline must choose who will be denied boarding. The first to get bumped are passengers who checked in late and those flying on discounted tickets, so get to the gate and check in as early as possible, especially during peak periods.

Always **bring a government-issued photo ID** to the airport; even when it's not required, a passport is best.

Security measures at Canadian airports are similar to those in the United States. Be sure you're not carrying anything that could be construed as a weapon: a letter opener, Swiss Army knife, or a toy weapon, for example.

Passengers departing from Vancouver must pay an airport-improvement fee before they can board their plane. The fee is C$5 for flights within British Columbia and the Yukon, C$15 for all other flights. Cash and credit cards are accepted.

CUTTING COSTS

The least expensive airfares to Canada are often priced for round-trip travel and must usually be purchased in advance. Airlines generally allow you to change your return date for a fee; most low-fare tickets, however, are nonrefundable. It's smart to call a number of airlines and check the Internet; when you are quoted a good price, book it on the spot—the same fare may not be available the next day, or even the next hour. Always check different routings and look into using alternate airports. Also, price off-peak flights and red-eye, which may be significantly less expensive than others. Travel agents, especially low-fare specialists (⇨ Discounts & Deals), are helpful.

Consolidators are another good source. They buy tickets for scheduled flights at reduced rates from the airlines, then sell them at prices that beat the best fare available directly from the airlines. (Many also offer reduced car-rental and hotel rates.) Sometimes you can even get your money back if you need to return the ticket. Carefully read the fine print detailing penalties for changes and cancellations, purchase the ticket with a credit card, and confirm your consolidator reservation with the airline.

🔁 Consolidators **AirlineConsolidator.com** ☎ 888/468-5385 ⊕ www.airlineconsolidator.com; for international tickets. **Best Fares** ☎ 800/880-1234 ⊕ www.bestfares.com; $59.90 annual membership. **Cheap Tickets** ☎ 800/377-1000 or 800/652-4327 ⊕ www.cheaptickets.com. **Expedia** ☎ 800/397-3342 or 404/728-8787 ⊕ www.expedia.com. **Hotwire** ☎ 866/468-9473 or 920/330-9418 ⊕ www.hotwire.com. **Now, Voyager** ☎ 212/459-1616 ⊕ www.nowvoyager.com. **Onetravel.com** ⊕ www.onetravel.com. **Orbitz** ☎ 888/656-4546 ⊕ www.orbitz.com. **Priceline.com** ⊕ www.priceline.com. **Travelocity** ☎ 888/709-5983, 877/282-2925 in Canada, 0870/111-7061 in U.K. ⊕ www.travelocity.com.

🔁 Courier Resources **Air Courier Association/Cheaptrips.com** ☎ 800/211-5119 ⊕ www.aircourier.org or www.cheaptrips.com; $20 annual membership. **Davis Travel Services** ⊕ www.couriertravel.org; $40 lifetime membership. **International Association of Air Travel Couriers** ✉ Box 1832 Ames IA 50010 ☎ 515/292-2458 🖷 515/292-2157 ⊕ www.courier.org; $45 annual membership.

ENJOYING THE FLIGHT

State your seat preference when purchasing your ticket, and then repeat it when you confirm and when you check in. For more legroom, you can request one of the few emergency-aisle seats at check-in, if you're capable of moving obstacles comparable in weight to an airplane exit door (usually between 35 pounds and 60 pounds)—a Federal Aviation Administration requirement of passengers in these seats. Seats behind a bulkhead also offer more legroom, but they don't have underseat storage. Don't sit in the row in front of the emergency aisle or in front of a bulkhead, where seats may not recline. SeatGuru.com has more information about specific seat configurations, which vary by aircraft.

Ask the airline whether a snack or meal is served on the flight. If you have dietary concerns, request special meals when booking. These can be vegetarian, low-cholesterol, or kosher, for example. It's a good idea to pack some healthful snacks and a small (plastic) bottle of water in your carry-on bag. On long flights, try to maintain a normal routine, to help fight jet lag. At night, get some sleep. By day, eat light meals, drink water (not alcohol), and **move around the cabin** to stretch your legs. For additional jet-lag tips consult *Fodor's FYI: Travel Fit & Healthy* (available at bookstores everywhere).

Smoking policies vary from carrier to carrier. Most airlines prohibit smoking on all of their flights; others allow smoking only on certain routes or certain departures. Ask your carrier about its policy. None of the major airlines or charter lines permit smoking, and all Canadian carriers ban smoking.

FLYING TIMES

Flying time to Vancouver is 5½ hours from New York, 6½ hours from Montréal, 4 hours from Chicago, and 2½ hours from Los Angeles.

HOW TO COMPLAIN

If your baggage goes astray or your flight goes awry, complain right away. Most carriers require that you **file a claim immediately.** The Aviation Consumer Protection Division of the Department of Transportation publishes *Fly-Rights*, which discusses airlines and consumer issues and is available online. You can also find articles and information on mytravelrights.com, the Web site of the nonprofit Consumer Travel Rights Center.

⚑ Airline Complaints **Aviation Consumer Protection Division** ✉ U.S. Department of Transportation, Office of Aviation Enforcement and Proceedings, C-75, Room 4107, 400 7th St. SW, Washington, DC 20590 ☎ 202/366-2220 ⊕ airconsumer.ost.dot.gov. **Federal Aviation Administration Consumer Protection Hotline** ✉ For inquiries: FAA, 800 Independence Ave. SW, Washington, DC 20591 ☎ 800/322-7873 ⊕ www.faa.gov.

RECONFIRMING

Check the status of your flight before you leave for the airport. You can do this on your carrier's Web site, by linking to a flight-status checker (many Web-booking services offer these), or by calling your carrier or travel agent. Always confirm international flights at least 72 hours ahead of the scheduled departure time.

AIRPORTS

The major airport is Vancouver International Airport (YVR). For information on regional airports, *see* the A to Z sections in each chapter.

⚑ Airport Information **Vancouver International Airport** ✉ Grant McConachie Way, Richmond ☎ 604/207-7077 ⊕ www.yvr.ca.

BIKE TRAVEL

Despite British Columbia's demanding landscape, bicycle travel is very popular. One of the most spectacular routes follows the abandoned 600-km-long (370-mi-long) Kettle Valley Railway through the mountains of the B.C. interior. Although the whole trail is no longer passable after a fire destroyed several trestles in 2003, large sections are still open. Tourism Kelowna has details. Gentler options include the 100-km (62-mi) Galloping Goose Regional Trail near Victoria and the rolling hills of the Gulf Islands. Cycle Vancouver Island has information about bike touring on Vancouver Island and the Gulf Islands.

⚑ Bike Maps **Cycle Vancouver Island** ☎ 250/888-2456 ⊕ www.cyclevancouverisland.ca. **Galloping Goose Regional Trail** ☎ 250/478-3344

⊕ www.crd.bc.ca/parks. **Tourism Kelowna** ☎ 250/861-1515 or 800/663-4345 ⊕ tourismkelowna.com.

BIKES IN FLIGHT

Most airlines accommodate bikes as luggage, provided they are dismantled and boxed; check with individual airlines about packing requirements. Some airlines sell bike boxes, which are often free at bike shops, for about $20 (bike bags can be considerably more expensive). International travelers often can substitute a bike for a piece of checked luggage at no charge; otherwise, the cost is about $100. Most U.S. and Canadian airlines charge $40–$80 each way.

BOAT & FERRY TRAVEL

Ferries play a central role in British Columbia's transportation network. In some areas, ferries provide the only access (besides floatplanes) into and out of communities. For visitors, ferries are one of the best ways to get a feel for the region and its ties to the sea. The British Columbia (BC) Ferry Corporation operates one of the largest ferry fleets in the world, serving about 40 ports of call on B.C.'s west coast. The ferries carry all vehicles as well as bicycles and foot passengers.

Reservations are required for vehicles on BC Ferries' Inside Passage and Queen Charlotte Island services; they are optional on services between Vancouver and Vancouver Island and on most sailings between Vancouver and the Southern Gulf Islands. Most other services do not accept reservations and load vehicles on a first-come, first-served basis.

Other companies operate ferries between the state of Washington and British Columbia's Vancouver Island, and coastal freighters take passengers and supplies to remote Vancouver Island outports. The Ministry of Highways operates several lake-crossing ferries in the Kootenays region. Foot-passenger ferries are also handy ways to get around Vancouver and Victoria. For additional information about regional ferry service, *see* individual chapters.

FARES & SCHEDULES

Payments and reservations are accepted in advance via phone or the Internet on reservable routes; for other routes, you must purchase tickets at the terminal before sailing time. BC Ferries accepts cash and traveler's checks in Canadian and U.S. funds at all of its terminals; American Express, MasterCard, and Visa are accepted at all but the smallest terminals. Direct debit or Interac payments are not accepted. Always check with BC Ferries before traveling; check-in times vary by route and season.

⚓ Boat & Ferry Information British Columbia (BC) Ferry Corporation ⊠ 1112 Fort St., Victoria, BC V8V 4V2 ☎ 250/386-3431, 888/223-3779 in Alberta, Washington State, and British Columbia outside Victoria ⊕ www.bcferries.com.

BUSINESS HOURS

BANKS & OFFICES

Most banks in British Columbia are open Monday–Thursday 10–3 and Friday 10–5 or 6. Some banks are open longer hours and also on Saturday morning. All banks are closed on national holidays. Most banks (and some gas stations and convenience stores) have automatic teller machines (ATMs) that are accessible around the clock. Many small islands and rural areas, however, do not have ATMs.

MUSEUMS & SIGHTS

Hours at museums vary, but most open at 10 or 11 and close in the evening. Some smaller museums close for lunch. Many museums are closed on Monday; some make up for it by staying open late on Wednesday or Thursday, often waiving admission.

SHOPS

Stores in B.C. are usually open Monday–Saturday 9–6. Shops in the major cities and in areas frequented by tourists are usually open Sunday as well. Stores often stay open Thursday and Friday evenings, most shopping malls until 9 PM. Many supermarkets are open 7:30 AM– 9 PM, and some food and convenience stores in Vancouver are open 24 hours.

BUS TRAVEL

Greyhound serves most towns in the province and provides frequent service on popular runs. Gray Line of Victoria oper-

ates bus service to most towns on Vancouver Island, Malaspina Coach Lines provides service from Vancouver and Vancouver International Airport to towns on the Sunshine Coast, and Pacific Coach Lines operates frequent service between Victoria and Vancouver on BC Ferries. The Tofino Bus offers daily service from Victoria and Nanaimo to Port Alberni, Tofino and Ucluelet. All bus companies ban smoking, and most long-distance buses have washrooms on board. Some long-haul buses even play videos.

CUTTING COSTS

Greyhound's Domestic Canada Pass provides unlimited bus travel for 7, 10, 15, 21, 30, 45, or 60 days anywhere in Canada served by Greyhound. You can purchase these passes online or at any Greyhound terminal in the United States or Canada. Greyhound also has passes that allow unlimited travel throughout North America or travel throughout the western or eastern half of the continent. All these passes are an excellent value for travelers who want to wander the highways and byways of the country, packing a lot of miles into a relatively short period of time. However, for occasional, short day trips, they're hardly worth it.

⚓ Discount Passes Greyhound Lines ⊠ 877 Greyhound Way SW, Calgary, AB T3C 3V8 ☎ 800/661-8747 in Canada, 800/231-2222 in U.S. ⊕ www.greyhound.ca.

FARES & SCHEDULES

Bus terminals in major cities and even in many smaller ones are usually efficient operations with service all week and plenty of agents on hand to handle ticket sales. In villages and some smaller towns, the bus station is simply a counter in a local convenience store, gas station, or snack bar. Getting information on schedules beyond the local ones is sometimes difficult in these places. For information on specific destinations within British Columbia, *see* the A to Z sections at the end of each chapter.

PAYING

In major bus terminals, most bus lines accept at least some of the major credit cards. Some smaller lines require cash or take only Visa or MasterCard. All accept traveler's checks in U.S. or Canadian currency with suitable identification, but it's advisable to exchange foreign currency (including U.S. currency) at a bank or exchange office. To buy a ticket in really small centers, it's best to use cash.

RESERVATIONS

Most bus lines do not accept reservations. You should plan on picking up your tickets at least 45 minutes before the bus's scheduled departure time.

🚌 **Bus Information Greyhound Lines** ✉ 877 Greyhound Way SW, Calgary, AB T3C 3V8 ☎ 800/661-8747 in Canada, 800/231-2222 in U.S. ⊕ www.greyhound.ca. **Gray Line of Victoria** ☎ 250/385-4411 or 800/318-0818 ⊕ www.graylinewest.com. **Malaspina Coach Lines** ☎ 877/227-8287 or 604/885-2217 ⊕ www.malaspinacoach.com. **Pacific Coach Lines** ☎ 604/662-8074 or 800/661-1725 ⊕ www.pacificcoach.com. **Tofino Bus** ☎ 250/725-2871 or 866/986-3466 ⊕ www.tofinobus.com

CAMERAS & PHOTOGRAPHY

Canada is one of the world's most scenic countries, and the misty light of B.C.'s west coast is particularly intriguing for photographers. The natural splendor of British Columbia vies for the attention of your camera lens.

The *Kodak Guide to Shooting Great Travel Pictures* (available at bookstores everywhere) is loaded with tips.

🚩 **Photo Help Kodak Information Center** ☎ 800/242-2424 ⊕ www.kodak.com.

EQUIPMENT PRECAUTIONS

Water, whether from rain, atmospheric humidity, sea, or river spray, is the camera's biggest enemy in British Columbia. Local photographers tuck silica gel packs into their camera cases to absorb moisture and take a small hand towel to wipe off raindrops. On rafting or whale-watching trips (where salt spray is especially damaging to equipment), consider taking a waterproof or a disposable camera instead of your usual equipment. Light conditions can change rapidly in B.C., so you may want to pack a variety of film speeds. Be sure to stock up on slide and high-speed film in cities; both are hard to find in the back-

country. Also, consider packing something red for your traveling companion to wear: it makes a nice contrast to the province's pervasive greens and blues.

Don't pack film or equipment in checked luggage, where it is much more susceptible to damage. X-ray machines used to view checked luggage are extremely powerful and therefore are likely to ruin your film. Try to ask for hand inspection of film, which becomes clouded after repeated exposure to airport X-ray machines, and keep videotapes and computer disks away from metal detectors. Always keep film, tape, and computer disks out of the sun. Carry an extra supply of batteries, and be prepared to turn on your camera, camcorder, or laptop to prove to airport-security personnel that the device is real.

CAR RENTAL

Rates in Vancouver begin at about C$40 a day or C$230 a week, usually including unlimited mileage. Car rentals in B.C. also incur a 7% sales tax, a C$1.50-per-day social-services tax, a C$0.70 per day Air Conditioning Excise Tax, and a vehicle-licensing fee of C$0.84 per day. An additional 15.27% Concession Recovery Fee, an extra fee charged by the airport authority for retail space in the terminal, is levied at airport locations. If you prefer a manual-transmission car, check whether the rental agency of your choice offers stick shifts; some companies, such as Avis, don't in Canada.

🚗 **Major Agencies Alamo** ☎ 800/522-9696 ⊕ www.alamo.com. **Avis** ☎ 800/331-1084, 800/879-2847 in Canada, 0870/606-0100 in U.K., 02/9353-9000 in Australia, 09/526-2847 in New Zealand ⊕ www.avis.com. **Budget** ☎ 800/472-3325, 800/268-8900 in Canada, 1300/794-344 in Australia, 0800/283-438 in New Zealand ⊕ www.budget.com. **Dollar** ☎ 800/800-6000, 0800/085-4578 in U.K. ⊕ www.dollar.com. **Hertz** ☎ 800/654-3001, 800/263-0600 in Canada, 0870/844-8844 in U.K., 02/9669-2444 in Australia, 09/256-8690 in New Zealand ⊕ www.hertz.com. **National Car Rental** ☎ 800/227-7368 ⊕ www.nationalcar.com.

CUTTING COSTS

Car-rental rates vary by supply and demand, so it pays to shop around and to reserve well in advance. Vancouver's airport and downtown locations usually have the best selection. Some car-rental agencies itemize fees, and some roll it into their rental rates. When comparing costs, take into account any mileage charges: an arrangement with unlimited mileage is usually the best deal if you plan to tour the province.

For a good deal, book through a travel agent who will shop around. Also, price local car-rental companies—whose prices may be lower still, although their service and maintenance may not be as good as those of major rental agencies—and research rates on the Internet. Consolidators that specialize in air travel can offer good rates on cars as well (⇨ Air Travel). Remember to ask about required deposits, cancellation penalties, and drop-off charges if you're planning to pick up the car in one city and leave it in another. If you're traveling during a holiday period, also make sure that a confirmed reservation guarantees you a car.

INSURANCE

When driving a rented car you are generally responsible for any damage to or loss of the vehicle. You also may be liable for any property damage or personal injury that you may cause while driving. Before you rent, see what coverage you already have under the terms of your personal auto-insurance policy and credit cards.

REQUIREMENTS & RESTRICTIONS

In Canada your own driver's license is acceptable. In B.C., children up to 40 pounds or 18 kilos in weight must use a child seat. Car seats cost about C$8 per day; fees vary, however, by agency. Additional drivers are charged about C$5 per day. Some agencies put a cap on these fees for longer rentals.

SURCHARGES

Before you pick up a car in one city and leave it in another, ask about drop-off charges or one-way service fees, which can be substantial. Also inquire about early return policies; some rental agencies charge extra if you return the car before the time specified in your contract, whereas others give you a refund for the days not used. Most agencies note the tank's fuel level on your contract; to avoid a hefty refueling fee, return the car with the same tank level. If the tank was full, refill it just before you turn in the car, but be aware that gas stations near the rental outlet may overcharge. It's almost never a deal to buy a tank of gas with the car when you rent it; the understanding is that you'll return it empty, but some fuel usually remains.

CAR TRAVEL

Canada's highway system is excellent. It includes the Trans-Canada Highway, or Highway 1, the longest highway in the world—running about 8,000 km (5,000 mi) from Victoria, British Columbia, to St. John's, Newfoundland, using ferries to bridge coastal waters at each end. The second-longest Canadian highway, the Yellowhead Highway (Highway 16), follows a route from the Pacific Coast and over the Rockies to the prairies. North of the population centers, roads become fewer and less developed.

FROM THE U.S.

Drivers must carry owner registration and proof of insurance coverage, which is compulsory in Canada. The Canadian Non-Resident Inter-Provincial Motor Vehicle Liability Insurance Card, available from any U.S. insurance company, is accepted as evidence of financial responsibility in Canada. If you're driving a car that is not registered in your name, carry a letter from the owner that authorizes your use of the vehicle.

The main entry point into British Columbia from the United States by car is on Interstate 5 at Blaine, Washington, 48 km (30 mi) south of Vancouver. Three highways enter British Columbia from the east: Highway 1, or the Trans-Canada Highway; Highway 3, or the Crowsnest Highway, which crosses southern British Columbia; and Highway 16, the Yellowhead Highway, which runs through northern British Columbia from the Rocky Mountains to Prince Rupert. From Alaska and the Yukon, take the Alaska Highway (from Fairbanks) or the Klondike Highway (from Skagway or Dawson City).

Border-crossing procedures are usually quick and simple (⇨ Passports & Visas). Every British Columbia border crossing (except the one at Aldergrove, which is open 8 AM to midnight) is open 24 hours. The Interstate 5 border crossing at Blaine, Washington (also known as the Douglas, or Peace Arch, border crossing), is one of the busiest border crossings between the United States and Canada. Weekend and holiday traffic tends to be heaviest; listen to local radio traffic reports for information about wait times. The Canada Border Services Agency posts estimated wait times on its Web site.

◪ Insurance Information **Canada Border Services Agency** ⊕ www.cbsa-asfc.gc.ca/menu-e.html. **Insurance Corporation of British Columbia (ICBC)** ☎ 604/661-2800 or 800/663-1466 ⊕ www.icbc. com.

EMERGENCY SERVICES

In case of emergency anywhere in B.C., call **911**; if you are not connected immediately, dial "0" and ask for the operator. The British Columbia Automobile Association (BCAA) provides 24-hour roadside assistance to AAA and CAA members.

◪ Roadside Assistance **BCAA** ☎ 604/268-5555 or 800/663-1956 nonemergencies, 604/293-2222 or 800/222-4357 emergencies ⊕ www.bcaa.com.

RULES OF THE ROAD

By law, you're required to wear seat belts (and to use infant seats). Motorcycle and bicycle helmets are mandatory. Right turns are permitted on red signals. Speed limits, given in kilometers, are usually within the 50–110 kph (30–66 mph) range outside the cities.

WINTER DRIVING

In coastal areas, the mild, damp climate contributes to roadways that are frequently wet. Winter snowfalls are not common (generally only once or twice a year), but when snow does fall, traffic grinds to a halt and the roadways become treacherous and stay that way until the snow melts. The high-altitude Coquihalla Highway (Highway 5), between Hope and Merritt, can see snow at any time of year.

Tire chains, studs, or snow tires are essential equipment for winter travel in the north and in mountain areas such as Whistler, the Kootenays, or the Rockies. If you're planning to drive into high elevations, be sure to check the weather forecast beforehand. Even the main-highway mountain passes can be forced to close because of snow conditions. The Ministry of Transportation Web site has up-to-date road reports.

◪ Road Reports **BC Ministry of Transportation** ⊕ www.th.gov.bc.ca/bchighways/roadreports/ roadreports.htm.

CHILDREN IN BRITISH COLUMBIA

Travelers crossing the border with children should **carry identification for them** similar to that required by adults (i.e., passport or birth certificate). Children traveling with one parent or other adult should **bring a letter of permission** from the other parent, parents, or legal guardian. Divorced parents with shared custody rights should **carry legal documents establishing their status.**

If you are renting a car, don't forget to arrange for a car seat when you reserve. For general advice about traveling with children, consult *Fodor's FYI: Travel with Your Baby* (available in bookstores everywhere).

◪ Local Information **Tourism Vancouver**'s free *Kids Guide Vancouver* is available at the Vancouver Tourist Info Centre. Tourism Vancouver's Web site, www.tourismvancouver.com, and the site www. kidsvancouver.com are both good sources of information on entertaining kids in the city. In Victoria, watch for the free *Kids' Guide to Victoria*.

FLYING

If your children are two or older, ask about children's airfares. As a general rule, infants under two not occupying a seat fly at greatly reduced fares or even for free. But if you want to guarantee a seat for an infant, you have to pay full fare. Consider flying during off-peak days and times; most airlines will grant an infant a seat without a ticket if there are available seats. When booking, confirm carry-on allowances if you're traveling with infants. In general, for babies charged 10% to 50% of the adult fare you are allowed one carry-on bag and a collapsible stroller; if the flight is full, the stroller may have to be checked or you may be limited to less.

Experts agree that it's a good idea to use safety seats aloft for children weighing less than 40 pounds. Airlines set their own policies: if you use a safety seat, U.S. carriers usually require that the child be ticketed, even if he or she is young enough to ride free, because the seats must be strapped into regular seats. And even if you pay the full adult fare for the seat, it may be worth it, especially on longer trips. Do **check your airline's policy about using safety seats during takeoff and landing.** Safety seats are not allowed everywhere in the plane, so get your seat assignments as early as possible.

When reserving, request children's meals or a freestanding bassinet (not available at all airlines) if you need them. But note that bulkhead seats, where you must sit to use the bassinet, may lack an overhead bin or storage space on the floor.

LODGING

Most hotels in British Columbia allow children under a certain age to stay in their parents' room at no extra charge, but others charge for them as extra adults; be sure to find out the cutoff age for children's discounts.

Most hotels will supply portable cribs or playpens, though it's a good idea to request these when you book.
🖪 Best Choices Lake Okanagan Resort ☎ 250/769-3511 or 800/663-3273 ⊕ www.lakeokanagan.com. **Manteo Resort Waterfront Hotel and Villas** ☎ 250/860-1031 or 800/445-5255 ⊕ www.manteo.com. **Tigh-na-Mara Resort** ☎ 250/248-2072 or 800/663-7373 ⊕ www.tigh-na-mara.com.

SIGHTS & ATTRACTIONS

Places that are especially appealing to children are indicated by a rubber-duckie icon (🐤) in the margin. In Vancouver, Granville Island has both a children's water park and the toy-and-games-filled Kids' Market. Stanley Park, with its aquarium, miniature train, petting zoo, and beaches, is also a must-see for kids, as are the science-oriented exhibits at Science World

and the H. R. MacMillan Space Centre. In Victoria, must-sees are the Bug Zoo and the lifelike exhibits at the Royal British Columbia Museum. Farther afield, the sandy beaches and warm waters of Okanagan Lake and the eastern shore of Vancouver Island make these two top family destinations. Whistler Resort is justifiably famous for its year-round family activities, but the smaller, less expensive ski resorts in the Okanagan and the Kootenays are good value and have plenty of kid-oriented activities.

CONSUMER PROTECTION

Whether you're shopping for gifts or purchasing travel services, **pay with a major credit card** whenever possible, so you can cancel payment or get reimbursed if there's a problem (and you can provide documentation). If you're doing business with a particular company for the first time, contact your local Better Business Bureau and the attorney general's offices in your state and (for U.S. businesses) the company's home state as well. Have any complaints been filed? Finally, if you're buying a package or tour, always consider travel insurance that includes default coverage (⇨ Insurance).
🖪 BBBs Council of Better Business Bureaus ✉ 4200 Wilson Blvd., Suite 800, Arlington, VA 22203 ☎ 703/276-0100 🖷 703/525-8277 ⊕ www.bbb.org.

CRUISE TRAVEL

Vancouver is, with Seattle, a major embarkation point for Alaska cruises, and virtually all Alaska-bound cruise ships call there; some also call at Victoria and Prince Rupert. Once leaving Vancouver, however, most luxury liners make straight for Alaska, leaving the fjords and islands of B.C. to smaller vessels and expedition ships. One exception is Celebrity Cruises, which offers three- to five-day fall cruises along B.C.'s southern coast. Some operators lead sailing trips around B.C.'s islands; independent travelers can explore the coast on BC Ferries or on one of the coastal freighters serving remote outposts. (*See* individual chapters for more information about ferry and freighter travel.)

To learn how to plan, choose, and book a cruise-ship voyage, consult *Fodor's FYI: Plan & Enjoy Your Cruise* (available in bookstores everywhere).

🚢 Cruise Lines **Carnival Cruise Lines** ☎ 800/327-9501 ⊕ www.carnival.com. **Crystal Cruises** ☎ 310/785-9300 or 800/446-6620 ⊕ www.crystalcruises.com. **Celebrity Cruises** ☎ 800/437-3111 ⊕ www.celebritycruises.com. **Holland America** ☎ 206/281-3535 or 877/932-4259 ⊕ www.hollandamerica.com. **Norwegian Cruise Line** ☎ 305/436-4000 or 800/327-7030 ⊕ www.ncl.com. **Princess Cruise Line** ☎ 661/753-0000 or 800/774-6237 ⊕ www.princess.com. **Radisson Seven Seas Cruises** ☎ 954/776-6123 or 800/285-1835 ⊕ www.rssc.com. **Royal Caribbean International** ☎ 305/539-6000 or 800/327-6700 ⊕ www.royalcaribbean.com.

The small, expedition-style ships operated by American Safari Cruises, Clipper Cruise Lines, and Cruise West explore the British Columbia coast on their way to Alaska; some offer cruises exclusively in B.C. Bluewater Adventures has 8- to 10-day sailing cruises of the B.C. coastline, including the Queen Charlotte Islands.

🚢 Local Cruise Lines **American Safari Cruises** ✉ 19221 36th Ave. W, Suite 208, Lynnwood, WA 98036 ☎ 425/776-4700 or 888/862-8881 ⊕ www.amsafari.com. **Bluewater Adventures** ✉ 3-252 E. 1st St., North Vancouver V7L 1B3 ☎ 604/980-3800 or 888/877-1770 ⊕ www.bluewateradventures.ca. **Clipper Cruise Line** ✉ 11969 Westline Industrial Dr., St. Louis, MO 63146-3220 ☎ 314/655-6700 or 800/325-0010 ⊕ www.clippercruise.com. **Cruise West** ✉ 2301 5th Ave., Suite 401, Seattle, WA 98121-1438 ☎ 206/441-8687 or 800/888-9378 ⊕ www.cruisewest.com.

CUSTOMS & DUTIES

When shopping abroad, keep receipts for all purchases. Upon reentering the country, **be ready to show customs officials what you've bought.** Pack purchases together in an easily accessible place. If you think a duty is incorrect, appeal the assessment. If you object to the way your clearance was handled, note the inspector's badge number. In either case, first ask to see a supervisor. If the problem isn't resolved, write to the appropriate authorities, beginning with the port director at your point of entry.

IN AUSTRALIA

Australian residents who are 18 or older may bring home A$900 worth of souvenirs and gifts (including jewelry), 250 cigarettes or 250 grams of cigars or other tobacco products, and 2.25 liters of alcohol (including wine, beer, and spirits). Residents under 18 may bring back A$450 worth of goods. If any of these individual allowances are exceeded, you must pay duty for the entire amount (of the group of products in which the allowance was exceeded). Members of the same family traveling together may pool their allowances. Prohibited items include meat products. Seeds, plants, and fruits need to be declared upon arrival.

🛂 **Australian Customs Service** ⊡ Customs House, 10 Cooks River Dr., Sydney International Airport, Sydney, NSW 2020 ☎ 02/6275-6666 or 1300/363-263, 02/8334-7444 or 1800/020-504 quarantine-inquiry line ᐧ 02/8339-6714 ⊕ www.customs.gov.au.

IN CANADA

Visitors may bring certain goods into Canada for their own use as "personal baggage." Clothing, camping and sports equipment, cameras, tape recorders, and even personal computers are considered to be personal baggage. Vehicles, vessels, and aircraft may also be imported. Provided these goods are declared upon arrival and taken back out of Canada when you leave, they will not be subject to any duties or taxes. A (refundable) deposit is sometimes required. A visitor's goods cannot be used by a resident of Canada, or on behalf of a business based in Canada.

Visitors may bring in the following items duty-free: 200 cigarettes, 50 cigars, and 7 ounces of tobacco; 1 bottle (1.14 liters or 40 imperial ounces) of liquor or 1.5 liters of wine, or 24 355-milliliter (12-ounce) bottles or cans of beer for personal consumption. Any alcohol and tobacco products in excess of these amounts are subject to duty, provincial fees, and taxes. You can also bring in gifts up to a total value of C$60 per gift as long as the gifts do not include alcohol or tobacco.

Cats and dogs must have a certificate issued by a licensed veterinarian that clearly identifies the animal and certifies that it has been vaccinated against rabies during the preceding 36 months. Seeing Eye and other assistance dogs are allowed into Canada without restriction. Plant material must be declared and inspected. There may be restrictions on some live plants, bulbs, and seeds. With certain restrictions or prohibitions on some fruits and vegetables, visitors may bring food with them for their own use, providing the quantity is consistent with the duration of the visit.

Canada's firearms laws are significantly stricter than those in the United States, and it's strongly advised that, if you do plan to bring a gun into Canada, you contact the Canadian Firearms Centre for up-to-date information before leaving home. All handguns and semiautomatic and fully automatic weapons are prohibited and cannot be brought into the country. Sporting rifles and shotguns may be imported provided they are to be used for sporting, hunting, protecting oneself from wildlife in remote areas, or competing while in Canada. All firearms must be declared to Canada Customs at the first point of entry. Failure to declare firearms will result in their seizure, and criminal charges may be made. Regulations require visitors to have a confirmed "Firearms Declaration" to bring any guns into Canada; a fee of C$50 applies, good for one year.

🏛 **Canada Border Services Agency** ✉ Customs Information Services, 191 Laurier Ave. W, 15th fl., Ottawa, Ontario K1A 0L5 ☎ 204/983-3500, 800/461-9999 in Canada ⊕ www.cbsa.gc.ca. **Canadian Firearms Centre** ☎ 800/731-4000 ⊕ www.cfc.gc.ca.

IN NEW ZEALAND
All homeward-bound residents may bring back NZ$700 worth of souvenirs and gifts; passengers may not pool their allowances, and children can claim only the concession on goods intended for their own use. For those 17 or older, the duty-free allowance also includes 4.5 liters of wine or beer; one 1,125-milliliter bottle of spirits; and either 200 cigarettes, 250 grams of tobacco, 50 cigars, *or* a combination of the three up to 250 grams. Meat products, seeds, plants, and fruits must be

declared upon arrival to the Agricultural Services Department.

🏛 **New Zealand Customs Service** ✉ Head office: The Customhouse, 17-21 Whitmore St., Box 2218, Wellington ☎ 09/300-5399 or 0800/428-786 ⊕ www.customs.govt.nz.

IN THE U.K.
From countries outside the European Union, including Canada, you may bring home, duty-free, 200 cigarettes, 50 cigars, 100 cigarillos, or 250 grams of tobacco; 1 liter of spirits or 2 liters of fortified or sparkling wine or liqueurs; 2 liters of still table wine; 60 milliliters of perfume; 250 milliliters of toilet water; plus £145 worth of other goods, including gifts and souvenirs. Prohibited items include meat and dairy products, seeds, plants, and fruits.

🏛 **HM Revenue & Customs** ✉ Portcullis House, 21 Cowbridge Rd. E, Cardiff CF11 9SR ☎ 0845/010-9000 or 0208/929-0152 advice service, 0208/929-6731 or 0208/910-3602 complaints ⊕ www.hmce.gov.uk.

IN THE U.S.
U.S. residents who have been out of the country for at least 48 hours may bring home, for personal use, $800 worth of foreign goods duty-free, as long as they haven't used the $800 allowance or any part of it in the past 30 days. This exemption may include 1 liter of alcohol (for travelers 21 and older), 200 cigarettes, and 100 non-Cuban cigars. Family members from the same household who are traveling together may pool their $800 personal exemptions. For fewer than 48 hours, the duty-free allowance drops to $200, which may include 50 cigarettes, 10 non-Cuban cigars, and 150 milliliters of alcohol (or 150 milliliters of perfume containing alcohol). The $200 allowance cannot be combined with other individuals' exemptions, and if you exceed it, the full value of all the goods will be taxed. Antiques, which the U.S. Customs and Border Protection defines as objects more than 100 years old, enter duty-free, as do original works of art done entirely by hand, including paintings, drawings, and sculptures. This doesn't apply to folk art or handicrafts, which are in general dutiable.

You may also send packages home duty-free, with a limit of one parcel per addressee per day (except alcohol or tobacco products or perfume worth more than $5). You can mail up to $200 worth of goods for personal use; label the package PERSONAL USE and attach a list of its contents and their retail value. If the package contains your used personal belongings, mark it AMERICAN GOODS RETURNED to avoid paying duties. You may send up to $100 worth of goods as a gift; mark the package UNSOLICITED GIFT. Mailed items do not affect your duty-free allowance on your return.

To avoid paying duty on foreign-made high-ticket items you already own and will take on your trip, register them with a local customs office before you leave the country. Consider filing a Certificate of Registration for laptops, cameras, watches, and other digital devices identified with serial numbers or other permanent markings; you can keep the certificate for other trips. Otherwise, bring a sales receipt or insurance form to show that you owned the item before you left the United States.

For more about duties, restricted items, and other information about international travel, check out U.S. Customs and Border Protection's online brochure, *Know Before You Go*. You can also file complaints on the U.S. Customs and Border Protection Web site, listed below.

U.S. Customs and Border Protection ✉ For inquiries and complaints, 1300 Pennsylvania Ave. NW, Washington, DC 20229 ⊕ www.cbp.gov ☎ 877/227-5551 or 202/354-1000.

DISABILITIES & ACCESSIBILITY
Canadian legislation with respect to access and provision of services for travelers with disabilities is similar to that in the United States. Most transportation facilities are navigable by wheelchair, and restaurants and hotels that are amenable to wheelchairs are also relatively easy to find, especially in the Vancouver area. Most major attractions—museums, galleries, theaters—are equipped with ramps and lifts to handle wheelchairs. Almost all national and provincial institutions—parks, public monuments, and government buildings—can be accessed by wheelchair.

The British Columbia Paraplegic Association has information about touring in the province. The government of Canada's Access to Travel Web site has information about travel in Canada for people with all manner of disabilities. You can also use this site to file a complaint about transportation obstacles in Canada.

Local Resources Access to Travel ⊕ www.accesstotravel.gc.ca. **British Columbia Paraplegic Association** ✉ 780 S.W. Marine Dr., Vancouver V6P 5Y7 ☎ 604/324-3611 or 877/324-3611 ⊕ www.canparaplegic.org/bc.

RESERVATIONS
When discussing accessibility with an operator or reservations agent, ask hard questions. Are there any stairs, inside *or* out? Are there grab bars next to the toilet *and* in the shower/tub? How wide is the doorway to the room? To the bathroom? For the most extensive facilities meeting the latest legal specifications, opt for newer accommodations. If you reserve through a toll-free number, consider also calling the hotel's local number to confirm the information from the central-reservations office. Get confirmation in writing when you can.

The Access Canada program rates accommodations by accessibility. The ratings are published in the British Columbia Accommodations Guide, available from Tourism B.C. Note that grab bars are common in B.C. hotels, but wheel-in showers are rare and bath benches are not normally provided.

Accommodation Information Hello BC (Tourism B.C.) ☎ 800/435-5622 ⊕ www.hellobc.com.

SIGHTS & ATTRACTIONS
Most city attractions, such as museums and galleries are wheelchair accessible. In summer, you can tour Stanley Park on the free, wheelchair-accessible Stanley Park Shuttle. Stanley Park Horse-Drawn Tours are also wheelchair accessible, and the Grouse Mountain Skyride offers accessibility with 24 hours notice (call 604/984-0661).

TRANSPORTATION
More than half of Vancouver's TransLink buses are equipped with wheelchair lifts.

The SeaBus ferry is wheelchair accessible, as is the SkyTrain system, with the exception of the Granville Street Station. BC Ferries' larger vessels, including those sailing between Vancouver and Vancouver Island and through the Inside Passage, are equipped with elevators. Tell the ticket agent before boarding that you would like to be parked near the elevator. Some smaller vessels on shorter routes do not have accessible washrooms or passengers lounges. Greyhound Bus lines have lift-equipped service to most towns on the B.C. mainland; reservations are essential. Pacific Coach Lines provides accessible service between Vancouver and Victoria. Rocky Mountain Railtours offers accessible two-day trips from Vancouver to Jasper with a stop at an accessible hotel en route. Avis Rent a Car (⇨ Car Rental) rents hand-controlled cars with at least 48 hours notice. To rent a lift-equipped van, contact Freedom Accessible Van Rentals (☎ 604/952–4499; ⊕ www. wheelchairvanrentals.com) or Sidewinder Conversions (☎ 888/266–2299; www. sidewinder-conversions.com). Most Vancouver cab companies have some vans with ramps or lifts. Disabled-parking stickers (windshield cards) from anywhere in North America are recognized in B.C.

The U.S. Department of Transportation Aviation Consumer Protection Division's online publication *New Horizons: Information for the Air Traveler with a Disability* offers advice for travelers with a disability, and outlines basic rights. Visit DisabilityInfo.gov for general information. ⚡ Information & Complaints **Aviation Consumer Protection Division** (⇨ Air Travel) for airline-related problems; ⊕ airconsumer.ost.dot.gov/publications/ horizons.htm for airline travel advice and rights. **Departmental Office of Civil Rights** ⊠ for general inquiries, U.S. Department of Transportation, S-30, 400 7th St. SW, Room 10215, Washington, DC 20590 ☎ 202/366-4648, 202/366-8538 TTY 🖶 202/366-9371 ⊕ www.dotcr.ost.dot.gov. **Disability Rights Section** ⊠ NYAV, U.S. Department of Justice, Civil Rights Division, 950 Pennsylvania Ave. NW, Washington, DC 20530 ☎ ADA information line 202/514-0301, 800/514-0301, 202/514-0383 TTY, 800/514-0383 TTY ⊕ www.ada.gov. **U.S. Department of Trans-** **portation Hotline** ☎ For disability-related air-travel problems, 800/778-4838 or 866/754-4368.

TRAVEL AGENCIES

In the United States, the Americans with Disabilities Act requires that travel firms serve the needs of all travelers. Some agencies specialize in working with people with disabilities. ⚡ Travelers with Mobility Problems **Access Adventures/B. Roberts Travel** ⊠ 1876 East Ave., Rochester, NY 14610 ☎ 800/444-6540 ⊕ www. brobertstravel.com. **CareVacations** ⊠ No. 5, 5110-50 Ave., Leduc, Alberta, Canada, T9E 6V4 ☎ 780/986-6404 or 877/478-7827 🖶 780/986-6485 ⊕ www.carevacations.com, for group tours and cruise vacations. **Flying Wheels Travel** ⊠ 143 W. Bridge St., Box 382, Owatonna, MN 55060 ☎ 507/451-5005 🖶 507/451-1685 ⊕ www. flyingwheelstravel.com.

DISCOUNTS & DEALS

Be a smart shopper and compare all your options before making decisions. A plane ticket bought with a promotional coupon from travel clubs, coupon books, and direct-mail offers or purchased on the Internet may not be cheaper than the least expensive fare from a discount-ticket agency. And always keep in mind that what you get is just as important as what you save.

If you plan to do much sightseeing, check out the Smartvisit Card attractions pass, which allows unlimited entry to over 40 attractions, tours, and outdoor adventures in Vancouver, Victoria, Squamish, and Whistler for a single price. The cards cost C$99 for two days, C$129 for three, or C$189 for five days; and can be purchased online or at several outlets in B.C., including the airport visitor-information booth. ⚡ **Smartvisit** ☎ 604/295-1157 ⊕ www. seevancouvercard.com.

DISCOUNT RESERVATIONS

To save money, look into discount-reservations services with Web sites and toll-free numbers, which use their buying power to get a better price on hotels, airline tickets (⇨ Air Travel), even car rentals. When booking a room, always **call the hotel's local toll-free number** (if one is available) rather than the central-reservations number—you'll often get a better price. Always ask about special packages or corporate rates.

When shopping for the best deal on hotels and car rentals, look for guaranteed exchange rates, which protect you against a falling dollar. With your rate locked in, you won't pay more, even if the price goes up in the local currency.

🖪 Hotel Rooms **Accommodations Express** ☎ 800/444-7666 or 800/277-1064. **Hotels.com** ☎ 800/246-8357 ⊕ www.hotels.com. **Quikbook** ☎ 800/789-9887 ⊕ www.quikbook.com. **Turbotrip.com** ⊕ w3.turbotrip.com. **World Hotels** ☎ 800/223-5652 ⊕ www.worldhotels.com.

PACKAGE DEALS

Don't confuse packages and guided tours. When you buy a package, you travel on your own, just as though you had planned the trip yourself. Fly–drive packages, which combine airfare and car rental, are often a good deal. In cities, ask the local visitor's bureau about hotel and local transportation packages that include tickets to major museum exhibits or other special events.

EATING & DRINKING

The restaurants we list are the cream of the crop in each price category. Properties indicated by an ✕▥ are lodging establishments whose restaurant warrants a special trip.

In Vancouver, where several thousand eateries represent almost every cuisine on the planet, deciding what to eat is as important as deciding what to see and do. Vancouverites are a health-conscious lot, so light, organic, and vegetarian meals are easy to find, and every restaurant and even most of the pubs in the province ban smoking indoors. Good coffee is everywhere—downtown you'll never have to walk more than half a block for a cup of high-test cappuccino. You won't find much street food in town (only hot dog vendors are permitted on city streets), but you can grab a takeout and picnic at any city beach or park.

In Victoria and on Vancouver Island, many chefs work with local organic farmers to create a distinctive regional cuisine; Whistler has some of the most highly regarded, and priciest, restaurants in the province. Elsewhere, excellent food is found in the most out of the way places, as chefs passionate about their ingredients locate close to the source and let their diners come to them. Neighborhood pubs, both in and outside cities, are your best bet for a casual meal. Many have a separate restaurant section where you can take kids.

To experience the province like a native, make dining a priority, and keep the following things in mind.

WHAT IT COSTS

Although the Canadian dollar isn't quite the steal it once was, dining in British Columbia is still one of North America's great bargains. Although high-end entrées, especially where seafood is involved, can top C$35, C$20 to C$25 is more the norm. At the other end of the scale, you can get a filling Chinese lunch special, or a country pub burger and fries, for C$5 to C$10. But even though food is a deal in B.C., alcohol is pricey. A bottle of wine can easily double your bill.

Bargains, however, abound: the densest cluster of cheap eats in Vancouver is along Denman Street in the West End. Another budget option is to check out the lunch specials at any of the little Asian restaurants lining Vancouver's streets and shopping malls. They serve healthy, hot meals for about the same cost as a take-out burger and fries.

If you eat early you may be able to take advantage of a prix-fixe deal not offered at peak hours. At many upscale restaurants, the lunch menus are similar to the dinner menus, with lower prices and smaller portions. Several of the most fashionable places have tapas-style bar menus, where you can sample smaller portions of top-notch cuisine at proportionately lower prices.

Credit cards are widely accepted, but a few smaller restaurants accept only cash. Discover Cards are little known in Canada, and many restaurants outside of Vancouver do not accept American Express. Our restaurant reviews indicate what credit cards are accepted (or not) at each establishment, but if you plan to use a credit card it's a good idea to double-check its acceptability when making reservations or before sitting down to eat.

MEALTIMES

Most upscale restaurants in Vancouver, Victoria, and Whistler observe standard North American meal times (5:30 to 9 or so for dinner, roughly noon to 2 if open for lunch); though some offer a lighter tapas-style menu (or, in Victoria, afternoon tea) in the afternoon. Casual places and pubs typically serve food all afternoon and into the evening. Restaurants that do stay open late (meaning midnight or 1 AM) usually morph into bars after about 9 PM, but the kitchen stays open. In Vancouver, the West End and Kitsilano have the most late-night choices; pubs are your best bet if you're eating late in Victoria. Unless otherwise noted, the restaurants listed in this guide are open daily for lunch and dinner.

RESERVATIONS & DRESS

At the hottest restaurants in Vancouver, Victoria, and Whistler, you need to make reservations at least a few days in advance, especially if you want to dine between 7 and 9, or on a Friday or Saturday night. On weeknights or outside of the peak tourist season, you can usually secure a table by calling the same day. Just showing up can work, too, though of course there's no guarantee you'll get a table.

If you want to dine, but not sleep, at one of B.C.'s better-known country inns, such as the Sooke Harbour House, the Aerie, or the Wickaninnish Inn, you should make your reservation as far ahead as possible. Guests staying at these inns are given first choice for dining reservations, which means spaces for nonguests are limited. When calling a restaurant, double-check that the information listed in these reviews hasn't changed. Credit card acceptance, hours of operation, chefs, and prices are subject to (and often do) change. Remember also to call the restaurant should you need to cancel your reservation—it's only courteous.

Reservations are always a good idea; we mention them only when they're essential or not accepted. Book as far ahead as you can, and reconfirm as soon as you arrive. (Large parties should always call ahead to check the reservations policy.) We mention dress only when men are required to wear a jacket or a jacket and tie.

SPECIALTIES

Despite dwindling stocks, wild Pacific salmon—fresh, smoked, dried, candied, barbecued, or grilled on an alderwood plank in the First Nations fashion—remains British Columbia's signature dish. Other local delicacies served at B.C.'s up-market restaurants include Fanny Bay or Long Beach oysters and Salt Spring Island lamb. Another homegrown treat is the Nanaimo Bar. Once a Christmas bake-sale standard, this chocolate-and-icing concoction has made its way to trendy city cafés.

WINE, BEER & SPIRITS

Though little known and virtually unobtainable outside the province, British Columbia wines have beaten many more established regions in international competitions. A tasting tour of B.C.'s Okanagan wine region is a scenic way to experience some of these vintages. British Columbians are also choosy about their beer, brewing and drinking (per capita) more micro-brewed ales and lagers than anyone else in the country. The liquor stores sell a daunting selection of oddly named brews, but many cottage breweries produce only enough for their local pubs, so it's always worth asking what's on draft.

EMBASSIES & CONSULATES

🛂 Australia **Australian Consulate** ✉ 888 Dunsmuir St., Suite 1225, Vancouver V6C 3K4 ☎ 604/684-1177. **Australian High Commission** ✉ 50 O'Connor St., Suite 710, Ottawa K1P 6L2 ☎ 613/236-0841.

🛂 New Zealand **New Zealand Consulate** ✉ 888 Dunsmuir St., Suite 1200, Vancouver V6C 3K4 ☎ 604/684-7388. **New Zealand High Commission** ✉ 99 Bank St., Suite 727, Ottawa K1P 6G3 ☎ 613/238-5991 ⊕ www.nzhcottawa.org.

🛂 United Kingdom **British Consulate General** ✉ 1111 Melville St., Suite 800, Vancouver V6E 3V6 ☎ 604/683-4421. **British High Commission** ✉ 80

Elgin St., Ottawa K1P 5K7 ☎ 613/237-1530 ⊕ www.britainincanada.org. ▮ United States **U.S. Consulate General** ✉ 1095 W. Pender St., 21st fl., Vancouver V6E 2M6 ☎ 604/685-4311. **U.S. Embassy** ✉ 490 Sussex Dr., Ottawa K1N 1G8 ☎ 613/238-5335 ⊕ www.usembassycanada.gov.

GAY & LESBIAN TRAVEL

Canada is a tolerant country, and same-sex couples should face few problems in Vancouver, where there's a large, visible, and very active gay and lesbian community.

The epicenter of Vancouver's gay scene is the stretch of Davie Street between Burrard and Jervis streets—a cluster of cafés, casual eating places, and shops offering designer T-shirts and sleek housewares. The city's lesbian community centers on Commercial Drive, a neighborhood shared with the Italian and Latin American community. Vancouver Pride Week, held in late July and early August, features parties, dances, and cruises and culminates in a parade on Sunday.

Same-sex couples can holiday happily anywhere in British Columbia, although Whistler, the Gulf Islands, Tofino and Victoria are especially gay-friendly destinations. Same-sex marriage is legal in British Columbia so couples from around the world travel here to exchange vows.

The Web sites www.gayvancouver.net and www.gayvan.com have the latest on gay events, nightlife, and travel in B.C., including information about destination weddings. You can also pick up a free copy of *Gay Friendly Vancouver* at the Vancouver Tourist InfoCentre and brochure racks around town.

For details about the gay and lesbian scene, consult *Fodor's Gay Guide to the USA* (available in bookstores everywhere). ▮ Gay- & Lesbian-Friendly Travel Agencies **Different Roads Travel** ✉ 1555 Palm Colony, Palm Springs, CA 92264 ☎ 760/325-6964 or 800/429-8747, Ext. 14 ⎙ 310/855-0323 ✉ lgernert@tzell.com. **Kennedy Travel** ✉ 130 W. 42nd St., Suite 401, New York, NY 10036 ☎ 800/237-7433 or 212/840-8659 ⎙ 212/730-2269 ⊕ www.kennedytravel.com. **Now, Voyager** ✉ 4406 18th St., San Francisco, CA 94114 ☎ 415/626-1169 or 800/255-6951 ⎙ 415/626-8626 ⊕ www.nowvoyager.com. **Skylink Travel and Tour/Flying Dutchmen Travel** ✉ 1455 N. Dutton Ave., Suite A, Santa Rosa, CA 95401 ☎ 707/546-9888 or 800/225-5759 ⎙ 707/636-0951; serving lesbian travelers.

HOLIDAYS

Canadian national holidays for 2006 are as follows: New Year's Day, Good Friday (April 14), Easter Monday (April 17), Victoria Day (May 22), Canada Day (July 1), Labour Day (September 4), Thanksgiving (October 9), Remembrance Day (November 11), and Christmas and Boxing Day (December 26). British Columbia Day (August 7) is a provincial holiday.

INSURANCE

The most useful travel-insurance plan is a comprehensive policy that includes coverage for trip cancellation and interruption, default, trip delay, and medical expenses (with a waiver for preexisting conditions).

Without insurance you'll lose all or most of your money if you cancel your trip, regardless of the reason. Default insurance covers you if your tour operator, airline, or cruise line goes out of business—the chances of which have been increasing. Trip-delay covers expenses that arise because of bad weather or mechanical delays. Study the fine print when comparing policies.

U.K. residents can buy a travel-insurance policy valid for most vacations taken during the year in which it's purchased (but check preexisting-condition coverage). British and Australian citizens need extra medical coverage when traveling overseas.

Always **buy travel policies directly from the insurance company**; if you buy them from a cruise line, airline, or tour operator that goes out of business you probably won't be covered for the agency or operator's default, a major risk. Before making any purchase, review your existing health and home-owner's policies to find what they cover away from home. ▮ Travel Insurers In the U.S.: **Access America** ✉ 2805 N. Parham Rd., Richmond, VA 23294 ☎ 800/284-8300 ⎙ 804/673-1469 for claims or 800/346-9265 for sales ⊕ www.accessamerica.com. **Travel Guard International** ✉ 1145 Clark St.,

Stevens Point, WI 54481 ☎ 800/826-1300 or 715/345-1041 🖷 715/345-2915 ⊕ www.travelguard.com. 🔃 In the U.K.: **Association of British Insurers** ✉ 51 Gresham St., London EC2V 7HQ ☎ 020/7600-3333 🖷 020/7696-8999 ⊕ www.abi.org.uk. In Canada: **RBC Insurance** ✉ 6880 Financial Dr., Mississauga, Ontario L5N 7Y5 ☎ 800/387-4357 or 905/816-2559 🖷 888/298-6458 ⊕ www.rbcinsurance.com. In Australia: **Insurance Council of Australia** ✉ Level 3, 56 Pitt St. Sydney, NSW 2000 ☎ 02/9253-5100 🖷 02/9253-5111 ⊕ www.ica.com.au. In New Zealand: **Insurance Council of New Zealand** ✉ Level 7, 111-115 Customhouse Quay, Box 474, Wellington ☎ 04/472-5230 🖷 04/473-3011 ⊕ www.icnz.org.nz.

LODGING

In Vancouver and Victoria you have a choice of luxury hotels; moderately priced modern properties; bed-and-breakfasts, both simple and luxurious; and smaller, older hotels with perhaps fewer conveniences but more charm. Options in smaller towns and in the country include large, full-service resorts; remote wilderness lodges; small, privately owned hotels; roadside motels; and B&Bs. Even here you need to make reservations at least on the day on which you plan to pull into town.

Canada doesn't have a national government-rating system for hotels, but in British Columbia, a blue Approved Accommodation decal on the window or door of a hotel or motel indicates that it has met provincial hotel-association standards for courtesy, comfort, and cleanliness.

Expect accommodations to cost more in summer than in the off-season (except for places such as ski resorts, where winter and spring break are high season). If you're planning to visit a major city or resort area in high season, **book well in advance.** Also be aware of any special events or festivals that may coincide with your visit and fill every room for miles around. Note also that many out-of-the-way lodgings are closed during the winter.

The lodgings we list are the cream of the crop in each price category. We always list the facilities that are available, but we don't specify whether they cost extra; when pricing accommodations, always ask what's included and what costs extra.

Properties are assigned price categories based on the range between their least and most expensive standard double rooms at high season (excluding holidays). Properties marked ✕⌂ are lodging establishments whose restaurants warrant a special trip. Assume that hotels operate on the European Plan (EP, with no meals) unless we specify that they use the Continental Plan (CP, with a continental breakfast), Modified American Plan (MAP, with breakfast and dinner), or the Full American Plan (FAP, with all meals).

APARTMENT & VILLA (OR HOUSE) RENTALS

If you want a home base that's roomy enough for a family and comes with cooking facilities, consider a furnished rental. These can save you money, especially if you're traveling with a group. Home-exchange directories sometimes list rentals as well as exchanges.

Rental houses, apartments, and cottages are popular in B.C., particularly on the coast, the islands, and in Whistler. Whistler condos are usually time-share or consortium arrangements and can be booked directly through Tourism Whistler. Vacation rentals elsewhere are usually privately owned and range from simple summer cottages to luxurious waterfront homes. Rates range from C$800 per week to several thousand; popular places book up as much as a year in advance. 🔃 International Agents **Hideaways International** ✉ 767 Islington St., Portsmouth, NH 03801 ☎ 603/430-4433 or 800/843-4433 🖷 603/430-4444 ⊕ www.hideaways.com, annual membership $185. 🔃 Local Agents **Chalet Select** ✉ 1673 Cyrville Rd., Glouster ON K1B 3L7 ☎ 613/747-6200 or 888/468-0329 ⊕ www.chaletselect.com. **5 Star Accommodation** ✉ 1821 Cook St., 2nd fl., Victoria V8T 3P5 ☎ 250/479-8600 or 888/479-8600 ⊕ www.bcacc.com. **Tourism Whistler** ✉ 4010 Whistler Way, Whistler V0N 1B4 ☎ 604/664-5625 or 800/944-7853 ⊕ www.tourismwhistler.com.

BED & BREAKFASTS

B&Bs can be found in both the country and the cities. For assistance in booking these, **contact Tourism British Columbia.** Be sure to **check out the B&B's Web site,** which may have useful information, although you should also find out how up-to-date it is. Room quality varies from house to house as well, so you should **ask to see a room before making a choice.**

F Reservation Services **Blue Dolphin Travel**
✉ 322 Marshall Bay, Winnipeg R3T 0R9 ☎ 866/247-2421 ⊕ www.bluedolphin-travel.com. **Hello BC (Tourism B.C.)** ☎ 800/435-5622 ⊕ www.hellobc.com.

CAMPING
Camping is one of the most popular ways to see British Columbia. To book a campsite in a provincial park, contact Discover Camping, operated by B.C. Parks. See National & Provincial Parks *below* for more information.

F Campsite Reservations **Discover Camping**
☎ 800/689-9025 ⊕ www.discovercamping.ca.

CUTTING COSTS
When making reservations, **ask about special deals and packages.** Big-city hotels that cater to business travelers often offer weekend packages, and many city hotels offer rooms at up to 50% off in winter. Hello BC, run by B.C.'s Tourism Ministry, lists discount packages.

F Hello BC (Tourism B.C.) ☎ 800/435-5622
⊕ www.hellobc.com.

HOME EXCHANGES
If you would like to exchange your home for someone else's, join a home-exchange organization, which will send you its updated listings of available exchanges for a year and will include your own listing in at least one of them. It's up to you to make specific arrangements.

F Exchange Clubs **HomeLink USA** ✉ 2937 NW 9th Terrace, Wilton Manors, FL 33311 ☎ 954/566-2687 or 800/638-3841 🖷 954/566-2783 ⊕ www.homelink.org; $80 yearly for a listing and online access; $45 additional to receive directories. **Intervac U.S.** ✉ 30 Corte San Fernando, Tiburon, CA 94920 ☎ 800/756-4663 🖷 415/435-7440 ⊕ www.intervacus.com; $128 yearly for a listing, online access, and a catalog; $68 without catalog.

HOSTELS
No matter what your age, you can save on lodging costs by staying at hostels. In some 4,500 locations in more than 70 countries

around the world, Hostelling International (HI), the umbrella group for a number of national youth-hostel associations, offers single-sex, dorm-style beds and, at many hostels, rooms for couples and family accommodations. British Columbia's 20 Hostelling International locations are clean, well equipped, and, for the most part, set in prime resort, island, and city-center locations. Most have kitchen facilities, family and private accommodations, and low-cost tours and outdoor activities. Chores are not required (as they are in some European hostels), and nonmembers are welcome (at slightly higher rates). B.C. also has a number of unofficial, or non-HI, hostels. Most are similar to HI hostels, though the quality varies and some of Vancouver's non-HI hostels are in rough neighborhoods.

Membership in any HI national hostel association, open to travelers of all ages, allows you to stay in HI-affiliated hostels at member rates; one-year membership is about $28 for adults (C$35 for a two-year minimum membership in Canada, £15 in the U.K., A$52 in Australia, and NZ$40 in New Zealand); hostels charge about $10–$30 per night. Members have priority if the hostel is full; they're also eligible for discounts around the world, even on rail and bus travel in some countries.

F Organizations **Hostelling International–USA**
✉ 8401 Colesville Rd., Suite 600, Silver Spring, MD 20910 ☎ 301/495-1240 🖷 301/495-6697 ⊕ www.hiusa.org. **Hostelling International–Canada** ✉ 205 Catherine St., Suite 400, Ottawa, Ontario K2P 1C3 ☎ 613/237-7884 or 800/663-5777 🖷 613/237-7868 ⊕ www.hihostels.ca. **YHA England and Wales** ✉ Trevelyan House, Dimple Rd., Matlock, Derbyshire DE4 3YH, U.K. ☎ 0870/870-8808, 0870/770-8868, 0162/959-2600 🖷 0870/770-6127 ⊕ www.yha.org.uk. **YHA Australia** ✉ 422 Kent St., Sydney, NSW 2001 ☎ 02/9261-1111 🖷 02/9261-1969 ⊕ www.yha.com.au. **YHA New Zealand** ✉ Level 1, Moorhouse City, 166 Moorhouse Ave., Box 436, Christchurch ☎ 03/379-9970 or 0800/278-299 🖷 03/365-4476 ⊕ www.yha.org.nz.

HOTELS
Because of British Columbia's cool climate, air-conditioning is usually found only in climate-controlled modern hotels

or in the Okanagan, where summers do get hot. All hotels listed have air-conditioning unless otherwise noted. All hotels listed have private bath unless otherwise noted. Bathrooms almost always have a shower but don't necessarily have a bathtub. Queen beds are the norm, and many chain hotels have two queen beds in each room to cover all the accommodation options. Fishing and hunting lodges are the exception: they typically have twin beds, though this is changing as these lodges increasingly cater to families rather than to just anglers. Most hotels can provide your choice of queen or twin beds if you book ahead. You should reserve well ahead for accommodation in British Columbia during July and August, except in ski areas, where the peak season is December–April.

🄵 **Toll-Free Numbers Best Western** ☎ 800/528-1234 ⊕ www.bestwestern.com. **Choice** ☎ 800/424-6423 ⊕ www.choicehotels.com. **Coast Hotels and Resorts** ☎ 800/663-1144 ⊕ www.coasthotels.com. **Comfort Inn** ☎ 800/424-6423 ⊕ www.choicehotels.com. **Days Inn** ☎ 800/325-2525 ⊕ www.daysinn.com. **Four Seasons** ☎ 800/332-3442 ⊕ www.fourseasons.com. **Hilton** ☎ 800/445-8667 ⊕ www.hilton.com. **Holiday Inn** ☎ 800/465-4329 ⊕ www.ichotelsgroup.com. **Howard Johnson** ☎ 800/446-4656 ⊕ www.hojo.com. **Hyatt Hotels & Resorts** ☎ 800/233-1234 ⊕ www.hyatt.com. **Marriott** ☎ 800/228-9290 ⊕ www.marriott.com. **Quality Inn** ☎ 800/424-6423 ⊕ www.choicehotels.com. **Radisson** ☎ 800/333-3333 ⊕ www.radisson.com. **Ramada** ☎ 800/228-2828, 800/854-7854 international reservations ⊕ www.ramada.com. **Red Lion and WestCoast Hotels and Inns** ☎ 800/733-5466 ⊕ www.redlion.com. **Relais & Châteaux** ☎ 800/735-2478 ⊕ www.relaischateaux.com. **Renaissance Hotels & Resorts** ☎ 800/468-3571 ⊕ www.marriott.com. **Sheraton** ☎ 800/325-3535 ⊕ www.starwood.com/sheraton. **Westin Hotels & Resorts** ☎ 800/228-3000 ⊕ www.starwood.com/westin.

MAIL & SHIPPING

In British Columbia you can buy stamps at the post office or from many retail outlets and some newsstands. If you're sending mail to or within Canada, **be sure to include the postal code** (six digits and letters). Note that the suite number often appears before the street number in an address, followed by a hyphen. The postal abbreviation for British Columbia is BC.

POSTAL RATES

Within Canada, postcards and letters up to 30 grams cost C$0.50; between 31 grams and 50 grams, the cost is C$0.85. Oversize letters up to 100 grams cost C$1. Letters and postcards to the United States cost C$0.85 for up to 30 grams, C$1 for between 31 and 50 grams, and C$1.70 for 51 to 100 grams. Prices do not include GST (Goods and Services Tax).

International mail and postcards run C$1.45 for up to 30 grams, C$2 for 31 to 50 grams, and C$3.40 for 51 to 100 grams.

RECEIVING MAIL

Visitors may have mail sent to them c/o General Delivery in the town they are visiting, for pickup in person within 15 days, after which it will be returned to the sender.

SHIPPING PARCELS

Small packages can be sent via the Small Packets service offered by Canada Post. Up to 250 grams to the United States is C$5.60 by air and C$3.95 surface; 250g–500g is C$7.50 by air and C$5.75 surface; 500g–1kg is C$11.75 by air and C$8.95 surface. Internationally, up to 250 grams is C$6.95 by air and C$4.95 surface; 250g–500g is C$13.40 by air and C$6.85 surface; 550g–1kg is C$26.25 by air and C$11.50 surface.

MEDIA

NEWSPAPERS & MAGAZINES

Maclean's is Canada's main general-interest magazine. It covers arts and culture as well as politics. Canada has two national newspapers, the *National Post* and the *Globe and Mail*—both are published in Toronto and both are available at newsstands in major foreign cities. Both have Web sites with limited information on cultural events. For more-detailed information, consult the two major daily newspapers in British Columbia, the *Vancouver Sun* and the *Province*.

RADIO & TELEVISION

U.S. television dominates Canada's airwaves. In border areas—where most people live—Fox, PBS, NBC, CBS, and ABC are readily available. Canada's two major networks, the state-owned Canadian Broadcasting Corporation (CBC) and the private CTV, and the smaller Global Network broadcast a steady diet of U.S. sitcoms and dramas in prime time with only a scattering of Canadian-produced dramas and comedies. The selection of Canadian-produced current-affairs programs, however, is much wider. Cable subscribers in British Columbia have the usual vast menu of specialty channels to choose from, including the all-news outlets operated by CTV and CBC.

The CBC operates the country's only truly national radio network. In fact, it operates four of them, two in English and two in French. Its Radio 1 network, usually broadcast on the AM band, has a daily schedule rich in news, current affairs, and discussion programs. One of the most popular shows, "As It Happens," takes a quirky and highly entertaining look at national, world, and weird events every evening at 6:30. Radio 2, usually broadcast on FM, emphasizes music and often features live classical concerts by some of Canada's best orchestras, opera companies, and choral groups.

MONEY MATTERS

Throughout this book, unless otherwise stated, all prices, including dining and lodging, are given in Canadian dollars.

Prices throughout this guide are given for adults. Substantially reduced fees are almost always available for children, students, and senior citizens. For information on taxes, *see* Taxes.

ATMS

ATMs are available in most bank and credit-union branches across the country, as well as in many convenience stores, malls, and gas stations.

CREDIT CARDS

Visa and MasterCard are widely accepted throughout British Columbia. Diners Club, also known as En Route, is less widely accepted. Discover is little known in Canada outside the major hotel chains. Many small retailers are reluctant to accept American Express cards because of the high fees charged.

Throughout this guide, the following abbreviations are used: **AE**, American Express; **D**, Discover; **DC**, Diners Club; **MC**, MasterCard; and **V**, Visa.

🔢 Reporting Lost Cards **American Express** ☎ 800/528-4800. **Diners Club** ☎ 800/234-6377. **Discover** ☎ 800/347-2683. **MasterCard** ☎ 800/307-7309. **Visa** ☎ 800/336-8472.

CURRENCY

U.S. dollars are widely accepted in much of Canada (especially in communities near the border) but you won't get the exchange rate offered at banks. Traveler's checks (some are available in Canadian dollars) and major U.S. credit cards are accepted in most areas.

The units of currency in Canada are the Canadian dollar (C$) and the cent, in almost the same denominations as U.S. currency ($5, $10, $20, 1¢, 5¢, 10¢, 25¢, etc.). The C$1 and C$2 bill are no longer used; they have been replaced by C$1 and C$2 coins (known as a "loonie," because of the loon that appears on the coin, and a "toonie," respectively).

CURRENCY EXCHANGE

For the most favorable rates, **change money through banks.** Although ATM transaction fees may be higher abroad than at home, ATM rates are excellent because they're based on wholesale rates offered only by major banks. You won't do as well at exchange booths in airports or rail and bus stations, in hotels, in restaurants, or in stores. To avoid lines at airport exchange booths, get a bit of local currency before you leave home.

🔢 Exchange Services **International Currency Express** ✉ 427 N. Camden Dr., Suite F, Beverly Hills, CA 90210 ☎ 888/278-6628 orders ☎ 310/278-6410 🌐 www.foreignmoney.com. **Travel Ex Currency Services** ☎ 800/287-7362 orders and retail locations 🌐 www.travelex.com.

NATIONAL & PROVINCIAL PARKS

If you plan to visit several national parks in Canada, you may be able to **save money on park fees by buying a multipark**

pass. Parks Canada sells a National Parks of Canada pass, good for 12 months at most Canadian national parks, for C$45. You can buy passes at the parks covered by the pass. Contact Parks Canada or the park you plan to visit for information. A National Historic Sites of Canada pass, offered by Parks Canada for C$35, is good for a year's admission to national historic sites. A Discovery package, which provides admission to national parks and national historic sites, is C$59 per year.

Most parks in B.C. are provincial parks. Most are free for day users, but 41 of the more popular parks on southern Vancouver Island, on the Lower Mainland, and in the Okanagan charge a C$3–C$5 per-vehicle, per-day parking fee. Camping fees range from C$9 to C$22 per vehicle, per night, and this includes the daily parking fee. Only cash is accepted at the parks, though you can use MasterCard or Visa to reserve a site by phone with Discover Camping. A C$50 Annual Parking Pass allows unlimited free parking in these parks, though you would need to visit frequently to make it worthwhile. The pass is available at provincial parks, through Discover Camping, and at Tourism B.C. InfoCentres.

🛈 **Park Passes BC Parks** ⊕ www.bcparks.ca. **Discover Camping** ☎ 800/689-9025 ⊕ www.discovercamping.ca. **Parks Canada** National office ✉ 25 Eddy St., Gatineau, QC K1A 0M5 ☎ 888/773-8888 ⊕ www.pc.gc.ca.

PACKING

Weather in British Columbia is changeable and varied; you can expect cool evenings and some chance of rain even in summer. If you plan on camping or hiking in the deep woods in summer, particularly in northern British Columbia, **always carry insect repellent.** In wilderness areas it's also a good idea to carry bear spray and/or wear bells to warn bears of your presence. Both are available in camping and hardware stores in B.C.

In your carry-on luggage, pack an extra pair of eyeglasses or contact lenses and enough of any medication you take to last a few days longer than the entire trip. You may also ask your doctor to write a spare prescription using the drug's generic name,

as brand names may vary from country to country. In luggage to be checked, **never pack prescription drugs, valuables, or undeveloped film.** And don't forget to carry with you the addresses of offices that handle refunds of lost traveler's checks. Check *Fodor's How to Pack* (available at online retailers and bookstores everywhere) for more tips.

To avoid customs and security delays, carry medications in their original packaging. Don't pack any sharp objects in your carry-on luggage, including knives of any size or material, scissors, nail clippers, and corkscrews, or anything else that might arouse suspicion.

To avoid having your checked luggage chosen for hand inspection, don't cram bags full. The U.S. Transportation Security Administration suggests packing shoes on top and placing personal items you don't want touched in clear plastic bags.

CHECKING LUGGAGE

You're allowed to carry aboard one bag and one personal article, such as a purse or a laptop computer. Make sure what you carry on fits under your seat or in the overhead bin. Get to the gate early, so you can board as soon as possible, before the overhead bins fill up.

Baggage allowances vary by carrier, destination, and ticket class. On international flights, you're usually allowed to check two bags weighing up to 70 pounds (32 kilograms) each, although a few airlines allow checked bags of up to 88 pounds (40 kilograms) in first class. Some international carriers don't allow more than 66 pounds (30 kilograms) per bag in business class and 44 pounds (20 kilograms) in economy. If you're flying to or through the United Kingdom, your luggage cannot exceed 70 pounds (32 kilograms) per bag. On domestic flights, the limit is usually 50 to 70 pounds (23 to 32 kilograms) per bag. In general, carry-on bags shouldn't exceed 40 pounds (18 kilograms). Most airlines won't accept bags that weigh more than 100 pounds (45 kilograms) on domestic or international flights. Expect to pay a fee for baggage that exceeds weight limits. Check baggage restrictions with your carrier before you pack.

Airline liability for baggage is limited to $2,500 per person on flights within the United States. On international flights it amounts to $9.07 per pound or $20 per kilogram for checked baggage (roughly $640 per 70-pound bag), with a maximum of $634.90 per piece, and $400 per passenger for unchecked baggage. You can buy additional coverage at check-in for about $10 per $1,000 of coverage, but it often excludes a rather extensive list of items, shown on your airline ticket.

Before departure, itemize your bags' contents and their worth, and label the bags with your name, address, and phone number. (If you use your home address, cover it so potential thieves can't see it readily.) Include a label inside each bag and **pack a copy of your itinerary.** At check-in, make sure each bag is correctly tagged with the destination airport's three-letter code. Because some checked bags will be opened for hand inspection, the U.S. Transportation Security Administration recommends that you leave luggage unlocked or use the plastic locks offered at check-in. TSA screeners place an inspection notice inside searched bags, which are resealed with a special lock.

If your bag has been searched and contents are missing or damaged, file a claim with the TSA Consumer Response Center as soon as possible. If your bags arrive damaged or fail to arrive at all, file a written report with the airline before leaving the airport.

⊞ Complaints U.S. Transportation Security Administration Contact Center ☎ 866/289-9673 ⊕ www.tsa.gov.

PASSPORTS & VISAS

When traveling internationally, carry your passport even if you don't need one. Not only is it the best form of ID, but it's also being required more and more. As of December 31, 2005, for instance, Americans need a passport to reenter the country from Bermuda, the Caribbean, and Panama. Such requirements also affect reentry from Canada and Mexico by air

and sea (as of December 31, 2006) and land (as of December 31, 2007). **Make two photocopies of the data page** (one for someone at home and another for you, carried separately from your passport). If you lose your passport, promptly call the nearest embassy or consulate and the local police.

U.S. passport applications for children under age 14 require consent from both parents or legal guardians; both parents must appear together to sign the application. If only one parent appears, he or she must submit a written statement from the other parent authorizing passport issuance for the child. A parent with sole authority must present evidence of it when applying; acceptable documentation includes the child's certified birth certificate listing only the applying parent, a court order specifically permitting this parent's travel with the child, or a death certificate for the nonapplying parent. Application forms and instructions are available on the Web site of the U.S. State Department's Bureau of Consular Affairs (⊕ travel.state.gov).

ENTERING CANADA

Citizens and legal residents of the United States don't need a passport or visa to enter Canada, but other proof of citizenship (a birth certificate) and some form of photo identification is requested. Naturalized U.S. residents should carry their naturalization certificate. Permanent residents who aren't citizens should carry their "green card." U.S. residents entering Canada from a third country must have a valid passport, naturalization certificate, or "green card."

Citizens of the United Kingdom need only a valid passport to enter Canada for stays of up to six months.

PASSPORT OFFICES

The best time to apply for a passport or to renew is in fall and winter. Before any trip, check your passport's expiration date, and, if necessary, renew it as soon as possible. **⊞ Australian Citizens Passports Australia** Australian Department of Foreign Affairs and Trade ☎ 131-232 ⊕ www.passports.gov.au.

📶 New Zealand Citizens **New Zealand Passports Office** ☎ 0800/22-5050 or 04/474-8100 ⊕ www. passports.govt.nz.
📶 U.K. Citizens **U.K. Passport Service** ☎ 0870/ 521-0410 ⊕ www.passport.gov.uk.

SENIOR-CITIZEN TRAVEL

To qualify for age-related discounts, mention your senior-citizen status up front when booking hotel reservations (not when checking out) and before you're seated in restaurants (not when paying the bill). Be sure to have identification on hand. When renting a car, ask about promotional car-rental discounts, which can be cheaper than senior-citizen rates.

📶 Educational Programs **Elderhostel** ⊠ 11 Ave. de Lafayette, Boston, MA 02111 ☎ 877/426-8056, 978/323-4141 international callers, 877/426-2167 TTY 📠 877/426-2166 ⊕ www.elderhostel.org.

SHOPPING

The low Canadian dollar has made B.C. a favorite shopping destination. Although the selection of manufactured goods isn't as wide as it is in the United States, B.C. towns have a wide range of independent shops selling handmade and imported goods. Popular souvenirs include hand-crafted items made by First Nations and other local artists.

KEY DESTINATIONS

Victoria's British heritage has left a legacy of import shops selling sweets, tea, tweeds, and linens from the British Isles. Salt Spring Island is known for its wealth of handcrafted items sold through artists' studios or at the island's Saturday market. At Okanagan wineries, you can pick up bottles of hard-to-find B.C. wines. Vancouver has the greatest selection of shops: Pacific Centre Mall in downtown Vancouver and Metrotown Mall in Burnaby are among the largest area malls.

SMART SOUVENIRS

Frozen fish may seem an odd souvenir, but given the price of salmon elsewhere in the world, Pacific salmon, at C$3–C$5 a pound, is one of the more popular items to take home from B.C. Most fishmongers in areas frequented by tourists will pack your salmon for travel, as will your fishing out-

fitter if you've caught your own. First Nations (particularly Haida) art and hand-crafted items are available at galleries, shops, and artists' studios throughout the province. Look for cedar boxes or silver jewelry with traditional designs, or items carved from argillite, a black slate unique to the Queen Charlotte Islands. Items can range from under C$100 to several thousand. Heavy sweaters knit with traditional designs are made by the Cowichan people near Duncan; they start at about C$200.

WATCH OUT

Cuban cigars are sold legally in Canada, but it's still illegal to take them back to the United States.

SPORTS & OUTDOORS

BICYCLING

📶 Association **Canadian Cycling Association** ⊠ 702-2197 Riverside Dr., Ottawa, ON K1H 7X3 ☎ 613/248-1353 📠 613/248-9311 ⊕ www. canadian-cycling.com.

CANOEING & KAYAKING

📶 Association **Canadian Recreational Canoeing Association** ⊠ 446 Main St. W, Box 398, Merrickville, ON K0G 1N0 ☎ 613/269-2910 or 888/252-6292 📠 613/269-2908 ⊕ www.paddlingcanada.com.

CLIMBING–MOUNTAINEERING

📶 Association **Alpine Club of Canada** ⊠ Indian Flats Rd., Box 8040, Canmore, AB T1W 2T8 ☎ 403/678-3200 📠 403/678-3224 ⊕ www. alpineclubofcanada.ca.

DIVING

📶 Association **Underwater Council of British Columbia** ⊠ Vancouver Maritime Museum, 1905 Ogden Point Rd., Vancouver, BC V6J 1A3 ☎ No phone ⊕ www.ucbc.ca.

GOLF

📶 Association **Royal Canadian Golf Association** ⊠ 1333 Dorval Drive, Suite 1, Oakville, ON L6M 4X7 ☎ 905/849-9700 📠 905/845-7040 ⊕ www.rcga. org.

STUDENTS IN CANADA

Persons under 18 years of age who are not accompanied by their parents should **bring a letter from a parent or guardian** giving them permission to travel to Canada. Travel Cuts is an agency specializing in

Student Travel. Outlets can be found on most Canadian college campuses and in most major Canadian cities. Student IDs can often be used for discounts at sights and entertainment venues.

🚩 **IDs & Services STA Travel** ✉ 10 Downing St., New York, NY 10014 ☎ 212/627-3111, 800/777-0112 24-hr service center 🖨 212/627-3387 ⊕ www.sta.com. **Travel Cuts** ✉ 187 College St., Toronto, Ontario M5T 1P7, Canada ☎ 800/592-2887 in U.S., 416/979-2406 or 866/246-9762 in Canada 🖨 416/979-8167 ⊕ www.travelcuts.com.

TAXES

A Goods and Services Tax (GST) of 7% applies on virtually every transaction in Canada except for the purchase of basic groceries. Prices in this book do not normally include taxes.

In addition to the GST, British Columbia levies a sales tax of 7% on most items (although groceries, children's clothes, and restaurant meals are exempt). Instead of the 7% PST, accommodations are subject to an 8% tax (in addition to the GST), and some municipalities levy an additional 1% or 2%. Wine, beer, and spirits purchased in bars and restaurants are subject to a 10% tax. Some restaurants build this into the price of the beverage, but others add it to the bill.

GST REFUNDS

You can **get a GST refund** on purchases taken out of the country and on short-term accommodations, including camping, of less than one month, but not on food, drink, tobacco, car or motor-home rentals, or transportation; rebate forms, which must be submitted within a year of leaving Canada, may be obtained from certain retailers, duty-free shops, customs officials, or from the Canada Customs and Revenue Agency. Most provinces do not tax goods that are shipped directly by the vendor to the purchaser's home. Always **save your original receipts** from stores and hotels (not just credit-card receipts), and **be sure the name and address of the establishment are shown on the receipt.** Original receipts are not returned. For you to be eligible for a refund, your receipts must total at least C$200, each individual receipt for goods

must show a minimum purchase of C$50 before tax, and the goods must have been removed from Canada within 60 days of purchase. You will also need proof of export, meaning that you must have your goods inspected and your receipts validated when you leave the country. Some agencies in Vancouver and Whistler offer on-the-spot cash GST refunds. Although they charge a commission of about 20%, some visitors may find it worth it for the convenience, especially as Canadian Government checks may be difficult to cash in some countries. *See* the shopping sections of individual chapters for locations.

🚩 **Canada Customs and Revenue Agency** ✉ Visitor Rebate Program, Summerside Tax Centre, 275 Pope Rd., Suite 104, Summerside, PE C1N 6C6 ☎ 902/432-5608, 800/668-4748 in Canada ⊕ www.cra-arc.gc.ca/tax/nonresidents/visitors.

TIME

Most of British Columbia lies within the Pacific time zone and is on the same time as Los Angeles and Seattle. It's 19 hours behind Sydney, 8 hours behind London, 3 hours behind New York City and Toronto, 2 hours behind Chicago, and 1 hour ahead of Alaska. B.C.'s Rocky Mountain region is on Mountain time, which is one hour ahead of Pacific time.

TIPPING

Tips and service charges are not usually added to a bill in Canada. In general, tip 15% of the total bill. This goes for waiters, barbers and hairdressers, and taxi drivers. Porters and doormen should get about C$2 a bag. For maid service, leave at least C$2 per person a day (C$3 in luxury hotels).

TOURS & PACKAGES

Because everything is prearranged on a prepackaged tour or independent vacation, you spend less time planning—and often get it all at a good price.

BOOKING WITH AN AGENT

Travel agents are excellent resources. But it's a good idea to collect brochures from several agencies, as some agents' suggestions may be influenced by relationships with tour and package firms that reward them for volume sales. If you have a special interest, find an agent with expertise in that area. The American Society of Travel Agents (ASTA) has a database of specialists worldwide; you can log on to the group's Web site to find one near you.

Make sure your travel agent knows the accommodations and other services of the place being recommended. Ask about the hotel's location, room size, beds, and whether it has a pool, room service, or programs for children, if you care about these. Has your agent been there in person or sent others whom you can contact?

Do some homework on your own, too: local tourism boards can provide information about lesser-known and small-niche operators, some of which may sell only direct.

BUYER BEWARE

Each year consumers are stranded or lose their money when tour operators—even large ones with excellent reputations—go out of business. So check out the operator. Ask several travel agents about its reputation, and try to **book with a company that has a consumer-protection program.** (Look for information in the company's brochure.) In the United States, members of the United States Tour Operators Association are required to set aside funds (up to $1 million) to help eligible customers cover payments and travel arrangements in the event that the company defaults. It's also a good idea to choose a company that participates in the American Society of Travel Agents' Tour Operator Program; ASTA will act as mediator in any disputes between you and your tour operator.

Remember that the more your package or tour includes, the better you can predict the ultimate cost of your vacation. Make sure you know exactly what is covered, and beware of hidden costs. Are taxes, tips, and transfers included? Entertainment and excursions? These can add up.

🚆 Tour-Operator Recommendations **American Society of Travel Agents** (⇨ Travel Agencies). **National Tour Association—The Global Association for Packaged Travel** ✉ 546 E. Main St., Lexington, KY 40508 ☎ 859/226-4444 or 800/682-8886 🖷 859/226-4414 ⊕ www.ntaonline.com. **United States Tour Operators Association** (USTOA) ✉ 275 Madison Ave., Suite

2014, New York, NY 10016 ☎ 212/599-6599 🖷 212/599-6744 ⊕ www.ustoa.com.

TRAIN TRAVEL

Amtrak has service from Seattle to Vancouver, providing connections between Amtrak's U.S.-wide network and VIA Rail's Canadian routes. VIA Rail Canada provides transcontinental rail service. In B.C. VIA Rail has two routes: Vancouver to Jasper, and Jasper to Prince Rupert with an overnight stop in Prince George. Rocky Mountaineer Vacations operates a variety of spectacular all-daylight rail trips between the Canadian Rockies and the west coast.

CUTTING COSTS

If you're planning to travel much by train, **look into the Canrail pass.** It allows 12 days of coach-class travel within a 30-day period; sleeping cars are available, but they sell out early and must be reserved at least a month in advance during the high season (June through mid-October), when the pass is C$763. Low-season rates (October 16 through May) are C$475. For more information and reservations, contact VIA Rail, or a travel agent in the United States or Canada.

Train travelers can **check out the 30-day North American RailPass** offered by Amtrak and VIA Rail. It allows unlimited coach-economy travel in the United States and Canada. The cost is C$899 from June to October 15, C$637 at other times.

FARES & SCHEDULES

🚆 Train Information **Amtrak** ☎ 800/872-7245 ⊕ www.amtrak.com. **Rocky Mountaineer Vacations** ☎ 800/665-7245 ⊕ www.rockymountaineer. com. **VIA Rail Canada** ☎ 888/842-7245 ⊕ www. viarail.ca.

PAYING

All the train services accept major credit cards, traveler's checks, and cash. VIA Rail will accept U.S. and Canadian currency.

RESERVATIONS

Reservations are essential on the Rocky Mountaineer and highly recommended on Amtrak and VIA routes. There's no extra charge for reservations on any of the train services listed.

TRANSPORTATION AROUND BRITISH COLUMBIA

Although cars and motor homes give the most freedom to tour B.C.'s byways, a combination of train tours, long-distance buses, internal flights, and coastal ferries makes it possible to see this huge region car-free. Among the roadless fjords and islands of the coast, ferries, private boats, and floatplanes provide the only access to many communities. In pedestrian-friendly Vancouver and Victoria, simply strolling is the best way to see the sights.

TRAVEL AGENCIES

A good travel agent puts your needs first. Look for an agency that has been in business at least five years, emphasizes customer service, and has someone on staff who specializes in your destination. In addition, **make sure the agency belongs to a professional trade organization.** The American Society of Travel Agents (ASTA) has more than 10,000 members in some 140 countries, enforces a strict code of ethics, and will step in to mediate agent-client disputes involving ASTA members. ASTA also maintains a directory of agents on its Web site; ASTA's TravelSense.org, a trip-planning and travel-advice site, can also help to locate a travel agent who caters to your needs. (If a travel agency is also acting as your tour operator, *see* Buyer Beware *in* Tours & Packages.)

🔁 Local Agent Referrals **American Society of Travel Agents (ASTA)** ✉ 1101 King St., Suite 200, Alexandria, VA 22314 ☎ 703/739-2782 🖨 703/684-8319 ⊕ www.astanet.com and www.travelsense.org. **Association of British Travel Agents** ✉ 68-71 Newman St., London W1T 3AH ☎ 020/7637-2444 🖨 020/7637-0713 ⊕ www.abta.com. **Association of Canadian Travel Agencies** ✉ 130 Albert St., Suite 1705, Ottawa, Ontario K1P 5G4 ☎ 613/237-3657 🖨 613/237-7052 ⊕ www.acta.ca. **Australian Federation of Travel Agents** ✉ Level 3, 309 Pitt St.,

Sydney, NSW 2000 ☎ 02/9264-3299 or 1300/363-416 🖨 02/9264-1085 ⊕ www.afta.com.au. **Travel Agents' Association of New Zealand** ✉ Level 5, Tourism and Travel House, 79 Boulcott St., Box 1888, Wellington 6001 ☎ 04/499-0104 🖨 04/499-0786 ⊕ www.taanz.org.nz.

VISITOR INFORMATION

Learn more about foreign destinations by checking government-issued travel advisories and country information. For a broader picture, consider information from more than one country.

🔁 Tourist Information **Canadian Tourism Commission** ☎ 613/946-1000 ⊕ www.travelcanada.ca. **Hello BC (Tourism B.C.)** ☎ 800/435-5622 ⊕ www.hellobc.com. **Vancouver Tourist InfoCentre** ✉ Plaza Level, 200 Burrard St., Vancouver V6C 3L6 ☎ 604/683-2000 ⊕ www.tourismvancouver.com. 🔁 Government Advisories **U.K. Foreign and Commonwealth Office** ✉ Travel Advice Unit, Consular Directorate, Old Admiralty Bldg., London SW1A 2PA ☎ 0870/606-0290 or 020/7008-1500 ⊕ www.fco.gov.uk/travel. **Australian Department of Foreign Affairs and Trade** ☎ 300/139-281 travel advisories, 02/6261-1299 Consular Travel Advice ⊕ www.smartraveller.gov.au or www.dfat.gov.au. **New Zealand Ministry of Foreign Affairs and Trade** ☎ 04/439-8000 ⊕ www.mft.govt.nz.

WEB SITES

Do check out the World Wide Web when planning your trip. You can find everything from weather forecasts to virtual tours of famous cities. Be sure to visit Fodors.com (⊕ www.fodors.com), a complete travel-planning site. You can research prices and book plane tickets, hotel rooms, rental cars, vacation packages, and more. In addition, you can post your pressing questions in the Travel Talk section. Other planning tools include a currency converter and weather reports, and there are loads of links to travel resources.

Vancouver

WORD OF MOUTH

"On a clear day or evening the views of the city of Vancouver from Grouse Mountain are magnificent. . . . But if it's cloudy, unless you are going to get there early in the day, give it a miss."
—Keith from Vancouver

"I love going down to Granville Island. . . . Wander through the market and enjoy the smells and colors . . . stick your head into the jewelry galleries . . . the prices are very fair and the art is unique! Take public transit, or if you are looking for something more interesting, take the little boat that connects Granville Island to Yaletown and other nearby areas."
—Aline from Vancouver

By Carolyn B.
Heller and Sue
Kernaghan

VANCOUVER IS A YOUNG CITY, even by North American standards. It was not yet a town when British Columbia became part of the Canadian confederation in 1871. The city's history, such as it is, remains visible to the naked eye: eras are stacked east to west along the waterfront, from cobblestone late-Victorian Gastown to shiny postmodern glass cathedrals of commerce.

The Chinese, among the first to recognize the possibilities of Vancouver's setting, came to British Columbia during the 1850s seeking the gold that inspired them to name the province Gum-shan, or Gold Mountain. They subsequently built the Canadian Pacific Railway, the transcontinental link that persuaded British Columbians to join that new nation back east called Canada. The railway chose the townsite of Granville, a ramshackle collection of shacks on the edge of Burrard Inlet, as its Pacific terminus.

The coming of the railway inspired the loggers and saloon-owners of Granville to incorporate as a city. They also chose a more dignified name: On April 6,1886, Granville Townsite, with a population of about 400, became the City of Vancouver, after the British explorer who had famously toured the inlet here in 1792. Just two months later, however, the new city burned to the ground after a brush fire. By the time the first transcontinental passenger train rolled in May 1887, the city had been rebuilt, and grew rapidly.

The railway, along with Canadian Pacific's fleet of clipper ships, gave Vancouver a full week's edge over the California ports in shipping tea and silk to New York at the end of the 19th century. Lumber, fish, and coal from British Columbia's hinterland also flowed through the port to world markets. The same ships and trains brought immigrants from all corners of the earth, helping the population grow exponentially to today's 2 million.

Long a port city in a resource-based province, Vancouver is relatively new to tourism and, for that matter, to its famous laid-back West Coast lifestyle. Most locals mark Expo '86, when the city cleaned up old industrial sites and generated new tourism infrastructure, as the turning point. Another makeover is in the works now, as Vancouver, with Whistler, prepares to host the 2010 Winter Olympics.

The mild climate, exquisite natural scenery, and relaxed outdoor lifestyle continually attract new residents, and the number of visitors is increasing for the same reasons. People often get their first glimpse of Vancouver when catching an Alaskan cruise, and many return at some point to spend more time here.

EXPLORING VANCOUVER

The heart of Vancouver, which includes downtown, Stanley Park, Yaletown, and the West End, sits on a peninsula bordered by English Bay and the Pacific Ocean to the west; by False Creek, the inlet home to

If you have
1 or 2
days

If you have only one day in Vancouver, start with an early morning walk, bike, or shuttle ride through **Stanley Park** ㉒– ㉙ to see the **Vancouver Aquarium Marine Science Centre** ㉓, enjoy the views from **Prospect Point** ㉗, and take a stroll along the seawall. If you leave the park at English Bay, you can have lunch on Denman or **Robson Street** ❶, meander on foot past the trendy shops between Jervis and Burrard streets, and then walk northeast on Burrard to view the many buildings of architectural interest. Alternatively, you can exit the the park at Coal Harbour and follow the Seawall Walk to **Canada Place** ❿, stopping for lunch at a seaside pub or restaurant. From Canada Place, follow Burrard Street southwest to Robson. Either way, the **Vancouver Art Gallery** ❸ and the **Vancouver Lookout!** ❽ at Harbour Centre also make good stops. On Day 2 take a leisurely walking tour of the shops, eateries, and cobblestone streets of Gastown, Chinatown, and Yaletown.

1

If you have
3 or 4
days

If you have another day to tour Vancouver and have followed the itinerary above, head to the south side of False Creek and English Bay on Day 3 to delve into the public market and the many boutiques, eateries, and theaters of **Granville Island** ㉟– ㊶. Buses and ferries provide easy transit, and touring the island is best accomplished on foot. (If you drive, parking is available, but traffic to the island can be congested, especially on weekends.)

On Day 4, tour other sights beyond downtown Vancouver. Make time for the **Museum of Anthropology** ㊵ on the campus of the University of British Columbia. Also visit the **Vancouver Museum** ㊷, the **H. R. MacMillan Space Centre** ㊸, and the **Vancouver Maritime Museum** ㊹, all in the Kitsilano area. Plan to dine at one of the innovative restaurants in Kitsilano or in the upscale South Granville neighborhood. If you'd rather play outside, head to the North Shore Mountains, where you can swing high above the Capilano River on the **Capilano Suspension Bridge** ㊾ and take in the panoramic city views as you ride the Skyride to the top of **Grouse Mountain** ㊿. Or, venture to the East Side and browse the funky boutiques along Main Street or Commercial Drive.

Granville Island, to the south; and by Burrard Inlet, the city's working port, to the north, where the North Shore Mountains loom. The oldest parts of the city, Gastown and Chinatown, lie at the edge of Burrard Inlet, around Main Street, which runs north–south and is roughly the dividing line between the east and west sides. All the avenues, which are numbered, have east and west designations. One note about printed Vancouver street addresses: suite numbers often appear *before* the street number, followed by a hyphen.

Other places of interest exist elsewhere in the city as well, such as the North Shore across Burrard Inlet, south of downtown across English Bay, and on Granville Island.

Robson to the Waterfront

Numbers in the text correspond to numbers in the margin and on the Downtown Vancouver map.

Museums and buildings of architectural and historical significance are the primary draw in downtown Vancouver, but there's also plenty of fine shopping.

a good walk

Begin on **Robson Street❶** ☛, at Bute or Thurlow Street. Follow Robson southeast to Hornby Street to reach **Robson Square❷**, on your right. The **Vancouver Art Gallery❸** is on the left. Head northeast on Hornby Street to get to the **Fairmont Hotel Vancouver❹**, a city landmark.

The **HSBC Bank Building** is at Georgia and Hornby streets, catercorner to the Hotel Vancouver. Its five-story-high public lobby atrium has a café, regularly changing art exhibitions, and one of the city's more intriguing public-art installations; *Pendulum,* by B.C. artist Alan Storey, is a 90-foot-long hollow aluminum sculpture that arcs hypnotically overhead. The **Cathedral Place** office tower, on the other side of Hornby Street, is one of Vancouver's most attractive postmodern buildings. The three large sculptures of nurses at the corners of the building are replicas of the statues that adorned the Georgia Medical–Dental Building, the art deco structure that previously occupied this site; the faux copper roof mimics that of the Fairmont Hotel Vancouver. Step into the lobby to see another interesting sculpture, Robert Studer's *Navigational Device,* suspended from high on the north wall.

The north exit of Cathedral Place (beside the café) leads to a peaceful green courtyard. Immediately next door (to the west) is the Gothic-style **Christ Church Cathedral❺**. About three blocks north (toward the water), the art deco **Marine Building❻** is on the left side of Burrard Street.

Facing the water, make a right onto Hastings Street and follow it east less than a half block for a look at the exterior of the exclusive Vancouver Club (on the waterside of the street). The club marks the start of the old financial district, which runs southeast along Hastings. The district's older temple-style banks, investment houses, and business-people's clubs are the surviving legacy of the city's sophisticated pre–World War II architecture.

Continue along Hastings to **Sinclair Centre❼**, between Howe and Granville streets. The magnificently restored complex of government buildings houses offices and retail shops. At 698 West Hastings Street, just past Granville Street, the jewelry store Birks now occupies the Roman-influenced former headquarters of the Canadian Imperial Bank of Commerce (CIBC). The 1907 cast-iron clock that stands outside was, at its previous location at Granville and Georgia streets, a favorite rendezvous point for generations of Vancouverites. The imposing 1931 Royal Bank building stands directly across the street. The elevator to the **Vancouver Lookout!❽** is at Hastings and Seymour streets, a block southeast of here.

On Seymour, head toward Burrard Inlet to **Waterfront Station❾**. Take a peek at the murals inside the 19th-century structure, and then exit by

The Great Outdoors

Nature has truly blessed this city, surrounding it with verdant forests, towering mountains, coves, inlets, rivers, and the wide sea. Diving, biking, hiking, skiing, snowboarding, and sailing are among the many outdoor activities possible in or near the city. Whether you prefer to relax on a beach by yourself or join a kayaking tour with an outfitter, Vancouver has plenty to offer.

Nightlife & the Arts

Vancouver residents support the arts enthusiastically, especially during the city's film, jazz, folk, and theater festivals, most of which take place between June and October. The city also covers the spectrum of arts and nightlife, from opera, ballet, and symphonies to live music, theater venues, pubs, and vibrant nightclubs.

1

the west staircase (to your left). This takes you out to Granville Square with its views of the working harbor and cruise-ship terminal. Head directly across Granville Square to the staircase on the far side. The stairs will take you down to Howe Street. Turn right to see the soaring canopies of **Canada Place** ⑩, where you can stroll around the cruise-ship-style decks for great ocean and mountain views, visit the Port Authority Interpretive Centre, or catch a film at the IMAX theater. The **Vancouver Tourist Info Centre** ⑪ is across Canada Place Way (next door to the Fairmont Waterfront Hotel). Canada Place is also the starting point of Vancouver's **Seawall Walk,** a pedestrian and bike route that follows most of the city's coastline. The first mile takes you past the waterfront parks, marinas, and condominiums of Coal Harbour to Stanley Park. Until 2008 you'll have to detour around the construction site next to Canada Place, but it's smooth sailing from there.

TIMING This tour takes about an hour to walk, not counting stops along the way. Allow an hour or more for the Vancouver Art Gallery, depending on the exhibits, and about 30 minutes for the Vancouver Lookout. Add another 30 minutes to an hour if you add a stroll along the Seawall Walk.

What to See

⑩ **Canada Place.** When Vancouver hosted the Expo '86 world's fair, this former cargo pier was transformed into the Canadian pavilion. Extending four city blocks north into Burrard Inlet, the complex mimics the style and size of a luxury ocean liner, with exterior promenades and open deck space. The Teflon-coated fiberglass roof, shaped like five sails, has become a Vancouver skyline landmark. Home to Vancouver's main cruise-ship terminal, Canada Place can accommodate up to three luxury liners at once. It's also home to the luxurious **Pan Pacific Hotel,** and, for the time being, the **Vancouver Convention and Exhibition Centre** (a new convention center, due to open in 2008, is under construction next door). You can stroll the exterior promenade and admire views of Burrard Inlet, Stanley Park, and the North Shore

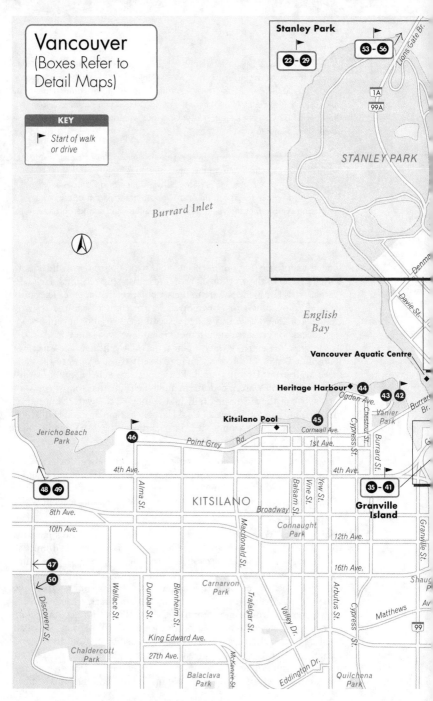

Vancouver
(Boxes Refer to
Detail Maps)

KEY

▶ *Start of walk
or drive*

Stanley Park

22 - 29

53 - 56

Lions Gate Br.

1A
99A

STANLEY PARK

Denma

Davie St.

Burrard Inlet

*English
Bay*

Vancouver Aquatic Centre

Heritage Harbour ◆ **44**

43 **42**

Ogden Ave.

Chestnut St.

*Vanier
Park*

Burra
Br.

Kitsilano Pool ◆

45

Cornwall Ave.

Cypress St.

Burrard St.

1st Ave.

*Jericho Beach
Park*

46

Point Grey Rd.

4th Ave.

4th Ave.

35 - 41

48 **49**

Alma St.

KITSILANO

Balsam St.

Vine St.

Yew St.

**Granville
Island**

8th Ave.

Broadway

Granville St.

10th Ave.

Macdonald St.

*Connaught
Park*

12th Ave.

47

16th Ave.

50

Discovery St.

Wallace St.

Dunbar St.

Blenheim St.

*Carnarvon
Park*

Trafalgar St.

Valley Dr.

Arbutus St.

Cypress St.

Matthews

Shaug
P

Av

99

King Edward Ave.

*Chaldercott
Park*

27th Ave.

McKenzie St.

Eddington Dr.

*Balaclava
Park*

*Quilchena
Park*

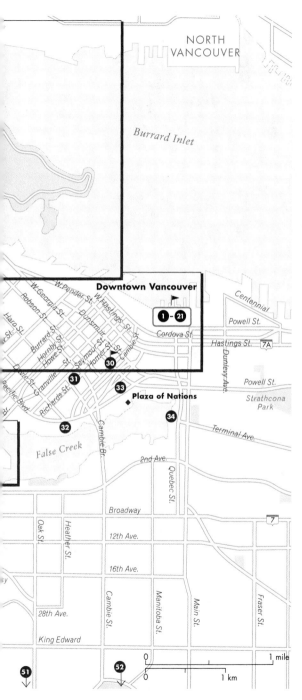

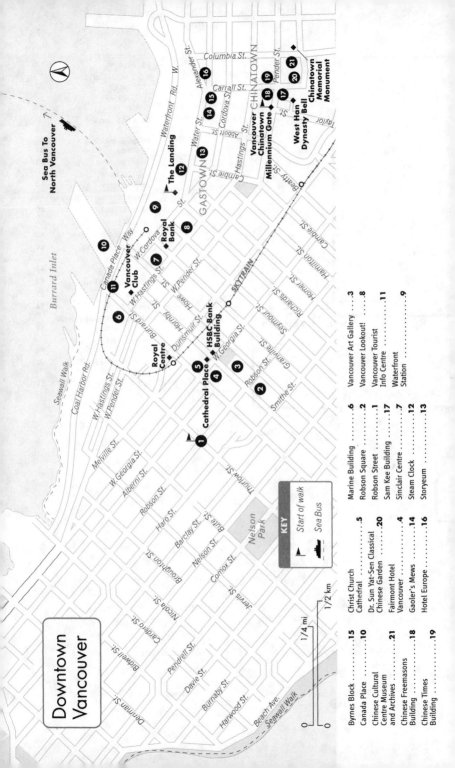

Downtown Vancouver

KEY

▲ Start of walk

⊷ Sea Bus

Byrnes Block **15**
Canada Place **10**
Chinese Cultural
Centre Museum
and Archives **21**
Chinese Freemasons
Building **18**
Chinese Times
Building **19**

Christ Church
Cathedral **5**
Dr. Sun Yat-Sen Classical
Chinese Garden **20**
Fairmont Hotel
Vancouver **4**
Gaoler's Mews **14**
Hotel Europe **16**

Marine Building **6**
Robson Square **2**
Robson Street **1**
Sam Kee Building **17**
Sinclair Centre **7**
Steam Clock **12**
Storyeum **13**

Vancouver Art Gallery **3**
Vancouver Lookout! **8**
Vancouver Tourist
Info Centre **11**
Waterfront
Station **9**

mountains; plaques posted at intervals offer historical information about the city and its waterfront. At the **Port Authority Interpretive Centre** (☎ 604/665–9177 or 604/665–9179 ☞ Free ☉ Weekdays 9–5) you can catch a video about the workings of the port, see some historic images of Vancouver's waterfront, or try your hand at a virtual container-loading game. The **CN IMAX Theatre** (☎ 604/682–4629 ☞ C$11.50, higher prices for some films) shows films on a five-story-high screen. ✉ 999 *Canada Place Way, Downtown* ☎ 604/647–7390 or 604/775–7200 ⊕ *www.canadaplace.ca.*

⑤ Christ Church Cathedral. The oldest church in Vancouver was built between 1889 and 1895. Constructed in the Gothic style, this Anglican church looks like the parish church of an English village from the outside, though underneath its sandstone-clad exterior it's made of Douglas fir from what is now south Vancouver. The 32 stained-glass windows depict Old and New Testament scenes, often set against Vancouver landmarks (St. Nicholas presiding over the Lions Gate Bridge, for example). The building's excellent acoustics enhance the choral evensong and carols frequently sung here. Gregorian chants are sung every Sunday evening at 9:30. ✉ *690 Burrard St., Downtown* ☎ 604/682–3848 ⊕ *www.cathedral.vancouver.bc.ca* ☉ *Weekdays 10–4. Services Sun. at 8 AM, 10:30 AM, and 9:30 PM; weekdays at 12:10 PM.*

④ Fairmont Hotel Vancouver. One of the last railway-built hotels in Canada, the Fairmont Hotel Vancouver was designed in the château style, its architectural details reminiscent of a medieval French castle. Construction began in 1929 and wrapped up just in time for King George VI of England's 1939 visit. The exterior of the building, one of the most recognizable in Vancouver's skyline, has carvings of malevolent-looking gargoyles at the corners, native chiefs on the Hornby Street side, and an assortment of figures from classical mythology decorating the building's facade. ✉ *900 W. Georgia St., Downtown* ☎ 604/684–3131 ⊕ *www.fairmont.com.*

⑥ Marine Building. Terra-cotta bas-reliefs depicting the history of transportation, such as airships, steamships, locomotives, and submarines, as well as Maya and Egyptian motifs and images of marine life adorn this 1930 art deco structure. Step inside for a look at the beautifully restored interior, and then walk to the corner of Hastings and Hornby streets for the best view of the building. ✉ *355 Burrard St., Downtown.*

② Robson Square. Architect Arthur Erickson designed this plaza, which was completed in 1979, to be *the* gathering place of downtown Vancouver. Landscaped walkways connect the Vancouver Art Gallery, government offices, and law courts. A University of British Columbia satellite campus and bookstore occupy the level below the street. Political protests and impromptu demonstrations take place on the gallery stairs, a tradition that dates from the days when the building was a courthouse. ✉ *Bordered by Howe, Hornby, Robson, and Smithe Sts., Downtown.*

⍎ ① Robson Street. Robson Street, Vancouver's busiest shopping street, is lined with see-and-be-seen sidewalk cafés, chain fashion stores, and high-end boutiques. The street, which links downtown to the West End, is particularly lively between Jervis and Burrard streets and stays that way into the evening.

off the beaten path

ROEDDE HOUSE MUSEUM – Two blocks south of Robson Street is the Roedde (pronounced *roh*-dee) House Museum, an 1893 house in the Queen Anne Revival style, set among Victorian-style gardens. Tours of the restored, antiques-furnished interior take about an hour. On Sunday, tours are followed by tea and cookies. The gardens (free) can be visited anytime. ⊠ *1415 Barclay St., between Broughton and Nicola, West End* ☎ *604/684–7040* ⊕ *www.roeddehouse.org* ☜ *C$4, Sun. C$5, including tea* ☉ *Wed.–Fri. 2–4, Sun. 2–4; longer hrs in summer.*

need a break?

The pastry chefs at **Sen5es Bakery** (⊠ 801 W. Georgia St., Downtown ☎ 604/633–0138) create some of Vancouver's most decadent treats. Stop in for a piece of champagne truffle cake, some hand-rolled chocolates, a raspberry financier tart, or whatever else suits your fancy. You can also grab coffee or a soup-and-sandwich lunch here.

❼ Sinclair Centre. Vancouver architect Richard Henriquez knitted four government office buildings into Sinclair Centre, an office-retail complex that takes up an entire city block between Cordova and Hastings, and Howe and Granville streets. Inside are designer-clothing shops, federal government offices, and a number of fast-food outlets. The two Hastings Street buildings—the 1910 **Post Office,** which has an elegant clock tower, and the 1911 **Winch Building**—are linked with the 1937 **Post Office Extension** and the 1913 **Customs Examining Warehouse** to the north. As part of a meticulous restoration in the mid-1980s, the post-office facade was moved to the Granville Street side of the complex. The original clockwork from the old clock tower is on display inside, on the upper level of the arcade. ⊠ *757 W. Hastings St., Downtown.*

❸ Vancouver Art Gallery. Painter Emily Carr's haunting evocations of the British Columbian hinterland are among the attractions at Western Canada's largest art gallery. Carr (1871–1945), a grocer's daughter from Victoria, fell in love with the wilderness around her and shocked middle-class Victorian society by running off to paint it. Her work accentuates the mysticism and the danger of B.C.'s wilderness and records the passing of native cultures. The gallery, which also hosts touring historical and contemporary exhibitions, is housed in a 1911 courthouse that Arthur Erickson redesigned in the early 1980s. Stone lions guard the steps at the parklike Georgia Street side; the main entrance is from Robson Square. For a break, try the Gallery Café's terrace. ⊠ *750 Hornby St., Downtown* ☎ *604/662–4719* ⊕ *www.vanartgallery.bc.ca* ☜ *C$15; may be higher for some exhibits; donation Thurs. 5–9* ☉ *Mon.–Wed. and Fri.–Sun. 10–5:30, Thurs. 10–9.*

❽ Vancouver Lookout! The lookout looks like a flying saucer stuck atop a high-rise. At 553 feet high, it affords one of the best views of Vancouver. A glass elevator whizzes you up 50 stories to the circular observation deck, where knowledgeable guides point out the sights and give a tour every hour on the hour. On a clear day you can see Vancouver Island and Mount Baker in Washington State. The top-floor restaurant makes one complete revolution per hour; the elevator ride up is free for diners. Tickets are good all day, so you can visit in daytime and return for another look after dark. ⊠ *555 W. Hastings St., Downtown* ☎ *604/689–0421* ⊕ *www.vancouverlookout.com* ⊑ *C$10* ☉ *May–Sept., daily 8:30 AM–10:30 PM; Oct.–Apr., daily 9–9.*

⓫ **Vancouver Tourist Info Centre.** Here you can find brochures and personnel to answer questions, book tours, reserve accommodations, buy event tickets, and see a nice view of the Burrard Inlet and the North Shore mountains. ⊠ *200 Burrard St., Downtown* ☎ *604/683–2000* ⊕ *www.tourismvancouver.com* ☉ *Mid-Sept.–mid-May, Mon.–Sat. 8:30–5; mid-May–mid-Sept., daily 8:30–7.*

❾ **Waterfront Station.** This former Canadian Pacific Railway passenger terminal was built between 1912 and 1914 as the western terminus for Canada's transcontinental railway. After Canada's railways merged, the station became obsolete, but a 1978 renovation turned it into an office–retail complex and depot for SkyTrain, SeaBus, and West Coast Express passengers. In the main concourse, panels near the ceiling depict the scenery travelers once saw on journeys across Canada. Here you can catch a 13-minute SeaBus trip across the harbor to the waterfront public market at Lonsdale Quay in North Vancouver. ⊠ *601 W. Cordova St., Downtown* ☎ *604/953–3333 SeaBus and SkyTrain, 604/683–7245 West Coast Express.*

Gastown

Gastown is where Vancouver originated after "Gassy" Jack Deighton canoed into Burrard Inlet in 1867 with his wife, some whiskey, and a few amenities. The smooth-talking Deighton convinced local mill workers into building him a saloon in exchange for a barrel of whiskey. (It didn't take much convincing. His saloon was on the edge of lumber-company land, where alcohol was forbidden.) In 1885, when the Canadian Pacific Railway announced that Burrard Inlet would be the terminus for the new transcontinental railway, the little town—called Granville Townsite at the time—saw its population grow fivefold over a few months. But on June 13, 1886, two short months after Granville's incorporation as the City of Vancouver, a clearing fire got out of control and burned down the entire town. It was rebuilt by the time the first transcontinental train arrived, in May 1887, and Vancouver became a transfer point for trade with the Far East and soon was crowded with hotels, warehouses, brothels, and saloons. The Klondike gold rush encouraged further development that lasted until 1912, when the so-called golden years ended. From the 1930s to the 1950s, hotels were converted into rooming houses, and the warehouse district shifted elsewhere. The neglected area gradually became run down. These days, Gastown, which along with Chinatown was declared a historic district in 1971, has been revitalized and is home to boutiques, cafés, loft apartments, and souvenir shops.

Numbers in the text correspond to numbers in the margin and on the Downtown Vancouver map.

Start at the **Landing** ☞, a former warehouse at the corner of Water and Richards streets, downtown. Built in 1905 with gold-rush money, it was renovated in 1988 to include shops and a brewpub. From the window at the rear of the lobby you can see Burrard Inlet and the North Shore Mountains. A block east, at the corner of Water and Cambie streets, stands the world's first **steam clock** ⑫. Half a block along, on the south side of the street is the entrance to **Storyeum** ⑬, a multimedia historical attraction. **Gaoler's Mews** ⑭ is about 1½ blocks east, tucked behind 12 Water Street. **Byrnes Block** ⑮, on the corner of Water and Carrall streets, and the **Hotel Europe** ⑯, at Powell and Alexander streets, are two buildings of historical and architectural interest. A statue of Gassy Jack Deighton stands on the west side of Maple Tree Square, at the intersection of Water, Powell, Alexander, and Carrall streets, where he built his first saloon.

Vancouver's downtown east side—the area between Gastown and Chinatown roughly bordered by West Cordova and West Hastings between Cambie and Gore—is Vancouver's roughest neighborhood and best avoided if you're on foot. If you're interested in law and order, though, consider a detour to the **Vancouver Police Centennial Museum** at Cordova and Gore streets, just east of Main Street.

TIMING The walk itself will take less than a half hour each way; allow at least 90 minutes for Storyeum and extra time for shopping. Although Gastown itself is quite safe during the day, you may want to avoid walking through the area after dark.

What to See

⑮ **Byrnes Block.** George Byrnes constructed Vancouver's oldest brick building on the site of Gassy Jack Deighton's second saloon after the 1886 Great Fire, which wiped out most of the fledgling settlement of Vancouver. For a while this building was Vancouver's top luxury hotel, the Alhambra Hotel, charging a dollar a night. The site of Deighton's original saloon, east of the Byrnes Block where his statue now stands, is the zero point from which all Vancouver street addresses start. ⊠ *2 Water St., Gastown.*

⑭ **Gaoler's Mews.** Once the site of the city's first civic buildings—the constable's cabin and customs house, and a two-cell log jail—this atmospheric brick-paved courtyard today is home to cafés, an Irish pub, and architectural offices. ⊠ *Behind 12 Water St., Gastown.*

⑯ **Hotel Europe.** Once billed as the best hotel in the city, this 1908 flatiron building is one of the world's best examples of triangular architecture. Now used for government-subsidized housing and not open to the public, the hotel still has its original Italian tile work and lead-glass windows. The glass tiles in the sidewalk on Alexander Street once provided light for an underground saloon. ⊠ *43 Powell St., Gastown.*

⑫ **Steam clock.** An underground steam system, which also heats many local buildings, supplies the world's first steam clock—possibly Vancouver's most-photographed attraction. On the quarter hour a steam whistle rings out the Westminster chimes, and on the hour a huge cloud of steam spews from the apparatus. The original design, based on an 1875 mechanism, was built in 1977 by Ray Saunders of Landmark Clocks (at 123 Cambie Street) to commemorate the community effort that saved Gastown from demolition. ⊠ *Water and Cambie Sts., Gastown.*

⑬ Storyeum. Live theater and life-size sets animate British Columbia's history in this ambitious underground attraction. A 65-minute walkthrough starts with a two-story descent in a massive cylindrical elevator. You then move through a series of sets—complete with live performances and sound effects—depicting an ancient rain forest, aboriginal legends, a gold-rush town, a merchant ship, a steam train, and more. A free exhibit of historic photos in the lobby is also worth a look. Book ahead, as numbers are limited for each show. ⊠ *142 Water St., Gastown* ☎ *604/687–8142 or 800/687–8142* ⊕ *www.storyeum.com* ⊠ *C$21.95* ⊙ *Daily 10–5, tours every ½ hr.*

off the beaten path

VANCOUVER POLICE CENTENNIAL MUSEUM – It's not in the best neighborhood, and its morgue and autopsy areas may be off-putting to some, but this museum provides an intriguing glimpse into the history of the Vancouver police. Firearms and counterfeit money are on exhibit, as are clues from some of the city's unsolved crimes. ⊠ *240 E. Cordova St., Downtown East Side* ☎ *604/665–3346* ⊕ *www.city. vancouver.bc.ca/police/museum* ⊠ *C$7* ⊙ *Mon.–Sat. 9–5.*

Chinatown

Vancouver's Chinatown, declared a historic district in 1971, is one of the oldest and largest such areas in North America. Chinese immigrants were among the first to recognize the possibilities of Vancouver's setting and have played an important role here since the 18th century. Many came to British Columbia during the 1850s seeking their fortunes in the Cariboo gold rush. Thousands more arrived in the 1880s, recruited as laborers to build the Canadian Pacific Railway.

Though they were performing the valuable and hazardous task of blasting the rail bed through the Rocky Mountains, the Chinese were discriminated against. The Anti-Asiatic Riots of 1907 stopped population growth in Chinatown for 50 years, and immigration from China was discouraged by increasingly restrictive policies that climaxed in a C$500-per-head tax during the 1920s. In the 1960s the city council planned bulldozer urban renewal for Strathcona, the residential part of Chinatown, as well as freeway connections through the most historic blocks of the district. Fortunately the project was halted. Though much of Vancouver's Chinese community has now shifted to suburban Richmond, Chinatown is still a vital neighborhood. The style of architecture in Vancouver's Chinatown is patterned on that of Guangzhou (Canton).

Although Chinatown is only a few blocks from Gastown, it's best to get there by cab, bus, or SkyTrain to avoid walking through the city's rough skid-row neighborhood. The No. 19 Metrotown and No. 22 Knight buses travel east to Chinatown from stops along West Pender Street; the No. 3 Main and No. 8 Fraser serve Chinatown from Cordova and Seymour near Waterfront Station. The Stadium-Chinatown SkyTrain station is a five-minute walk from Chinatown. From the station head down the Keefer Street steps, and turn left at Abbott Street. This will take you to the Millennium Gate.

Another option is to take the Silk Road Walking Tour, a self-guided route marked with banners that starts at the Vancouver Public Library downtown and leads to the main attractions in Chinatown.

a good walk

At the intersection of West Pender and Taylor streets, the **Vancouver Chinatown Millennium Gate** ► marks the western boundary of Chinatown. This four-pillar, three-story high, brightly painted arch spanning Pender Street was erected in 2002 to mark the millennium and commemorate the Chinese community's role in Vancouver's history. The gate incorporates both Eastern and Western symbols, and both traditional and modern Chinese themes.

Just east of the Millennium Gate, a right turn will take you into Shanghai Alley. Also known as Chinatown Heritage Alley, this was the site of the first Chinese settlement in the Vancouver area. By 1890 Shanghai Alley and neighboring Canton Alley were home to about 1,000 Chinese residents. At the end of the alley is a replica of the West Han Dynasty Bell, a gift to Vancouver from the city of Guangzhou, China. Surrounding the bell are a series of panels relaying some of the area's early history.

Return to Pender Street and turn right. The first building you pass is the **Sam Kee Building** ⑰, the world's narrowest office building. Across the street, at 1 West Pender Street, is the **Chinese Freemasons Building** ⑱, notable for its two different facades. Directly across Carrall Street is the **Chinese Times Building** ⑲.

The **Dr. Sun Yat-Sen Classical Chinese Garden** ⑳ is about a half block east and across Pender, tucked into a courtyard behind the Chinese Cultural Centre. The free, public Dr. Sun Yat-Sen Park is next to the garden. A short path through the park takes you out to Columbia Street, where the entrance to the **Chinese Cultural Centre Museum and Archives** ㉑ (not to be confused with the Chinese Cultural Centre that fronts Pender Street) is on your left. Across Columbia Street is the Chinatown Memorial Monument, commemorating the Chinese-Canadian community's contribution to the city, province, and country. The monument, shaped in the Chinese character "zhong," symbolizing moderation and harmony, is flanked by bronze statues of a railroad worker and a WWII soldier.

Finish your tour of Chinatown by poking around in the open-front markets, bakeries, and herbalist and import shops that line several blocks of Pender and Keefer streets running east. Ming Wo Cookware, at 23 East Pender, has a great selection of Eastern and Western culinary supplies. Ten Ren Tea and Ginseng Company, at 550 Main, and Ten Lee Hong Tea and Ginseng, at 500 Main, carry all kinds of exotic tea blends. For art, ceramics, and rosewood furniture, have a look at Yeu

Hua Handicraft Ltd., at 173 East Pender. If you're in the area in summer on a Friday, Saturday, or Sunday, check out the bustling Night Market, for which the 200 block of East Pender and Keefer are closed to traffic 6:30–11 PM (until midnight on Saturday). The Web site www. vancouver-chinatown.com has details.

TIMING The walk itself will take about 20 minutes. Allow about an hour each for the garden and the museum and extra time for shopping.

What to See

㉑ Chinese Cultural Centre Museum and Archives. This Ming Dynasty–style facility is dedicated to promoting an understanding of Chinese-Canadian history and culture. A compelling permanent exhibit on the first floor traces the history of Chinese Canadians in British Columbia. The art gallery upstairs hosts traveling exhibits by Chinese and Canadian artists, and an on-site military museum recalls the role of Chinese Canadians in the last two world wars. ⊠ *555 Columbia St., Chinatown* ☎ *604/658–8880* ⊕ *www.cccvan.com* ⊠ *C$4, Tues. by donation* ☺ *Tues.–Sun. 11–5.*

⑱ Chinese Freemasons Building. Two completely different facades distinguish this structure on the northwest corner of Pender and Carrall streets. The side facing Pender represents a fine example of Cantonese recessed balconies. The Carrall Street side displays the standard Victorian style common throughout the British Empire. Dr. Sun Yat-Sen hid for months in this building from agents of the Manchu Dynasty while he raised funds for its overthrow, which he accomplished in 1911. ⊠ *3 W. Pender St., Chinatown.*

⑲ Chinese Times Building. Police officers during the early 20th century could hear the clicking sounds of clandestine mah-jongg games played after sunset on the hidden mezzanine floor of this 1902 structure. But attempts by vice squads to enforce restrictive policies against the Chinese gamblers proved fruitless because police were unable to find the players. The office building isn't open to the public. ⊠ *1 E. Pender St., Chinatown.*

⑳ Dr. Sun Yat-Sen Classical Chinese Garden. The first authentic Ming Dy-
Fodor'sChoice nasty–style garden outside China, this garden was built in 1986 by 52
★ artisans from Suzhou, China. It incorporates design elements and traditional materials from several of Suzhou's centuries-old private gardens. No power tools, screws, or nails were used in the construction. Guided tours (45 minutes long), included in the ticket price, are conducted on the hour between mid-June and the end of August (call ahead for off-season tour times); they are valuable in understanding the philosophy and symbolism that are central to the garden's design. A concert series, including classical, Asian, world, jazz, and sacred music, plays on Friday evenings in July, August, and September. The free public park next door is also designed as a traditional Chinese garden. Covered walkways make this a good rainy-day choice. ⊠ *578 Carrall St., Chinatown* ☎ *604/662–3207* ⊕ *www.vancouverchinesegarden.com* ⊠ *C$8.25* ☺ *May–mid-June and Sept., daily 10–6; mid-June–Aug., daily 9:30–7; Oct., daily 10–4:30; Nov.–Apr., Tues.–Sun. 10–4:30.*

⑰ Sam Kee Building. *Ripley's Believe It or Not!* recognizes this 6-foot-wide structure as the narrowest office building in the world. In 1913, after the city confiscated most of the then-owner's land to widen Pender Street, he built a store on what was left, in protest. Customers had to be served through the windows. These days the building houses an insurance agency, whose employees make do within the 4-foot-10-inch-wide interior. The glass panes in the sidewalk on Pender Street once provided light for Chinatown's public baths, which, in the early 20th century, were in the basement here. The presence of this and other underground sites has fueled rumors that Chinatown and Gastown were connected by tunnels that enabled residents of the latter to anonymously enjoy the vices of the former. Tunnels haven't been found, however. ⊠ *8 W. Pender St., Chinatown.*

Stanley Park

Fodor's Choice
★

A 1,000-acre wilderness park only blocks from the downtown section of a major city is both a rarity and a treasure. In the 1860s, because of a threat of American invasion, the area that is now Stanley Park was designated a military reserve, though it was never needed. When the city of Vancouver was incorporated in 1886, the council's first act was to request that the land be set aside as a park. In 1888 permission was granted and the grounds were named Stanley Park after Lord Stanley, then governor general of Canada.

If you're driving to Stanley Park, head northwest on Georgia Street from downtown. If you're taking public transit, catch any bus labeled STANLEY PARK at the corner of Pender and Howe streets downtown.

You can also catch North Vancouver Bus 240 or 246 from anywhere on West Georgia Street to the park entrance at Georgia and Chilco streets, or a Robson Bus 5 to Robson and Denman streets, where there are a number of bicycle-rental outlets.

Once at the park, you can bike, walk, drive, or take the free park shuttle to reach the main attractions. The seawall path, a 9-km (5½-mi) paved shoreline route popular with walkers, cyclists, and in-line skaters, is one of several car-free zones within the park. If you have the time (about a half day) and the energy, strolling the entire seawall is an exhilarating experience. It extends an additional mile east past the marinas, cafés, and waterfront condominiums of Coal Harbour to Canada Place downtown, so you could start your walk or ride from there. From the south side of the park, the seawall continues for another 28 km (17 mi) along Vancouver's waterfront as far at the University of British Columbia; allowing for a pleasant, if ambitious, day's ride. Anywhere on the seawall, cyclists must wear helmets and stay on their side of their path. Within Stanley Park, cyclists must ride in a counterclockwise direction.

Parking is available at or near all the major attractions; one ticket (C$6 April–September, C$3 October–March) allows you to park all day and to move between lots.

The free **Stanley Park Shuttle** (☎ 604/257–8400 ⊕ www.vancouver.ca/parks/) operates mid-June to mid-September, providing frequent (15-

minute intervals) transportation between 14 major park sights. Pick it up on Pipeline Road, near the Georgia Street park entrance, or at any of the stops in the park. For information about guided nature walks in the park, contact the **Lost Lagoon Nature House** (☎ 604/257–8544 or 604/718–6522 ⊕ www.stanleyparkecology.ca) on the south shore of Lost Lagoon, at the foot of Alberni Street.

Numbers in the text correspond to numbers in the margin and on the Stanley Park map.

a good tour

If you're walking or cycling, start at the foot of **Alberni Street** ►, beside Lost Lagoon. Go through the underpass and veer right, following the cycle-path markings, to the seawall. If you're driving, enter the park at the foot of Georgia Street. For direct access to the main parking lot, the **Miniature Railway and Children's Farmyard** ㉒, the **Vancouver Aquarium Marine Science Centre** ㉓, and the Stanley Park Shuttle, veer left up Pipeline Road. To continue the tour, keep right and go under the underpass. This puts you on scenic Stanley Park Drive, which circles the park.

Whether you're on the seawall or Stanley Park Drive, the old wooden structure that you pass on your right is the Vancouver Rowing Club, a private athletic club established in 1903. Just ahead and to your left is a parking lot, an information booth (staffed year-round, weather permitting), and a turnoff to the aquarium and Painters' Corner, where artists sell their work. A Salmon Demonstration Stream, near the information booth, presents facts about the life cycle of this important fish.

Continue along past the Royal Vancouver Yacht Club. The causeway to Deadman's Island, a former burial ground for local Salish people and early settlers, is about ½ km (¼ mi) farther. It's now a small naval installation, HMCS *Discovery,* and isn't open to the public. The **totem poles** ㉔, which are a bit farther down Stanley Park Drive and on your left, are a popular photo stop. The **Nine O'Clock Gun** ㉕ is ahead at the water's edge, just past the sign for Hallelujah Point. Brockton Point and its small lighthouse and foghorn are to the north.

Brockton Oval, where you can catch a rugby game in winter or cricket in summer, is inland on your left. Next, on the waterside, watch for the *Girl in a Wetsuit,* a sculpture on a rock offshore that mimics Copenhagen's *Little Mermaid.* A little farther along the seashore stands a replica of the dragon-shape figurehead from the SS *Empress of Japan,* which plied these waters between 1891 and 1922.

Lumbermen's Arch ㉖, a log archway, is at Km 3 (Mi 2) of the drive. There's a picnic area, a snack bar, and a small beach here. The Children's Water Park, across the road, is a big draw throughout summer. Cyclists and walkers can turn off here for a shortcut back to the aquarium, the Miniature Railway and Children's Farmyard, and the park entrance.

The Lions Gate Bridge is about 2 km (1 mi) farther along the seawall or Stanley Park Drive. Here drivers and cyclists part company. Cyclists ride under the bridge and past the cormorants' nests tucked beneath **Prospect Point** ㉗. Drivers pass over the bridge and reach a viewpoint and café at the top of Prospect Point. Both routes then continue around to

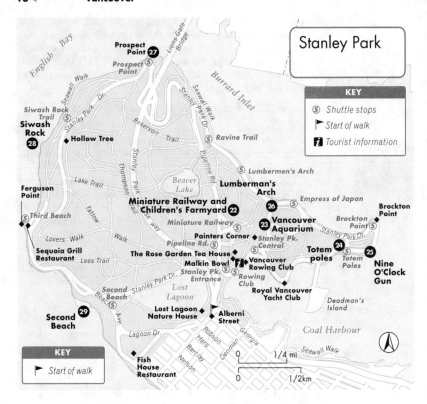

the English Bay side of the park and the beginning of sandy beaches. The imposing monolith offshore (though not visible from the road) is **Siwash Rock** ㉘, the focus of a native legend. If you're driving, watch for a sign for the Hollow Tree. This 56-foot-wide burnt cedar stump has shrunk over the years but still gives an idea of how large some of the old-growth trees were. Continue along to reach the swimming area and snack bar at Third Beach.

The next attraction along the seawall is the large heated pool at **Second Beach** ㉙. If you're walking or cycling, you can take a shortcut from here back to Lost Lagoon by taking the perpendicular pathway behind the pool that cuts into the park. Either of the footbridges ahead leads to a path along the south side of the lagoon that takes you back to your starting point at the foot of Alberni or Georgia Street. If you continue along the seawall from Second Beach, you will emerge from the park into a residential neighborhood of high-rises, the West End. You can walk back to Alberni Street along Denman Street, where you can stop at one of the many cafés, or continue along the seawall to Yaletown, Granville Island, and beyond.

TIMING   The driving tour takes about an hour. Parking is available near most of the sights in the park. Biking time depends on your speed, but with stops to see the sights, expect the ride to take several hours. It takes at least two hours to see the aquarium thoroughly. If you're going to walk the park and take in most of the sights, plan on spending the day. The seawall can get crowded on summer weekends, but inside the park is a 28-km (17-mi) network of peaceful walking and cycling paths through old- and second-growth forest. The wheelchair-accessible Beaver Lake Interpretive Trail is a good choice if you're interested in park ecology. Take a map—they're available at the park-information booth and many of the concession stands—and don't go into the woods alone or after dusk.

What to See

㉖ **Lumbermen's Arch.** Made of one massive log, this archway, erected in 1952, is dedicated to the workers in Vancouver's first industry. Beside the arch is an asphalt path that leads back to Lost Lagoon and the Vancouver Aquarium.

㉒ **Miniature Railway and Children's Farmyard.** A child-size steam train takes kids and adults on a ride through the woods. Next door is a farmyard full of critters, including goats, rabbits, and pigs. At Christmastime, an elaborate light display illuminates the route, and Halloween displays draw crowds throughout October. A family ticket gets everyone in for the child's rate. ⊠ *Off Pipeline Rd., Stanley Park* ☎ *604/257–8531* 🎫 *Each site C$5, C$2.50 for adults accompanying children* ☉ *June–early Sept., daily 11–4; Oct., daily 6 PM–10 PM; Dec., daily 3 PM–10 PM; Jan.–May, weekends 11–4, weather permitting.*

㉕ **Nine O'Clock Gun.** This cannonlike apparatus by the water was installed in 1890 to alert fishermen to a curfew ending weekend fishing. Now it signals 9 o'clock every night.

> **need a break?**
>
> The **The Rose Garden Tea House** (☎ 604/602–3088), in a 1911 manor house near the Children's Farmyard, serves traditional afternoon tea, complete with scones, pastries, and sandwiches, in its tearoom daily 11–5. The C$30 meal includes a choice of 200 loose leaf teas. Reservations are recommended. Also on-site is the family-friendly Verandah Bar and Grill, serving burgers, nachos, and pasta lunches and dinners on a wide garden-view verandah ($–$$$).

㉗ **Prospect Point.** At 211 feet, Prospect Point is the highest point in the park and provides striking views of the North Shore and Burrard Inlet. There's also a souvenir shop, a snack bar, and a restaurant here. From the seawall, you can see where cormorants build their seaweed nests along the cliff ledges.

> **need a break?**
>
> **Prospect Point Café** (☎ 604/669–2737) is at the top of Prospect Point, with a deck overlooking the Lions Gate Bridge. It specializes in salmon dishes and makes a good lunch stop, though it's often fully booked with tour groups ($–$$$).

㉙ **Second Beach.** The 50-meter pool, which has lifeguards and waterslides, is a popular spot in summer. The sandy beach also has a playground and covered picnic areas. ☎ *604/257–8371 summer only* ⊕ *www.*

vancouver.ca/parks/ ⊠ *Beach free, pool C$4.50* ☺ *Pool mid-May–mid-June, weekdays noon–8:45; weekends 10–8:45; mid-June–late July, daily 10–8:45; late July–Labor Day, Mon., Wed., Fri. 7 AM–8:45 PM, Tues., Thurs., and weekends 10–8:45.*

㉘ Siwash Rock. According to a local First Nations legend, this 50-foot-high offshore promontory is a monument to a man who was turned into stone as a reward for his unselfishness. The rock is visible from the seawall; if you're driving, you need to park and take a short path through the woods.

㉔ Totem poles. Totem poles are an important art form among native peoples along British Columbia's coast. These eight poles, all carved in the latter half of the 20th century, include replicas of poles originally brought to the park from the north coast in the 1920s, as well as poles carved specifically for the park by First Nations artists. The several styles of poles represent a cross section of B.C. native groups, including the Kwakwaka'wakw, Haida, and Nisga'a. The combination of carved animals, fish, birds, and mythological creatures represents clan history. An information center near the site has a snack bar, a gift shop, and information about B.C.'s First Nations.

★ ☕ **㉓ Vancouver Aquarium Marine Science Centre.** Massive pools with windows below the water level let you come face to face with beluga whales, sea otters, sea lions, dolphins, and harbor seals at this research and educational facility. In the Amazon rain-forest gallery you can walk through a jungle setting populated with piranhas, caimans, and tropical birds and vegetation and, in summer, hundreds of free-flying butterflies. Other displays, many with hands-on features for kids, show the underwater life of coastal British Columbia and the Canadian Arctic. A Tropic Zone is home to exotic freshwater and saltwater life, including clownfish, moray eels, and black-tip reef sharks. Beluga whale, sea lion, and dolphin shows, as well as dive shows (where divers swim with aquatic life, including sharks) are held daily. For an extra fee, you can help the trainers feed and train otters, belugas, and sea lions. There's also a café and a gift shop. Be prepared for lines on weekends and school holidays. ☎ 604/659–3474 ⊕ *www.vanaqua.org* ⊠ *C$17.50* ☺ *July–Labor Day, daily 9:30–7; Labor Day–June, daily 10–5:30.*

Yaletown & False Creek

In 1985–86 the provincial government cleared up a derelict industrial site on the north shore of False Creek, built a world's fair, and invited everyone. Twenty million people showed up at Expo '86. Now the site of the fair has become one of the largest urban-redevelopment projects in North America.

Tucked in among the forest of green-glass, high-rise condo towers is the old warehouse district of Yaletown. First settled by railroad workers who had followed the newly laid tracks from the town of Yale in the Fraser Canyon, Yaletown in the 1880s and '90s was probably the most lawless place in Canada; the Royal Canadian Mounted Police complained it was too far through the forest for them to police it. It's now one of the city's most fashionable neighborhoods, and the Victorian brick-loading docks have become terraces for cappuccino bars. The area—which also has restaurants, brewpubs, day spas, retail and whole-sale fashion outlets, and shops selling upscale home decor—makes the most of its waterfront location, with a seaside walk and cycle path that runs completely around the shore of False Creek. Parking is tight in Yaletown, though there's a lot at Library Square. It's easier to walk or come by False Creek or Aquabus Ferry.

Numbers in the text correspond to numbers in the margin and on the Vancouver map.

a good walk

Start at **Library Square** ➌⓪ ➤ at Homer and Georgia streets. Leave by the Robson Street (east) exit, cross Robson, and continue south on Hamilton Street. Cross Smithe Street and continue down Mainland Street to Nelson Street; you're now in the heart of Yaletown. Three blocks west (to your right) along Nelson Street will take you to the **Contemporary Art Gallery** ➌①. Stop for a coffee at one of Yaletown's loading-dock cafés or poke around the shops on Hamilton and Mainland streets.

From the foot of Mainland Street, turn left on Davie Street and cross Pacific Boulevard. This takes you to the **Roundhouse** ➌②, a former turnaround point for trains that is now a showcase for local arts groups. David Lam Park, Yaletown's waterfront green space, is behind the Roundhouse. Continue to the waterfront at the foot of Davie Street. Here, an intriguing iron-and-concrete sculpture with panels displays archival images of events around False Creek. Also at the foot of Davie Street is the Yaletown dock for Aquabus Ferries (☎ 604/689–5858), where you can catch a boat to Granville Island, Science World, Hornby Street, David Lam Park, or Stamp's Landing and Spyglass Place on the south shore of False Creek. Ferries run every 15 minutes from 7 AM to 10 PM.

From here you can access Vancouver's seaside path, a car-free bike, in-line skating, and pedestrian pathway that continues all the way around False Creek. You can rent a bike or in-line skates at the foot of Davie. A right turn takes you, in about 3 km (2 mi), to the West End and Stanley Park.

To continue this tour, turn left. After about 1 km (½ mi) is the Plaza of Nations, the heart of the old Expo site and now a waterfront plaza little used except for special events. Cross the plaza toward Pacific Boulevard and take the pedestrian overpass to B.C. Place Stadium. The stadium's massive fiberglass and Teflon roof is held up by nothing more than air, making this 60,000-seat venue the largest air-supported domed stadium in the world. Walk around to Gate A and the **B.C. Sports Hall of Fame and Museum** ➌③. As you leave the museum, the Terry Fox Memorial is to your left. This archway at the foot of Robson Street was built in honor of Terry Fox (1958–81), a local student whose cross-Canada run raised millions of dollars for cancer research. From here you can continue two blocks west to return to Library Square. To continue the tour, walk two blocks north on Beatty Street to Stadium Station and take the SkyTrain one stop east to Main Street–Science World station, or return to the waterfront and walk another 1 km (½ mi) east to **Science**

World ㉞, a hands-on museum. From Science World, the SkyTrain takes you back downtown, or you can catch a ferry back to Yaletown or to other stops on False Creek.

If you're at Science World on a summer weekend, you can catch the **Downtown Historic Railway** (☎ 604/665–3903 ⊕ www.trams.bc.ca) to Granville Island. These antique trams stop at Quebec Street and Terminal Avenue, in front of Science World.

TIMING   It takes about 1½ hours to walk around all the sights. Allow about an hour for the B.C. Sports Hall of Fame and museum and two hours for Science World.

What to See

☺ ㉝ **B.C. Sports Hall of Fame and Museum.** Inside the B.C. Place Stadium complex, this museum celebrates the province's sports achievers in a series of historical displays. You can test your sprinting, climbing, and throwing prowess in the high-tech participation gallery. An hour-long audio tour is included with admission. ⊠ *B.C. Place, 777 Pacific Blvd. S, Gate A, at Beatty and Robson Sts., Downtown* ☎ *604/687–5520* ⊕ *www. bcsportshalloffame.com* ⊠ *C$8* ☉ *Daily 10–5.*

㉛ **Contemporary Art Gallery.** This nonprofit public gallery in a purpose-built modern building has regularly changing exhibits of the latest in contemporary local and international visual art. Other events include artists talks, lectures, and tours. ⊠ *555 Nelson St., Downtown* ☎ *604/681–2700* ⊕ *www.contemporaryartgallery.ca* ⊠ *By donation* ☉ *Wed. and Fri. noon–6, Thurs. noon–8, weekends noon–5.*

▶ ㉚ **Library Square.** The spiraling library building, open plazas, and lofty atrium of Library Square, completed in the mid-1990s, were built to evoke images of the Colosseum in Rome. A high-tech library is the core of the structure; the outer edge of the spiral houses cafés and boutiques. ⊠ *350 W. Georgia St., Downtown* ☎ *604/331–3600* ⊕ *www.vpl.vancouver. bc.ca* ☉ *Mon.–Thurs. 10–9, Fri. and Sat. 10–6, Sun. 1–5.*

㉜ **Roundhouse.** This round brick structure was built in 1888 as the turnaround point for transcontinental trains reaching the end of the line at Vancouver. A spirited local campaign helped to create a home here (in a glass pavilion on the Davie Street side) for **Engine 374,** which pulled the first passenger train into Vancouver on May 23, 1887. Now a community center, the Roundhouse hosts festivals and exhibitions. ⊠ *181 Roundhouse Mews, Yaletown* ☎ *604/713–1800* ⊕ *www.roundhouse. ca* ⊠ *Free, admission may be charged to some events* ☉ *Weekdays 9 AM–10 PM, weekends 9–5.*

need a break?
Across from the Roundhouse, **Urban Fare** (⊠ 177 Davie St., Yaletown ☎ 604/975–7550) supplies, among other things, truffles, foie gras, and bread air-freighted from France to Yaletown's Francophiles and foodies. It's open daily 6 AM–midnight. You can sample the wares at the café.

☺ ㉞ **Science World.** In a gigantic, shiny dome built over the Omnimax theater, this hands-on science center encourages children to participate in interactive exhibits and demonstrations. Exhibits change throughout the year, so there's always something new to see. ⊠ *1455 Québec St., False Creek* 📞 *604/443–7443 or 604/443–7440* ⊕ *www.scienceworld.bc.ca* 📧 *Science World C$13.75, Science World and Omnimax theater C$18.75* 🕐 *July–Labor Day, daily 10–6; Sept.–June, weekdays 10–5, weekends 10–6.*

Granville Island

Fodor'sChoice ★ One of North America's most successful urban-redevelopment schemes was just a sandbar until World War I, when the federal government dredged False Creek for access to the sawmills that lined the shore. The sludge from the creek was heaped onto the sandbar to create the island. It was used to house much-needed industrial and logging-equipment plants, but the businesses began to deteriorate by the 1960s. In the early '70s, the federal government came up with a creative plan to redevelop the island with a public market, marine activities, and artisans' studios but to retain the architecture's industrial character. The refurbished Granville Island opened to the public in 1979 and was an immediate hit with locals and visitors alike.

Besides the popular public market, the island is home to a marina, an art college, theaters, restaurants, pubs, park space, playgrounds, and dozens of crafts shops and artisans studios. It's also among the venues for Vancouver's many performing arts festivals—and is a great place to catch top-quality street entertainment.

Though the 35-acre island is now technically a peninsula, connected years ago by landfill to the south shore of False Creek, its distinct atmosphere sets it apart from the rest of the city.

Numbers in the text correspond to numbers in the margin and on the Granville Island map.

a good walk

To reach Granville Island on foot, make the 15-minute walk from downtown Vancouver to the south end of Hornby Street. Aquabus Ferries depart from here and deliver passengers across False Creek at the **Granville Island Public Market** ☺ ☞, which has a slew of food and other stalls. False Creek ferries leave every five minutes for Granville Island from a dock behind the Vancouver Aquatic Centre, on Beach Avenue, and deliver passengers between the Bridges pub and the Public Market. Still another option is to take a 20-minute ride on a TransLink bus; from Waterfront Station or stops on Granville Street, take False Creek South Bus 50 to the edge of the island. Buses 4 UBC and 7 Dunbar will also take you within a few minutes' walk of the island. The market is a short walk from the bus, ferry, or tram stop. If you drive, parking is free for up to three hours, and paid parking is available in four garages on the island.

Another way to travel is to hop the **Downtown Historic Railway** (📞 604/665–3903 ⊕ www.trams.bc.ca), two early-20th-century electric trams that on summer weekends and holiday afternoons run from Science World to Granville Island.

From the market, to start a clockwise tour of the island, walk south on Johnston Street or take the waterside boardwalk behind the Arts Club

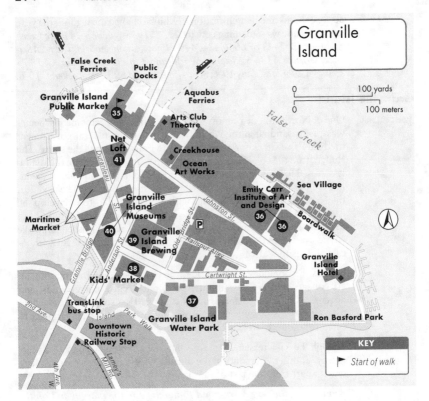

Theatre and around the Creekhouse building. Either way, past the shops and studios in the Creekhouse building is Ocean Art Works, an open-sided longhouse-style structure where you can watch First Nations artists at work. Continue south to the **Emily Carr Institute of Art and Design** ㊱, the province's leading art college. To the right of the main entrance is the Charles H. Scott Gallery, which hosts contemporary exhibitions in various media. Just past the gallery, turn left and follow a covered walkway along the south side of the art school to Sea Village, one of the few houseboat communities in Vancouver. Then take the boardwalk that starts at the houseboats and continues partway around the island. Behind the Granville Island Hotel is a small hill that used to be called the Mound, but was renamed Ron Basford Park. It's a natural amphitheater for outdoor performances.

From the Granville Island Hotel, turn right onto Cartwright Street; then take the right fork into Railspur Alley. This part of the island is home to a mix of crafts galleries, studios, and workshops. Railspur Alley alone is home to about a dozen studios and galleries, producing everything from guitars, to leather work and model dragons. You can see wooden boats being built at the Alder Bay Boat Company (✉ 1247 Cartwright St.), watch glassblowers at work at New-Small & Sterling Studio Glass (✉ 1440 Old Bridge St.), and check out the kinetic sculptures in progress at i.e. creative (✉ 1399 Railspur Alley). The Federation of Canadian Artists Gallery, the Crafts Association of B.C. Crafthouse, and the Gallery of B.C. Ceramics—all on Cartwright Street—showcase local works.

Also on Cartwright Street are two great attractions for kids: the **Granville Island Water Park** ㊲ and the **Kids' Market** ㊳. Adults can head for the microbrewery tour at **Granville Island Brewing** ㊴, across the street from the Kids' Market.

Cross Anderson Street and walk north on Duranleau Street. The **Granville Island Museums** ㊵, with train and model-boat displays, is on your left. The sea-oriented shops of the Maritime Market are next. The **Net Loft** ㊶ shopping arcade is the last place to explore. Once you have come full circle, you can either take the ferry back to downtown Vancouver or stay for dinner and catch a play at the Arts Club or the Waterfront Theatre.

TIMING If your schedule is tight, you can tour Granville Island in three to four hours. If you like to shop, or if a festival is in progress, you'll likely need a full day.

Sights to See

㊱ **Emily Carr Institute of Art and Design.** The institute's three main buildings—tin-plated structures formerly used for industrial purposes—were renovated in the 1970s. The **Charles H. Scott Gallery** to the right of the main entrance hosts contemporary exhibitions in various media. ✉ *1399 Johnston St., Granville Island* ☎ *604/844–3811* ⊕ *www.eciad.ca* ▣ *Free* ☉ *Weekdays noon–5, weekends 10–5.*

㊴ **Granville Island Brewing.** Tours of Canada's first modern microbrewery last about 45 minutes and include a taste of four brews. Kids are welcome; they get a taste of root beer. ✉ *1441 Cartwright St., Granville Island* ☎ *604/687–2739* ⊕ *www.gib.ca* ▣ *C$9.75* ☉ *Daily 10–8; tours daily at noon, 2, and 4.*

㊵ **Granville Island Museums.** Here are two museums under one roof. The collection of the **Model Ships Museum** includes exquisitely detailed early-20th-century military and working vessels, including a 13-foot replica of the HMS *Hood,* the British Royal Navy ship that was sunk by the German warship *Bismarck* in 1941, and a model of the *Hunley,* an 1863 Confederate submarine that was the first to sink a surface vessel. The **Model Trains Museum,** the world's largest toy-train collection on public display, includes a diorama of the Fraser Canyon and the Kettle Valley that involves 1,000 feet of track and some large-scale (3-foot-high) model trains. ✉ *1502 Duranleau St., Granville Island* ☎ *604/683–1939* ⊕ *www.granvilleislandmuseums.com* ▣ *Both museums C$7.50* ☉ *Mid-May–mid-Oct., daily 10–5:30; mid-Oct.–mid-May, Tues.–Sun. 10–5:30.*

★ ▶ ㊲ **Granville Island Public Market.** Because no chain stores are allowed in this 50,000-square-foot building, each outlet here is unique. Dozens of stalls sell locally grown produce direct from the farm; others sell crafts, chocolates, cheeses, fish, meat, flowers, and exotic foods. On Thursday in summer, market gardeners sell fruit and vegetables from trucks outside. On the north end of the market you can pick up a snack, lunch, or coffee at one of the many food stalls. The Market Courtyard, on the waterside, is a good place to catch street entertainers. Weekends can get madly busy. ⊠ *1689 Johnston St., Granville Island* ☎ *604/666–6477* ⊕ *www.granvilleisland.com* ⊙ *Daily 9–7.*

☪ ❸ **Granville Island Water Park.** North America's largest free public water park has slides, pipes, and sprinklers for children to shower one another. Kids can also join in free daily craft activities. ⊠ *1318 Cartwright St., Granville Island* ☎ *604/257–8195* ⊠ *Free* ⊙ *Mid-May–Labor Day, daily 10–6; slides open mid-June.*

☪ ❸ **Kids' Market.** A slice of kids' heaven on Granville Island, the Kids' Market has an indoor play area and two floors of small shops that sell all kinds of toys, magic gear, books, and other fun stuff. ⊠ *1496 Cartwright St., Granville Island* ☎ *604/689–8447* ⊙ *Daily 10–6.*

❹ **Net Loft.** This blue-and-red building includes a bookstore, a café, and a collection of high-quality boutiques selling imported and locally made crafts, exotic fabrics, handmade paper, and First Nations art. ⊠ *1666 Johnston St., Granville Island* ☎ *No phone* ⊙ *Daily 10–7.*

Kitsilano

The beachfront district of Kitsilano (popularly known as Kits), south of downtown Vancouver, is among the trendiest of Canadian neighborhoods. Originally inhabited by the Squamish people, whose Chief Khahtsahlanough gave the area its name, Kitsilano began to attract day-trippers from Vancouver in the early part of the 20th century. Some stayed and built lavish waterfront mansions; others built simpler Craftsman-style houses farther up the slope. After a period of decline in the mid-20th century, Kits, which contains many restored wood-frame Craftsman-style houses, is once again chic.

Kitsilano is home to three museums, some fashionable shops, and popular pubs and cafés. Kits has hidden treasures, too: rare boats moored at Heritage Harbour, stately mansions on forested lots, and, all along the waterfront, quiet coves and shady paths within a stone's throw of Canada's liveliest beach.

Numbers in the text correspond to numbers in the margin and on the Vancouver map.

a good walk

Vanier Park, the grassy beachside setting for three museums and the best kite-flying venue in Vancouver, is the logical gateway to Kits. The most enjoyable way to get here is by False Creek Ferries, from Granville Island or from behind the Vancouver Aquatic Centre, on Beach Avenue. The ferries dock at Heritage Harbour behind the Vancouver Maritime Museum. You can also walk or cycle about 1 km (½ mi) along the waterfront pathway from Granville Island (leave the island by Anderson Street and keep to your right along the waterfront, following the Seaside Bike Path signs). If you prefer to come by road, drive over the Burrard Street Bridge, turn right at Chestnut Street, and park in either of the museum parking lots; or take Bus 2, or 22 traveling south on Burrard Street downtown, get off at Cypress Street and Cornwall Avenue, and walk over to the park.

Vancouver Museum ㊷ ☞, which showcases the city's natural and cultural history, shares a building with the **H. R. MacMillan Space Centre** ㊸, a high-tech museum focusing on outer space. The **Vancouver Maritime Museum** ㊹, which traces the maritime history of the West Coast, is to the west and toward the water. Each museum has hands-on exhibits that appeal to kids.

The massive white-and-yellow contraption behind the Maritime Museum is the Ben Franklin submersible. It looks like something a Jules Verne character would put to sea but was actually built in 1968 as a marine research tool and was once the largest of its kind in America. Beside the submersible is the boiler and paddle wheel shaft from the SS *Beaver,* the first steamship on the B.C. coast. On the water, where the ferries dock, is Heritage Harbour, home to a rotating series of boats of historical interest. In summer the big tent, set up in Vanier Park, is the venue for the Bard on the Beach Shakespeare series.

West of the Maritime Museum is a quiet, grassy beach. A staircase leads up from the beach to a paved walkway. Take a moment to look at the 100-foot-tall replica Kwakiutl totem pole in front of the museum, and then follow the walkway west to popular **Kitsilano Beach** ㊺. Across the water you can see Stanley Park and Vancouver's downtown core. Stroll along the beach about 1 km (½ mi) past the restaurant and playground, to the outdoor pool at the far end. Continue past the pool, along the water, and enter a shady pathway lined with blackberry bushes that runs behind the Kitsilano Yacht Club. Soon the lane opens up to a viewpoint and gives access to another sandy cove.

About ½ km (¼ mi) from the yacht club, the path ends at a staircase. This leads up to a viewpoint and a tiny park on Point Grey Road. Double back the way you came, heading east toward Kits Beach, but this time follow Point Grey Road for a look at the front of the homes you could see from the beach path. The 1909 Logan House, at 2530 Point Grey Road, is an Edwardian dream home with a massive curved balcony.

Follow Point Grey Road as it curves to the right, and cross Cornwall Avenue at Balsam Street. Turn left on either York or 1st Avenue and walk two blocks to Yew Street, where in summer you can find one of the biggest concentrations of sidewalk pubs and cafés in Greater Vancouver. Alternatively, you can hike up the hill to 4th Avenue, once the heart of the hippie district, and explore the shops between Balsam and Burrard streets. You can catch a bus back to downtown Vancouver on Cornwall or 4th Avenue, or cut across Kits Beach Park back to Vanier Park.

TIMING The walk alone takes about an hour. Add two hours to see the MacMillan Space Centre and an hour for each of the other museums. With time out for shopping or swimming, a visit to Kitsilano could fill a whole day.

What to See

🕲 ㊺ **Kitsilano Beach.** Picnic sites, a playground, tennis courts, beach volleyball, a restaurant, take-out concessions, Vancouver's biggest outdoor pool, and some fine people-watching can all be found at Kits Beach. Inland from the pool, the **Kitsilano Showboat,** an outdoor amphitheater, hosts free music and dance performances in summer. ⊠ *2305 Cornwall Ave., Kitsilano* ☎ *Pool 604/731–0011 summer only* ⊕ *www.vancouver.ca/ parks/* ☼ *Beach free, pool C$4.50* ☉ *Pool late May–mid-June, weekdays noon–8:45, weekends 10–8:45; mid-June–Labor Day, weekdays 7 AM–8:45 PM, weekends 10–8:45; Labor Day–mid-Sept., weekdays 7 AM–7:15 PM, weekends 10–7:15.*

🐚 ❹❸ **H. R. MacMillan Space Centre.** The interactive exhibits and high-tech learning systems at this museum include a Virtual Voyages ride, where visitors can take a simulated space journey (definitely not for those afraid of flying); GroundStation Canada, showcasing Canada's achievements in space; and the Cosmic Courtyard, full of hands-on space-oriented exhibits including a moon rock and a program that shows what you would look like as an alien. You can catch daytime astronomy shows or evening music and laser shows at the **H. R. MacMillan Planetarium.** When the sky is clear, the ½-meter telescope at the **Gordon MacMillan Southam Observatory** (☎ 604/738–2855) is focused on whatever stars or planets are worth watching that night. Admission to the observatory is by donation, and it's open year-round Friday and Saturday evenings, from 8 PM to 11 PM, weather permitting. ⊠ *Vanier Park, 1100 Chestnut St., Kitsilano* ☎*604/738–7827* ⊕*www.hrmacmillanspacecentre.com* ☎*C$13.50* ☉ *July and Aug., daily 10–5; Sept.–June, Tues.–Sun. 10–5.*

🐚 ❹❹ **Vancouver Maritime Museum.** About a third of the museum has been turned over to kids, with touchable displays that provide a chance to drive a tug, maneuver an underwater robot, or dress up as a seafarer. Toddlers and school-age children can work the hands-on displays in Pirates' Cove and the Children's Maritime Discovery Centre. The museum also has an extensive collection of model ships and is the last moorage for the *RCMP Arctic St. Roch,* the first ship to sail in both directions through the treacherous Northwest Passage and the first to circumnavigate North America. ⊠ *Vanier Park, 1905 Ogden Ave., north end of Cypress St., Kitsilano* ☎*604/257–8300* ⊕*www.vancouvermaritimemuseum. com* ☎ *C$10* ☉ *Mid-May–Labor Day, daily 10–5; Labor Day–mid-May, Tues.–Sat. 10–5, Sun. noon–5.*

🐚 ▶ ❹❷ **Vancouver Museum.** Vancouver's short but funky history comes to life at this seaside museum. The 1950's Gallery boasts a 1955 Ford Fairlane Victoria and a Seeburg select-o-matic jukebox, and the 1960s-theme Revolution Gallery revisits the city's days at the hippie capital of Canada. Visitors can hear local bands from the '60s and poke around a re-created communal house. At this writing a war-years gallery was in the works. At the on-site Joyce Whalley Learning Centre, kids and adults can handle artifacts relating to immigration, First Nations, and the history of childhood. Watch for intriguing temporary exhibits. ⊠ *Vanier Park, 1100 Chestnut St., Kitsilano* ☎ *604/736–4431* ⊕ *www.vanmuseum.bc.ca* ☎ *C$10* ☉ *June–Sept., Fri.–Wed. 10–5, Thurs. 10–9; Oct.–June, Tues., Wed., and Fri.–Sun. 10–5, Thurs. 10–9.*

need a break? Just steps from the sand, **Watermark on Kits Beach** (☎ 604/738–5487) serves lunch and dinner inside and on its big oceanview deck. There's also a take-out concession at the same site.

South Vancouver & Point Grey

Some of Vancouver's best gardens, natural sights, and museums, including the renowned Museum of Anthropology, are south of downtown, on the campus of the University of BC and in the city's southern residential districts. Individual attractions are easily reached by TransLink buses, but you need a car to see them all comfortably in a day.

Numbers in the text correspond to numbers in the margin and on the Vancouver map.

a good drive

From downtown Vancouver, cross the Burrard Street Bridge and follow the marked scenic drive (to the right). This takes you along Cornwall Avenue, which becomes Point Grey Road and follows the waterfront to Alma Street. The little wooden structure in the park at the corner of Point Grey Road and Alma Street is the **Old Hastings Mill Store Museum** ㊼ ▶, Vancouver's oldest building. If you're a golf fan, you might take a detour to the **British Columbia Golf Museum** ㊼, on Blanca Street at the edge of the University Golf Course.

The scenic drive continues south on Alma Street and then west (to the right) on 4th Avenue. Take the right fork onto Northwest Marine Drive, which winds past Jericho, Locarno, and Spanish Banks beaches and up to the University of British Columbia (UBC). The **Museum of Anthropology** ㊽ is here (opposite Gate 4) and houses one of the world's best collections of Pacific Northwest First Nations artifacts. **Nitobe Memorial Garden** ㊾, a Japanese-style strolling garden, is across Marine Drive. Limited metered parking is available at the Museum of Anthropology; pay parking is available in the Rose Garden parking lot, across Marine Drive from the museum.

The **University of British Columbia Botanical Garden** ㊿, which has plenty of parking, is 2 km (1.2 mi) farther along Marine Drive. For more gardens, follow Marine Drive through the university grounds and take the left fork onto 41st Avenue. Turn left again onto Oak Street to reach the entrance of the **VanDusen Botanical Garden** ㊿, at 37th Avenue and Oak Street on your left. The complex is planted with an English-style maze, water and herb gardens, and more. Return to 41st Avenue, continue farther east (turn left), and then turn left again on Cambie Street to reach **Queen Elizabeth Park** ㊿, which overlooks the city. To get back downtown, continue north on Cambie Street and over the Cambie Street Bridge.

TIMING Except during rush hour, it takes about 30 minutes to drive from downtown to the University of British Columbia. You should add another 30 to 45 minutes of driving time for the rest of the tour and about two hours to visit each of the main attractions.

What to See

㊼ **British Columbia Golf Museum.** This offbeat museum at the edge of the University Golf Club is a treat for those who can't get enough of the game. Housed in a 1930 colonial bungalow that once served as the course clubhouse, the museum has a fine collection of historic photos, trophies, antique clubs, and other golfing memorabilia. The exhibits are arranged like a golf course in 18 sections, or holes, with a theme for each. ✉ *2545*

Blanca St., at 10th Ave., Point Grey ☎ 604/222–4653 ⊕ *www. bcgolfmuseum.org* 🖃 *Free* ⊙ *Tues.–Sun. noon–4.*

48 **Museum of Anthropology.** Part of the University of British Columbia, the
Fodor'sChoice MOA has one of the world's leading collections of Northwest Coast First
★ Nations Art. The Great Hall displays dramatic cedar poles, bentwood
boxes, and canoes adorned with traditional Northwest Coast painted
designs. On clear days, the gallery's 50-foot-tall windows provide a striking backdrop of mountains and sea. Another highlight is the work of
the late Bill Reid, one of Canada's most respected Haida artists. In *The
Raven and the First Men* (1980), carved in yellow cedar, he tells a Haida
story of creation. Reid's gold-and-silver jewelry work is also on display,
as are exquisite carvings of gold, silver, and argillite (a black shale found
on Haida Gwaii, also known as the Queen Charlotte Islands) by other
First Nations artists. The museum's visible storage section displays, in
drawers and cases, thousands of examples of tools, textiles, masks, and
other artifacts from around the world. The Koerner Ceramics Gallery
contains 600 pieces from 15th- to 19th-century Europe. Behind the museum are two Haida houses, set on the cliff over the water. Free guided
tours—given twice daily in summer, usually at 11 and 2 (call to confirm times)—are very informative. For an extra C$5 you can rent a
VUEguide, an electronic device which senses where you are in the museum and shows relevant artist interviews, archival footage, and photographs of the artifacts in their original settings, on a hand-held screen.
Arthur Erickson designed the cliff-top structure that houses the MOA,
which also has a book and fine-art shop and a summertime café. To reach
the museum by transit, take UBC Bus 4 from Granville Street or Bus 44
from Burrard Street downtown to the university loop, a 10-minute
walk from the museum. ⊠ *University of British Columbia, 6393 N.W.
Marine Dr., Point Grey* ☎ 604/822–5087 ⊕ *www.moa.ubc.ca* 🖃 *C$9,
free Tues. 5–9* ⊙ *Memorial Day–Labor Day, Tues. 10–9, Wed.–Mon.
10–5; Labor Day–Memorial Day, Tues. 11–9, Wed.–Sun. 11–5.*

49 **Nitobe Memorial Garden.** Opened in 1960 in memory of Japanese scholar
and diplomat Dr. Inazo Nitobe (1862–1933), this 2½-acre walled garden,
which includes a pond, a stream with a small waterfall, and a ceremonial
teahouse, is considered one of the most authentic Japanese tea and strolling
gardens outside Japan. Designed by Professor Kannosuke Mori of Japan's
Chiba University, the garden incorporates many native British Columbia
trees and shrubs, pruned and trained in the Japanese fashion and inter-
planted with Japanese maples and flowering shrubs. The circular path
around the park symbolizes the cycle of life and provides a tranquil view
from every direction. Cherry blossoms are the highlight in April and May,
and in June the irises are magnificent. ⊠ *University of British Columbia,
1903 West Mall, Point Grey* ☎ 604/822–9666 ⊕ *www.nitobe.org* 🖃 *$C4
mid-Mar.–mid-Oct., $C8 includes admission to the UBC Botanical Gar-
dens; by donation mid-Oct.–mid-Mar.* ⊙ *Mid-Mar.–mid-Oct., daily 10–6;
mid-Oct.–mid-Mar., weekdays 10–2:30.*

46 **Old Hastings Mill Store Museum.** Vancouver's first store and oldest building was built in 1865 at the foot of Dunlevy Street in Gastown and moved
to this seaside spot in 1930. The only building to predate the 1886 Great

Fire, the site is now a museum with displays of First Nations artifacts and pioneer household goods. ✉ *1575 Alma St., Point Grey* ☎ *604/734-1212* 🖅 *Donation* ☉ *Mid-June–mid-Sept., Tues.–Sun. 11–4; mid-Sept.–mid-Dec. and Feb.–mid-June, weekends 1–4.*

52 **Queen Elizabeth Park.** Besides views of downtown, the park has lavish sunken gardens, a rose garden, and an abundance of grassy picnicking spots. Other park facilities include 20 tennis courts, pitch and putt, and a restaurant. In the **Bloedel Floral Conservatory** you can see tropical and desert plants and 65 species of free-flying tropical birds in a glass triodetic dome. To reach the park by public transportation, take a Cambie Bus 15 from the corner of Robson and Burrard streets downtown to 33rd Avenue. ✉ *Cambie St. and 33rd Ave., South Vancouver* ☎ *604/257-8570* ⊕ *www.vancouver.ca/parks/* 🖅 *Conservatory C$4.25* ☉ *Apr.–Sept., weekdays 9–8, weekends 10–9; Oct.–Mar., daily 10–5.*

50 **University of British Columbia Botanical Garden.** Ten thousand trees, shrubs, and rare plants from around the world thrive on this 70-acre research site on the university campus. The complex includes an Asian garden, a garden of medicinal plants, and an alpine garden with some of the world's rarest plants. Guided tours can be arranged in advance. ✉ *6804 S. W. Marine Dr., Point Grey* ☎ *604/822-9666* ⊕ *www.ubcbotanicalgarden.org* 🖅 *Mid-Mar.–mid-Oct., C$6, $8 includes admission to Nitobe Memorial Garden; mid-Oct.–mid-Mar. free* ☉ *Mid-Mar.–mid-Oct., daily 10–6; mid-Oct.–mid-Mar., daily 10–3.*

51 **VanDusen Botanical Garden.** An Elizabethan maze, a formal rose garden, a meditation garden, and a collection of Canadian heritage plants are among the many themed displays at this 55-acre site. The collections include flora from every continent and many rare and endangered species. The new Phyllis Bentall Garden area features hybrid water lilies and carnivorous plants (a hit with kids). From mid-May to early June the Laburnum Walk forms a canopy of gold; in August and September the wildflower meadow is in bloom. The wheelchair-accessible site is also home to five lakes, a garden shop, a library, and a restaurant. In June the garden hosts North America's largest (in attendance and area) outdoor flower and garden show. During the last three weeks of December, the garden is illuminated for the Christmas-theme Festival of Lights (daily 5–9 PM). An Oak Bus 17 gets you here from downtown. Queen Elizabeth Park is a 1-km (½-mi) walk away, along West 37th Avenue. ✉ *5251 Oak St., at W. 37th Ave., South Vancouver* ☎ *604/878-9274 garden, 604/261-0011 restaurant* ⊕ *www.vandusengarden.org* 🖅 *C$7.75 Apr.–Sept., C$5.50 Oct.–Mar.* ☉ *June–Aug., daily 10–9; Sept.–May, daily (call for hrs).*

North Vancouver

The mountains that form a stunning backdrop to Vancouver lie in the district of North Vancouver, a bridge or SeaBus ride away on the North Shore of Burrard Inlet. Although the area is part suburb, the mountainous terrain has kept large parts of North Vancouver forested. This is where Vancouverites and visitors go for easily accessible hiking, skiing, and viewing the city lights.

Numbers in the text correspond to numbers in the margin and on the Vancouver map.

a good drive

From downtown, drive west down Georgia Street to Stanley Park and across the Lions Gate Bridge to North Vancouver. Stay in the right lane, take the North Vancouver exit, and then turn left onto Capilano Road. In about 2 km (1 mi), you come to the **Capilano Suspension Bridge** ⑤ ▶. A few hundred yards up Capilano Road, on the left, is the entrance to **Capilano River Regional Park** ⑤. About 1½ km (1 mi) along the park access road you'll find the Capilano Salmon Hatchery. Returning to Capilano Road and continuing north, you'll reach Cleveland Dam (also part of the park), where you can stop for great mountain views. As you continue north, Capilano Road becomes Nancy Greene Way, which ends at the base of **Grouse Mountain** ⑤. From here, a cable car to the summit gives you great city views.

Alternatively, you can take the SeaBus from Waterfront Station to **Lonsdale Quay** ⑤ and then catch a Grouse Mountain Bus 236. This stops at the Capilano Suspension Bridge and near the Salmon Hatchery on its way to the base of Grouse Mountain.

TIMING You need a half day to see the sights, a full day if you want to hike at Grouse Mountain or Capilano River Regional Park. To save a lot of time, avoid crossing the Lions Gate Bridge during weekday rush hours (about 7–9 AM and 3–6 PM).

What to See

☺ ⑤ **Capilano River Regional Park.** The park contains hiking trails and footbridges over the Capilano River, where it cuts through a dramatic gorge. At the park's **Capilano Salmon Hatchery** (⊠ 4500 Capilano Park Rd., North Vancouver ☎ 604/666–1790), viewing areas and exhibits illustrate the life cycle of the salmon. The best time to see the salmon run is between July and November. The **Cleveland Dam** (⊠ Capilano Rd., about 1½ km [1 mi] past main park entrance) is at the north end of the park. Built in 1954 and named for Dr. E. A. Cleveland, a former chief commissioner of the Greater Vancouver Water District, it dams the Capilano River to create the 5½-km-long (3½-mi-long) Capilano Reservoir. A hundred yards from the parking lot, you can walk across the top of the dam to enjoy striking views of the reservoir and mountains behind it. The two sharp peaks to the west are the Lions, for which the Lions Gate Bridge is named. ⊠ *Capilano Rd., North Vancouver* ☎ *604/224–5739* ⊕ *www.gvrd.bc.ca/parks/CapilanoRiver.htm* ☜ *Free* ☉ *Park daily 8 AM–5 PM; hatchery June–Aug., daily 8–8; May and Sept., daily 8 AM–7 PM; Apr. and Oct., daily 8 AM–6 PM; Nov.–Mar. daily 8 AM–4 PM.*

☺ ▶ ⑤ **Capilano Suspension Bridge.** At Vancouver's oldest tourist attraction (the original bridge was built in 1889), you can get a taste of rain-forest scenery and test your mettle on the swaying, 450-foot cedar-plank suspension bridge that hangs 230 feet above the rushing Capilano River. Across the bridge is the Treetops Adventure, where you can walk along 650 feet of cable bridges suspended among the trees; there's also a scenic pathway along the canyon's edge. Without crossing the bridge, you can enjoy the site's viewing decks, nature trails, totem park, and carving center (where you can watch First Nations carvers at work), as well as history and forestry exhibits, a massive gift shop in the original 1911 teahouse, and a restaurant. May through October, guides in 19th-century costumes conduct free tours on such themes as history, nature, or ecology, and fiddle bands, First Nations dancers, and other entertainers keep things lively. ✉ *3735 Capilano Rd., North Vancouver* ☎ *604/985–7474* ⊕ *www.capbridge.com* ✉ *Mid-May–Oct. C$26.95, Nov.–mid-May C$22.95, plus C$3 for parking* ☉ *Mid-May–Labor Day, daily 8:30–8; Nov.–Mar., daily 9–5; Sept., Oct., and Apr.–mid-May call for hrs.*

★ ☾ ⑤⑤ **Grouse Mountain.** North America's largest aerial tramway, the **Skyride** is a great way to take in the city, sea, and mountain vistas (be sure to pick a clear day or evening). The Skyride makes the 2-km (1-mi) climb to the peak of Grouse Mountain every 15 minutes. Once at the top you can take in a half-hour video presentation at the Theatre in the Sky (it's included with your Skyride ticket). Other free mountaintop activities include, in summer, lumberjack shows, chairlift rides, walking tours, hiking, falconry demonstrations, and a chance to visit the grizzly bears and grey wolves in the mountain's wildlife refuge. For an extra fee you can also try tandem paragliding, or helicopter tours. In winter you can ski, snowshoe, snowboard, ice-skate on a mountaintop pond, or take Sno-Cat-drawn sleigh rides. A stone-and-cedar lodge is home to a café, a pub-style bistro, and a high-end restaurant, all with expansive city views. ✉ *6400 Nancy Greene Way, North Vancouver* ☎ *604/980–9311* ⊕ *www.grousemountain.com* ✉ *Skyride and most activities C$29.95* ☉ *Daily 9 AM–10 PM.*

off the beaten path

LYNN CANYON PARK – With a steep canyon landscape, a temperate rain forest complete with waterfalls, and a suspension bridge 166½ feet above raging Lynn Creek, this park provides thrills to go with its scenic views. The on-site Ecology Centre distributes maps of area hiking trails and has information about the local flora and fauna. There's also a gift shop and a café on site. To get to the park, take the Lions Gate Bridge and Capilano Road, go east on Highway 1, take the Lynn Valley Road exit, and turn right on Peters Road. From downtown Vancouver, you can take the SeaBus to Lonsdale Quay, then Bus 228 or 229 from the quay; both stop near the park. ✉ *3663 Park Rd., at end of Peters Rd., North Vancouver* ☎ *604/981–3103 ecology center, 604/984–9311 café* ⊕ *www.dnv.org/ecology* ✉ *Ecology Centre by donation, suspension bridge free* ☉ *Park: daily, dawn to dusk; Ecology Centre: June–Sept., daily 10–5; Oct.–May, weekdays 10–5, weekends noon–4.*

☾ ⑤⑥ **Lonsdale Quay.** Of the many public markets in the Greater Vancouver area, this indoor seaside market is one of the most popular. Stalls selling fresh produce, exotic fare, and ready-to-eat food fill the lower level; upstairs are boutiques, toy stores, and a kids' play area. Outside you can wander the quay, admire the fishing boats and tugs moored here, and enjoy the views of the downtown skyline across the water. The SeaBus foot passenger ferry (☎ 604/953–3333 ⊕ www.translink.bc.ca) part of the city's public transit system, leaves the quay every 15 to 30 minutes for the 13-minute ride to Waterfront Station downtown. ✉ *123 Carrie Cates Ct., foot of Lonsdale Ave.* ☎ *604/985–6261* ⊕ *www. lonsdalequay.com* ✉ *Free* ☼ *May–Aug., daily 9:30–7; Sept.–Apr., daily 9:30–6:30.*

WHERE TO EAT

From inventive downtown bistros to waterfront seafood palaces, to Asian restaurants that rival those in Asia, Vancouver has a diverse array of gastronomical options. Many cutting-edge establishments are perfecting and defining Pacific Northwest fare, which incorporates regional seafood—notably salmon—and locally grown produce, often accompanied by British Columbian wines. Small plates are big, too—an increasing number of restaurants offer tapas-style portions designed for sharing; order several to make a meal and enjoy a variety of tastes.

With at least a third of the city's population of Asian heritage, it's no surprise that Asian eateries abound in Vancouver. From mom-and-pop noodle shops, curry houses, and corner sushi bars to elegant and upscale dining rooms, cuisine from China, Japan, and India (and to a lesser extent, from Taiwan, Korea, Thailand, Vietnam, and Malaysia) can be found all over town. Look for restaurants emphasizing Chinese regional cuisine, contemporary Indian-influenced fare, and different styles of Japanese cooking, from elaborate multicourse *kaiseki* dinners with their prescribed sequence of small courses, to light meals at casual *izakayas* (Japanese tapas bars). Even in restaurants that are not specifically "Asian," you'll find abundant Asian influences—your grilled salmon may be served with *gai lan* (Chinese broccoli), black rice, or a coconut-milk curry.

British Columbia's wine industry is enjoying great popularity, and many restaurants feature locally produced wines. The Okanagan Valley in the province's interior and Vancouver Island are the main wine-producing areas. Merlot, pinot noir, and chardonnay are among the major varieties; also look for ice wine, a dessert wine made from grapes that are picked while they are frozen on the vines.

If you'd like to stroll and scope out your dining options downtown, try Robson Street for everything from upscale Italian dining rooms to cheap, friendly Asian cafés and noodle shops, or explore Denman and Davie streets for a variety of ethnic eats. In Yaletown, both Hamilton and Mainland streets are lined with restaurants and upscale bars, many with outdoor terraces. In Kitsilano, West 4th Avenue between Burrard and Balsam streets has plenty of restaurant choices. Broadway, which runs across the city from the East Side toward the University of British Columbia, is lined with places to eat; the blocks around the Granville Street and Cambie Street intersections are particularly food-friendly.

Dining is fairly informal here. Casual but neat dress is appropriate everywhere. Smoking is prohibited by law in all Vancouver restaurants (indoors). *See* the Downtown Vancouver Dining map to locate downtown restaurants and the Greater Vancouver Dining map to locate restaurants in Kitsilano, Granville Island, and other neighborhoods.

A 15% tip is expected. A 7% Goods and Services Tax (GST) is levied on the food portion of restaurant bills, and a 10% liquor tax is charged on wine, beer, and spirits. Some restaurants build the liquor tax into the price of the beverage, but others add it to the bill.

WHAT IT COSTS In Canadian dollars				
	$$$$	$$$	$$	$	¢

	$$$$	$$$	$$	$	¢
AT DINNER	over $30	$21–$30	$13–$20	$8–$12	under $8

Prices are for a main course.

Downtown Vancouver

Belgian

$$ ✕ **Chambar.** Who would have predicted that a hip Belgian eatery in a high-ceiling space on a dreary block between Downtown and Gastown would take Vancouver by storm? A young, smartly dressed crowd hangs out at the bar sipping Belgian beer or funky cocktails (pink peppercorn daiquiri, anyone?), working up their appetites for chef Nico Schuermans's creative cooking, in which classic Belgian dishes are reinvented with flavors from North Africa and beyond. His *waterzoi* (seafood stew) is infused with vanilla, charred orange, and basil, while *moules* (mussels) might be sauced with smoked chilies, cilantro, and coconut cream. Unusual? Perhaps. Delicious? Definitely. ⊠ *562 Beatty St., Downtown* ☎ *604/879–7119* ⊟ *AE, MC, V* ⊗ *Closed Sun. No lunch.*

Cafés

¢–$ ✕ **Lupo Caffé Bar.** The deep red walls and upholstered bar stools give this Italian-style café an expensive feel, but the light meals are moderately priced. In the morning you can stop in for an espresso, poached eggs on toasted brioche, or a slab of rustic bread with jam. Midday, the menu includes panini, salads, and soups (including a light and peppery Tuscan bean), and several pasta dishes. ⊠ *1014 W. Georgia St., Downtown* ☎ *604/685–1131* ⊕ *www.lupos.ca* ⌕ *Reservations not accepted* ⊟ *MC, V* ⊗ *Closed Sun. No dinner.*

¢ ✕ **The Kolachy Shop.** At this casual café near B.C. Place, owners Kevin and Jason Thibert have taken *kolachy,* a slightly sweet, filled dough of Eastern European origin, and transformed it into a popular—and portable—light meal. Breakfast kolachy include a bacon-and-egg version and a "veggie scramble" stuffed with eggs, potatoes, mushrooms, and cheese. At lunch, fillings range from creamy mushroom to BBQ beef to a Greek-style mix of feta, spinach, and artichoke hearts. Come early for the best selection, and save room for dessert—kolachy (of course), stuffed with apricot, cherry, or poppy seed. ⊠ *888 Beatty St., Yaletown* ☎ *604/488–0200* ⊕ *www.kolachy.com* ⌕ *Reservations not accepted* ⊟ *MC, V* ⊗ *Closed Sun. No dinner.*

Casual

¢–$ ✕ **The Elbow Room.** Known for the good-natured abuse that the staff occasionally dishes out to customers, this entertaining diner-style joint, where the lime-green walls are decorated with celebrity photos, is a Vancou-

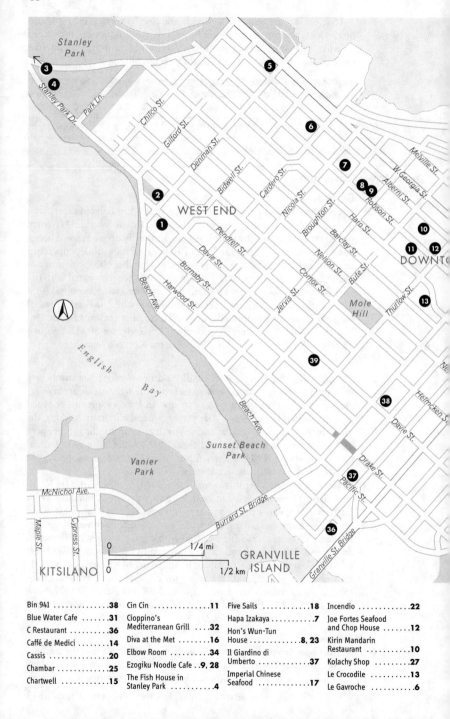

Where to Eat in Downtown Vancouver

WHERE TO REFUEL

WITH SUSHI BARS ON EVERY CORNER (or so it often seems), cafés all across the city, and plenty of burger joints, Vancouver has no shortage of places to grab a quick bite to eat. Although many U.S. fast-food franchises have sprouted up across Canada, the local chains listed below may provide more distinctive alternatives.

Café Crêpe. Crêpes are a popular snack or light meal in Vancouver, and these petits cafés serve both savory and sweet varieties.

De Dutch Pannekoek House. Specializing in Dutch pannekoeken (thin dinner-plate-size pancakes that come in nearly 50 combinations), these casual diner-style places serve burgers and sandwiches as well as breakfast items.

Earl's. Big cheery rooms, upbeat music, chipper service, and a vast menu of burgers, salads, sandwiches, pastas, steaks, and vegetarian options make this local chain a favorite, especially for groups and families.

Flying Wedge. Why opt for a basic cheese pizza when you can get "extreme" slices like the Sexi Mexi (topped with refried beans, salsa, and olives), the spicy Szechuan Chicken, or the Spinach Fettucine, a carbo-loader's dream topped with pasta, pesto, and sun-dried tomatoes?

White Spot. Founded in Vancouver in 1928 as Canada's first drive-in restaurant, this chain with more than 60 locations in B.C. and Alberta is a classic "spot" for burgers and fries, although salads, sandwiches, steaks, grilled chicken, and plenty of breakfast items round out the menu.

Wrap Zone. For a quick, portable bite to eat, stop into this B.C.-based minichain of sandwich-and-smoothie bars. The menu is particularly vegetarian-friendly, and they make a few kid-size wraps, too.

ver institution. They serve breakfast all day—the omelets are fluffy, the bacon is crisp, and the portions are generous—as well as burgers, sandwiches, and salads. If you don't finish your meal, you may be asked to make a donation to the local food bank. ⊠ *560 Davie St., Downtown* ☎ *604/685–3628* ⊕ *www.theelbowroomcafe.com* ⌨ *Reservations not accepted* ☰ *AE, MC, V* ☼ *No dinner.*

Chinese

$$–$$$ ✕ **Imperial Chinese Seafood.** The two-story floor-to-ceiling windows at this Cantonese restaurant in the art deco Marine Building have lovely views of Stanley Park and the North Shore Mountains across Coal Harbour. Any dish with lobster, crab, or shrimp from the live tanks is recommended, as is the dim sum, served daily 11 AM to 2:30 PM. ⊠ *355 Burrard St., Downtown* ☎ *604/688–8191* ⊕ *www.imperialrest.com* ☰ *DC, MC, V.*

$$–$$$ ✕ **Kirin Mandarin Restaurant.** A striking silver mural of a *kirin*, a mythical dragonlike creature, presides over this elegant two-tier restaurant. The specialties here are northern Chinese (Mandarin and Szechuan) dishes, which tend to be richer and spicier than the Cantonese cuisine served at Kirin's other locations. Try the Peking duck, or the kung pao lobster: sautéed lobster meat served with a deep-fried lobster claw. Dim sum is served daily. ⊠ *1166 Alberni St., Downtown* ☏ *604/682–8833* ⊕ *www. kirinrestaurant.com* ⊟ *AE, DC, MC, V.*

$$ ✕ **Wild Rice.** The look is decadent postmodern, with lounging couches and a glowing aquamarine bar; the food, served in tasting portions or on larger plates meant for sharing, borrows from China and across Asia but adds a decidedly contemporary spin. You might find pot stickers filled with kabocha squash, kung pao chicken paired with three types of broccoli, or coconut milk crème brûlée. A wide-ranging tea and martini selection augments the short but well-chosen wine list. ⊠ *117 W. Pender St., Chinatown* ☏ *604/642–2882* ⊕ *www.wildricevancouver.com* ⌃ *Reservations not accepted* ⊟ *AE, MC, V* ⊙ *No lunch weekends.*

¢–$$ ✕ **Hon's Wun-Tun House.** Mr. Hon has been keeping Vancouver residents in Chinese comfort food since the 1970s. The best bets on the 300-item menu are the wonton and noodle dishes, any of the Chinese vegetables, and anything with barbecued meat. The Robson Street outlet has a separate kitchen for vegetarians and an army of fast-moving waitresses. The original Keefer Street location is in the heart of Chinatown. ⊠ *1339 Robson St., West End* ☏ *604/685–0871* ⌃ *Reservations not accepted* ⊟ *MC, V* ✕ ⊠ *268 Keefer St., Chinatown* ☏ *604/688–0871* ⌃ *Reservations not accepted* ⊟ *No credit cards.*

Contemporary

$$$$ ✕ **Five Sails.** This special-occasion restaurant at the Pan Pacific Hotel commands a sweeping view of Canada Place, Lions Gate Bridge, and the lights of the North Shore. The broad-reaching, seasonally changing menu takes its inspiration from both Europe and the Pacific Rim. Highlights have included grilled B.C. salmon, beef tenderloin wrapped in pancetta and topped with foie gras, and sautéed prawns paired with Dungeness crab ravioli. ⊠ *Pan Pacific Hotel, 999 Canada Pl., Downtown* ☏ *604/891–2892* ⊕ *www.dinepanpacific.com* ⊟ *AE, DC, MC, V* ⊙ *No lunch.*

$$$–$$$$ ✕ **Chartwell.** Named after Sir Winston Churchill's country home (a painting of it hangs over one of this elegant restaurant's two fireplaces), the flagship dining room at the Four Seasons hotel has rich wood paneling, deep leather chairs, and a reputation for innovative cuisine. The seasonally changing menu makes the most of western Canada's regional bounty, notably lamb, beef, and seafood; grilled items, served with your choice of vegetable, starch, and sauce, are a specialty. ⊠ *791 W. Georgia St., Downtown* ☏ *604/844–6715* ⊕ *www.fourseasons.com/ vancouver* ⊟ *AE, D, DC, MC, V* ⊙ *No lunch.*

$$$–$$$$ ✕ **Diva at the Met.** Regional cuisine shines at this chic, modern restaurant in the Metropolitan Hotel. The menu changes frequently but focuses on the best local seafood, produce, and wines; you might find wild salmon served with a tomato tart, Pacific halibut paired with fennel-onion ravioli, or lamb loin served with a lamb terrine and a lentil cassoulet. Choose a table at the back for an intimate evening, near the front or on the patio for a more lively scene. A light lounge menu is available all evening, and the after-theater crowd heads here for late-evening snacks and desserts. The creative breakfasts are popular, too. ⊠ *645 Howe St., Downtown* ☏ *604/602–7788* ⊕ *www.metropolitan.com/ diva* ⊟ *AE, D, DC, MC, V.*

★ **$$$-$$$$**   ✕ **Raincity Grill.** One of the best places to try British Columbian food and wine is this pretty candlelighted bistro overlooking English Bay. The menu, which owner Harry Kambolis likes to call "stubbornly regional," changes seasonally and relies almost completely on local and regional products, from salmon and shellfish to game and fresh organic vegetables. Vegetarian selections are always on the menu, and the exclusively Pacific Northwest and Californian wine list has 100 choices by the glass. The prix-fixe early dinner (C$25) served from 5 to 6 PM is a steal. ⊠ *1193 Denman St., West End* ☎ *604/685–7337* ⊕ *www.raincitygrill. com* ⊟ *AE, DC, MC, V* ⊘ *No lunch weekdays.*

$$$ ✕ **Sequoia Grill at the Teahouse.** The former officers' mess in Stanley Park is perfectly poised for watching sunsets over the water. The Pacific Northwest menu includes such specialties as roasted pear salad and grilled ahi tuna, as well as seasonally changing treatments of duck breast, B.C. salmon, and rack of lamb. In summer you can dine on the patio; afternoon tapas are served year-round. ⊠ *7501 Stanley Park Dr., Ferguson Point, Stanley Park* ☎ *604/669–3281 or 800/280–9893* ⊕ *www. vancouverdine.com* ⊟ *AE, MC, V.*

$$-$$$ ✕ **Water Street Café.** The tables at this casual tourist-friendly Gastown bistro spill out onto the sidewalk for front-row views of the steam clock across the street. Tall windows on two sides of the lofty blue-and-white interior take in the Gastown streetscape. It's tempting to pick one of the 13 varieties of pasta, but the crab chowder, West Coast crab cakes, and the Fanny Bay oysters also are good choices. Although the basics are done well here, don't expect culinary innovation. ⊠ *300 Water St., Gastown* ☎ *604/689–2832* ⊟ *AE, MC, V.*

Continental

$$$-$$$$ ✕ **William Tell.** Silver-service plates, brass chandeliers, and vintage Swiss maps on hunter-green walls set a tone of Swiss luxury at this long-established restaurant in the Georgian Court Hotel. Continental classics, such as filet mignon, chateaubriand, and steak tartare (prepared tableside), share menu space with such Swiss dishes as cheese fondue and thinly sliced veal with mushrooms in a light white-wine sauce. Sunday night is all-you-can-eat Swiss buffet. Lunch is served only in the bistro area, which caters to a more casual crowd than the main restaurant. ⊠ *765 Beatty St., Downtown* ☎ *604/688–3504* ⊕ *www.thewmtell.com* ⊟ *AE, DC, MC, V* ⊘ *Main dining room closed Mon.*

Eclectic

$-$$ ✕ **Umami Tapas & Wine Bar.** Named for the Japanese term for the "fifth taste"—a dark woodsy note that complements salty, sweet, bitter, and sour flavors—this jewel box of a wine bar mixes Mediterranean and Japanese influences on moderately sized plates meant for sharing. Try the tuna spring rolls (fresh fish wrapped in nori and shiso leaves and sauced with a mirin-balsamic vinegar reduction), or the Dungeness crab sticks (luscious fried crab served with wasabi mayonnaise on an avocado and tomato salad). Ask owner Hiro Shintaku, an experienced sommelier, to recommend wines to match the eclectic dishes. ⊠ *572 Davie St., Downtown* ☎ *604/696–9563* ⊟ *AE, MC, V* ⊘ *No lunch.*

$ ✕ **Bin 941.** Part tapas restaurant, part up-tempo bar, this bustling, often noisy hole in the wall claims to have launched Vancouver's small plates trend. Among the adventurous snack-size dishes, you might find grilled smoked sablefish paired with black rice and spicy lime-glaze bok choy, or lamb sirloin served with a torta of smoked gouda, roasted vegetables, and potatoes. Snack on a couple, or have several and make a feast of it. The Bin serves food until 1:30 AM. Bin 942, a sister spot in Kitsilano, is a touch more subdued (⇨ Dining, Greater Vancouver). ✉ *941 Davie St., Downtown* ☎ *604/683–1246* ⊕ *www.bin941.com* ⌕ *Reservations not accepted* ▤ *MC, V* ☻ *No lunch.*

French

$$$–$$$$ ✗ **Le Crocodile.** Chefs prepare classic Alsatian-inspired food (such as the signature onion tart) at this long-established downtown restaurant. Golden yellow walls, café curtains, and burgundy banquettes keep things cozy. Favorite dishes, many of which also appear at lower prices at lunch, include saffron-lobster fricassee, veal medallions with morel sauce, and pan-seared Dover sole with lemon butter. ✉ *100–909 Burrard St., Downtown* ☎ *604/669–4298* ⊕ *www.lecrocodilerestaurant. com* ▤ *AE, DC, MC, V* ☻ *Closed Sun. No lunch Sat.*

$$$–$$$$ ✗ **Le Gavroche.** Classic French cuisine receives contemporary accents at this romantic restaurant, set in an early-20th-century house with mountain views. Seafood entrées range from roasted sturgeon with cauliflower puree to smoked sablefish with pink peppercorn sauce; meat options include rich beef tenderloin and rack of lamb. Vegetarian choices are always available. One of the few places with tableside service of steak tartare and Caesar salad, Le Gavroche also has a 5,000-label wine cellar. ✉ *1616 Alberni St., West End* ☎ *604/685–3924* ⊕ *www.legavroche. com* ▤ *AE, DC, MC, V* ☻ *No lunch weekends.*

$–$$ ✗ **Cassis.** French home-cooking meets downtown chic at this good-value bistro, where the high ceilings and rough wooden floors give it a stripped-down, loftlike feel. The highlights of the French regional menu, where most dishes are under C$12, are garlicky bouillabaisse, bright with orange peel and brimming with fresh fish; salade niçoise updated with thinly sliced ahi carpaccio; and *choucroute* that pairs a mild stewed cabbage with a rosy smoked pork chop. More businesslike midday, the place lets down its hair in the evenings, when a DJ spins tunes late on some nights. ✉ *420 W. Pender St., Downtown* ☎ *604/605–0420* ⊕ *www.cassisvancouver.com* ▤ *MC, V* ☻ *No lunch weekends.*

Greek

¢–$ ✗ **Stepho's Souvlaki.** Regulars swear by, and are quite prepared to wait in line for, Stepho's inexpensive and tasty roast lamb, moussaka, and souvlaki, served in a bustling taverna. The take-out menu is handy for picnics on the beach just down the street. ✉ *1124 Davie St., West End* ☎ *604/683–2555* ⌕ *Reservations not accepted* ▤ *AE, MC, V.*

Italian

$$$–$$$$ ✗ **Cin Cin.** With its gold walls, arched windows, and terra-cotta tiles— and its crowd-pleasing modern Italian menu—this Tuscan-inspired restaurant is appropriate for a business meal, a romantic tête-à-tête, or simply a relaxing dinner at the end of a long day. The heated terrace, shielded by greenery, feels a long way from busy Robson Street below. Inside, there's a lively scene around the hand-carved marble bar. The food, from the open kitchen and the wood-fire grill, oven, and rotisserie, changes seasonally, but might include panko-crusted Pacific halibut with a limoncello vinaigrette, Dungeness crab with carrot-and-tarragon risotto, and thin-crust wood-fired pizza. An early-evening prix-fixe menu is good value, at C$35. ⊠ *1154 Robson St., upstairs, West End* ☎ *604/688–7338* ⊕ *www.cincin.net* ⊟ *AE, DC, MC, V* ⊘ *No lunch weekends.*

$$–$$$$ ✕ **Caffé de Medici.** Run by the same family since 1980, this elegant northern Italian restaurant is—despite its location on Vancouver's most fashionable street—pleasantly free of attitude. Tomato salad made with buffalo mozzarella is a popular starter, and main courses might include gnocchi with chorizo sausage, black olives, and pine nuts; lamb osso buco served over risotto; or wild salmon paired with braised greens and lobster-crab ravioli. There's a separate vegetarian menu, too. The quiet atmosphere (it's set back from busy Robson Street) and gracious service make this a good choice for business lunches or romantic dinners. ⊠ *1025 Robson St., West End* ☎ *604/669–9322* ⊕ *www.caffedemedici. com* ⊟ *AE, DC, MC, V* ⊘ *No lunch weekends.*

★ **$$–$$$$** ✕ **Il Giardino di Umberto.** The vine-draped terrace with a wood-burning oven or any of the four terra-cotta-tile rooms inside are attractive places to enjoy this long-established restaurateur's traditional Tuscan cuisine. The frequently changing menu includes a variety of pasta dishes, osso buco Milanese with saffron risotto, grilled salmon with saffron and fennel vinaigrette, and roast reindeer loin with a wine reduction. Dine here with someone special. ⊠ *1382 Hornby St., Downtown* ☎ *604/669–2422* ⊕ *www.umberto.com* ⊟ *AE, DC, MC, V* ⊘ *Closed Sun. No lunch Sat.*

Japanese

$–$$$ ✕ **Yoshi.** Sushi and sashimi are the specialties at this traditional Japanese restaurant, where picture windows face Stanley Park and the North Shore mountains—try the fresh wild salmon, crab, or whatever is on special. Interesting items come from the *robata* (grill), too, including meltingly tender black cod. The gracious staff is quick to refill your green tea or explain menu items. The restaurant is on the second floor, and in warm weather, you can dine on the terrace. With advance notice, you can order a *kaiseki* dinner, a classic meal with a prescribed sequence of small courses. ⊠ *689 Denman St., West End* ☎ *604/738–8226* ⊕ *www.yoshijapaneserestaurant.com* ⊟ *AE, DC, MC, V* ⊘ *No lunch weekends.*

★ **$** ✕ **Hapa Izakaya.** *Izakayas* are Japanese pubs that serve tapas-style small plates designed for sharing, and they have sprouted up all over Vancouver. One of the best places to sample the izakaya phenomenon is in this sleek space popular with festive groups of twenty- and thirtysomethings. Try the mackerel (cooked tableside—with a blowtorch—and served with hot mustard), udon noodles coated with briny cod roe, or the Korean-style stone bowl filled with rice, pork, and vegetables. Sake or Japanese beer are the drinks of choice. If you're dining alone, sit at the counter facing the open kitchen to watch the action. ⊠ *1479 Robson St., West End* ☎ *604/689–4272* ⊟ *AE, MC, V* ⊘ *No lunch.*

¢–$ ✕ **Ezogiku Noodle Cafe.** Noodles—or, more precisely, Japanese ramen noodles—are the specialty at these cheap and cheerful hole-in-the-wall cafés. The two Robson Street locations fill quickly with hungry shoppers and homesick Japanese students. Some say the noodles and soups here are just like those in Tokyo. With nothing over C$10, Ezogiku is one of the best values on this chic shopping strip. ⊠ *270 Robson St., at Hamilton St., Yaletown* ☎ *604/685–9466* ⊠ *1329 Robson St., at Jervis St., West End* ☎ *604/685–8606* ⚠ *Reservations not accepted* ⊟ *No credit cards.*

Mediterranean

$$–$$$$ ✕ **Cioppino's Mediterranean Grill.** Cioppino, a fragrant seafood stew, is the signature dish at this lofty, candlelight room. Chef Pino Posteraro impresses with homemade pastas and such Italian-Mediterranean dishes as a casserole of sea bass and vegetables, and duck breast with chorizo and cannellini beans. Mr. Posteraro also serves more rustic Italian fare, such as charbroiled lamb chops and braised beef short ribs, at **Enoteca** (⊠ 1129 Hamilton St., Yaletown ☎ 604/685–8462), a brick-walled sister restaurant next door. Both restaurants have streetside patios. ⊠ *1133 Hamilton St., Yaletown* ☎ *604/688–7466* ⊕ *www.cioppinosyaletown.com* ⊟ *AE, DC, MC, V* ⊗ *Both closed Sun. No lunch at Cioppino's, no lunch weekends at Enoteca.*

$$–$$$$ ✕ **Provence Marinaside.** This airy, modern Mediterranean-style eatery on Yaletown's waterfront presents French and Italian takes on seafood, including a delicious bouillabaisse and lush, garlicky tiger prawns, though the rack of lamb and an extensive antipasti selection are also popular. The marina-view patio makes a sunny breakfast or lunch spot, and the take-out counter is a great place to put together a picnic. ⊠ *1177 Marinaside Crescent, at foot of Davie St., Yaletown* ☎ *604/681–4144* ⊕ *www.provencevancouver.com* ⊟ *AE, DC, MC, V.*

Native American

$$–$$$
Fodor'sChoice
★

✕ **Liliget Feast House.** This intimate room looks like the interior of a longhouse, with wooden walkways across pebble floors, contemporary First Nations art on the walls, and cedar-plank tables with tatami-style benches. Liliget is one of the few places in the world serving the original Northwest Coast First Nations cuisine. A feast platter lets you try most of the fare, which includes bannock bread, baked sweet potato with hazelnuts, alder-grilled salmon, buffalo smokies (smoked buffalo sausages), venison strips, duck breast, oysters, mussels, and steamed fern shoots. ⊠ *1724 Davie St., West End* ☎ *604/681–7044* ⊕ *www.liliget.com* ⊟ *AE, DC, MC, V* ⊗ *Closed Mon. and Tues. Oct.–Feb. No lunch.*

Pizza

$–$$ ✕ **Incendio.** The hand-flipped thin-crust pizzas, with innovative toppings including Asiago cheese, prosciutto, roasted garlic, and sun-dried tomatoes, and the mix-and-match pastas and sauces (try the hot smoked-duck sausage, artichoke, and tomato combination or the broccoli and pine nuts in a creamy gorgonzola cheese sauce) draw crowds to this Gastown eatery. The room, in a circa-1900 heritage building, with exposed brick, local artwork, and big curved windows, has plenty of atmosphere. ⊠ *103 Columbia St., Gastown* ☎ *604/688–8694* ⊕ *www.incendio.ca* ⊟ *AE, MC, V* ⊗ *No lunch weekends.*

Seafood

$$$$ ✕ **C Restaurant.** Save your pennies, fish fans—dishes such as scallops
Fodor'sChoice   wrapped with octopus bacon or lightly smoked Skeena wild salmon (which
★   might be paired with pumpkin or fried bread with preserved lemon) have
established this spot as Vancouver's most innovative seafood restaurant.
Start with shucked oysters from the raw bar, or try C's Taster Box, in
which several morsels are served dramatically on a four-tier display. An
eight-course tasting menu (C$90 per person) highlights local and ex-
otic seafood. Both the chic, ultramodern interior and the waterside
patio overlook False Creek. ⊠ 2–1600 Howe St., Downtown ☎ 604/
681–1164 ⊕ www.crestaurant.com ⊟ AE, DC, MC, V ⊘ No lunch weekends or Oct.–Apr.

$$$–$$$$ ✕ **Blue Water Cafe.** This fashionable restaurant shows its architectural
bones with exposed timbers and brick that arrived in the 1890s as
ships' ballast. Fresh, local seafood is the theme, with catch such as
Queen Charlotte Island halibut and B.C. sturgeon, though steaks, in-
cluding Canadian prime beef, are also available. There's a good selec-
tion of raw oysters, and the sushi chef turns out both classic and new
creations using local seafood. You could dress up a bit, whether you dine
in the candlelighted interior or outside on the former loading dock
that's now an attractive terrace. An early-evening prix-fixe menu is a
good value at C$35. ⊠ 1095 Hamilton St., Yaletown ☎ 604/688–
8078 ⊕ www.bluewatercafe.net ⊟ AE, DC, MC, V.

$$$–$$$$ ✕ **Joe Fortes Seafood and Chop House.** Named for a much-loved English
Bay lifeguard, this lively San Francisco–style brasserie just off Robson
Street has a piano bar, a bistro, an oyster bar, and a delightful covered
rooftop patio. The menu is wide-ranging, but steaks, chops, and gen-
erous portions of fresh seafood are the main draw. Try the cedar-smoked
salmon, the cioppino (a seafood stew), or the Seafood Tower on Ice—
a starter of oysters, tuna sashimi, mussels, clams, scallops, shrimp, lob-
ster, and crab that's meant to be shared. ⊠ 777 Thurlow St., Downtown
☎ 604/669–1940 ⊕ www.joefortes.ca ⊟ AE, D, DC, MC, V.

$$–$$$ ✕ **The Fish House in Stanley Park.** This 1930s former sports pavilion
with two verandas and a fireplace is tucked between Stanley Park's ten-
nis courts and putting green. The food, including simply grilled ahi tuna
steak and corn-husk-wrapped salmon with a maple glaze, is flavorful
and unpretentious. Chef Karen Barnaby, author of The Low-Carb
Gourmet cookbook, also offers a seafood-focused low-carb menu. Be-
fore dinner head for the oyster bar, or arrive between 5 and 6 weeknights
for the early-bird specials. Traditional English afternoon tea is served
between 2 and 4 daily. ⊠ 8901 Stanley Park Dr., enter park from foot
of Robson St., Stanley Park ☎ 604/681–7275 or 877/681–7275 ⊕ www.
fishhousestanleypark.com ⊟ AE, D, DC, MC, V.

$–$$$ ✕ **Rodney's Oyster House.** This fishing-shack look-alike in Yaletown has
one of the widest selections of oysters in town (up to 18 varieties), from
locally harvested bivalves to exotic Japanese kumamotos. You can pick
your oysters individually—they're laid out on ice behind the bar and priced
at C$1.50 to about C$3 each—or try the clams, scallops, mussels, and
other mollusks from the steamer kettles. Oyster lovers can also relax over
martinis and appetizers in the attached Mermaid Room lounge. ⊠ 1228

FUELED BY CAFFEINE

FUELLED BY CAFFEINE" is the slogan for a Vancouver-based minichain of coffeehouses, and it also seems an apt description of this city. Meeting for coffee is a year-round social ritual, and when the sun shines, practically every scrap of sidewalk sprouts a café table with at least a couple of latte sippers.

Although the Starbucks invasion is nearly complete there are plenty of more colorful places—from sleek and modern to comfortably bohemian. You'll find the same variety of coffee drinks that you can get across North America, though some places refer to an "americano" as a "canadiano." An increasing number of cafés offers free Wi-Fi, too.

Bean Around the World (✉ 1945 Cornwall Ave., Kitsilano ☎ 604/739–1069 ✉ 2977 Granville St., South Granville ☎ 604/730–9555 ✉ 4456 W. 10th Ave., Point Grey ☎ 604/222–1400 ✉ 3598 Main St., East Side ☎ 604/875–9199), of the "Fuelled by Caffeine" slogan, runs a number of comfortable coffeehouses (some with fireplaces) around the city.

Granville Island has several coffee places, but only the **Blue Parrot Café** (✉ Granville Island Public Market, 1689 Johnston St., Granville Island ☎ 604/688–5127), provides such sweeping views of the boats on False Creek.

Cushy couches and wholesome goodies make **Bojangles Café** (✉ 785 Denman St., West End ☎ 604/687–3622 ✉ 1506 Coal Harbour Quay, Coal Harbour ☎ 604/687–6599) a good place to rest after a walk around Stanley Park. There's another location in Yaletown (✉ 1097 Marinaside Crescent, Yaletown ☎ 604/683–7556).

Some of Vancouver's best coffee is served at the several city-center locales of **Caffè**

Artigiano (✉ 1101 W. Pender ☎ 604/685–5333 ✉ 763 Hornby ☎ 604/696–9222 ✉ 740 W. Hastings St. ☎ 604/915–7200), where the baristas have won prizes for their "Latte Art," making patterns in the froth. **Delaney's on Denman** (✉ 1105 Denman St., West End ☎ 604/662–3344) is a friendly and often crowded coffee bar near English Bay, in the heart of Vancouver's gay community.

Serious coffee drinkers head for Commercial Drive on the city's East Side. This increasingly bohemian neighborhood is full of spots to fuel your caffeine habit. With its marble-top tables and dark espresso drinks, **Caffe Calabria** (✉ 1745 Commercial Dr., East Side ☎ 604/253–7017) is one of the many traditional Italian cafés along "The Drive." **Continental Coffee** (✉ 1806 Commercial Dr., East Side ☎ 604/255–0712) has a funky, boho vibe, but the weekend lineups attest to the first-rate coffee; they make a particularly good americano. **Prado Café** (✉ 1938 Commercial Dr., East Side ☎ 604/255–5537) feels industrial-chic, with gun-metal grey chairs and blond-wood tables.

Vancouverites don't live by coffee alone, as proven by the proliferation of tea shops. At its two contemporary city-center teahouses, **Infuze** (✉ 870 W. Cordova St., Downtown ☎ 604/689–3188 ✉ 1114 Denman St., West End ☎ 604/689–3177) specializes in matcha (Japanese green tea), as well as other green, black, and oolong teas and herbal infusions. Tiny **O-Cha Tea Bar** (✉ 1116 Homer St., Yaletown ☎ 604/633–3929) serves 60 of its own blends, including rich, milky "Lat-Teas." At **T** (✉ 1568 W. Broadway, South Granville ☎ 604/730–8390), which sells a vast selection of teas and related paraphernalia, you can sample a cup in the serene, vaguely Japanese-style tearoom.

Hamilton St., Yaletown ☎ 604/609–0080 ▭ *AE, DC, MC, V* ☺ *Restaurant closed Sun., lounge closed Mon.–Wed. No lunch in lounge.*

Greater Vancouver

Cafés

¢–$ ✕ **Soupspoons Urban Soup Bar.** This deli-style soup bar serves about 10 homemade varieties along with cheese, bread (made daily in-house), pastries, and Euro-sandwiches such as croque monsieurs, focaccia, and panini. It's a convenient refueling stop if you're shopping on Kitsilano's 4th Avenue. ✉ *2278 W. 4th Ave., Kitsilano* ☎ 604/328–7687 ⊕ *www.soupspoons. com* ⚑ *Reservations not accepted* ▭ *V.*

Chinese

$$–$$$ ✕ **Kirin Seafood Restaurant.** You can take in cityscapes and mountain views from this room opposite City Hall. The focus is on seafood, including crab and lobster from live tanks, and on Cantonese creations, which are milder than the northern Chinese cuisine served at Kirin Mandarin Restaurant downtown. Dim sum is served daily. There's another location in suburban Richmond, not far from the airport. ✉ *555 W. 12th Ave., 2nd fl., City Sq. Shopping Centre, Fairview* ☎ 604/879–8038 ✉ *3 W. Centre, 2nd fl., 7900 Westminster Hwy., Richmond* ☎ 604/ 303–8833 ⊕ *www.kirinrestaurant.com* ▭ *AE, DC, MC, V.*

$$–$$$ ✕ **Sun Sui Wah Seafood Restaurant.** Sails grace the ceiling of this bright and bustling Cantonese restaurant with locations on the East Side and in suburban Richmond. Sun Sui Wah is best known for its excellent dim sum (served 10–3 daily), which ranges from traditional handmade dumplings to some highly adventurous fare. Dinner specialties include roasted squab and enormous king crab from the live tanks. ✉ *3888 Main St., East Side* ☎ 604/872–8822 *or* 866/872–8822 ✉ *4940 No. 3 Rd., Richmond* ☎ 604/273–8208 *or* 866/683–8208 ⊕ *www.sunsuiwah. com* ▭ *AE, DC, MC, V.*

$–$$ ✕ **Shiang Garden Seafood Restaurant.** Dim sum aficionados make the trek to this upscale Cantonese restaurant in suburban Richmond for some of the tastiest tidbits in town. Order from the menu (there are no carts circling the dining rooms), or just point at what the other tables are having. In the evenings, Hong Kong–style seafood is the specialty. The multilevel restaurant, which is popular with Asian families, is in a shopping plaza, set back from No. 3 Road at Leslie Road. ✉ *4540 No. 3 Rd., Richmond* ☎ 604/273–8858 ▭ *DC, MC, V.*

Contemporary

★ $$$$ ✕ **Bishop's.** This highly regarded room serves West Coast cuisine with an emphasis on organic, regional produce. The menu changes weekly, but highlights have included such starters as house-cured gravlax and such mains as steamed smoked sablefish, Dungeness crab cakes, and locally raised lamb. All are beautifully presented and impeccably served with suggestions from Bishop's extensive local wine list. The split-level room displays elaborate flower arrangements and selections from owner John Bishop's art collection. ✉ *2183 W. 4th Ave., Kitsilano* ☎ 604/738– 2025 ⊕ *www.bishopsonline.com* ▭ *AE, DC, MC, V* ☺ *Closed 1st wk in Jan. No lunch.*

$$$$
Fodor'sChoice
★ ✕ **West.** Contemporary regional cuisine is the theme at this chic restaurant, one of the city's most innovative dining rooms. Among chef David Hawksworth's creations are an Asian-inspired salad of BBQ duck, watercress, radish, and pea shoots; sablefish with wild ramps; and "Tongue & Cheek"—braised veal cheeks and roast tongue served with a sweetbread-shallot ravioli. Marble floors, high ceilings, and warm caramel leather set into red walls make the space feel simultaneously energetic and cozy. Multicourse tasting menus, a small-plates menu, and a good-value (C$35) early-evening set menu, served before 6 PM, make for plenty of dining options. ⌂*2881 Granville St., South Granville* ☎*604/738–8938* ⊕*www. westrestaurant.com* ▭ *AE, DC, MC, V* ⊘ *No lunch weekends.*

$$$–$$$$ ✕ **The Beach House.** It's worth the drive over the Lions Gate Bridge to West Vancouver for an evening meal or lunch at this 1912 seaside house. Whether inside the terraced room or on the heated beachside patio, most every table has views over Burrard Inlet and Stanley Park. The Pacific Northwest menu changes seasonally but creates accessible takes on meat, poultry, and seafood, including wild B.C. salmon. After your meal, you can take a stroll along the pier or the seaside walkway. ⌂ *150–25th St. off Marine Dr., West Vancouver* ☎ *604/922–1414* ⊕ *www.atthebeachhouse.com* ▭ *AE, DC, MC, V.*

$$–$$$ ✕ **Seasons in the Park.** Tiered seating and tall windows allow virtually every table here a commanding view over the gardens in Queen Elizabeth Park, to the city and mountains beyond. Wood paneling and wrought iron make for an elegant atmosphere that's mirrored in the contemporary Pacific Northwest fare. The menu might include black cod with Asian vegetables or herb-crusted rack of lamb, as well as daily-changing treatments of wild B.C. salmon. Weekend brunch is popular, and three fireplaces on the patio allow for year-round outdoor dining. ⌂*Queen Elizabeth Park, W. 33rd Ave. and Cambie St., South Vancouver* ☎*604/874–8008 or 800/632–9422* ⊕*www.vancouverdine.com* ▭ *AE, MC, V.*

★ **$$** ✕ **Cru.** "Small plates and big glasses" is the motto of this tapas- and wine-focused restaurant, stylishly outfitted with tan banquettes and romantic low lighting. More than 35 wines by the glass (plus more by the bottle) complement the inventive designed-to-share dishes. There's a wonderfully crispy duck confit served on a frisée salad with warm bacon dressing, a trio of bruschetta that might be topped with fig and walnut tapenade or pancetta and fennel, and an assortment of cheeses from B.C., Quebec, and beyond. Save room for dessert, perhaps the decadent bittersweet chocolate torte or the goat cheese cake with sour-cherry compote. ⌂ *1459 W. Broadway, South Granville* ☎ *604/677–4111* ⊕ *www. cru.ca* ▭ *AE, MC, V* ⊘ *No lunch.*

$$ ✕ **Feenie's.** Owned by Robert Feenie of Lumière fame, this fashionable bistro next door serves the chef's contemporary creations in a more relaxed setting. The colorful space, with deep red and gold walls and blond wood tables, fills nightly with young trendies who graze on the Feenie burger (with mushrooms, cheese, and bacon), grilled wild salmon (paired with lemon, pea, and mint risotto), or the heartier pappardelle with braised beef, pine nuts, and arugula. ⌂ *2563 W. Broadway, Kitsilano* ☎ *604/ 739–7115* ⊕ *www.feenies.com* ▭ *AE, DC, MC, V.*

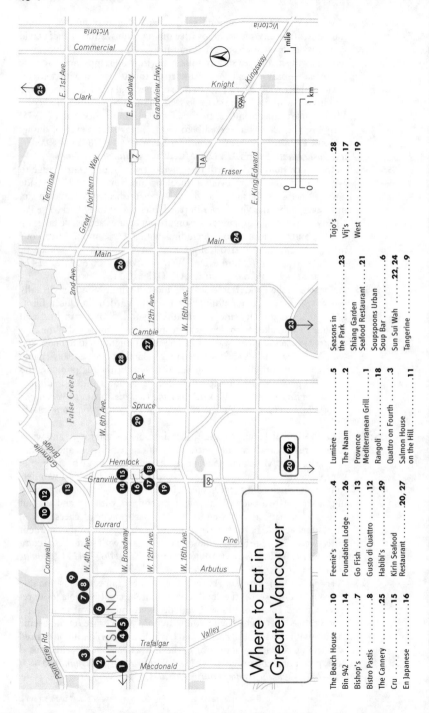

Where to Eat in Greater Vancouver

Eclectic

$ ✕ **Bin 942.** High-energy murals, low lights, and up-tempo (sometimes loud) music draw crowds to this tiny tapas bar. The real star here, though, is the food. From the scallop and tiger-prawn tournedos to the beef tenderloin phyllo Wellington, the chef creates some of the most eclectic small plates in town. Fun is also part of the deal: the chocolate fruit fondue, for example, comes with a paintbrush. Food is served until 1:30 AM (until midnight on Sunday), and the excellent, affordable, wines are all available by the glass. ⊠ *1521 W. Broadway, South Granville* ☎ *604/ 734–9421* ⊕ *www.bin941.com* ⌲ *Reservations not accepted* ▤ *MC, V* ⊗ *No lunch.*

French

$$$$ ✕ **Lumière.** Chef Robert Feenie is the Vancouver food community's
Fodor's Choice golden boy; he stars in his own Food Network show, and earned fur-
★   ther kudos for his winning appearance on the *Iron Chef.* The contemporary French cuisine at this light and airy restaurant isn't so much served as it's orchestrated, arranged in one of the chef's frequently changing multicourse set menus. The menus, whether seafood, vegetarian, or the elaborate 12-course signature menu, present creative takes on French cuisine, using regionally sourced organic produce. Although the main dining room offers only a prix-fixe option, you can sample menu items at the tasting bar. ⊠ *2551 W. Broadway, Kitsilano* ☎ *604/739–8185* ⊕ *www.lumiere.ca* ▤ *AE, DC, MC, V* ⊗ *No lunch.*

$$$ ✕ **Bistro Pastis.** This intimate 15-table French bistro sticks to its roots with a signature steak tartare and great frites but has some innovative dishes, too: try the Belgian endive and Roquefort salad with hazelnut vinaigrette, or the roasted duck breast, which might come with walnut gnocchi. There's a large selection of wines by the glass. Finish on a sweet note with crêpes Suzette, lemon tart, or a basket of madeleines. The decor is simple and homey, with white tablecloths, brown wicker chairs, a fireplace, and French doors opening onto the sidewalk. ⊠ *2153 W. 4th Ave., Kitsilano* ☎ *604/731–5020* ⊕ *www.bistropastis.com* ▤ *AE, DC, MC, V* ⊗ *Closed Mon.*

Indian

$$–$$$ ✕ **Vij's.** Vikram Vij, the genial proprietor of Vancouver's most innovative Indian restaurant, uses local ingredients to create exciting takes on South Asian cuisine. The dishes, such as lamb "popsicles" in a creamy fenugreek-scented curry, or sautéed arugula with paneer cheese and roasted cashews, are far from traditional but are spiced beautifully. Mr. Vij circulates through the room, which is decorated with Indian antiques and whimsical elephant-pattern lanterns, greeting guests and suggesting dishes or cocktail pairings. Expect to cool your heels at the bar or stroll around the neighborhood while you wait for a table, but if you favor creative Indian fare, it's worth it. ⊠ *1480 W. 11th Ave., South Granville* ☎ *604/736–6664* ⊕ *www.vijs.ca* ⌲ *Reservations not accepted* ▤ *AE, DC, MC, V* ⊗ *No lunch.*

$ ✕ **Rangoli.** Next door to Vij's, and under the same ownership, this storefront bistro serves up similarly innovative Indian fare in a much more relaxed setting. Nab a table on the sidewalk or in the small but modern interior space, and sample tamarind-marinated grilled chicken, eggplant and green onion curry, or mutton kebobs with apple chaat (a spiced apple condiment), washed down with ginger lemonade or a maharaja pilsner. Come early, though; they close at 8 PM. ☒ *1488 W. 11th Ave., South Granville* ☎ *604/736–5711* ⊕ *www.vijsrangoli.ca* ⚑ *Reservations not accepted* ▤ *MC, V.*

Italian

$$–$$$$ ✕ **Quattro on Fourth.** Central Italian cuisine shines at this family-run neighborhood favorite. The signature Spaghetti Quattro comes with hot chilies, minced chicken, black beans, olive oil, and generous lashings of garlic. Mains include Cornish hen grilled with herbs, garlic, and spicy peppers; rack of lamb with a fig and Dijon demi-glace and pistachio-crusted sea bass with roasted sweet pepper sauce. Mahogany tables, chandeliers, candlelight, and a hand-painted floor glow indoors; a patio beckons in summer. The cellar has 400 wine varieties and an extensive grappa selection. The same owners also run the similar **Gusto di Quattro** (☒ 1 Lonsdale Ave., next to Lonsdale Quay, North Vancouver ☎ 604/924–4444) a quick SeaBus ride across the harbor from downtown. ☒ *2611 W. 4th Ave., Kitsilano* ☎ *604/734–4444* ⊕ *www.quattrorestaurants.com* ▤ *AE, DC, MC, V* ⊘ *No lunch.*

Japanese

★ **$$–$$$$** ✕ **Tojo's.** Hidekazu Tojo is a sushi-making legend in Vancouver, with more than 2,000 special preparations stored in his creative mind. His handsome tatami rooms and city-view dining room provide the proper setting for intimate dining, but Tojo's 10-seat sushi bar is a convivial ringside seat for watching the creation of edible art. The best way to experience Tojo's creativity is to reserve a spot at the sushi bar and order *omakase* (chef's choice); chef Tojo will keep offering you wildly more adventurous fare until you cry uncle. Budget a minimum of C$50 per person (before drinks) for the omakase option; tabs topping C$100 per person are routine. ☒ *202–777 W. Broadway, Fairview* ☎ *604/872–8050* ⊕ *www.tojos.com* ▤ *AE, DC, MC, V* ⚑ *Reservations required for omakase* ⊘ *Closed Sun. No lunch.*

$–$$$ ✕ **En Japanese.** Modern West Coast takes on Japanese food are served in geometrically arranged portions that range from small to larger (order several and experiment) at this simple space. An avocado salad comes with a miso-wasabi dressing, and barbecued eel is layered with fish, cucumber, and egg. The sushi, tempura, and noodle dishes all come with surprising twists. The taupe-and-white candlelight room is almost austere, though watching the elaborate creations come from the kitchen is half the fun. ☒ *2686 Granville St., South Granville* ☎ *604/730–0330* ▤ *AE, DC, MC, V* ⊘ *Closed Mon. No lunch.*

Mediterranean

$$–$$$ ✕ **Provence Mediterranean Grill.** This West Side bistro, decorated in sunny shades of gold, is run by a French-Italian husband-wife team of chefs (who also own Yaletown's Provence Marinaside). Together they bring the tastes of the Mediterranean—garlic, parsley, mussels, goat cheese, olive oil, tapenade, bouillabaisse, and fresh seafood—to grateful Vancouverites. You can have a full meal, with wine skillfully paired by the helpful staff, or graze from more than a dozen grilled and marinated choices in the antipasti bar. If you want takeout, a day's notice will get you a picnic basket worthy of an afternoon in Arles. ⊠ *4473 W. 10th Ave., Point Grey* ☎ *604/222–1980* ⊕ *www.provencevancouver.com* ⊟ *AE, DC, MC, V.*

Middle Eastern

¢ ✕ **Habibi's.** The Lebanese home cooking at this storefront café is one of the area's best values. All the dishes are vegetarian, and most are meze-size (appetizer-size)—try several, and experiment with such specialties as *lebneh* (a yogurt cheese with spices), *balila* (warm chickpeas with garlic and olive oil), and *warak anab* (rice-stuffed grape leaves marinated in lemon juice). Wooden tables, soft blues music, and family photos from the old country make a welcome change from most eateries in this price range. ⊠ *1128 W. Broadway, Fairview* ☎ *604/732–7487* ⊕ *www. habibis.com* ⌔ *Reservations not accepted* ⊟ *V* ☺ *Closed Sun.*

Seafood

$$$–$$$$ ✕ **The Cannery.** This long-established East Side favorite has striking views over the harbor and the mountains beyond. Though the tables are set with white linen and china, the rustic nautical decor, including a retired fishing boat out front, indicates the specialty here. Most diners come for the seafood classics: bouillabaisse, Dungeness crab, Nova Scotia lobster, treats from the daily fresh sheet, or the Cannery's signature salmon Wellington with a pinot-noir sauce. To get here, take Hastings Street east from downtown, and turn left onto Clark Drive. Cross the bridge into the port area, notify the guard that you're headed for the Cannery, and turn left (east) onto Commissioner. ⊠ *2205 Commissioner St., East Side* ☎ *604/254–9606 or 877/254–9606* ⊕ *www. canneryseafood.com* ⊟ *AE, D, DC, MC, V* ☺ *No lunch weekends.*

$$$–$$$$ ✕ **Salmon House on the Hill.** Perched halfway up a mountain, this restaurant has stunning water and city views by day and expansive vistas of city lights by night. The Salmon House is best known for its alder-grilled salmon, though the grilled oysters, British Columbia prawns, and treats from the daily fresh sheet are also tempting. The Northwest Coast First Nations–theme decor is tastefully done, though it can hardly compete with what's outside the windows. The Salmon House is about 15 to 30 minutes from Vancouver by car (depending on traffic). Go over the Lions Gate Bridge and take the Folkestone Way exit off Highway 1 west. ⊠ *2229 Folkestone Way, West Vancouver* ☎ *604/926–3212* ⊕ *www.salmonhouse. com* ⊟ *AE, DC, MC, V.*

★ **$** ✕ **Go Fish.** If the weather's fine, head for this seafood stand on the docks near Granville Island. It's owned by Gord Martin, of Bin 941/ 942 fame, so it's not your ordinary chippie. The menu is short—highlights include fish-and-chips, grilled salmon or tuna sandwiches, and oyster po' boys—but the quality is first-rate, and the accompanying Asian-flavored slaw leaves ordinary cole slaw in the dust. There are just a few (outdoor) tables, so go early or be prepared to wait. To get here, walk along the waterfront path from Granville Island; by car, drive east from Burrard on 1st Avenue until it ends at the docks. ⊠ *1505 W. 1st Ave., Fisherman's Wharf, Kitsilano* ☎ *604/730–5039* ⊟ *MC, V* ☺ *Closed Mon. and Tues. No dinner.*

Vegetarian

¢–$ ✕ **Foundation Lounge.** The decor at this East Side vegetarian joint—mismatched formica tables, 1950s-style vinyl chairs, a cinderblock bar—may not win any design prizes, but the bohemian vibe is friendly and the meat-free fare is tasty. Try the satay salad—mixed greens, tofu, and broccoli topped with a warm, tangy peanut sauce—or opt for a hearty veggie burger or the tofu-and-mango scramble. Though it's on a dreary (if gentrifying) block, this storefront restaurant is hopping from midday until 1 AM. ✉ *2301 Main St., East Side* ☎ *604/708–0881* 🖃 *MC, V.*

¢–$ ✕ **The Naam.** Vancouver's oldest natural-foods eatery is open 24 hours, so if you need to satisfy a late-night craving for a veggie burger, rest easy. The Naam also serves Thai noodle dishes, burritos, enchiladas, wicked chocolate desserts, wine, beer, and fresh-squeezed juices. Try the famous baked fries with miso gravy. Wood tables, an open fireplace, and live blues, folk, and jazz most evenings keep things homey. Reservations are accepted only for groups of six or more and only between Monday and Thursday. ✉ *2724 W. 4th Ave., Kitsilano* ☎ *604/738–7151* ⊕ *www. thenaam.com* 🖃 *AE, DC, MC, V.*

WHERE TO STAY

Accommodations in Vancouver range from luxurious waterfront hotels to neighborhood B&Bs, chain hotels (both luxury and budget), basic European-style pensions, and backpacker's hostels.

Although the city is quite compact, each area has its distinct character and accommodation options. The central business district, between Robson Street and the waterfront, offers mid-to-high-end hotels, which cater to both tourists and business travelers. The area is within walking distance of most downtown sights and handy to the Canada Place cruise ship terminal, though it can be a little dull in the evenings as few people live in the area. Also downtown, you can find a cluster of low-to-mid-price hotels along Granville Street south of Robson. Good for those who prefer nightlife to quiet, this part of Granville is lined with bars, nightclubs, and movie theaters. Yaletown, also centrally located on the downtown peninsula, is a trendy area with lots of high-end shopping and dining. The West End, a high-rise residential district tucked between the downtown core and Stanley Park, and just blocks from either, is also an excellent option. Here you can find hotels in all price ranges on the main arteries and historic hotels and B&Bs on tree-lined back streets. Because so many people live in the area, you can find plenty of shops, cafés, and street life in the evenings. There are plenty of cheap hotels in the downtown core east of Cambie, but this is a rough neighborhood, best avoided at night. Outside the downtown peninsula, a bed in North Vancouver will put you close to hiking and skiing; accommodations on the West Side—in Kitsilano and on the University of British Columbia campus—are handy to beaches, parks, gardens, and the shopping and cafés of Kitsilano and Granville Island.

Most hotels let children under 18 stay free in their parents' room, although you may be charged extra for more than two adults. Other things to budget for include parking, which runs about C$20 per day at downtown hotels, and is usually free outside the downtown core; a one-time cleaning fee if you bring a pet, which can cost from C$10 to C$70; phone and Internet charges; and health club admission (these are usually free for guests, but some high-end hotels charge extra to use the gym and pool facilities). You'll also be charged a 10% accommodations tax and a 7% Goods and Services Tax (GST). Keep your original hotel receipts as you may be able to reclaim the 7% GST portion of the tax. *See* Smart Travel Tips for details about reclaiming GST.

The chart below shows high-season prices, but from mid-October through March, rates throughout the city can drop as much as 50%.

WHAT IT COSTS In Canadian dollars				
$$$$	**$$$**	**$$**	**$**	**¢**
FOR 2 PEOPLE over $250	$176–$250	$126–$175	$75–$125	under $75

Prices are for a standard double room in high season, excluding 10% room tax and 7% GST.

$$$$ 🏨 **Delta Vancouver Suites.** Attached to the Morris J. Wosk Centre for Dialogue (a conference center), this modern all-suite hotel is a nice example of early millennial chic. The striking marble and cherrywood lobby soars three stories. The suites aren't large, but the minimalist blond furnishings, efficient layout, and floor-to-ceiling windows in most rooms create a sense of space. Slightly pricier Signature Club suites have a private lounge, continental breakfast, and evening refreshments. The hotel's restaurant, Manhattan ($–$$$), is hidden away from the madding crowd. ⊠ *550 W. Hastings St., vehicle entrance on Seymour St., Downtown, V6B 1L6* ☎ *604/689–8188* 🖷 *604/605–8881* ⊕ *www. deltavancouversuites.ca* ↪ *226 suites* ♙ *Restaurant, room service, IDD phones, minibars, cable TV with movies and video games, in-room broadband, indoor pool, gym, hot tub, sauna, spa, steam room, lounge, shop, babysitting, dry cleaning, laundry service, concierge, concierge floor, business services, meeting rooms, parking (fee), some pets allowed, no-smoking floors* ▭ *AE, D, DC, MC, V.*

$$$$ 🏨 **Fairmont Hotel Vancouver.** The copper roof of this 1939 château-style hotel dominates Vancouver's skyline. Guest rooms vary in size, but even the standard rooms have an air of prestige, with high ceilings, lush draperies, and 19th-century-style mahogany furniture. A friendly dog on staff is available for petting and walks and the full-service spa here is Canada's first to cater to men, with big screen TVs, wireless Internet, and black leather pedicure chairs. Rooms on the Fairmont Gold floor have extra services, including a private lounge and its own concierge. ⊠ *900 W. Georgia St., Downtown, V6C 2W6* ☎ *604/684–3131* 🖷 *604/ 662–1929* ⊕ *www.fairmont.com* ↪ *556 rooms, 37 suites* ♙ *2 restaurants, room service, IDD phones, some minibars, cable TV with movies and video games, in-room broadband, Wi-Fi, indoor pool, wading pool, gym, hair salon, hot tub, massage, sauna, spa, lobby lounge, wine bar, shops, babysitting, dry cleaning, laundry service, concierge, concierge floor, business services, meeting rooms, parking (fee), some pets allowed (fee), no-smoking floors* ▭ *AE, D, DC, MC, V.*

$$$$ 🏨 **Fairmont Vancouver Airport.** Vancouver's most luxurious airport hotel is actually part of the international terminal building. Rooms and public areas are chic, modern, and minimalist, with pale woods, calming neutrals, extensive use of local cedar and slate, and artworks commissioned from local artists. One floor is completely hypoallergenic—where rooms have hypoallergenic pillows and comforters, water and air purifiers, and central vacuum systems that reduce dust—and all rooms have floor-to-ceiling windows—the triple-pane construction provides near-perfect soundproofing. Rooms on the north side have mountain views; some rooms have jetted tubs for two. ⊠ *Vancouver International Airport, 3311 N. Service Rd., Box 23798, Richmond V7B 1X9* ☎ *604/207–5200* 🖷 *604/248–3219* ⊕ *www.fairmont.com* ⚓ *398 rooms, 21 suites* ⚒ *Restaurant, room service, IDD phones, in-room safes, minibars, cable TV with movies and video games, in-room broadband, Wi-Fi, indoor pool, wading pool, gym, hot tub, steam room, spa, lounge, piano, babysitting, dry cleaning, laundry service, concierge, concierge floor, business services, meeting rooms, parking (fee), some pets allowed (fee), no-smoking floors* ⊟ *AE, D, DC, MC, V.*

$$$$ 🏨 **Fairmont Waterfront.** This modern 23-story hotel is across the street from the Trade and Convention Centre and the Canada Place cruise-ship terminal but it's the floor-to-ceiling windows with ocean, park, and mountain views from most of the guest rooms that really make this hotel. Adorned with blond-wood furniture, warm earth-tone or blue and apricot fabrics, and contemporary Canadian artwork, each room has a window that opens. Next to the mountain-view pool is a rooftop herb garden—an aromatic retreat open to guests. Two hotel dogs are on hand for petting, pampering, and taking for strolls. ⊠ *900 Canada Pl. Way, Downtown, V6C 3L5* ☎ *604/691–1991* 🖷 *604/691–1999* ⊕ *www.fairmont.com/waterfront* ⚓ *489 rooms, 29 suites* ⚒ *Restaurant, room service, IDD phones, some in-room safes, some kitchenettes, minibars, cable TV with movies and video games, in-room broadband, Wi-Fi, pool, gym, hot tub, massage, steam room, lounge, shops, babysitting, dry cleaning, laundry service, concierge, concierge floor, business services, meeting rooms, parking (fee), some pets allowed (fee), no-smoking floors* ⊟ *AE, D, DC, MC, V.*

$$$$ 🏨 **Four Seasons.** This 29-story downtown luxury hotel is famous for pampering guests. The lobby, which connects to the Pacific Centre shopping mall, is lavish, with a fountain in the atrium-style lounge. Standard rooms, with understated color schemes, marble bathroom fixtures, and tall windows with city views, are spacious and traditionally furnished, as are the even more spacious corner rooms with sitting areas. Service at the Four Seasons is top-notch; the many amenities include free evening limousine service. The dining room, Chartwell ($$$–$$$$), is one of the best in the city. ⊠ *791 W. Georgia St., vehicle entrance on Howe St., Downtown, V6C 2T4* ☎ *604/689–9333* 🖷 *604/684–4555* ⊕ *www.fourseasons.com* ⚓ *306 rooms, 70 suites* ⚒ *2 restaurants, room service, IDD phones, in-room safes, minibars, cable TV with movies and video games, in-room broadband, Wi-Fi, indoor-outdoor pool, gym, hot tub, massage, sauna, lounge, shops, babysitting, dry cleaning, laundry service, concierge, business services, meeting rooms, parking (fee), some pets allowed (fee), no-smoking floors* ⊟ *AE, DC, MC, V.*

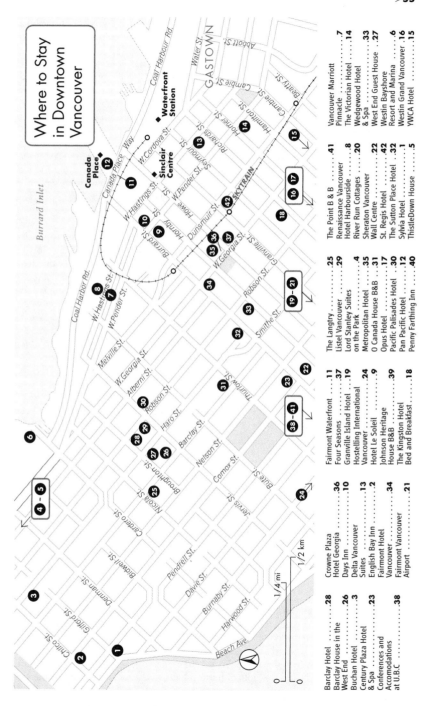

Where to Stay in Downtown Vancouver

Barclay Hotel **28**
Barclay House in the
West End **26**
Buchan Hotel **3**
Century Plaza Hotel
& Spa **23**
Conferences and
Accomodations
at U.B.C **38**

Crowne Plaza
Hotel Georgia **36**
Days Inn **10**
Delta Vancouver
Suites **13**
English Bay Inn **2**
Fairmont Hotel
Vancouver **34**
Fairmont Vancouver
Airport **21**

Fairmont Waterfront **11**
Four Seasons **37**
Granville Island Hotel ... **19**
Hostelling International
Vancouver **24**
Hotel Le Soleil **9**
Johnson Heritage
House B&B **39**
The Kingston Hotel
Bed and Breakfast **18**

The Langtry **25**
Listel Vancouver **29**
Lord Stanley Suites
on the Park **4**
Metropolitan Hotel **35**
O Canada House B&B **31**
Opus Hotel **17**
Pacific Palisades Hotel .. **30**
Pan Pacific Hotel **12**
Penny Farthing Inn **40**

The Point B & B **41**
Renaissance Vancouver
Hotel Harbourside **8**
River Run Cottages **20**
Sheraton Vancouver
Wall Centre **22**
St. Regis Hotel **42**
The Sutton Place Hotel . **32**
Sylvia Hotel **1**
ThistleDown House **5**

Vancouver Marriott
Pinnacle **7**
The Victorian Hotel **14**
Wedgewood Hotel
& Spa **33**
West End Guest House .. **27**
Westin Bayshore
Resort and Marina **6**
Westin Grand Vancouver **16**
YWCA Hotel **15**

$$$$ ⊞ **Hotel Le Soleil.** The staff at this stylish business-district boutique hotel prides itself on attentive, personal service. The golden decor and intimate fireplace in the neoclassical lobby and the vibrant gold-and-crimson fabrics in the guest rooms—most are small suites—radiate warmth. Luxurious touches, such as 300-thread-count Egyptian cotton sheets, marble bathrooms, and custom-designed Biedermeier-style furniture, abound. Two penthouse suites have 24-foot ceilings and wraparound terraces. The hotel doesn't have a pool or fitness facilities, but guests have access to the extensive facilities at the YWCA next door for a fee. ⊠ *567 Hornby St., Downtown, V6C 2E8* ☏ *604/632–3000 or 877/632–3030* ᵬ *604/632–3001* ⊕ *www.hotellesoleil.com* ☞ *10 rooms, 109 suites* ⌂ *Restaurant, room service, IDD phones, in-room safes, cable TV with movies, in-room broadband, Web TV, massage, bar, babysitting, dry cleaning, laundry service, concierge, meeting rooms, parking (fee), some pets allowed (fee), no-smoking floors* ☰ *AE, DC, MC, V.*

$$$$ ⊞ **Listel Vancouver.** Art and jazz adorn this elegant hotel on Vancouver's most vibrant shopping street. Gallery-floor guest rooms and suites display original or limited-edition works by artists such as Carmelo Sortino and Bernard Cathelin; rooms on the Museum floor are decorated with work from contemporary First Nations artists such as Susan Point and Eugene Alfred. Custom-made furniture in both Gallery and Museum rooms complements the art. You can catch live jazz nightly at O'Doul's Restaurant & Bar downstairs. ⊠ *1300 Robson St., West End, V6E 1C5* ☏ *604/684–8461 or 800/663–5491* ᵬ *604/684–7092* ⊕ *www.listel-vancouver.com* ☞ *119 rooms, 10 suites* ⌂ *Restaurant, room service, IDD phones, minibars, cable TV with movies, Wi-Fi, gym, hot tub, massage, bar, shop, babysitting, dry cleaning, laundry service, meeting rooms, travel services, parking (fee); no smoking* ☰ *AE, D, DC, MC, V.*

$$$$ ⊞ **Metropolitan Hotel.** Two lions guard the entrance, and a striking antique gold-leaf temple carving graces the lobby of this full-service business district hotel. The spacious rooms, all designed according to the principles of feng shui, are decorated in muted colors, and even the standard rooms have such luxurious extras as duvets and Italian-made Frette bathrobes. Business-class rooms come with printers, fax machines, and ergonometric chairs. Extensive fitness facilities include a putting green on a third-floor terrace. The restaurant, Diva ($$$–$$$$), is one of the city's finest. ⊠ *645 Howe St., Downtown, V6C 2Y9* ☏ *604/687–1122 or 800/667–2300* ᵬ *604/689–7044* ⊕ *www.metropolitan.com* ☞ *179 rooms, 18 suites* ⌂ *Restaurant, room service, IDD phones, in-room safes, minibars, cable TV with movies and video games, in-room broadband, Wi-Fi, indoor pool, gym, hot tub, sauna, steam room, racquetball, squash, bar, babysitting, dry cleaning, laundry service, concierge, business services, meeting rooms, parking (fee), some pets allowed (fee), no-smoking floors* ☰ *AE, D, DC, MC, V.*

★ **$$$$** ⊞ **Opus Hotel.** The design team had a good time with this boutique hotel, creating fictitious characters and designing rooms for each. Billy's room is fun and offbeat, with pop art and lime-green accents. Dede's room boasts lepoard skin, velveteen, and faux fur accents, whereas Bob and Carol's place has softer edges and golden tones. Most rooms have a full wall of windows, lots of natural light, and views of the city or the Japanese garden in the courtyard. Two rooms have private access to the garden; seventh-floor rooms have balconies. Other perks include dog-walking, personal shopping, and free car service anywhere downtown. ⊠ *322 Davie St., Yaletown, V6B 5Z6* ☎ *604/642–6787 or 866/642–6787* 🖷 *604/642–6780* ⊕ *www.opushotel.com* ➼ *85 rooms, 11 suites* ⟋ *Restaurant, coffee shop, room service, IDD phones, in-room safes, minibars, cable TV with movies and video games, some in-room DVD/VCRs, in-room broadband, Wi-Fi, gym, bar, lounge, babysitting, dry cleaning, laundry service, concierge, business services, meeting rooms, parking (fee), some pets allowed, no-smoking floors* ⊟ *AE, DC, MC, V.*

★ **$$$$** 🖬 **Pan Pacific Hotel.** A centerpiece of the waterfront Canada Place, the luxurious Pan Pacific shares a complex with the Vancouver Convention and Exhibition Centre and Vancouver's main cruise-ship terminal. The rooms are large and modern, with maplewood throughout, marble vanities, Italian linens, and stunning ocean, mountain, or skyline views. The high-end suites, some with a private steam room, sauna, or baby-grand piano, are popular with visiting celebrities. In 2005 the 26-room, Roman-bath–theme Spa Utopia and Salon and a new state-of-the-art health and fitness center opened. ⊠ *999 Canada Pl., Downtown, V6C 3B5* ☎ *604/662–8111, 800/663–1515 in Canada, 800/937–1515 in U.S.* 🖷 *604/685–8690* ⊕ *www.panpacific.com* ➼ *465 rooms, 39 suites* ⟋ *2 restaurants, coffee shop, room service, some in-room faxes, in-room safes, some kitchens, minibars, cable TV with movies and video games, in-room broadband, in-room data ports, Wi-Fi, pool, health club, hair salon, outdoor hot tub, massage, sauna, spa, steam room, lounge, shops, babysitting, dry cleaning, laundry service, concierge, business services, car rental, parking (fee), some pets allowed (fee), no-smoking floors* ⊟ *AE, DC, MC, V.*

$$$$ 🖬 **Sheraton Vancouver Wall Centre.** These two ultramodern glass highrises and their landscaped grounds take up an entire city block. Rooms in both the north tower—Vancouver's tallest building—and the south have floor-to-ceiling windows with views of water, mountains, and city. The best views are above the 14th floor or in one of the corner rooms with two walls of glass. Rooms are chic and spacious with a blond-wood, blue, or burgundy Ralph Lauren color scheme; exceptionally comfortable beds; and original, often local, artwork. The upbeat, modern public areas are decorated with bright colors and an eclectic collection of art (including the world's largest collection of African pygmy art). ⊠ *1088 Burrard St., Downtown V6Z 2R9* ☎ *604/331–1000 or 800/663–9255* 🖷 *604/893–7200* ⊕ *www.sheratonwallcentre.com* ➼ *673 rooms, 60 suites* ⟋ *2 restaurants, coffee shop, room service, some in-room faxes, in-room safes, minibars, refrigerators, cable TV with movies and video games, in-room broadband, Web TV, Wi-Fi, indoor pool, health club, hair salon, hot tubs, sauna, spa, steam room, 2 bars, shops, babysitting, dry cleaning, laundry service, concierge, concierge floor, convention center, parking (fee), some pets allowed (fee), no-smoking floors* ⊟ *AE, DC, MC, V.*

$$$$ 🖬 **The Sutton Place Hotel.** The feel here is more of an exclusive European ★ guesthouse than a large modern hotel. Guest rooms are furnished in a traditional European style with soft neutrals and lush fabrics, and the service is gracious and attentive. A full spa (also open to nonguests) offers a wide menu. La Grande Résidence (part of Sutton Place), an apartment hotel suitable for stays of at least a week, is next door, at 855 Burrard. The hotel's Fleuri restaurant (⇨ Dining, Downtown Vancouver) serves continental cuisine. ⊠ *845 Burrard St., Downtown, V6Z 2K6* ☎ *604/682–5511 or 800/961–7555* 🖶 *604/682–5513* ⊕ *www. suttonplace.com* ➷ *350 rooms, 46 suites, 164 apartments* ⚴ *Restaurant, coffee shop, room service, IDD phones, in-room safes, minibars, cable TV with movies and video games, in-room DVDs, in-room broadband, Web TV, indoor pool, gym, hot tub, spa, steam room, lounge, piano bar, shop, babysitting, dry cleaning, laundry service, concierge, business services, meeting rooms, parking (fee), some pets allowed (fee), no-smoking floors* ⊟ *AE, D, DC, MC, V.*

$$$$
Fodor'sChoice
★

🏨 **Wedgewood Hotel & Spa.** The small, lavish Wedgewood is run by an owner who cares fervently about her guests. The lobby and guest rooms are decorated in a traditional European style with original artwork and antiques selected by the proprietor on her European travels. Guest rooms are capacious, and each has a balcony. The four penthouse suites have fireplaces. All the extra touches are here, too: afternoon ice delivery, dark-out drapes, CD players, robes, and a morning newspaper. The turndown service includes homemade cookies and bottled water. The sensuous Bacchus restaurant and lounge ($$$–$$$$) is in the lobby. The luxurious on-site spa is very popular—book ahead for an appointment. ⊠ *845 Hornby St., Downtown, V6Z 1V1* ☎ *604/689–7777 or 800/ 663–0666* 🖶 *604/608–5348* ⊕ *www.wedgewoodhotel.com* ➷ *41 rooms, 43 suites* ⚴ *Restaurant, room service, IDD phones, in-room safes, minibars, cable TV with movies and video games, in-room broadband, Wi-Fi, gym, spa, steam room, lounge, babysitting, dry cleaning, laundry facilities, laundry service, business services, meeting rooms, parking (fee), no-smoking floors* ⊟ *AE, D, DC, MC, V.*

★ $$$$

🏨 **Westin Bayshore Resort and Marina.** Perched on Coal Harbour beside Stanley Park, the Bayshore has sweeping harbor and mountain views. Most rooms take full advantage of this, with floor-to-ceiling windows that open to a railing or a step-out balcony. Interiors are cheery and comfortable, with rich modern blue-and-gold fabrics, plush armchairs, and exceptionally comfortable beds. The only downtown resort hotel, the Bayshore is also rich with recreational facilities, including fishing charters, sightseeing cruises and poolside yoga. Vancouver's Seawall Walk connects the resort to Stanley Park and the Vancouver Convention and Exhibition Centre. ⊠ *1601 Bayshore Dr., off Cardero St., West End, V6G 2V4* ☎ *604/682–3377* 🖶 *604/687–3102* ⊕ *www.westinbayshore. com* ➷ *482 rooms, 28 suites* ⚴ *2 restaurants, coffee shop, room service, IDD phones, some in-room faxes, some in-room safes, minibars, cable TV with movies and video games, in-room broadband, Wi-Fi, 2 pools (1 indoor), fitness classes, health club, hair salon, hot tub, massage, sauna, steam room, boating, marina, fishing, bar, lounge, shops, babysitting, dry cleaning, laundry service, concierge, business services, convention center, car rental, parking (fee), some pets allowed, no-smoking floors* ⊟ *AE, D, DC, MC, V.*

$$$$

🏨 **Westin Grand Vancouver.** With its striking modern decor and all-suites layout, the Westin Grand, shaped like a grand piano, is one of Vancouver's more stylish hotels. Most of the compact studios and one-bedroom suites have floor-to-ceiling windows with skyline views. Corner suites are larger and half have small balconies. Deluxe suites have marble baths; all units have a deep soaker tub and kitchenettes. The hotel is close to the main sports-and-entertainment district and to the fashionable restaurants of Yaletown. ⊠ *433 Robson St., Downtown, V6B 6L9* ☎ *604/602–1999 or 888/680–9393* 🖷 *604/647–2502* ⊕ *www.westingrandvancouver. com* ↘ *23 rooms, 184 suites* ⚘ *Restaurant, room service, IDD phones, in-room safes, kitchenettes, minibars, microwaves, cable TV with movies and video games, some in-room VCRs, in-room broadband, Wi-Fi, pool, gym, outdoor hot tub, sauna, spa, steam room, bar, nightclub, piano, shop, babysitting, dry cleaning, laundry service, concierge, business services, meeting rooms, travel services, parking (fee), some pets allowed (fee), no-smoking floors* ▤ *AE, D, DC, MC, V.*

$$$–$$$$ 🖭 **Century Plaza Hotel & Spa.** Full kitchens and an indoor pool make this 30-story downtown high-rise a good family choice. The taupe-and-green decor is on the bland side, but all the amenities are here, including a highly rated full-service spa. The pricier one-bedroom suites are enlivened with French doors and spalike bathrooms. Corner suites have balconies, and north-facing rooms above the seventh floor have mountain and ocean views. ⊠ *1015 Burrard St., Downtown V6Z 1Y5* ☎ *604/687–0575 or 800/663–1818* 🖷 *604/687–0578* ⊕ *www.century-plaza. com* ↘ *135 rooms, 135 suites* ⚘ *Restaurant, café, IDD phones, some kitchens, microwaves, refrigerators, cable TV with movies and video games, some in-room DVDs, in-room broadband, Wi-Fi, indoor pool, hair salon, spa, steam rooms, lounge, comedy club, shops, babysitting, dry cleaning, laundry facilities, laundry service, concierge, Internet room, meeting rooms, parking (fee), some pets allowed, no smoking floors* ▤ *AE, DC, MC, V.*

$$$–$$$$ 🖭 **Crowne Plaza Hotel Georgia.** Mahogany paneling, brass chandeliers, terrazzo floors, and other faithful restorations recall the days when the Georgia, a registered historic property, was Vancouver's hotel of choice for visiting celebrities. Frank Sinatra and Elvis Presley, among others, have enjoyed the comforts of this 1927 beaux arts building across from the Vancouver Art Gallery. Art deco guest rooms evoke the 1920s, but modern amenities, such as high-speed Internet access, down duvets, and CD players, are here, too. A traditional afternoon tea is served daily in the lounge. ⊠ *801 W. Georgia St., Downtown V6C 1P7* ☎ *604/682–5566 or 800/663–1111* 🖷 *604/642–5579* ⊕ *www.hotelgeorgia.bc.ca* ↘ *311 rooms, 2 suites* ⚘ *Restaurant, room service, IDD phones, cable TV with movies and video games, in-room broadband, Wi-Fi, gym, lounge, shop, babysitting, dry cleaning, laundry service, concierge, concierge floor, business services, meeting rooms, parking (fee), some pets allowed, no-smoking floors* ▤ *AE, D, DC, MC, V.*

$$$–$$$$ 🖭 **Lord Stanley Suites on the Park.** These small, attractive, fully equipped suites are right at the edge of Stanley Park. Each has in-suite laundry, an office nook, a sitting room, and one or two bedrooms. Suites overlooking busy Georgia Street have an enclosed sunroom; those backing onto quieter Alberni Street have balconies. You're also close to many restaurants on Denman Street, a block away. ⊠ *1889 Alberni St., West*

End ☎ *604/688–9299 or 888/767–7829* 🖨 *604/688–9297* ⊕ *www. lordstanley.com* 🛏 *95 suites* ᗢ *IDD phones, kitchens, cable TV, in-room VCRs, in-room broadband, gym, sauna, babysitting, dry cleaning, laundry service, concierge, meeting rooms, parking (fee), no-smoking floors* 🖃 *AE, DC, MC, V* ⫟⚪ *CP.*

$$$–$$$$ 🏨 **Pacific Palisades Hotel.** Bright citrus colors, abstract art, and geometric patterns create a high-energy South Beach look at this chic Robson Street hotel. The cheerful decor extends to the spacious guest rooms and suites, where big balconies and wall-to-wall windows keep things light and airy and, on the higher floors, bring in sweeping water and mountain views. Fun is the idea here, from the playful decor to the minibars stocked with toys, the in-room yoga kits, and the free evening wine receptions. Pet-sitting, Frisbees, dog cookies, and a pet-services directory are all offered. ☒ *1277 Robson St., entrance at Jervis St., West End, V6E 1C4* ☎ *604/688–0461 or 800/663–1815* 🖨 *604/688–4374* ⊕ *www. pacificpalisadeshotel.com* 🛏 *76 rooms, 157 suites* ᗢ *Restaurant, room service, IDD phones, some in-room faxes, some kitchens, some kitchenettes, minibars, microwaves, cable TV with movies and video games, in-room broadband, Wi-Fi, indoor pool, gym, hot tub, spa, steam room, lounge, shops, babysitting, dry cleaning, laundry facilities, laundry service, concierge, business services, meeting rooms, parking (fee), some pets allowed, no-smoking floors* 🖃 *AE, D, DC, MC, V.*

$$$–$$$$ 🏨 **O Canada House B&B** This beautifully restored 1897 Victorian, within walking distance of downtown, is where the first version of "O Canada," the national anthem, was written, in 1909. Each bedroom is appointed in late-Victorian antiques; modern comforts such as bathrobes help make things homey. The top-floor room is enormous, with two king beds and a private sitting area. A separate one-room coach house in the garden is a romantic option. Breakfast, served in the dining room, is a lavish affair. ☒ *1114 Barclay St., West End, V6E 1H1* ☎ *604/688–0555 or 877/688–1114* 🖨 *604/488–0556* ⊕ *www.ocanadahouse.com* 🛏 *7 rooms* ᗢ *IDD phones, fans, refrigerators, cable TV, in-room VCRs, Wi-Fi, free parking; no a/c, no kids under 12, no smoking* 🖃 *MC, V* ⫟⚪ *BP.*

$$$–$$$$ 🏨 **Vancouver Marriott Pinnacle.** The soaring 50-foot-high atrium lobby makes a striking entrance to this 38-story hotel a few blocks from the cruise-ship terminal and central business district. Decorated in modern pale woods and neutral tones, each room has almost a full wall of windows offering expansive views of Burrard Inlet and the North Shore Mountains or the city skyline. The hotel's Show Case restaurant and bar serves West Coast cuisine with global influences. ☒ *1128 W. Hastings St., Downtown V6E 4R5* ☎ *604/684–1128 or 800/207–4150* 🖨 *604/298–1128* ⊕ *www.vancouvermarriottpinnacle.com* 🛏 *424 rooms, 10 suites* ᗢ *Restaurant, room service, IDD phones, in-room safes, minibars, cable TV with movies and video games, in-room broadband, Wi-Fi, indoor pool, gym, hot tub, massage, sauna, steam room, lounge, shop, babysitting, dry cleaning, laundry service, concierge, concierge floor, Internet room, business services, meeting rooms, parking (fee), some pets allowed (fee), no-smoking floors* 🖃 *AE, D, DC, MC, V.*

$$–$$$$ 🏨 **The Langtry.** Inside this 1930 former apartment building near Robson Street and Stanley Park are six apartment-size suites furnished in a mix of modern and art deco styles with cathedral ceilings, inlaid-oak floors, and French doors. Each has a full kitchen, a dining area, and a feather bed. ✉ *968 Nicola St., West End, V6G 2C8* ☎ *604/687–7892* ⊕ *www.thelangtry.com* ⇱ *6 suites* ⚐ *IDD phones, fans, kitchens, microwaves, cable TV, in-room VCRs, Wi-Fi, laundry facilities, free parking, some pets allowed; no a/c, no smoking* ▭ *AE, MC, V.*

$$–$$$$ 🏨 **Renaissance Vancouver Hotel Harbourside.** An indoor pool and play area, direct access to a waterside park, big rooms, and a "kids under 12 eat free" policy in the casual restaurant make this oceanside high-rise a good choice for families. It's also handy to the cruise-ship terminal and central business district. Rooms are all 350 square feet and have either step-out or full-size glassed-in balconies; many have sweeping water and mountain views. The modern mustard and burgundy decor includes an ergonometric desk chair, an armchair, and heated bathroom floors. ✉ *1133 W. Hastings St., Downtown V6E 2T3* ☎ *604/689–9211 or 800/905–8582* 🖷 *604/689–4358* ⊕ *www.renaissancevancouver.com* ⇱ *437 rooms, 12 suites* ⚐ *2 restaurants, coffee shop, IDD phones, some in-room safes, minibars, cable TV with movies and video games, in-room broadband, Web TV, Wi-Fi, indoor pool, gym, hot tub, massage, lounge, sports bar, piano, shop, babysitting, dry cleaning, laundry service, concierge, concierge floor, business services, meeting rooms, car rental, parking (fee), some pets allowed, no-smoking floors* ▭ *AE, D, DC, MC, V.*

★ **$$–$$$$** 🏨 **ThistleDown House.** This 1920 Arts and Crafts house with its private, sunny garden, is handy to North Shore hiking and skiing, but just 15 to 30 minutes from downtown. Furnished with a low-key, eclectic arrangement of antiques, art deco touches, local art, and treasures gathered from the hosts' travels, each room has its own charm: under the Apple Tree, with its private patio, gas fireplace and air-jet tub, is a romantic choice; Mulberry Peek, an octagonal tower room, has four walls of windows and a private balcony; Pages, the former library, has a cast-iron pedestal tub and book-lined walls. ✉ *3910 Capilano Rd., North Vancouver, V7R 4J2* ☎ *604/986–7173 or 888/633–7173* 🖷 *604/980–2939* ⊕ *www.thistle-down.com* ⇱ *6 rooms* ⚐ *Cable TV, laundry service, Internet room, free parking; no a/c, no room phones, no kids under 12, no smoking* ▭ *MC, V* ☉ *Closed Dec. and Jan.* ❍l *BP.*

$$$ 🏨 **English Bay Inn.** European antiques, stained-glass windows, and touches of Asian art furnish this 1930s Tudor-style house near Stanley Park. The inn has a Chippendale dining table in the breakfast room, sleigh beds in three of the guest rooms, and a tiny Italianate garden out back. One suite winds up two levels and has its own fireplace. A lower-level suite has a private entrance, an antique four-poster bed, and its own kitchen and dining area. Port and sherry are served by the living-room fire each evening, and homemade scones are prepared daily for the four-course breakfasts. ✉ *1968 Comox St., West End, V6G 1R4* ☎ *604/683–8002 or 866/683–8002* 🖷 *604/683–8089* ⊕ *www.englishbayinn.com* ⇱ *4 rooms, 2 suites* ⚐ *IDD phones, some fans, cable TV, some in-room VCRs, dry cleaning, laundry service, free parking; no a/c, no smoking* ▭ *AE, DC, MC, V* ❍l *BP.*

$$$ 🏨 **Granville Island Hotel.** Granville Island is one of Vancouver's more entertaining neighborhoods, but unless you've moored up in a houseboat, the only overnight option is the Granville Island Hotel. The exterior of this offbeat water's-edge building is part Mission style, part industrial tin plate. Inside, marble floors and Persian rugs grace many of the guest rooms. Most rooms have water views through full-length windows, and those on the top floor (the third) have small balconies. The corridor in the east wing overlooks vats brewing away for the fashionable brew-pub and restaurant downstairs. ⊠ *1253 Johnston St., Granville Island, V6H 3R9* ☎ *604/683–7373 or 800/663–1840* 🖷 *604/683–3061* ⊕ *www. granvilleislandhotel.com* ⊅ *74 rooms, 8 suites* ⚫ *Restaurant, room service, IDD phones, minibars, some microwaves, cable TV with movies, in-room broadband, exercise equipment, hot tub, massage, sauna, mountain bikes (summer only), pub, babysitting, dry cleaning, laundry service, business services, meeting rooms, parking (fee), some pets allowed (fee), no-smoking floors* ▭ *AE, D, DC, MC, V.*

$$–$$$ 🏨 **Barclay House in the West End.** Stained glass, antiques, and art nouveau fixtures decorate this comfortable 1904 heritage house on a tree-lined residential street a few blocks from downtown or Stanley Park. Two pianos, a fireplace, leather wing chairs, and an extensive video library make this a cozy rainy-day hangout. Two units have private sitting rooms; several have claw-foot tubs and a brass, mahogany, or canopy queen bed. The West Room has its own little Juliette balcony. Peace is assured, as there are no adjoining walls between guest rooms. ⊠ *1351 Barclay St., West End, V6E 1H6* ☎ *604/605–1351 or 800/971–1351* 🖷 *604/605–1382* ⊕ *www.barclayhouse.com* ⊅ *4 rooms, 2 suites* ⚫ *IDD phones, refrigerators, cable TV, in-room VCRs, in-room broadband, free parking; no kids under 10, no smoking* ▭ *AE, MC, V* ⦿*BP.*

$$–$$$ 🏨 **Days Inn.** Convenient to Vancouver's convention center, the main cruise-ship terminal, and the U.S. consulate, this is one of the few moderately priced hotels in the business district. Rooms in the six-story, 1920 building are small but freshly decorated with duvets and cheerful colors. The two-bedroom, one-bathroom units are good value for groups and families. The hotel runs a free shuttle to the train and bus station and to both cruise-ship terminals. ⊠ *921 W. Pender St., Downtown, V6C 1M2* ☎ *604/681–4335 or 877/681–4335* 🖷 *604/681–7808* ⊕ *www. daysinnvancouver.com* ⊅ *80 rooms, 5 suites* ⚫ *Restaurant, in-room safes, some microwaves, some refrigerators, cable TV with movies, in-room data ports, Wi-Fi, lounge, pub, babysitting, dry cleaning, laundry facilities, laundry service, parking (fee), no-smoking* ▭ *AE, D, DC, MC, V.*

$$–$$$ 🏨 **Johnson Heritage House B&B.** This 1920 Craftsman-style house, on a quiet, tree-lined avenue 15 minutes from downtown, is filled with collectibles—gramophones, carousel horses, and antique Chinese statues—illustrating the hosts' antiques-dealing past. The enormous Carousel Suite also has a gas fireplace, mountain views, a jetted tub, and dozens of mermaid figurines from around the world. The Sunshine Room has a brass canopy bed and a small private deck; the Mountain Room has a claw-foot tub in a private bath across the hall. On the lower level, a two-bedroom, two-bathroom suite with a full kitchen, washer and dryer, and private entrance is ideal for families. ⊠ *2278 W. 34th Ave., Kerrisdale, V6M 1G6* ☎ *604/266–4175* 🖷 *604/266–4175* ⊕ *www.johnsons-inn-vancouver.com* ⊅ *3 rooms, 1 suite* ⚫ *IDD phones, some refrigerators, cable TV, some in-room VCRs, Internet room; no a/c, no smoking*

≡ *No credit cards* ⊘ *Rooms closed Nov.–Apr., suite may be available year-round* ⏏⬤⎮ *BP.*

$$–$$$ ⬚ **River Run Cottages.** This romantic riverside B&B is part of a historic floating-home community, 30-minutes south of downtown. Choose from a little floating house with a loft bed and an antique claw-foot tub; a two-level suite (once a net loft) with a Japanese soaking tub on the deck; or two river's-edge units, each with a woodstove and a waterside deck. Breakfasts are delivered to your room; in-room dinners are available with advance notice. Romance packages include champagne and a sprinkling of rose petals. ✉ *4551 River Rd. W, Ladner, V4K 1R9* ☎ *604/946–7778* 🖷 *604/940–1970* ⊕ *www.riverruncottages.com* ⬩⭤ *2 rooms, 2 suites* ⚘ *IDD phones, microwaves, refrigerators, boating, bicycles, free parking, some pets allowed (fee); no a/c, no room TVs, no smoking* ≡ *MC, V* ⏏⬤⎮ *BP.*

$$–$$$ ⬚ **West End Guest House.** This Victorian B&B, built in 1906, is a true "painted lady," from its gracious front parlor, cozy fireplace, and early 1900s furniture to its bright pink exterior. Most of the handsome rooms are furnished with antiques; two larger rooms have gas fireplaces and two have brass beds. The inn is in a residential neighborhood, a two-minute walk from Robson Street. The owners also have two suites in a modern building next door, and a cabin, a suite, and a room at **Inn Penzance** ($$$) a B&B set among award-winning gardens on the North Shore. ✉ *1362 Haro St., West End, V6E 1G2* ☎ *604/681–2889 or 888/546–3327* 🖷 *604/688–8812* ⊕ *www.westendguesthouse.com* ⬩⭤ *8 rooms* ⚘ *Fans, cable TV, some in-room VCRs, Wi-Fi, bicycles, Internet room, free parking; no a/c, no smoking* ≡ *AE, D, DC, MC, V* ⏏⬤⎮ *BP.*

$$ ⬚ **Penny Farthing Inn.** This bright turquoise 1910 Craftsman-style home, on a tree-lined street in trendy Kitsilano, a few minutes south of downtown, has loads of period charm, with stained-glass windows, hardwood floors, an antique piano and period furniture. Lace curtains and big brass beds or oak four-posters furnish the brightly painted rooms. Two have garden-view balconies and all have private baths, though one is across the hall. Abigail's Attic is a self-contained suite at the top of the house with mountains and skyline views. Shops, restaurants, and beaches are all nearby. ✉ *2855 W. 6th Ave., Kitsilano, V6K 1X2* ☎ *604/739–9002* 🖷 *604/739–9004* ⊕ *www.pennyfarthinginn.com* ⬩⭤ *3 rooms, 1 suite* ⚘ *Some refrigerators, Internet room; no TV in some rooms, no kids under 12, no smoking* ≡ *No credit cards* ⏏⬤⎮ *BP.*

$$ ⬚ **St. Regis Hotel.** This 1916 budget-boutique hotel offers good-value rooms in the downtown core. There's no view, but the clean, well-maintained rooms have fresh green-and-gold carpets and fabrics, modern furniture, and duvets on new king or queen beds. Some rooms can sleep six, and rates include fitness passes to the health club across the street. ✉ *602 Dunsmuir St., Downtown, V6B 1Y6* ☎ *604/681–1135 or 800/770–7929* 🖷 *604/683–1126* ⊕ *www.stregishotel.com* ⬩⭤ *72 rooms, 3 suites* ⚘ *Restaurant, coffee shop, room service, some refrigerators, cable TV, in-room data ports, Wi-Fi, pub, dry cleaning, laundry service, business services, no-smoking floors* ≡ *AE, DC, MC, V* ⏏⬤⎮ *CP.*

$–$$ ⬚ **Barclay Hotel.** A great location steps from the shops of Robson Street and low rates make this three-story former apartment building one of the city's best-value pension-style hotels. The guest rooms are clean if basic, but the 1930s building, with its wide corridors, skylights, and mahogany staircase, has a certain old-world charm. Most of the front rooms overlooking Robson Street have mountain views, but the back rooms are quieter. ⊠ *1348 Robson St., West End, V6E 1C5* ☎ *604/688–8850* 🖷 *604/688–2534* ⊕ *www.barclayhotel.com* ⊷ *76 rooms, 10 suites* ♿ *Some refrigerators, cable TV, bar, dry cleaning, laundry service, parking (fee), no-smoking floors* ☰ *AE, D, DC, MC, V.*

$–$$
Fodor'sChoice
★

🏨 **The Victorian Hotel.** Budget hotels can be beautiful, too, as proven by the gleaming hardwood floors, high ceilings, and chandeliers at this prettily restored 1898 European-style pension. Offering some of Vancouver's best value accommodations, guest rooms in the two connecting three-story buildings have down duvets, oriental rugs, lush draperies, and period furniture; some have bay windows or mountain views. Some of the private bathrooms are outfitted with marble tiles and granite countertops (though some have a shower and no tub). Even the shared baths are spotlessly clean and nicely appointed. At this writing, Wi-Fi was planned. ⊠ *514 Homer St., Downtown, V6B 2V6* ☎ *877/681–6369 or 604/681–6369* 🖷 *604/681–8776* ⊕ *www.victorian-hotel.com* ⊷ *39 rooms, 18 with bath* ♿ *IDD phones, fans, some refrigerators, some microwaves, cable TV, laundry service, parking (fee); no a/c, no smoking.* ☰ *MC, V* ⊙| *CP.*

¢–$$

🏨 **Buchan Hotel.** On a tree-lined residential street a block from Stanley Park, this 1926 pension-style hotel vies with the Sylvia Hotel as one of Vancouver's best values. Popular with cyclists thanks to its bike storage and low-traffic location, the Buchan also provides free coffee and tea, a lounge with a fireplace, and ski storage but no elevator. Rooms are simple but comfortable, with checked or floral fabrics and old-fashioned radiators. Rooms without baths have handbasins. ⊠ *1906 Haro St., West End, V6G 1H7* ☎ *604/685–5354 or 800/668–6654* 🖷 *604/685–5367* ⊕ *www.buchanhotel.com* ⊷ *60 rooms, 34 with bath* ♿ *Restaurant, fans, cable TV, bar, laundry facilities, parking (fee); no a/c, no room phones, no smoking* ☰ *AE, DC, MC, V.*

¢–$$

🏨 **Conferences and Accommodation at UBC.** Between May and August, the University of British Columbia opens its student housing to visitors. Budget travelers looking for clean and secure, if basic, accommodation can choose from single or twin dorm rooms with shared bathrooms at the Pacific Spirit Hostel, or single rooms with shared baths, shared kitchens (without dishes and pots), and some fabulous views in Gage Towers. Several freshly decorated studio and one-bedroom suites with private baths, balconies, and kitchenettes are also available on campus, some year-round. The campus, on a scenic point about 20 minutes from downtown, also has an indoor pool and student-priced eateries open to the public. ⊠ *5959 Student Union Blvd., University of British Columbia Campus, V6T 1K2* ☎ *604/822–1000* 🖷 *604/822–1001* ⊕ *www.ubcconferences.com* ⊷ *300 beds in Pacific Spirit Hostel, 946 single rooms in Gage Towers, 47 West Coast Suites* ♿ *Some kitchens, some kitchenettes, some in-room broadband, Wi-Fi, 2 tennis courts (at Pacific Spirit Hostel), basketball (at hostel), laundry facilities, parking (fee); no a/c, no phones in some rooms, no TV in some rooms, no smoking.* ☰ *AE, MC, V* ⊙ *Hostel and Gage, closed Sept.–Apr.; suites open year-round.*

¢–$$ 🖭 **The Kingston Hotel Bed & Breakfast.** Convenient to shopping, the Kingston is an old-style four-story elevator building, the type of establishment you'd find in Europe. Small and immaculate, the spartan rooms are decorated in a contemporary style, with flower-pattern bedspreads and pastel colors. Some rooms have private bathrooms; others have a sink in the room and share a bath down the hall. ⊠ *757 Richards St., Downtown, V6B 3A6* 🖀 *604/684–9024 or 888/713–3304* 🖶 *604/ 684–9917* ⊕ *www.kingstonhotelvancouver.com* ⤴ *52 rooms, 13 with bath* ♿ *Restaurant, IDD phones, some fans, cable TV, in-room data ports, sauna, pub, laundry facilities; no a/c, no TV in some rooms, no smoking* ⊟ *AE, MC, V* ⦾I *CP.*

★ **¢–$$** 🖭 **Sylvia Hotel.** To stay at the Sylvia in June through August, you must book six months to a year ahead. This Virginia-creeper-covered 1912 building is popular because of its low rates and near-perfect location: about 25 feet from the beach on scenic English Bay, 200 feet from Stanley Park, and a 20-minute walk from Robson Street. The rooms and apartment-style suites vary from tiny to spacious. Many of the basic but comfortable rooms are large enough to sleep four and all have windows that open. ⊠ *1154 Gilford St., West End, V6G 2P6* 🖀 *604/681–9321* 🖶 *604/ 682–3551* ⊕ *www.sylviahotel.com* ⤴ *97 rooms, 22 suites* ♿ *Restaurant, room service, in-room data ports, some kitchens, cable TV, Wi-Fi, lounge, dry cleaning, laundry service, Internet room, parking (fee), some pets allowed, no-smoking floors; no a/c* ⊟ *AE, DC, MC, V.*

¢–$$ 🖭 **YWCA Hotel.** A secure, modern high-rise in the heart of the entertainment district, the YWCA has bright, comfortable rooms—some big enough to sleep five. Some share a bath down the hall, some share a bath between two rooms, and others have private baths. TV lounges and shared kitchens are available for all guests, and rates include use of the YWCA adults-only pool and fitness facility, a 15-minute walk away at 535 Hornby Street. ⊠ *733 Beatty St., Downtown, V6B 2M4* 🖀 *604/895–5830 or 800/663–1424* 🖶 *604/681–2550* ⊕ *www.ywcahotel.com* ⤴ *155 rooms, 40 with bath* ♿ *Café, refrigerators, cable TV, in-room data ports, Wi-Fi, laundry facilities, Internet room, meeting rooms, parking (fee), no-smoking floors; no TV in some rooms* ⊟ *AE, MC, V.*

★ **$** 🖭 **The Point Bed and Breakfast.** Handy to Kitsilano beach, Granville Island, and Vanier Park, and a five-minute ferry hop from downtown Vancouver, this 1913 gabled home on a quiet tree-lined street makes a great hideaway. The freshly renovated rooms are bright, airy, serene—and much prettier than most in this price range—with pale walls, wicker armchairs, Ansel Adams prints, and duvet-topped queen beds made with 400-thread-count sheets and piled high with pillows; mosaic-tile bathrooms have showers but no tubs. Breakfast is delivered to your room. ⊠ *1855 Creelman Ave., Kitsilano, V6J 1B7* 🖀 *604/274–9693* ⊕ *www. thepointbandb.com* ⤴ *4 rooms* ♿ *Refrigerators, cable TV, in-room DVD, Wi-Fi, laundry facilities, some pets allowed (fee); no a/c, no kids under 14, no smoking* ⊟ *AE, MC, V* ⦾I *CP.*

¢–$ 🖭 **Hostelling International Vancouver.** Vancouver has three Hostelling International locations: a former hotel in the downtown core, a big hostel set in parkland at Jericho Beach in Kitsilano, and a smaller building near English Bay. Each has private rooms for two to four people; bunks in men's, women's, and coed dorms (with bedding and lockers); a shared kitchen, a TV lounge, and a range of free or low-cost tours and activities. The Central hostel has rooms with private baths and TVs; the West End hostel is accessible to people who use wheelchairs. ⊠ *HI Vancouver Central, 1025 Granville St., Downtown, V6Z 1L4* ☎ *604/685–5335 or 888/203–8333* 🖷 *604/685–5351* ⊕ *www.hihostels.ca* ⇌ *36 rooms, 26 with bath; 41 4-bed dorm rooms* ♿ *In-room broadband, pub, laundry facilities, Internet room; no a/c in some rooms, no room phones, no room TVs, no smoking* ☰ *MC, V* ⑩ *CP* ⊠ *HI Vancouver Downtown, 1114 Burnaby St., West End, V6E 1P1* ☎ *604/684–4565 or 888/203–4302* 🖷 *604/684–4540* ⊕ *www.hihostels.ca* ⇌ *23 rooms, 44 4-bed dorm rooms* ♿ *Wi-Fi, mountain bikes, billiards, library, recreation room, laundry facilities, meeting room, travel services, Internet room, free parking; no a/c, no room phones, no room TVs, no smoking* ☰ *MC, V* ⑩ *CP* ⊠ *HI Vancouver Jericho Beach, 1515 Discovery St., Kitsilano, V6R 4K5* ☎ *604/224–3208 or 888/203–4303* 🖷 *604/224–4852* ⊕ *www.hihostels.ca* ⇌ *10 rooms, 9 14-bed dorm rooms* ♿ *Café, mountain bikes, recreation room, video game room, laundry facilities, Internet room, parking (fee); no a/c, no room phones, no room TVs, no smoking* ☰ *MC, V* ⊘ *Closed Oct.–Apr.*

NIGHTLIFE & THE ARTS

For **events information,** pick up a copy of the free *Georgia Straight* (available at cafés and bookstores and street boxes around town) or look in the entertainment section of the *Vancouver Sun* (Thursday's paper has listings in the "Queue" section). Tickets for many venues can be booked through **Ticketmaster** (☎ 604/280–4444 ⊕ www.ticketmaster.ca).

Tickets Tonight (⊠ 200 Burrard St., Downtown ☎ 604/684–2787 ⊕ www.ticketstonight.ca), at the Vancouver Tourist Info Centre, sells half-price day-of-the-event tickets and full-price advance tickets to theater, concerts, festivals, and other performing-arts events in Vancouver.

Nightlife

Vancouver's bars, pubs, and lounges are usually open seven nights a week until 1 AM. Dance clubs get lively at about 10 PM and stay open until 3 AM on weekends many close on Sunday and Monday. Most dance clubs levy a cover charge of C$5 to C$10. Smart-casual dress will do for most Vancouver nightspots. No jeans or running shoes is the standard dress code in dance clubs, though patrons like to dress up for some of the smarter places. The legal drinking age in British Columbia is 19, and you'll need two pieces of ID to prove it. Some upscale clubs ask that patrons be at least 23. A bylaw bans smoking indoors in all public places in Vancouver, including pubs, bars, and dance clubs. The pubs listed here are good places for casual meals. Many have both an adults-only pub and a separate restaurant section where kids are welcome.

Bars, Pubs & Lounges

Yaletown locals and visiting celebrities lounge on sofas and sip martinis at the sensually lighted **Afterglow** (⊠ 1082 Hamilton St., Yaletown

☎ 604/602–0835), a lounge tucked behind Glowbal restaurant. The **Bacchus Lounge** (✉ 845 Hornby St., Downtown ☎ 604/608–5319), in the Wedgewood Hotel, is a relaxing place with plush couches, a fireplace, and a pianist. **Bridges** (✉ 1696 Duranleau St., Granville Island ☎ 604/687–4400), near the Public Market, has the city's biggest marina-side deck and a cozy nautical-theme pub.

Jazz, disco, soul, funk, R&B, and 44 kinds of bubbly appeal to an over-25 crowd at **Crush Champagne Lounge** (✉ 1180 Granville St., Downtown ☎ 604/684–0355) A martini-drinking crowd fills the multiroom, '60s-theme **ginger sixty-two** (✉ 1219 Granville St., Downtown ☎ 604/688–5494); weekend performance artists and elaborate cocktails and snacks add to the fun. For a pint of properly poured Guinness and live Irish music, try the **Irish Heather** (✉ 217 Carrall St., Gastown ☎ 604/688–9779 ⊕ www.irishheather.com). There's also a restaurant upstairs and, out back in an atmospheric coach house is **Shebeen,** or whiskey house, where you can try any of about 130 whiskies. Two big patios and plenty of comfy sofas draw locals to the easy-going **Jupiter Café** (✉ 1216 Bute St., West End ☎ 604/609–6665).

Near Stanley Park and attached to Cardero's restaurant, the **Marine Pub** (✉ 1583 Coal Harbour Quay, West End ☎ 604/669–7666) has deep leather couches, marina views, and recycled ship timbers and other nautical touches. The pub grub is top-notch. The **Mill Marine Bistro** (✉ 1199 W. Cordova St. ☎ 604/687–6455) is a waterfront pub and restaurant a 15-minute stroll west of Canada Place along the Coal Harbour Seawall Walk. The **900 West** (✉ 900 W. Georgia St., Downtown ☎ 604/669–9378) wine bar at the Fairmont Hotel Vancouver has 75 wines available by the glass.

Local hipsters and film industry types sip martinis and lounge on baroque and pop-art furniture at the hip **Opus Bar** (✉ 350 Davie St., in the Opus Hotel, Yaletown ☎ 604/642–0557). The multifaceted **Sand Bar** has a highly rated seafood restaurant, a wine bar, and dancing, Wednesday to Saturday nights in its **Teredo Bar** (✉ 1535 Johnson St., Granville Island ☎ 604/669–9030); a rooftop patio has dramatic views over False Creek. **Vistas** (✉ 1133 W. Hastings St., Downtown ☎ 604/691–2787), a revolving lounge and restaurant on the 19th floor of the Renaissance Vancouver Hotel Harbourside, takes in 360-degree views of the Stanley Park, Burrard Inlet, and the downtown core.

Brewpubs

Dix Barbecue and Brewery (✉ 871 Beatty St., Downtown ☎ 604/682–2739), near Yaletown and B.C. Place Stadium, is a relaxed and friendly place, with exposed brick and beams, a fireplace, a long mahogany bar, and vats brewing up a variety of ales and lagers. Dix also serves a fine southern-style barbecue, slow-smoked in-house in an apple- or cherry-wood smoker. The **Dockside Brewing Company** (✉ Granville Island Hotel, 1253 Johnston St., Granville Island ☎ 604/685–7070), with it's seaside patio, casual Pacific Northwest restaurant, and house-brewed German-style beer is a popular hangout. Harbor views, good food, and traditionally brewed beer are the draws at woodsy, paneled **Steamworks** (✉ 375 Water St., Gastown ☎ 604/689–2739), home to a pub, restaurant, and coffee bar. The **Yaletown Brewing Company** (✉ 1111 Mainland St., Yaletown ☎ 604/681–2739) is based in a renovated warehouse with a glassed-in brewery turning out several tasty beers. It also has a lively singles'-scene pub, a patio, and a restaurant.

Casinos

Vancouver has a few casinos; proceeds go to local charities and arts groups. No alcohol is served, and guests must be at least 19 years old. The **Edgewater Casino** (✉ 311–750 Pacific Blvd. S, Downtown ☎ 877/688–3343 or 604/687–3343 ⊕ www.edgewatercasino.ca) in the Plaza of Nations, has 600 slot machines, 48 table games, and a bistro. It's open 9 AM–6 AM daily. The **Royal City Star Riverboat Casino** (✉ 788 Quayside Dr., Westminster Quay, New Westminster ☎ 604/519–3660 ⊕ www.royalcitystar. bc.ca) is a Mississippi riverboat moored on the Fraser River. Its five decks include 24 gaming tables, a poker room, 300 slot machines, two bars, a lounge, and a restaurant. It's open 10 AM–4 AM daily. Admission is free.

Comedy

The **Vancouver International Comedy Festival** (☎ 604/683–0883 ⊕ www. comedyfest.com), held in late July and early August, brings an international collection of improv, stand-up, circus, and other acts to various downtown venues. The **Vancouver TheatreSports League** (☎ 604/738–7013 ⊕ www.vtsl.com), a hilarious improv troupe, performs at the New Revue Stage on Granville Island. Stand-up comedians perform Tuesday to Saturday evenings at **Yuk Yuk's** in the Century Plaza Hotel (✉ 1015 Burrard St., Downtown ☎ 604/696–9857 ⊕ www.crewcomedy.com).

Gay Nightlife

Vancouver's biggest gay dance club, the newly renovated **Celebrities** (✉ 1022 Davie St. ☎ 604/681–6180) has a huge dance floor and the latest in sound, lighting, and visuals. Music ranges from Top 40 to hip-hop and R&B; men and women are welcome. The **Fountainhead** is a friendly local pub, with a street-side patio ideally placed for Davie Street people-watching (✉ 1025 Davie St. ☎ 604/687–2222). **Lick** (✉ 455 Abbott St. ☎ 604/685–7777) is Vancouver's most popular lesbian dance bar. Two more dance clubs, **Honey** and **Lotus,** at the same site, are open to all.

A big, multitiered dance club, **Numbers** (✉ 1042 Davie St., West End ☎ 604/685–4077) features drag and theme nights. The **Oasis** (✉ 1240 Thurlow St., West End ☎ 604/685–1724) is a relaxed piano lounge with a tapas-style menu and a rooftop patio; it attracts a mixed local crowd. The **Odyssey** (✉ 1251 Howe St., Downtown ☎ 604/689–5256) is a dance club with drag shows, go-go boys, and theme nights. Anything from pool tournaments to leather and latex nights happens at the **PumpJack Pub** (✉ 1167 Davie St., West End ☎ 604/685–3417), a friendly neighborhood pub. **Sugar Daddy's** (✉ 1262 Davie St. ☎ 604/632–1646) is Vancouver's first gay video bar, with big-screen TVs showing sports and music videos.

Music

DANCE CLUBS A smartly dressed crowd flocks to dance and celebrity-spot at upscale **AuBAR** (✉ 674 Seymour St., Downtown ☎ 604/648–2227). **Caprice** (✉ 967 Granville St. ☎ 604/681–2114) is a two-level former movie theater with an restaurant and lounge where R&B and Top 40 play to a 21-plus crowd. The **Commodore Ballroom** (✉ 868 Granville St., Downtown ☎ 604/739–7469), a 1929 dance hall, has been restored to its art deco glory, complete with its massive sprung dance floor. Live bands play here six nights a week; Tuesday is DJ night.

There's plenty of room to dance at the 8,000 square foot **Plaza Cabaret** (✉ 881 Granville St., Downtown ☎ 604/646–0064). Top 40, dance, and hip-hop play for the crowd on the huge dance floor. You can also watch the action from the mezzanine, or relax in the upstairs lounge. **Shine** (✉ 364 Water St., Gastown ☎ 604/408–4321), a luminous, postmodern spot, draws a trendy crowd to its '80s classics, dancehall, rap, and rock-and-roll nights. On weekends, a well-dressed, over-25 crowd lines up for **Skybar** (✉ 670 Smithe St., Downtown ☎ 604/697–9199 ⊕ www.skybarvancouver.com), a chic three-level club including a lounge, a dance club, and a rooftop restaurant.

Top international DJs play house, R&B, hip-hop, and electronica for a dance-loving crowd at **Sonar** (✉ 66 Water St., Gastown ☎ 604/683–6695). The fashionable **Voda** (✉ 783 Homer St., Downtown ☎ 604/684–3003), in the Westin Grand Hotel, is one of the few places where Vancouverites dress up. The intimate club draws a thirtysomething professional crowd to its weekend Top 40 and house nights and a younger crowd for midweek hip-hop.

FOLK For folk and traditional Celtic concerts year-round, call the **Rogue Folk Club** (☎ 604/736–3022). The **Vancouver Folk Music Festival** (☎ 604/602–9798 or 800/985–8363 ⊕ www.thefestival.bc.ca), one of the world's leading folk- and world-music events, takes place at Jericho Beach Park in mid-July.

JAZZ & BLUES The hotline of the **Coastal Jazz and Blues Society** (☎ 604/872–5200 ⊕ www.coastaljazz.ca) has information about concerts and clubs. The society also runs the **Vancouver International Jazz Festival,** which lights up 40 venues around town every June. You can hear live jazz at the **Cellar Restaurant and Jazz Club** (✉ 3611 W. Broadway, Kitsilano ☎ 604/738–1959). A house band plays Thursday to Saturday at **Mo' Butta** (✉ 52 Powell St., Gastown ☎ 604/688–6439), a jazz-and-blues spot in a historic brick-lined building. Local art and a Southern-theme menu are also draws. The best of local jazz musicians play nightly at **O'Doul's Restaurant & Bar** (✉ 1300 Robson St., West End ☎ 604/661–1400) in the Listel Vancouver hotel.

ROCK & BLUES The **Backstage Lounge** (✉ 1585 Johnston St., Granville Island ☎ 604/687–1354) stages local bands Wednesday through Saturday nights. In the early evening, the **Railway Club** (✉ 579 Dunsmuir St., Downtown ☎ 604/681–1625) attracts film and media types to its pub-style rooms; after 8 it becomes a venue for local bands. Technically it's a private social club, so patrons must sign in, but everyone of age is welcome. The **Vogue Theatre** (✉ 918 Granville St., Downtown ☎ 604/331–7909), a former movie palace, hosts a variety of concerts by visiting performers. Vancouver's most established rhythm-and-blues bar, the **Yale** (✉ 1300 Granville St., Downtown ☎ 604/681–9253), has live bands most nights.

The Arts

Dance

A few of the many modern-dance companies in town are DanceArts Vancouver and New Performance Works; besides the Scotia Bank Dance Centre, the Firehall Arts Centre and the Vancouver East Cultural Centre are among their performance venues.

Ballet British Columbia (☎ 604/732–5003 ⊕ www.balletbc.com) mounts productions and hosts out-of-town companies from November through May. Most of its performances are at the Queen Elizabeth Theatre. The **Scotiabank Dance Centre** (✉ 677 Davie St., Downtown ☎ 604/606–6400 ⊕ www.thedancecentre.ca) is the hub of dance in British Columbia. The striking building, with an art deco facade, has performance and rehearsal space and provides information about dance in the province.

Film

Tickets are half-price Tuesday at most chain-owned Vancouver movie theaters. The **Fifth Avenue Cinemas** (✉ 2110 Burrard St., Kitsilano ☎ 604/734–7469 ⊕ www.allianceatlantiscinemas.com) is a small multiplex featuring foreign and independent films. **Pacific Cinématèque** (✉ 1131 Howe St., Downtown ☎ 604/688–3456 ⊕ www.cinematheque.bc.ca) shows independent and international features. The **Ridge Theatre** (✉ 3131 Arbutus St., Kitsilano ☎ 604/738–6311 ⊕ www.ridgetheatre.com) is a long-established art-house cinema.

The **Vancouver International Film Festival** (☎ 604/685–0260 ⊕ www. viff.org) is held in late September and early October in several theaters around town.

Music

CHAMBER MUSIC & SMALL ENSEMBLES

Early Music Vancouver (☎ 604/732–1610 ⊕ www.earlymusic.bc.ca) performs medieval, Renaissance, baroque, and early classical music on period instruments year-round and hosts the Vancouver Early Music Programme and Festival from mid-July to mid-August at the University of British Columbia. Concerts by the **Friends of Chamber Music** (☎ No phone ⊕ www.friendsofchambermusic.ca) are worth watching for in the local-newspaper entertainment listings. The **Vancouver Recital Society** (☎ 604/602–0363 ⊕ www.vanrecital.com) presents both emerging and well-known classical musicians in recital September–May at the Chan Centre for the Performing Arts, the Vancouver Playhouse, and the Orpheum Theater. In summer the society produces the Vancouver Chamber Music Festival, on the grounds of **Crofton House School** (✉ 3200 W. 41st Ave., South Vancouver) and at **Green College** (✉ 6201 Cecil Green Park Point Grey).

CHORAL GROUPS

The **Vancouver Bach Choir** (☎ 604/921–8012 ⊕ www.vancouverbachchoir. com) performs a five-concert series at the Orpheum Theatre between December and May. The **Vancouver Cantata Singers** (☎ 604/730–8856 ⊕ www.cantata.org) presents choral performances at various venues around town. The **Vancouver Chamber Choir** (☎ 604/738–6822 ⊕ www. vancouverchamberchoir.com) performs at several venues, including the Orpheum and the Chan Centre.

FESTIVALS **Festival Vancouver** (☎ 604/688–1152 ⊕ www.festivalvancouver.bc.ca) is Vancouver's biggest music event, with more than 50 performances of orchestral, chamber, choral, world, as well as opera and jazz in 10 venues around the city in early August.

ORCHESTRAS The **Vancouver Symphony Orchestra** (✉ 601 Smithe St., Downtown ☎ 604/876–3434 ⊕ www.vancouversymphony.ca) is the resident company at the **Orpheum Theatre.**

Opera

Vancouver Opera (☎ 604/682–2871 ⊕ www.vanopera.bc.ca) stages four productions a year from October through May at the Queen Elizabeth Theatre.

Theater

The **Arts Club Theatre Company** (✉ 1585 Johnston St., Granville Island ☎ 604/687–1644 ⊕ www.artsclub.com) operates two theaters. The **Arts Club Granville Island Stage** is an intimate venue and a good place to catch works by local playwrights. The **Stanley Industrial Alliance Stage,** at 2750 Granville Street, is a lavish former movie palace staging works by such perennial favorites as William Shakespeare and Noel Coward. Both operate year-round.

Carousel Theatre (☎ 604/685–6217 ⊕ www.carouseltheatre.ca) performs for children and young people at the **Waterfront Theatre** (✉ 1410 Cartwright St., Granville Island). Big international shows, from Broadway musicals to Chinese dance productions, play at the **Centre in Vancouver for Performing Arts** (✉ 777 Homer St., Downtown ☎ 604/602–0616 ⊕ www.centreinvancouver.com). The **Chan Centre for the Performing Arts** (✉ 6265 Crescent Rd., University of British Columbia Campus, Point Grey ☎ 604/822–2697 ⊕ www.chancentre.com) contains a 1,200-seat concert hall, a theater, and a cinema.

The **Firehall Arts Centre** (✉ 280 E. Cordova St., Downtown East Side ☎ 604/689–0926 ⊕ www.firehallartscentre.ca) showcases innovative theater and modern dance works in an intimate downtown Eastside space. The **Queen Elizabeth Theatre** (✉ 600 Hamilton St., Downtown ☎ 604/665–3050 ⊕ www.vancouver.ca/theatres) is a major venue for ballet, opera, and other events. **Vancouver East Cultural Centre** (✉ 1895 Venables St., East Vancouver ☎ 604/254–9578 ⊕ www.vecc.bc.ca) is a multipurpose performance space. In the same complex as the Queen Elizabeth Theatre, the **Vancouver Playhouse** (✉ 649 Cambie St., Downtown ☎ 604/665–3050 ⊕ www.vancouverplayhouse.com) is the leading venue in Vancouver for mainstream theater. The **Vogue Theatre** (✉ 918 Granville St., Downtown ☎ 604/331–7909 ⊕ www.voguetheatre.com), a former movie palace, hosts theater and live music events.

Bard on the Beach (☎ 604/739–0559 or 877/739–0559 ⊕ www.bardonthebeach.org) is a summer series of Shakespeare's plays performed in tents on the beach at Vanier Park. **Theatre Under the Stars** (☎ 604/687–0174 ⊕ www.tuts.bc.ca) performs such popular family-friendly musicals as *The Sound of Music* and *Kiss Me Kate* at Malkin Bowl, an outdoor amphitheater in Stanley Park, during July and August. You can watch the show from the lawn, or from the Rose Garden Tea House as part of a dinner-theater package. The **Vancouver Fringe Festival** (☎ 604/257–0350 ⊕ www.vancouverfringe.com), an annual theater festival, is staged in early September at various venues on and around Granville Island.

SPORTS & THE OUTDOORS

Blessed with a fabulous natural setting and excellent public facilities, it's not surprising that Vancouverites are a sporty lot. It's not uncommon for locals to commute to work by bike or even kayak and, after hours, they're as likely to hit the trails, ski slopes, or tennis courts as the bars or nightclubs.

In the downtown core, you can jog, bike, or in-line skate, hit the beach, or take a boat out on the bay. Top-rated skiing, snowboarding, mountain biking, fishing, diving, and golf are just minutes away.

And, though locals are more inclined to play their sports than watch them, the city also boasts several major league sports franchises.

For gear rental, maps, and local information, check out **Mountain Equipment Co-op** (✉ 130 W. Broadway, Fairview ☎ 604/872–7858 ⊕ www. mec.ca).

Ticketmaster (☎ 604/280–4400 ⊕ www.ticketmaster.ca) sells tickets to many local sports events.

Beaches

An almost continuous string of beaches runs from Stanley Park to the University of British Columbia. The water is cool, but the beaches are sandy, edged by grass. All have lifeguards, washrooms, concession stands, and limited parking, unless otherwise noted. The **Vancouver Parks Board** (⊕ http://vancouver.ca/parks/rec/beaches/) has details. Liquor is prohibited in parks and on beaches.

Ambleside Park, at the north end of the Lions Gate Bridge, with its long stretch of sand, is the North Shore's most popular beach. **Kitsilano Beach**, over the Burrard Bridge from downtown, is the city's busiest beach—in-line skaters, volleyball games, and sleek young people are ever present. The part of the beach nearest the Vancouver Maritime Museum is the quietest. Facilities include a playground, a restaurant and concession stand, tennis courts, and an enormous heated pool. The **Point Grey beaches**—Jericho, Locarno, and Spanish Banks—begin at the end of Point Grey Road and offer huge expanses of sand backed by wide lawns dotted with picnic tables. The shallow water, warmed slightly by sun and sand, is good for swimming. Jericho Beach is popular for windsurfing. Farther out, toward Spanish Banks, the beach becomes less crowded. The **Stanley Park Beaches**, along Stanley Park Drive in Stanley Park, draw families. Second Beach has a playground, a small sandy area, and a large, heated pool with a slide. Third beach has a larger stretch of sand, fairly warm water, and great sunset views. It's a popular evening picnic spot. The **West End beaches**, just outside Stanley Park, are within sight of the neighboring high-rises. A waterslide, street performers, and artists keep things interesting all summer at English Bay Beach, at the foot of Denman Street. Farther along Beach Drive, Sunset Beach is too close to the downtown core for clean, safe swimming, but is a great spot for an evening stroll. You can catch a ferry to Granville Island here, or swim at the **Vancouver Aquatic Centre** (⊠ 1050 Beach Ave. ☎ 604/665–3424), a public indoor pool and fitness center. You can reach **Wreck Beach,** Canada's largest clothing-optional beach, via a steep trail and flight of stairs from Gate 6, off Marine Drive on the University of British Columbia campus. This 6-km (4-mi) long wildernesslike beach, managed by a team of volunteers, has a delightfully anarchic culture of its own. The driftwood is tangled, bathing suits are optional, and vendors sell a wild array of food, goods, and services. Up to 14,000 people might visit on a summer weekend. There are no lifeguards. For details, see (⊕ www.wreckbeach.org).

Biking

Vancouver is a bike-friendly town. Many TransLink buses have bike racks and bikes are welcome on the SeaBus and on the SkyTrain at off-peak times. Aquabus Ferries transport bikes and riders across False Creek. Cycling maps are available from most bike shops and bike-rental outlets and on the TransLink Web site ⊕ www.translink.bc.ca. Helmets are required by law and a sturdy lock is essential.

Several **long-distance bikeways** lace the city. Designed as the safest way for cyclists to get around, they combine bike-only pathways with quiet side streets. The most popular, and scenic, of these bikeways, and really a must-ride for any visiting rider, is the **Seaside Path.** This 39-km (23-mi) flat, car-free route starts at Canada Place downtown, follows the waterfront around Stanley Park, and continues all the way around False Creek to Spanish Banks Beach. North Vancouver's **Seymour Valley Trailway** in the Lower Seymour Conservation Reserve (⊠ End of Lillooet Rd., North Vancouver ☎ 604/432–6286 ⊕ www.gvrd.bc.ca), is a 10-km (6-mi) paved pathway, suitable for cyclists, in-line skaters, and baby strollers, that meanders over streams and through woods.

BIKE RENTALS Most bike-rental outlets also rent Rollerblades and jogging strollers. Cycling helmets, a legal requirement in Vancouver, come with the rentals. Locks and maps are also normally supplied. If you're starting your bike ride near Stanley Park, try **Bayshore Bicycles** (⊠ 745 Denman St., West End ☎ 604/688–2453). It has a range of bikes and Rollerblades as well as baby joggers and bike trailers. **Reckless Bike Stores** (⊠ 110 Davie St., Yaletown ☎ 604/648–2600 ⊠ 1810 Fir St., at 2nd Ave., Kitsilano ☎ 604/731–2420) rents bikes on the Yaletown section of the bike path. To explore the Granville Island and Kitsilano area, stop at the Kitsilano branch. **Spokes Bicycle Rentals** (⊠ 1798 W. Georgia St., West End ☎ 604/688–5141), at Denman and Georgia, near Stanley Park, has a wide selection of bikes, including kids' bikes, tandems, mountain bikes, and Rollerblades.

BIKE TOURS **Spokes Bicycle Rentals** (⊠ 1798 W. Georgia St., West End ☎ 604/688–5141 ⊕ www.vancouverbikerental.com) offers 90-minute tours of Stanley Park for C$33 and 3 ½-hour rides around Stanley Park, False Creek, and Granville Island for C$66; rates include bike rentals.

MOUNTAIN
BIKING

Opened in 2005, the **Cypress Mountain Bike Park** (✉ Cypress Bowl Rd., West Vancouver, Exit 8 off Hwy. 1 westbound ☎ 604/913–2453 ⊕ www. cypressmountain.com ⊙ June–Sept., daily, call for hrs 🎫 C$32 for a 4-hr pass) has several kilometers of lift-accessed trails for all levels. Full face helmets are required and body protection is recommended. Equipment rentals, sales and repairs, as well as a restaurant and pub, are onsite. North Vancouver's **Lower Seymour Conservation Reserve** (✉ End of Lillooet Rd., North Vancouver ☎ 604/432–6286 ⊕ www.gvrd.bc.ca) has miles of rugged mountain trails. **Pacific Spirit Regional Park** (✉ 4915 W. 16th Ave., Point Grey ☎ 604/224–5739 ⊕ www.gvrd.bc.ca/parks/ PacificSprit.htm), bordering the University of British Columbia, has 38 km (23 mi) of challenging rain-forest trails.

Diving

Especially in winter, when water clarity allows visibility of up to 100 feet, the waters near Vancouver offer some of the most spectacular temperate water diving in the world.

BC Dive and Kayak Adventures (☎ 604/732–1344 or 800/960–0066 ⊕ www.bcdive.com) offers day trips from Vancouver to the flora- and fauna-rich waters of Howe Sound and Indian Arm. The trips run weekends, year-round.

Fishing

You can fish for salmon all year in coastal British Columbia. **Sewell's Marina Horseshoe Bay** (✉ 6409 Bay St., Horseshoe Bay ☎ 604/921–3474 ⊕ www.sewellsmarina.com) leads guided and self-driven salmon-fishing charters in Howe Sound. **Westin Bayshore Yacht Charters** (✉ 1601 Bayshore Dr., off W. Georgia St., West End ☎ 604/691–6936 ⊕ www. westinbayshoreyachts.com) operates fishing charters. For fishing license details, *see* British Columbia A to Z.

Football

The **B.C. Lions** (☎ 604/930–5466 ⊕ www.bclions.com) Canadian Football League team plays home games at **B.C. Place Stadium** (✉ 777 Pacific Blvd. S, Downtown ☎ 604/669–2300 ⊕ www.bcplacestadium.com).

Golf

Vancouver-area golf courses offer challenging golf with great scenery. Most are open year-round.

For advance tee-time bookings at any of about 75 British Columbia courses, or for a spur-of-the-moment game, call **Last Minute Golf** (☎ 604/878–1833 or 800/684–6344 ⊕ www.lastminutegolfbc.com). The company matches golfers and courses, sometimes at substantial greens-fee discounts. The facilities of the 18-hole, par-72, 6,700 yard **Fraserview Golf Course** (✉ 7800 Vivian Dr., South Vancouver ☎ 604/ 257–6923, 604/280–1818 advance bookings ⊕ www.city.vancouver. bc.ca/parks/golf/) include a driving range and a new club house. The greens fee is C$51–C$54. This newly renovated course is the best-equipped and most attractive of several run by the Vancouver Parks Board. The challenging 18-hole, par-72 course at **Furry Creek Golf and Country Club** (✉ Rte. 99, Furry Creek ☎ 604/896–2224 or 888/922–

9462 ⊕ www.furrycreekgolf.ca), a 45-minute drive north of Vancouver, has a C$109 peak-season greens fee that includes a mandatory cart. The course has stunning fjord-side scenery, but with many blind shots it can be tricky to play. For C$149 you can combine a round with an hour-long ecocruise from Horseshoe Bay. The course is closed late October to early March.

Northview Golf and Country Club (✉ 6857 168th St., Surrey ☎ 604/576–4653 or 888/574–2211 ⊕ www.northviewgolf.com) has two Arnold Palmer–designed 18-hole courses (both par 72, and both open year-round). The greens fee for the Ridge course is C$85–C$95; the fee for the more challenging Canal course is C$65–C$75. An optional cart at either course costs C$32. The semiprivate **Seymour Golf and Country Club** (✉ 3723 Mt. Seymour Pkwy., North Vancouver ☎ 604/929–2611 ⊕ www.seymourgolf.com) is set among old growth forest at the base of Mount Seymour. It's open to the public on Monday and Friday; greens fees run C$61 to C$66. On the city's west side, the recently renovated par 71, 6,560 yard **University Golf Club** (✉ 5185 University Blvd., Vancouver ☎ 604/224–1818 ⊕ www.universitygolf.com) has an excellent club house and dining facility; it's also home to the British Columbia Golf Museum (Exploring, *above*). Greens fees are C$60 to C$70. At the well-manicured, 18-hole, par 72 course (closed November through March) at the **Westwood Plateau Golf and Country Club** (✉ 3251 Plateau Blvd., Coquitlam ☎ 604/552–0777 or 800/580–0785 ⊕ www.westwoodplateaugolf.com), the greens fee, which includes a cart, is C$159. The club also has a restaurant open seasonally. The 9-hole **Academy Course** nearby (604/941–4236) is open year-round.

Health & Fitness Clubs

The **Bentall Centre Athletic Club** (✉ 1055 Dunsmuir St., lower plaza, Downtown ☎ 604/689–4424 ⊕ www.bentallcentreathleticclub.com) specializes in squash and also has racquetball courts and weight and cardio gyms; aerobics classes are given as well. The drop-in fee is C$15. The **YMCA** (✉ 955 Burrard St., Downtown ☎ 604/689–9622 ⊕ www.vanymca.org), downtown, has a daily rate of C$10. Facilities include two pools; a men's steam room and women's sauna; a weight room and cardio center; as well as yoga classes; a boxing room; racquetball, squash, and handball courts; and a sports medicine clinic. The **YWCA** (✉ 535 Hornby St., Downtown ☎ 604/895–5777 ⊕ www.ywcahealthandwellness.com) has an ozone pool, a cardio room, two coed and one women-only weight rooms, aerobics, yoga, and pilates classes, a whirlpool, and steam rooms. The day rate is C$16.

Hiking

Vancouver offers plenty of easy forest walks in city and regional parks, as well as challenging wilderness hikes just minutes from town in the North Shore mountains. If you're headed to the mountains, don't be swayed by their proximity to civilization; every year hikers are lost within sight of the city lights. For a mountain hike, pack warm clothes (even in summer) and extra food and water, and be sure to leave word with someone in the city as to your route and the time you expect to be back. Remember that weather can change quickly in the mountains. You can check for a weather forecast with **Environment Canada** (⊕ http://weatheroffice.ec.gc.ca).

International Travel Maps & Books (✉ 530 W. Broadway ☎ 604/879–3621 ⊕ www.itmb.com) has a good selection of local topographic maps.

For relatively easy walks, check out the seaside **Lighthouse Park** (✉ Beacon La. off Marine Dr., West Vancouver), which has fairly flat forested trails leading to the rocky shoreline. The rugged **Pacific Spirit Regional Park** (✉ 4915 W. 16th Ave., Point Grey ☎ 604/224–5739 ⊕ www.gvrd.bc.ca/parks/), near the University of British Columbia, has 54 km (32 mi) of fairly level forested trails. **Stanley Park** (☎ 604/257–8400 ⊕ www.vancouver.ca/parks/) has miles of trails to explore.

In the mountains of North Vancouver, **Capilano River Regional Park** (☎ 604/224–5739 ⊕ www.gvrd.bc.ca/parks) has trails along the edge of a dramatic gorge. **Cypress Provincial Park** (✉ Cypress Bowl Rd., West Vancouver ⊕ www.bcparks.ca) is a good choice for serious hikers. North Vancouver's **Lower Seymour Conservation Reserve** (✉ End of Lillooet Rd., North Vancouver ☎ 604/432–6286 ⊕ www.gvrd.bc.ca) has some easy rain-forest walks, including 10 km (6 mi) of paved paths. **Mount Seymour Provincial Park** (✉ Mount Seymour Rd. off Seymour Pkwy., North Vancouver ⊕ www.bcparks.ca) offers challenging mountain trails for experienced, well-equipped hikers.

The **Grouse Grind** (✉ 6400 Nancy Greene Way, North Vancouver ☎ 604/980–9311 ⊕ www.grousemountain.com) is a steep (rising 2,800 feet in less than 2 mi), grueling trail from the Grouse Mountain parking lot to the top of the mountain. The path, packed with fit Vancouverites most summer afternoons, is popular, but not very pleasant and not suitable for young children. There are some much more scenic trails at the top of the mountain, accessed via the Grouse Mountain Skyride. Grouse Grinders can take the Skyride down the mountain for a C$5; a round-trip ticket costs C$29.95.

GUIDED HIKES   Guided walks through the rain forests and canyons of the North Shore are run by **Rockwood Adventures** (☎ 604/980–7749 or 888/236–6606 ⊕ www.rockwoodadventures.com). The C$75 fee includes snacks and hotel pickup.

Hockey
The **Vancouver Canucks** (✉ 800 Griffiths Way, Downtown ☎ 604/899–7400) of the National Hockey League play at **General Motors Place.**

Jogging
The **Running Room** (✉ 679 Denman St., West End ☎ 604/684–9771) is a good source for information about fun runs in the area. Any part of the 39-km (23-mi) **Seaside Path,** which frames the city's coastline from Canada Place to Spanish Banks, offers a scenic car-free run. The 9-km-(5½-mi)- long section around **Stanley Park** (☎ 604/257–8400) is deservedly popular and provides an excellent minitour of the city. You can take a shorter run of 4 km (2½ mi) in the park around Lost Lagoon.

Skiing

CROSS-COUNTRY   The best cross-country skiing, with 19 km (11½ mi) of groomed trails, some of it lighted for night skiing, is at **Cypress Mountain** (⊠ Cypress Bowl Rd., West Vancouver, Exit 8 off Hwy. 1 westbound ☎ 604/419–7669 ⊕ www.cypressmountain.com).

DOWNHILL   Whistler Resort, a top-ranked ski destination, is a two-hour drive from
SKIING &   Vancouver. The North Shore Mountains hold three ski and snowboard
SNOWBOARDING   areas. All have rentals, lessons, night skiing, and a variety of runs suitable for all skill levels. The season runs December to April. Grouse Mountain can be reached by TransLink buses. Cypress and Seymour each run shuttle buses from Lonsdale Quay and other North Shore stops.

Cypress Mountain (⊠ Cypress Bowl Rd., West Vancouver, Exit 8 off Hwy. 1 westbound ☎ 604/419–7669 ⊕ www.cypressmountain.com) has 36 runs on two mountains, five chairlifts, two surface lifts, and a vertical drop of 1,750 feet. The mountain also has a snow-tubing area and snowshoe tours. Reached via a cable car, **Grouse Mountain** (⊠ 6400 Nancy Greene Way, North Vancouver ☎ 604/980–9311, 604/986–6262 snow report ⊕ www.grousemountain.com) is the only North Shore mountain with snow-making capabilities. It has 24 runs, a vertical drop of 1,210 feet, a snowshoeing park, an outdoor ice-skating pond, and great city views from the runs. There's also a choice of upscale and casual dining in a good-looking stone-and-timber lodge. **Mount Seymour** (⊠ 1700 Mt. Seymour Rd., North Vancouver ☎ 604/986–2261, 604/718–7771 snow report ⊕ www.mountseymour.com) has three chairlifts and a vertical drop of 1,042 feet. With a half-pipe and three terrain parks, it's popular with snowboarders. You can also take a snowshoeing tour or play in the tobogganing and snow-tubing areas.

Tennis

There are 181 free public courts in 44 parks around town. Contact the **Vancouver Board of Parks and Recreation** (☎ 604/257–8400 ⊕ www.vancouver.ca/parks/) for locations. Most courts are played on a drop-in basis, but six courts in **Stanley Park** (☎ 604/605–8224 May through Sept. only) can be reserved for a fee.

Water Sports

BOATING &   You can charter motorboats and sailboats from Granville Island through
SAILING   **Blue Pacific Yacht Charters** (⊠ 1519 Foreshore Walk, Granville Island ☎ 604/682–2161 or 800/237–2392 ⊕ www.bluepacificcharters.ca). **Cooper Boating** (⊠ 1620 Duranleau St., Granville Island ☎ 604/687–4110 or 888/999–6419 ⊕ www.cooperboating.com) charters sailboats and cabin cruisers, with or without skippers. It also provides sailing and power-boating lessons. You can charter a yacht at **Westin Bayshore Yacht Charters** (⊠ 1601 Bayshore Dr., off W. Georgia St., West End ☎ 604/691–6936 ⊕ www.westinbayshoreyachts.com).

CANOEING &   Kayaks are a fun way to explore the waters of False Creek and the shore-
KAYAKING   line of English Bay. **Ecomarine Ocean Kayak Centre** (⊠ 1668 Duranleau St., Granville Island ☎ 604/689–7575 or 888/425–2925 ⊕ www.ecomarine.com ⊠ English Bay ☎ 604/685–2925 ⊠ Jericho Beach

☎ 604/222–3565) offers lessons and rentals year-round from Granville Island, and from early May to early September at Jericho Beach and English Bay. From May to October **Deep Cove Canoe and Kayak Rentals** (✉ 2156 Banbury Rd., North Vancouver ☎ 604/929–2268 ⊕ www. deepcovekayak.com) offers rentals, guided trips, and lessons for kids and adults at their North Shore base. **Lotus Land Tours** (☎ 604/684–4922 or 800/528–3531 ⊕ www.VancouverNatureAdventures.com) leads kayaking tours in Indian Arm, north of Vancouver between May and October. The five-hour trip costs C$149 and includes a salmon barbecue lunch and hotel pick up. The company also offers kayaking day trips to the Gulf Islands, including a floatplane flight back to Vancouver. Experience is not required; the kayaks are easy for beginners to handle. With **Takaya Tours** (☎ 604/904–7410 ⊕ www.takayatours.com) you can paddle a 45-foot traditional-style Salish ocean-going canoe while First Nations guides relay local legends, sing traditional songs, and point out ancient village sites. The two-hour tours cost C$54 and leave from Cates Park in North Vancouver. Reservations are essential.

RIVER RAFTING   The **Canadian Outback Adventure Company** (☎ 604/921–7250 or 800/565–8735 ⊕ www.canadianoutback.com) runs white-water rafting and scenic, family-oriented (not white water) floats on day trips from Vancouver. A white-water day trip costs C$155 per person; family trips are C$95 per person; transportation to and from Vancouver is available for an extra C$40 per person. **Lotus Land Tours** (☎ 604/684–4922 or 800/528–3531 ⊕ www.VancouverNatureAdventures.com) runs river rafting day trips from Vancouver to Whistler, C$195 includes return transportation, four hours of guided rafting, and a barbecue lunch.

WINDSURFING   The winds aren't heavy on English Bay, making it a perfect locale for learning the sport. You have to travel north to Squamish for more challenging high-wind conditions. Sailboard rentals and lessons are available between May and September at **Windsure Windsurfing School** (✉ Jericho Beach, Kitsilano ☎ 604/224–0615 ⊕ www.windsure.com).

Wildlife Viewing

BIRD- & EAGLE-   Between mid-November and mid-February, the world's largest con-
WATCHING   centration of bald eagles gather to feed on salmon at **Brackendale Eagles' Park** (✉ Government Rd. off Hwy. 99, Brackendale), about an hour north of Vancouver. With **Canadian Outback Adventure Company** (☎ 604/921–7250 or 800/565–8735, ⊕ www.canadianoutback.com) you can watch and photograph the eagles from a slow-moving raft on the Cheakamus River. Transportation from Vancouver is available. Day trips to Brackendale with **Vancouver All-Terrain Adventures** (☎ 604/984–2374 or 888/754–5601 ⊕ www.all-terrain.com) include pick up in Vancouver in a four-wheel-drive Suburban, and an option to watch the eagles by raft or horseback.

More than 260 species of migratory birds visit the **George C. Reifel Bird Sanctuary** (✉ 5191 Robertson Rd., Ladner ☎ 604/946–6980 ⊕ www. reifelbirdsanctuary.com ⊆ C$4 ⊙ Daily 9–4), an 850-acre site on Westham Island, about an hour south of Vancouver.

WHALE- Between April and October pods of Orca whales travel through the Strait
WATCHING of Georgia, near Vancouver. The area is also home to harbor seals, elephant seals, bald eagles, minke whales, porpoises, and a wealth of birdlife.

Lotus Land Tours (☎ 604/684–4922 or 800/528–3531 ⊕ www.
VancouverNatureAdventures.com) can take you out in a high-speed covered boat to watch for whales and other wildlife in the Strait of Georgia. The three- to five-hour cruise cost C$149 and includes pick up
anywhere in Vancouver and an on-board lunch. **Wild Whales Vancouver**
(☎ 604/699–2011 ⊕ www.whalesvancouver.ca) leaves Granville Island
in search of Orca pods in Georgia Strait. Rates are C$109 for a three-
to seven-hour trip in either an open or glass-domed boat. Trips leave
twice daily, April through October.

SHOPPING

Unlike many cities where suburban malls have taken over, Vancouver
is full of individual boutiques and specialty shops. Antiques stores, ethnic markets, art galleries, gourmet-food shops, and high-fashion outlets abound, and both Asian and First Nations influences in crafts,
home furnishings, and foods are quite prevalent. Store hours vary but
are generally 9:30–6 Monday, Tuesday, Wednesday, and Saturday;
9:30–9 Thursday and Friday; and 10–5 Sunday. In Gastown and along
Main Street, many shops don't open until 11 or noon.

You'll pay both 7% Provincial Sales Tax (PST) and 7% Goods and Services Tax (GST) on most purchases. Nonresidents of Canada are enti-
tled to a refund of GST paid on many purchases, though you'll need to
keep your receipts to claim it (⇨ *see* Smart Travel Tips for more information about reclaiming GST). **Global Refund** (✉ 900 W. Georgia St. ☎ 604/
893–8478), on the lower level of the Fairmont Hotel Vancouver, can give
you an on-the-spot cash refund, though it charges 20% commission.

Shopping Neighborhoods

Robson Street

Robson Street, stretching from Burrard to Bute, is the city's main fash-
ion-shopping and people-watching artery. The Gap and Banana Republic
have their flagship stores here, as do Canadian fashion outlets Club
Monaco and Roots. Souvenir shops and cafés fill the gaps. West of Bute,
the shops cater to the thousands of Japanese and Korean students in town
to study English; Asian food shops, video outlets, and cheap noodle bars
abound.

Gastown & Chinatown

Treasure hunters like the 300 block of **West Cordova Street** in Gastown,
where offbeat shops sell curios, vintage clothing, and locally designed
clothes. Bustling **Chinatown**—centered on Pender and Main streets—is
full of Chinese bakeries, restaurants, herbalists, and import shops.

Yaletown

Frequently described as Vancouver's SoHo, this neighborhood on the
north bank of False Creek is home to boutiques, home stores, and

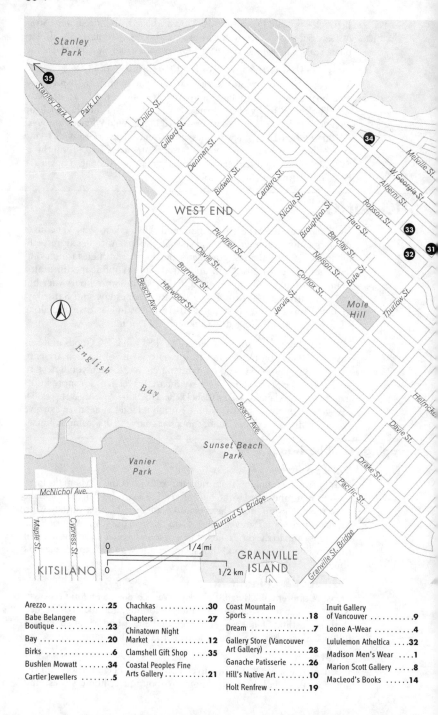

Where to Shop in Downtown Vancouver

restaurants, many in converted warehouses, that cater to a trendy, money-eyed crowd.

Granville Island

On the south side of False Creek, **Granville Island** has a lively food market and a wealth of galleries, crafts shops, and artisans' studios.

South Granville

About two-dozen high-end art galleries, antiques shops, and Oriental-rug emporiums are packed between 5th and 15th avenues on Granville Street, in an area known as **Gallery Row**. Granville Street, between Broadway and 16th Avenue, is known as **Granville Rise**, and it's also lined with chic fashion, home decor, and specialty food shops.

Kitsilano

West 4th Avenue, between Burrard and Balsam, is the main shopping strip in funky Kitsilano. You'll find clothing and shoe boutiques, as well as housewares and gift shops. Just east of Burrard, several stores sells ski and snowboard gear.

Main Street & the Punjabi Market

Main Street, between 20th and 30th avenues, is an up-and-coming neighborhood, rich with ethnic restaurants and antiques, collectibles, and vintage-fashion shops. A growing number of eclectic boutiques here showcase local designers' creations. In the **Punjabi Market** area, Vancouver's "Little India" on Main Street around 50th Avenue, curry houses, sweets shops, grocery stores, discount jewelers, and silk shops abound.

Commercial Drive

Guatemalan crafts, Italian shoes, and espresso bars with soccer matches broadcast live from Italy come together on **Commercial Drive,** between East 2nd Avenue and Venables Street, Vancouver's world-beat melting pot.

Richmond

In suburban **Richmond,** south of downtown Vancouver, several large shopping malls—centered on and around No. 3 Road between Cambie Road and Granville Avenue—mix chain stores with small boutiques and eateries that cater to the area's upscale Asian residents.

Department Stores & Shopping Centers

The best options for department stores in downtown Vancouver include mid-price the **Bay** (✉ 674 Granville St., at Georgia St., Downtown ☎ 604/681–6211), founded as part of the fur trade in the 17th century. **Holt Renfrew** (✉ 633 Granville St., Downtown ☎ 604/681–3121) focuses on high fashion for men and women.

In and around Vancouver are several shopping centers with an assortment of offerings. **Metrotown Centre** (✉ 4800 Kingsway, Burnaby ☎ 604/438–3610), one of the largest malls in the area, is 20 minutes from downtown by SkyTrain. **Oakridge Centre** (✉ 650 W. 41st Ave., at Cambie St., South Vancouver ☎ 604/261–2511) has a mix of trendy shops, mid-price boutiques, and North American chains. **Pacific Centre Mall** (✉ 700

W. Georgia St., Downtown ☎ 604/688–7236) takes up three city blocks in the heart of downtown. Mid-price, mainstream clothing shops predominate on the lower level; chicer, pricier items can be found on the upper floor. Shops in and around **Sinclair Centre** (✉ 757 W. Hastings St., Downtown) cater to sophisticated and pricey tastes.

The Vancouver area hosts two Asian-style summer night markets, which make entertaining shopping excursions. Chinatown is at its liveliest when the **Chinatown Night Market** (✉ Keefer St., between Columbia and Gore Sts., Chinatown ☎ 604/682–8998) sets up shop. It's open from late May to mid-September, 6:30 PM to 11 PM Friday through Sunday.

★ The **Richmond Night Market** (✉ 12631 Vulcan Way, off Bridgeport Rd. at Sweden Way, Richmond ☎ 604/244–8448) is an Asian-style extravaganza of food stalls offering noodle bowls, satay sticks, and bubble tea, and vendors selling everything from socks to mops. The market runs from 7 PM to midnight on Friday and Saturday, and from 7 PM to 11 PM on Sunday, from late May to late September. The market grounds are behind the Home Depot store.

Specialty Stores

Antiques

Key antiques hunting grounds are Gallery Row on Granville Street and along Main Street from 20th to 30th Avenues. The **Vancouver Antique Centre** (✉ 422 Richards St., Downtown ☎ 604/684–9822) has about a dozen antiques and collectibles dealers under one roof.

Art & Crafts Galleries

Gallery Row along Granville Street between 5th and 15th avenues is home to about a dozen high-end contemporary-art galleries. The **Diane Farris Gallery** (✉ 1590 W. 7th Ave., South Granville ☎ 604/737–2629) often showcases new Canadian and international artists. The **Douglas Reynolds Gallery** (✉ 2335 Granville St., South Granville ☎ 604/731–9292) has a fine collection of Northwest Coast First Nations art, specializing in woodwork and jewelry.

A number of notable galleries are also on the downtown peninsula. **Buschlen Mowatt** (✉ 1445 W. Georgia St., West End ☎ 604/682–1234) exhibits the works of contemporary Canadian and international artists.

★ **Coastal Peoples Fine Arts Gallery** (✉ 1024 Mainland St., Yaletown ☎ 604/685–9298) has an impressive collection of First Nations jewelry, ceremonial masks, prints, and carvings their beautiful books and postcards make affordable souvenirs. The **Inuit Gallery of Vancouver** (✉ 206 Cambie St., Gastown ☎ 888/615–8399 or 604/688–7323) exhibits Northwest Coast and Inuit art. The **Marion Scott Gallery** (✉ 308 Water St., Gastown ☎ 604/685–1934) specializes in Inuit art.

Granville Island is a don't-miss destination for craft aficionados. Stroll Railspur Alley (off Old Bridge Street), which is lined with working artists' studios; the Net Loft building opposite the Public Market also has several galleries. Pick up the "Artists & Artisans of Granville Island" brochure (available at shops around the island) for a complete listing of galleries and studios. **Circle Craft** (✉ 1–1666 Johnston St., Net Loft,

Granville Island ☎ 604/669–8021), an artists' co-op, sells textiles, wood pieces, jewelry, ceramics, and glass works. **Craft House** (✉ 1386 Cartwright St., Granville Island ☎ 604/687–7270), run by the Crafts Association of B.C., showcases works by local artisans. The **Gallery of B.C. Ceramics** (✉ 1359 Cartwright St., Granville Island ☎ 604/669–3906) displays functional and decorative ceramics by local artists.

Doctor Vigari Gallery (✉ 1312 Commercial Dr., East Side ☎ 604/255–9513) showcases an eclectic assortment of jewelry, crafts, paintings, and furniture, most by B.C. artists.

Books

★ **Barbara-Jo's Books to Cooks** (✉ 1740 W. 2nd Ave., Kitsilano ☎ 604/688–6755 ✉ 11–1666 Johnston St., Net Loft, Granville Island ☎ 604/684–6788) stocks scores of cookbooks, including many by Vancouver- and B.C.–based chefs. Vancouver's two **Chapters** (✉ 788 Robson St., Downtown ☎ 604/682–4066 ✉ 2505 Granville St., at Broadway, South Granville ☎ 604/731–7822) carry a vast selection of popular books and CDs, and often discount bestsellers. **Duthie Books** (✉ 2239 W. 4th Ave., Kitsilano ☎ 604/732–5344) is a long-established homegrown favorite.

★ **Kidsbooks** (✉ 3083 W. Broadway, Kitsilano ☎ 604/738–5335) has Vancouver's best selection of books for children, from toddlers to teens. **MacLeod's Books** (✉ 455 W. Pender St., Downtown ☎ 604/681–7654) is one of the city's best antiquarian and used-book stores. **Sophia Books** (✉ 450 W. Hastings St., Downtown ☎ 604/684–0484) specializes in French and other foreign-language titles. **Wanderlust** (✉ 1929 W. 4th Ave., Kitsilano ☎ 604/739–2182) carries thousands of travel books and maps, as well as luggage and travel accessories.

Clothes

CHILDREN'S CLOTHING   If you're shopping for style-conscious babies and toddlers, check out the new and "recycled" clothes at **Dandelion Kids** (✉ 1206 Commercial Dr., East Side ☎ 604/676–1862). In its stores across Canada, **Please Mum** (✉ 2951 W. Broadway, Kitsilano ☎ 604/732–4574 ✉ Oakridge Centre, 650 W. 41st Ave., South Vancouver ☎ 604/261–5440 ✉ Metropolis at Metrotown, 4700 Kingsway, Burnaby ☎ 604/430–1702) sells comfortable, colorful clothing for children from newborns to about age 10. At **Roots Kids** (✉ 1153 Robson St., West End ☎ 604/684–8801), you can find this Canadian company's signature casual wear in children's sizes.

MEN'S & WOMEN'S CLOTHING   West Coast casual is the predominant look in Vancouver, and the clothing stores reflect that, though chic designer outlets and shops selling more eclectic creations can also be found.

Babe Belangere Boutique (✉ 1092 Hamilton St., Yaletown ☎ 604/806–4010) sells women's clothing that's fashionable without being over-the-top, including velvety skirts from Nougat London, designer jeans, and Kenzie sweaters. The frilly feminine clothing, jewelry, and bags, some by local designers, at **Barefoot Contessa** (✉ 3715 Main St., East Side) make this pretty shop worth a look. A small department store for the design-conscious, **Caban** (✉ 2912 Granville St., South Granville ☎ 604/742–1522) stocks men's and women's clothing (as well some as housewares and gifts).

Dream (✉ 311 W. Cordova St., Gastown ☎ 604/683–7326) is where up-and-coming local designers sell their wares. Sun hats, rain hats, cowboy hats, fedoras, mountie hats, cloches, straw hats—**Edie Hats** (✉ 4–1666 Johnston St., Net Loft, Granville Island ☎ 604/683–4280 or 800/750–2134) has them all. Men's and women's fashions by Versace, Yves Saint Laurent Rive Gauche, Dior, Prada, and others are available at **Leone** (✉ 757 W. Hastings St., Downtown ☎ 604/683–1133), in Sinclair Centre. You'll find somewhat more affordable, locally made fashions—and an Italian café—at **A-Wear** (✉ 350 Howe St., Downtown ☎ 604/685–9327), on Leone's lower floor.

★ Everyone from power-yoga devotees to soccer moms covets the fashionable well-constructed workout wear from Vancouver-based **Lululemon Athletica** (✉ 1148 Robson St., West End ☎ 604/681–3118 ✉ 2113 W. 4th Ave., Kitsilano ☎ 604/732–6111 ✉ Metrotown Centre, Burnaby ☎ 604/430–4659); local preteens save their allowances for the signature headbands. For upscale menswear and made-to-measure suits try **Madison Men's Wear** (✉ 1050 W. Pender St., Downtown ☎ 604/683–2122).

For outdoorsy clothes that double as souvenirs (many sport maple leaf logos), check out the sweatshirts, leather jackets, and other comfy casuals at **Roots** (✉ 1001 Robson St., West End ☎ 604/683–4305), an outfitter to the Canadian Olympic team. Globetrotters like the practical, hard-wearing, Canadian-made travel clothing available at **Tilley Endurables** (✉ 2401 Granville St., South Granville ☎ 604/732–4287). **Twigg & Hottie** (✉ 3671 Main St., East Side ☎ 604/879–8595) stocks one-of-a-kind creations from local designers that resemble fabulously funky outfits your best friend the fasionista might whip up.

VINTAGE   Not much bigger than a walk-in closet, **Arezzo Consignment** (✉ 127–1208
CLOTHING   Homer St., Yaletown ☎ 604/689–2830) sells dressy women's wear; you might find beaded sweaters or strappy black dresses at far below normal Yaletown prices. **Turnabout** (✉ 3121 Granville St., South Granville ☎ 604/732–8115 ✉ 3060 W. Broadway, Kitsilano ☎ 604/731–7762) is a long-established vintage clothing store. The Granville Street location sells upscale women's wear; the Broadway branch sells more casual clothing, as well as clothes for men.

Food

FOOD MARKETS   Tourists and locals alike throng the **Granville Island Public Market**
Fodor's Choice   (✉ 1689 Johnston St., Granville Island ☎ 604/666–5784) in search of
★ fresh produce, meats, baked goods, and prepared foods. Check out **Oyama Sausage Co.** for fantastic pâtés, charcuterie, and fresh sausages. At the **Salmon Shop** (☎ 604/669–3474), you can pick up fresh or smoked salmon wrapped for travel. Stop into **South China Seas Trading Co.** (☎ 604/681–5402) for all types of Asian ingredients, as well as cookbooks. At **Lonsdale Quay** (✉ 123 Carrie Cates Ct., North Vancouver ☎ 604/985–6261), an indoor marketplace, vendors sell prepared foods, seafood, and fresh produce. You can picnic out on the terrace to enjoy the views of the downtown skyline. It's a short ride on the Seabus from downtown.

FOOD SHOPS
★

If you love cheese, don't miss **Les Amis du Fromage** (✉ 1752 W. 2nd Ave., Kitsilano ☎ 604/732–4218), which sells a mind-boggling array of cheeses from B.C., other provinces, France, and elsewhere. The extremely knowledgeable mother-and-daughter owners, Alice and Allison Spurrell, and their staff encourage you to taste before you buy. Although the selection of Italian cheeses, pastas, vinegars, and oils lures foodies to **La Grotta Del Formaggio** (✉ 1791 Commercial Dr., East Side ☎ 604/255–3911), an Italian-style deli and market, the real stars here are the made-to-order Italian sandwiches.

To pick up fixings for an elegant picnic or to find a gift for a foodie friend, stop into **Meinhardt Fine Foods** (✉ 3002 Granville St., South Granville ☎ 604/732–4405). The same owners run **Picnic** (✉ 3010 Granville St., South Granville ☎ 604/732–4405) next door, which sells sandwiches, wraps, and pastries to eat in or take out. **T&T Supermarket** (✉ 179 Keefer Pl., Chinatown ☎ 604/899–8836 ✉ 2800 E. 1st Ave., at Renfrew, East Side ☎ 604/254–9668 ✉ Metrotown Centre, Burnaby ☎ 604/436–4881 ✉ 8181 Cambie Rd., President Plaza, Richmond ☎ 604/279–1818), a minichain of maxi-size Asian supermarkets, sells exotic produce, Chinese baked goods, and prepared foods; you can assemble an inexpensive lunch-to-go from the hot food counter.

PASTRY &
CHOCOLATE
SHOPS

Looking for a present for a chocolate lover? Check out the chocolates in First Nations designs at **Chocolate Arts** (✉ 2037 W. 4th Ave., Kitsilano ☎ 604/739–0475 or 877/739–0475). At **Ganache Patisserie** (✉ 1262 Homer St., Yaletown ☎ 604/899–1098), chef Peter Fong creates decadently elegant desserts. A full cake—maybe chocolate banana cake or vanilla-chèvre cheesecake—would make a welcome gift; a slice would perk up your shopping day.

Gifts

Museum and gallery gift shops are among the best places to buy high-quality souvenirs—West Coast native art, books, music, jewelry, and other items. The **Clamshell Gift Shop** (✉ Vancouver Aquarium Marine Science Centre, Stanley Park ☎ 604/659–3413), in Stanley Park, has souvenir clothing and aquatic-theme toys and gifts. The **Gallery Store** (✉ 750 Hornby St., Downtown ☎ 604/662–4706), in the Vancouver Art Gallery, has a good selection of art books and locally designed jewelry. The **Museum of Anthropology Gift Shop** (✉ 6393 N.W. Marine Dr., University of British Columbia Campus, Point Grey ☎ 604/822–5087) has an excellent selection of Northwest Coast jewelry, carvings, and prints, as well as books on First Nations history and culture.

Chachkas (✉ 1075 Robson St., West End ☎ 604/688–6417) sells design-conscious jewelry, leather goods, housewares, and gifts; look for the vegan-friendly handbags by Montréal designers Matt & Nat. **Hill's Native Art** (✉ 165 Water St., Gastown ☎ 604/685–4249) has Vancouver's largest selection of First Nations art.

Lattimer Gallery (✉ 1590 W. 2nd Ave., False Creek ☎ 604/732–4556), near Granville Island, is full of native arts and crafts in all price ranges. **Roost Homeware** (✉ 1192 Hamilton St., Yaletown ☎ 604/708–0084) sells colorful resinware bowls, vases, and platters from Australia's Dinosaur

Designs, plus bath "bonbons," funky pocketbooks, and other contemporary gift items. **Salmon Village** (✉ 779 Thurlow St., West End ☎ 604/685–3378), just off Robson Street, has all manner of travel-ready Canadian delicacies, from maple syrup to salmon. One of Vancouver's most extensive, but least known, native-art collections is hidden in the back room at the **Three Vets** (✉ 2200 Yukon St., Fairview ☎ 604/872–5475), a camping-equipment store. Ask any staff member to show you. The **Wickaninnish Gallery** (✉ 14–1666 Johnston St., Net Loft, Granville Island ☎ 604/681–1057) sells prints, jewelry, T-shirts, and other items with designs by First Nations artists.

Jewelry

Vancouver's leading jewelry shops are clustered along Hastings Street. **Birks** (✉ 698 W. Hastings St., Downtown ☎ 604/669–3333) takes up the main floor and mezzanine of a neoclassical building that was the former headquarters of the Canadian Imperial Bank of Commerce. **Cartier Jewellers** (✉ 408 Howe St., Downtown ☎ 604/683–6878) is the Vancouver outlet of the famous jewelry chain. **Palladio** (✉ 855 W. Hastings St., Downtown ☎ 604/685–3885) carries high-fashion jewelry in gold and platinum. In Yaletown, **Posh** (✉ 1059 Mainland St., Yaletown ☎ 604/669–6167) sells spangly, vintage-inspired jewelry by B.C. designers.

Kitchenware

At long-standing local kitchenware shop **Ming Wo** (✉ 23 E. Pender St., Chinatown ☎ 604/683–7268 ✉ 2170 W. 4th Ave., Kitsilano ☎ 604/737–2624), dim-sum steamers and maple leaf–shape cookie cutters share shelf space with dishes, espresso machines, and sushi sets. There's an especially good selection of Asian cooking implements.

Outdoor Equipment

Outdoor-oriented Vancouver is a great place to pick up camping and hiking gear. There's a cluster of outdoor equipment shops on West Broadway between Yukon and Manitoba Streets.

Climate (✉ 223 W. Broadway, Fairview ☎ 604/216–8768) sells high-quality technical clothing for skiing, hiking, and other sports. **Coast Mountain Sports** (✉ 777 Dunsmuir St., Pacific Centre Mall, Downtown ☎ 604/687–7668 ✉ 2201 W. 4th Ave., Kitsilano ☎ 604/731–6181 ✉ Metrotown Centre, Burnaby ☎ 604/434–9397) has high-performance (and high-fashion) gear. The massive **Mountain Equipment Co-op** (✉ 130 W. Broadway, Fairview ☎ 604/872–7858) is a local institution with a good selection of high-performance and mid-price clothing and equipment. A onetime C$5 membership is required. Vancouver-based **Taiga** (✉ 301 W. Broadway, Fairview ☎ 604/875–8388) sells popular waterproof cycling gear, as well as other outdoor clothing, sleeping bags, and tents. **Three Vets** (✉ 2200 Yukon St., Fairview ☎ 604/872–5475), near Cambie Street and Broadway, is an army-surplus-style store with budget-price family camping equipment. They also have a native art collection worth seeing.

Shoes

Fashionable footwear emporium **Gravity Pope** (✉ 2205 W. 4th Ave., Kitsilano ☎ 604/731–7673) sells Camper, Puma, Kenneth Cole, and other international brands for men and women. From traditional leather sandals to fanciful purple pumps, Italian shoes are the specialty at family-run **Kalena's** (✉ 1526 Commercial Dr., East Side).

VANCOUVER A TO Z

To research prices, get advice from other travelers, and book travel arrangements, visit www.fodors.com.

AIR TRAVEL TO & FROM VANCOUVER

Air Canada, Air Canada Jazz, and WestJet Airlines serve destinations around Western Canada. West Coast Air and Harbour Air Seaplanes operate 35-minute harbor-to-harbor service (downtown Vancouver to downtown Victoria) several times a day. Planes leave from near the Pan Pacific Hotel at 300–999 Canada Place. West Coast Air also flies from Vancouver International Airport to downtown Victoria. Helijet International has helicopter service from downtown Vancouver and the Vancouver airport to Victoria. The heliport is near Vancouver's Pan Pacific Hotel.

🛫 Airlines & Contacts **Air Canada** ☎ 888/247-2262 ⊕ www.aircanada.ca. **Air Canada Jazz** ☎ 888/247-2262 ⊕ www.flyjazz.ca. **Harbour Air** ☎ 604/274-1277 or 800/665-0212 ⊕ www.harbour-air.com. **Helijet International** ☎ 800/665-4354 or 250/382-6222 ⊕ www.helijet.com. **West Coast Air** ☎ 604/606-6888 or 800/347-2222 ⊕ www.westcoastair.com. **WestJet Airlines** ☎ 800/538-5696 ⊕ www.westjet.com.

AIRPORTS & TRANSFERS

Vancouver International Airport is on Sea Island, about 23 km (14 mi) south of downtown off Highway 99. An airport-improvement fee is assessed on all flight departures: C$5 for flights within British Columbia or the Yukon; C$15 for all other flights. Major credit cards and Canadian and United States currencies are accepted. Alaska, American, British Airways, Continental, Northwest, Qantas, and United serve the airport. The two major domestic carriers are Air Canada and WestJet.

🛫 Airport Information **Vancouver International Airport** ✉ Grant McConachie Way, Richmond ☎ 604/207-7077 ⊕ www.yvr.ca.

AIRPORT TRANSFER   The drive from the airport to downtown takes 20 to 45 minutes, depending on the time of day. Airport hotels provide shuttle service to and from the airport. If you're driving, go over the Arthur Laing Bridge and north on Granville Street (also signposted as Highway 99). Signs direct you to Vancouver City Centre.

The Vancouver Airporter Service bus leaves the international- and domestic-arrivals levels of the terminal building approximately every half hour, stopping at major downtown hotels. The first bus arrives at the airport at 6:10 AM, and the service runs until 11:30 PM. The fare is C$12 one-way and C$18 round-trip.

Taxi stands are in front of the terminal building on domestic- and international-arrivals levels. The taxi fare to downtown is about C$25. Area cab companies include Black Top and Yellow.

Limousine service from LimoJet Gold costs about C$50 one-way.

To travel downtown by public transit, take any TransLink bus marked Airport Station; then transfer at Airport Station to a No. 98 Burrard Station bus. To return to the airport, take a No. 98 Richmond Centre bus and transfer at Airport Station.

🚹 Taxis & Shuttles **Black Top Cabs** ☎ 604/681-2181. **LimoJet Gold** ☎ 604/273-1331 or 800/278-8742 ⊕ www.limojetgold.com. **TransLink** ☎ 604/953-3333 ⊕ www.translink.bc.ca. **Vancouver Airporter Service** ☎ 604/946-8866 or 800/668-3141. **Yellow Cab** ☎ 604/681-1111.

BOAT & FERRY TRAVEL

BC Ferries operates two major ferry terminals outside Vancouver. From Tsawwassen to the south (an hour's drive from downtown), ferries sail to Swartz Bay near Victoria, to Nanaimo on Vancouver Island, and to the Gulf Islands (the small islands between the mainland and Vancouver Island). From Horseshoe Bay (45 minutes north of downtown), ferries sail to the Sunshine Coast and to Nanaimo on Vancouver Island. Vehicle reservations on Vancouver to Victoria and Nanaimo routes are optional and cost C$15 to C$17.50 in addition to the fare. There's no extra charge for reservations on Gulf Island routes.

HarbourLynx runs direct, high-speed, foot-passenger-only service between downtown Vancouver and downtown Nanaimo on Vancouver Island. The trip takes 80 minutes and costs C$25 plus tax each way.

The SeaBus is a 400-passenger commuter ferry that crosses Burrard Inlet from Waterfront Station downtown to the foot of Lonsdale Avenue in North Vancouver. Leaving every 15 to 30 minutes, the bus takes 13 minutes and costs the same as the TransLink bus. With a transfer, connection can be made to any TransLink bus or SkyTrain.

Aquabus Ferries connect several stations on False Creek, including Science World, Plaza of Nations, Granville Island, Stamp's Landing, Spyglass Place, Yaletown, and the Hornby Street dock. Some Aquabus ferries take bicycles, and the company also operates two historic wooden boats on some runs.

False Creek Ferries provides foot-passenger service between the Aquatic Centre on Beach Avenue, Granville Island, Science World, Stamp's Landing, and Vanier Park.

False Creek and Aquabus ferries are not part of the TransLink system, so bus transfers aren't accepted.

🚹 Boat & Ferry Information **Aquabus Ferries** ☎ 604/689-5858 ⊕ www.aquabus.bc.ca. **BC Ferries** ☎ 250/386-3431, 888/223-3779 in British Columbia, Alberta, and Washington State ⊕ www.bcferries.com. **False Creek Ferries** ☎ 604/684-7781 ⊕ www.granvilleislandferries.bc.ca. **HarbourLynx** ☎ 866/206-5969, 250/753-4443 in Nanaimo, 604/688-5465 in Vancouver ⊕ www.harbourlynx.com. **SeaBus** ☎ 604/953-3333 ⊕ www.translink.bc.ca.

BUS TRAVEL TO & FROM VANCOUVER

Pacific Coach Lines provides service from Vancouver to Victoria every two hours and hourly in July and August. Greyhound Lines serves most other towns in the province, including Whistler and Nanaimo on Van-

couver Island. Pacific Central Station is the depot for both bus companies. Quick Shuttle buses run service from downtown Vancouver and Vancouver Airport to Seattle (SeaTac) Airport and downtown Seattle. They leave five times a day in winter and up to eight times a day in summer. The downtown Vancouver depot is at the Holiday Inn, though the shuttle picks up at most downtown Vancouver hotels by prior arrangement.
🚌 **Greyhound Lines** ☎ 604/482–8747, 800/661–8747 in Canada, 800/231–2222 in U.S. ⊕ www.greyhound.ca. **Pacific Central Station** ✉ 1150 Station St., Downtown ☎ No phone. **Pacific Coach Lines** ☎ 604/662–8074 or 800/661–1725 ⊕ www.pacificcoach. com. **Quick Shuttle** ☎ 604/940–4428 or 800/665–2122 ⊕ www.quickcoach.com. **Quick Shuttle's Vancouver depot** ✉ 1110 Howe St., Downtown ☎ No phone.

BUS TRAVEL WITHIN VANCOUVER

TransLink buses provide regular service throughout Vancouver and its suburbs. Exact change is needed to ride TransLink buses: C$2.25 for regular adult fares within Vancouver or C$3.25–C$4.50 for weekday trips to the suburbs, including the SeaBus to the North Shore. Books of 10 tickets (FareSavers) are sold at convenience stores and newsstands; look for a blue-and-yellow FARE DEALER sign. Day passes, good for unlimited travel all day, cost C$8. They're available from fare dealers, the Tsawwassen ferry terminal, and at any SeaBus or SkyTrain station. Transfers (ask for one when you board) are valid for 90 minutes, allow travel in any direction, and are good on buses, SkyTrain, and SeaBus.
🚌 **TransLink** ☎ 604/953–3333 ⊕ www.translink.bc.ca.

CAR RENTAL

🚗 **Major Agencies Avis** ☎ 604/606–2847 or 800/331–1212. **Budget** ☎ 604/668–7000 or 800/268–8900. **Thrifty Car Rental** ☎ 604/606–1666 or 800/847–4389.

CAR TRAVEL

Interstate 5 in Washington State becomes Highway 99 at the U.S.–Canada border. Vancouver is a three-hour drive (226 km [140 mi]) from Seattle.

A car can be handy for touring areas outside the city center, but it isn't essential. On the compact downtown peninsula, however, it's generally easier to get around on foot or by public transport, especially in light of the congestion, limited parking, and many one-way streets.

EMERGENCY
SERVICES
The British Columbia Automobile Association provides 24-hour emergency road service for members of the American and the Canadian automobile associations.
🚗 **British Columbia Automobile Association** ☎ 604/293–2222 or 800/222–4357 ⊕ www.bcaa.com.

PARKING
Downtown Vancouver parking lots fill quickly. Two large underground pay parking garages that usually have space are the Library Square lot and the Pacific Centre lot. Parking fees run about C$3 an hour or C$7–C$14 a day. Don't leave anything in your car, even in the trunk; break-ins are quite common downtown (hotel parking tends to be more secure, though more expensive, than public lots). Parking outside the downtown core is an easier proposition.
🚗 **Library Square lot** ✉ 775 Hamilton St., off Robson St., Downtown ☎ 604/669–4183. **Pacific Centre lot** ✉ 700 block of Howe St., east side, Downtown ☎ 604/684–9715.

TRAFFIC It's best to avoid border crossings during peak times such as holidays and weekends. Highway 1, the Trans-Canada Highway, enters Vancouver from the east. To avoid traffic, arrive after rush hour (9 AM).

Vancouver's rush-hour traffic, about 7–9 weekday mornings and starting at 3 PM weekday afternoons, can be horrendous. The worst bottlenecks outside the city center are the North Shore bridges (especially the Lions Gate Bridge), the George Massey Tunnel on Highway 99 south of Vancouver, and Highway 1 through Coquitlam and Surrey.

Right turns are allowed at most red lights after you've come to a full stop.

EMERGENCIES

🔢 Emergency Services **Ambulance, fire, police** ☎ 911.
🔢 Hospitals **Ultima Medicentre** ✉ Bentall Centre, plaza level, 1055 Dunsmuir St., Downtown ☎ 604/683-8138, a drop-in clinic in Bentall Centre, is open weekdays 8 AM–4:30 PM. The emergency ward at **St. Paul's Hospital** ✉ 1081 Burrard St., Downtown ☎ 604/682-2344 is open 24 hours.
🔢 24-Hour Pharmacy **Shopper's Drug Mart** ✉ 1125 Davie St., West End ☎ 604/669-2424.

LODGING

Hello BC, operated by the provincial Ministry of Tourism, can book accommodations anywhere in British Columbia.
🔢 Reservation Services **Hello BC** ☎ 800/435-5622 ⊕ www.hellobc.com.

MAIL & INTERNET

There are several postal outlets in downtown Vancouver. The Bentall Centre outlet is open weekdays 8–5. There are also postal outlets in many stores, particularly Shopper's Drug Mart and Pharmasave branches, throughout the city. These outlets usually keep the same hours as the store they're in. Internet access is available free at the central branch of the Vancouver Public Library. Internet cafés can be found throughout the city; they charge about C$3 per half hour.
🔢 Post Office **Canada Post** ✉ Bentall Centre, 595 Burrard St., Downtown ☎ 800/267-1177 ⊕ www.canadapost.ca.
🔢 Public Library **Vancouver Public Library** ✉ 350 W. Georgia St., Downtown ☎ 604/331-3600.

RAPID-TRANSIT TRAVEL

A rapid-transit system called SkyTrain travels underground downtown and is elevated for the rest of its route to Coquitlam and Surrey. The system has two lines: the Expo Line and the Millennium Line. These lines stop at the same stations between downtown and Commercial Drive, so unless you're traveling east of Commercial Drive, it doesn't matter which line you use. Trains leave about every two to five minutes. Tickets, sold at each station from machines (correct change is not necessary), must be carried with you as proof of payment. You may use transfers from SkyTrain to SeaBus and TransLink buses and vice versa. SkyTrain is convenient for transit between downtown, B.C. Place Stadium, Pacific Central Station, and Science World.
🔢 **SkyTrain** ☎ 604/953-3333 ⊕ www.translink.bc.ca.

TAXIS

It's difficult to hail a cab in Vancouver. Unless you're near a hotel, you'll have better luck calling a taxi service. Try Black Top or Yellow.

🔳 Taxi Companies **Black Top Cabs** ☎ 604/681-2181. **Yellow Cab** ☎ 604/681-1111.

TOURS

Tour prices fluctuate, so inquire about rates when booking.

AIRPLANE TOURS Baxter Aviation conducts tours to the mountains, glaciers, and islands around the city from C$79 per person based on four people or more per plane. You can see Vancouver from the air for about C$99 for 20 minutes with Harbour Air Seaplanes.

🔳 Fees & Schedules **Baxter Aviation** ☎ 604/683-6525 or 800/661-5599 ⊕ www. baxterair.com. **Harbour Air Seaplanes** ☎ 604/233-3505 or 800/665-0212 ⊕ www. harbour-air.com.

BOAT TOURS Aquabus Ferries operates tours of False Creek on small covered boats and vintage wooden ferries. Twenty-five-minute tours cost C$6 and run year-round; 45-minute minicruises are offered May through October and cost C$9. The tours leave every 15 minutes from the Aquabus dock on Granville Island.

False Creek Ferries has a 40-minute tour for C$10. It leaves from Granville Island daily, every half hour. A 25-minute tour for C$6 runs weekends and holidays only. It leaves every 15 minutes from Granville Island.

Harbour Cruises, at the north foot of Denman Street on Coal Harbour, operates a 1¼-hour narrated tour of Burrard Inlet on a paddlewheeler. Tours are given from April through October and cost less than C$20. Harbour Cruises also offers sunset dinner cruises, four-hour lunch cruises up scenic Indian Arm, and four-hour brunch tours into Howe Sound.

Paddlewheeler Riverboat Tours, at the New Westminster Quay, can take you out on the Fraser River in an 1800s-style paddle wheeler. Tours run year-round, and include a variety of sightseeing and evening entertainment options, including cruises to historic Fort Langley.

🔳 Fees & Schedules **Aquabus Ferries** ☎ 604/689-5858 ⊕ www.aquabus.bc.ca. **False Creek Ferries** ☎ 604/684-7781 ⊕ www.granvilleislandferries.bc.ca. **Harbour Cruises** ✉ 1 North Foot of Denman St., at W. Georgia St., West End ☎ 604/688-7246 or 800/663-1500 ⊕ www.boatcruises.com. **Paddlewheeler Riverboat Tours** ✉ Unit 139, 810 Quayside Dr., New Westminster ☎ 604/525-4465 or 877/825-1302 ⊕ www. vancouverpaddlewheeler.com.

HELICOPTER
TOURS Tour Vancouver, the harbor, or the mountains of the North Shore by helicopter for C$140 to C$165 per person (minimum of four people). Most tours leave from the Harbour Heliport next to the Pan Pacific Hotel downtown. Tours are also available from the top of Grouse Mountain.

🔳 Fees & Schedules **Helijet Charters** ✉ 455 Waterfront Rd., Downtown ☎ 604/270-1484 or 800/987-4354 ⊕ www.helijet.com.

ORIENTATION
TOURS Gray Line conducts a 3½-hour Deluxe Grand City bus tour year-round. The tour picks up at all major downtown hotels and includes Stanley Park, Chinatown, Gastown, English Bay, and Granville Island. The fee is about C$55. From May through September, Gray Line also has a nar-

rated city tour with 21 stops around downtown, Stanley Park, and Granville Island aboard double-decker buses; passengers can get on and off as they choose and can travel free the next day. Adult fare is about C$30.

The one-hour Stanley Park Horse Drawn Tours operate March 1 to the end of October and cost C$22.42 per person. The tours leave every 20 to 30 minutes from the information booth on Stanley Park Drive. The tours include transport from downtown to Stanley Park. The Vancouver Trolley Company runs trolley-style buses through Vancouver on a two-hour narrated tour of Stanley Park, Gastown, English Bay, Granville Island, and Chinatown, among other sights. A day pass allows you to complete one full circuit, getting off and on as often as you like. Start the trip at any of the 23 stops and buy a ticket (C$30) on board. The four-hour City Highlights tour run by West Coast City and Nature Sightseeing is about C$54. A longer tour for C$65 includes a visit to the Capilano Suspension Bridge. Pickup is available from all major hotels downtown.

North Shore tours usually include a gondola ride up Grouse Mountain, a walk across the Capilano Suspension Bridge, a stop at a salmon hatchery, a visit to the Lonsdale Quay Market, and a ride back to town on the SeaBus. North Shore tours are offered early March through late October by Landsea Tours and mid-April through October by West Coast City and Nature Sightseeing. The five hour tours are about C$89.

🖪 Fees & Schedules **Gray Line** ☎ 604/879-3363 or 800/440-3885 ⊕ www.grayline. ca. **Landsea Tours** ☎ 604/255-7272 or 877/669-2277 ⊕ www.vancouvertours.com. **Stanley Park Horse-Drawn Tours** ☎ 604/681-5115 ⊕ www.stanleypark.com. **Vancouver Trolley Company** ☎ 604/801-5515 or 888/451-5581 ⊕ www.vancouvertrolley.com. **West Coast City and Nature Sightseeing** ☎ 604/451-1600 or 877/451-1777 ⊕ www. vancouversightseeing.com.

PRIVATE GUIDES   Early Motion Tours picks you up at your hotel for a spin through Vancouver in a 1930 Model-A Ford convertible. Vancouver All-Terrain Adventures offers customized city tours in a luxury four-wheel-drive Suburban at C$75 an hour for up to seven passengers. Group and individual tours in eight European languages are available from VIP Tourguide Services.

🖪 Fees & Schedules **Early Motion Tours** ☎ 604/687-5088. **Vancouver All Terrain Adventures** ☎ 604/984-2374 or 888/754-5601 ⊕ www.all-terrain.com. **VIP Tourguide Services** ☎ 604/214-4677 ⊕ www3.telus.net/tourguides.

SPECIAL-   If Vancouver looks familiar, chances are you've already seen it on screen,
INTEREST TOURS   posing as an American city in any of the hundreds of U.S. movies and TV shows filmed here. Vancouver Movie Tours will take you behind the scenes to locations made famous in film and video, including the apartment used by Agent Scully in *The X-Files*. Three-hour tours run daily, year-round, and cost C$75. A tour of Scully's apartment costs C$29.

🖪 Fees & Schedules **Vancouver Movie Tours** ☎ 604/609-2770 or 888/250-7211 ⊕ www.vanmovietours.com.

WALKING TOURS   Students from the Architectural Institute of British Columbia lead 90-minute walking tours of the city's top heritage sites Tuesday to Saturday, mid-June through August. Tours are C$5 per person and meet at 1 PM at various locations. Guides from the Chinese Cultural Centre offer 90-minute walking tours of Chinatown's heritage buildings, clan associations, shops, temples, and other attractions, many of which are not normally open to the public. Tours cost C$10 and run daily at 10 AM and 2 PM between June and September. Reservations are essential. The Gastown Business Improvement Society sponsors free 90-minute historical and architectural walking tours daily June through August. Meet the guide at 2 PM at the statue of "Gassy" Jack in Maple Tree Square. Guides with Walkabout Historic Vancouver dress in 19th-century costume for their two-hour historical walking tours around downtown and Gastown or Granville Island. Tours run March through October and cost C$25.

🖪 Fees & Schedules **Architectural Institute of British Columbia** ☎ 604/683-8588 or 800/667-0753 in BC ⊕ www.aibc.ca. **Chinese Cultural Centre** ⊠ 50 E. Pender St. ☎ 604/658-8883 ⊕ www.vancouver-chinatown.com

Gastown Business Improvement Society ☎ 604/683-5650 ⊕ www.gastown.org. **Walkabout Historic Vancouver** ☎ 604/720-0006 ⊕ www.walkabouthistoricvancouver.com.

TRAIN TRAVEL

The Pacific Central Station, at Main Street and Terminal Avenue, near the Main Street SkyTrain station, is the hub for rail service. Amtrak has daily service between Seattle and Vancouver. VIA Rail provides transcontinental service through Jasper to Toronto three times a week.

The volunteer-run Downtown Historic Railway operates two restored electric trams (built in 1905 and 1913) along a 5-km (3-mi) track between Science World and Granville Island. The trams, which also stop at 1st Avenue and Ontario Street and at Leg-in-Boot Square, near 6th Avenue and Moberly Street, operate every half hour between 12:30 PM and 5 PM weekends and holidays from mid-May to mid-October. The adult fare is C$2.

🖪 **Amtrak** ☎ 800/872-7245 ⊕ www.amtrak.com. **Downtown Historic Railway** ☎ 604/665-3903 ⊕ www.trams.bc.ca. **Pacific Central Station** ⊠ 1150 Station St., Downtown ☎ No phone. **VIA Rail** ☎ 888/842-7245 ⊕ www.viarail.ca.

VISITOR INFORMATION

Easily spotted on Vancouver streets in their red uniforms, Downtown Ambassadors, sponsored by the Downtown Vancouver Business Improvement Association, provide information, directions, safe walks, and emergency assistance to anyone visiting Vancouver's central business district. On Granville Island, roving ambassadors, wearing red hats, answer questions about the island.

🖪 **Downtown Ambassadors** ☎ 604/689-4357 ⊕ www.downtownvancouver.net. **Granville Island Information Services** ☎ 604/666-5784 ⊕ www.granvilleisland.com. **Hello BC** ☎ 800/435-5622 ⊕ www.hellobc.com. **Vancouver Tourist Info Centre** ⊠ 200 Burrard St., Downtown ☎ 604/683-2000 ⊕ www.tourismvancouver.com.

Victoria & Vancouver Island

WORD OF MOUTH

"Number one on my must-see list is Butchart Gardens—absolutely incredible! Plan to stay at least half a day and linger into the evening, when the gardens are illuminated. There are daily concerts, as well as fireworks displays on Saturday nights in the summer. You can also eat lunch, dinner, or have afternoon tea there."

—laurafromtexas

"The Tofino area is a must destination for nature lovers . . . with old-growth rain forests and miles of deserted beach (not for swimming—cold and often high surf—but great for walking and exploring)."

—mtjt

By Sue
Kernaghan

BEACHES, WILDERNESS PARKS, mountains, deep temperate rain forests, and a wealth of wildlife have long drawn adventurous visitors to the West Coast's largest island. These days, however, a slew of excellent restaurants, country inns, spas, and ecologically sensitive resorts means you can enjoy all that beauty in comfort—though roughing it is still an option.

Despite its growing popularity, the island rarely feels crowded. Fewer than a million people live here, and virtually all of them cluster on the island's sheltered eastern side, between Victoria and Campbell River; half live in Victoria itself. The island's west coast, facing the open ocean, is wild and often inhospitable, with few roads and only a handful of small settlements. Nevertheless, the old-growth forests, magnificent stretch of beach, and challenging trails of the Pacific Rim National Park Reserve, as well as the chance to see whales offshore, are major draws for campers, hikers, kayakers, and even surfers.

The cultural heritage of the Pacific Coast First Nations peoples—the Kwakiutl, Nootka, and others, who occupied the land for more than 12,000 years before the first Europeans arrived en masse in the late 19th century—is as rich as Vancouver Island's natural bounty. Their art and culture are on display throughout the island, in totems and petroglyphs, in city art galleries, and in the striking collections at the Royal British Columbia Museum in Victoria, the Quw'utsun' Cultural and Conference Centre in Duncan, and the U'mista Cultural Centre in Alert Bay.

Exploring Vancouver Island

Vancouver Island, touched by Pacific currents, has the mildest climate in Canada. Temperatures are usually above 32°F in winter and below 80°F in summer, although winter brings frequent rains (especially on the west coast). When traveling by car, keep in mind that Vancouver Island's west coast, beyond Port Renfrew, Ucluelet, and Tofino, has very few roads and is accessible mainly by sea or air.

About the Restaurants

"Fresh, local, organic" has become a mantra for many Vancouver Island chefs: some have even joined forces with local farmers to ensure supply of the freshest items. Wild salmon, locally made cheeses, Pacific oysters, forest-foraged mushrooms, organic vegetables in season, local microbrews, and even wines from the island's few family-run wineries can all be sampled here. Restaurants in the region are generally casual. Smoking is banned in all public places, including restaurants and bars, in Greater Victoria, and on the Southern Gulf Islands.

About the Hotels

Accommodations on Vancouver Island range from bed-and-breakfasts and country inns to rustic cabins to deluxe ecotourism lodges. Victoria in particular has a great selection of English-style B&Bs. Most small inns and B&Bs ban smoking indoors, and virtually all hotels in the area have no-smoking rooms. Most accommodations lack air-conditioning, as it rarely gets hot enough to need it. Advance reservations are always a good idea, especially in July and August, and in some of the more isolated

Numbers in the text correspond to numbers in the margin and on the Vancouver Island map.

If you have
1 to 3
days

For a short trip, 🖾 **Victoria ❶** –⓰ is a fine place to begin. There's plenty to explore, from the flower-fringed Inner Harbour and the museums and attractions nearby to Market Square and the shops and restaurants of Chinatown. World-famous Butchart Gardens on the **Saanich Peninsula ⓲** is only a half hour away by car, and you might take a full day to explore the beautiful grounds. On Day 3, head west to 🖾 **Sooke ⓱** or north, over the scenic Malahat region, to **Duncan ⓳**, **Chemainus ⓴**, or **Nanaimo ㉑**, which has ferry service to the mainland.

If you have
4 to 6
days

A brief stay in 🖾 **Victoria ❶** –⓰ can be followed by a tour of Vancouver Island. Follow the itinerary above, heading to **Sooke ⓱** on Day 3. Day 4 allows time to see the Quw'utsun' Cultural and Conference Centre in **Duncan ⓳** and the murals and restored Victorian buildings of 🖾 **Chemainus ⓴**. On Day 5, one alternative is to trek across the island to the scenic west coast to visit 🖾 **Ucluelet ㉔** and 🖾 **Tofino ㉕** (pick one for your overnight) and spend some time whale-watching or hiking around **Pacific Rim National Park Reserve ㉖**. Another choice is to continue up the east coast to visit **Strathcona Provincial Park ㉜** or to do some salmon fishing from 🖾 **Campbell River ㉚**. Spend Day 6 retracing your steps to Victoria or Nanaimo, for ferry service to the mainland.

If you have
7 to 10
days

A longer trip allows more time to explore the area in and around the **Pacific Rim National Park Reserve ㉖** or to visit **Bamfield ㉓** or the **Broken Group Islands** on the *Lady Rose*, a coastal freighter that sails from **Port Alberni ㉒**. If you're exploring the east coast, you could visit one of the rustic islands; **Quadra ㉛**, **Denman**, and **Hornby** islands as well as the Southern Gulf Islands of Salt Spring, Mayne, and Galiano (⇨ Chapter 4) are all easily reached by ferry. Otherwise, head north toward **Port Hardy ㉞** to see the resident whale pods near Telegraph Cove. From Port Hardy you can continue a tour of British Columbia on an Inside Passage cruise.

2

towns. Room rates are also levied a Goods & Services Tax (GST) of 7% plus B.C.-hotel tax of 8%. You can pick up a GST form at customs when you leave Canada to apply for a rebate on the GST portion.

WHAT IT COSTS in Canadian dollars					
	$$$$	**$$$**	**$$**	**$**	**¢**
RESTAURANTS	over $30	$21–$30	$13–$20	$8–$12	under $8
HOTELS	over $250	$176–$250	$126–$175	$75–$125	under $75

Restaurant prices are for a main course at dinner, not including 7% GST and 10% liquor tax. Hotel prices are for two people in a standard double room in high season, excluding 10% provincial accommodation tax, service charge, and 7% GST.

Timing

Though summer is the most popular time to visit, in winter the island has skiing at Mt. Washington, near Courtenay, and, off the west coast, dramatic storms that can be fun to watch from a cozy inn. March and April are the best time to see migrating whales off the west coast.

VICTORIA

Originally Fort Victoria, Victoria was the first European settlement on Vancouver Island. It was chosen to be the westernmost trading outpost of the British-owned Hudson's Bay Company in 1843 and became the capital of British Columbia in 1868. Victoria has since evolved into a walkable, livable seaside town of gardens, waterfront pathways, and restored 19th-century architecture. Often described as the country's most British city, Victoria is these days—except for the odd red phone booth, good beer, and well-mannered drivers—working to change that image, preferring to celebrate its combined native, Asian, and European heritage.

The city is 71 km (44 mi), or 1½ hours by ferry plus 1½ hours by car, south of Vancouver, or a 2½-hour ferry ride from Seattle.

Downtown Victoria

Numbers in the text correspond to numbers in the margin and on the Downtown Victoria map.

Begin on the waterfront at the **Visitor Information Centre** ☞, at 812 Wharf Street. Across the way on Government Street is the **Fairmont Empress ❶**, a majestic hotel that opened in 1908 (the public entrance is at the south end, off Belleville Street). A short walk around the harbor along the Inner Harbour Walk (take any of the staircases from Government Street down to the water level) takes you to the **Royal London Wax Museum ❷**. Floating in the harbor beside the wax museum are the **Pacific Undersea Gardens ❸**, an underwater exhibit of local sea life. Across Belleville Street is the **Parliament Buildings ❹** complex, seat of the provincial government. Cross Government Street to reach the **Royal British Columbia Museum ❺**, one of Canada's most impressive museums. Beside the museum and bordering Douglas Street are the totem poles and ceremonial longhouse of Thunderbird Park; Helmcken House, the oldest house in Victoria; and the tiny 19th-century St. Ann's Schoolhouse. A walk south on Douglas Street leads to the beautiful **Beacon Hill Park ❻**. A few blocks west of the park on Government Street is **Emily Carr House ❼**, the birthplace of one of British Columbia's best-known artists. Walk back to Beacon Hill Park, and then proceed north on Douglas Street until you reach Blanshard Street, on your right. Take Blanshard, where just past Academy Close (on the right) you can see the entrance to **St. Ann's Academy ❽**, a former convent school with parklike grounds. (There's also a footpath to the academy from Southgate Street.) From St. Ann's, follow Belleville Street west. The next stop, at the corner of Douglas and Belleville streets, is Victoria's newest attraction, **The BC Experience ❾**, where you can see a variety of high-tech, interactive exhibits about the province of B.C.

2

Canoeing & Kayaking

The island-dotted Strait of Georgia, on the east side of Vancouver Island, provides fairly protected seagoing, stunning scenery, and plenty of opportunities to spot orcas, eagles, and other local fauna. The Broken Group Islands, off the island's west coast, draw kayakers from around the world to their protected, wildlife-rich waters. The mountainous Strathcona Provincial Park offers scenic lake and river paddling.

Fishing

Miles of coastline and numerous lakes, rivers, and streams lure anglers to Vancouver Island. Though salmon doesn't run as thickly as it once did, both coasts of the island still have excellent salmon fishing, and many operators run fishing charters.

Hiking

The West Coast Trail, one of the world's most famous trails, runs along the western side of Vancouver Island. Other trails include the Juan de Fuca Marine Trail and those in Strathcona Provincial Park. But you can find fine hiking-trail networks in almost all of the island's many parks.

Whale-Watching

About 200 resident and nearly as many transient orcas, or killer whales, as well as humpback whales, minke whales, and other marine mammals travel the island's eastern coastal waters. These, and the gray whales that migrate along the west coast, are the primary focus of the many whale-watching boat tours leaving Victoria, Campbell River, Telegraph Cove, Ucluelet, Bamfield, and Tofino in spring and summer months. July, August, and September are the best months to see orcas; in March and April thousands of migrating gray whales pass close to the west coast of Vancouver Island on their way from Baja California to Alaska. Harbor seals, sea lions, porpoises, and marine-bird sightings are a safe bet anytime.

For a different kind of interaction, head two blocks north (uphill) on Douglas Street and turn left at Courtney Street. Half a block in on your left you'll find the **Victoria Bug Zoo** ⑩, a creepy-crawly attraction popular with children. From the Bug Zoo, continue west on Courtney Street to Government Street, Victoria's liveliest shopping street. Head north about three blocks to Government and View streets, where you can see the entrance to the cobblestone **Bastion Square** ⑪, the original site of Fort Victoria and the Hudson's Bay Company trading post, which now houses restaurants and offices. Just north of Government and View, on the right-hand side of Government Street, is the entrance to Trounce Alley, a pretty pedestrian-only shopping arcade.

At Bastion Square you can stop in the **Maritime Museum of British Columbia** ⑫ to learn about an important part of the province's history. North of Bastion Square a few blocks, on Store Street between Johnson Street and Pandora Avenue, is **Market Square** ⑬, one of the city's most picturesque shopping districts. Across Pandora Avenue is the entrance to the narrow, shop-lined Fan Tan Alley, which leads to Fisgard Street, the heart of **Chinatown** ⑭.

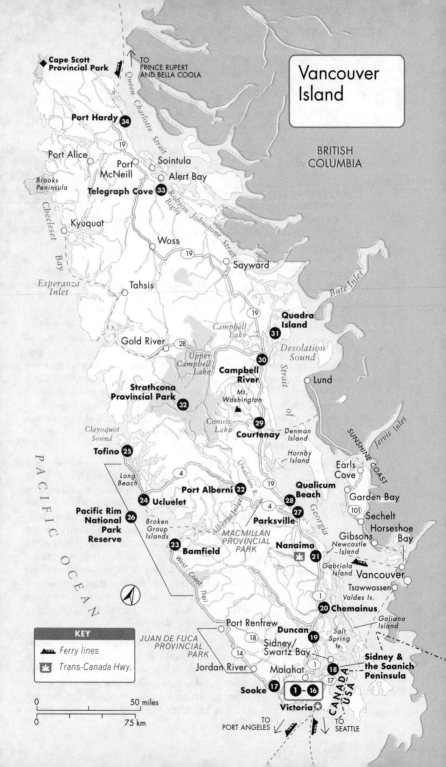

Head back south on Government Street until you hit Fort Street. From here, a 25-minute walk or a short drive east takes you to Joan Crescent and lavish **Craigdarroch Castle** ⓖ. Down the hill on Moss Street is the **Art Gallery of Greater Victoria** ⓰.

In summer, a ride on Victoria Harbour Ferries from the Inner Harbour takes you to Point Ellice House, a historic waterside home and garden.

TIMING Many of the attractions in downtown Victoria are within easy walking distance of one another. You can walk this tour in a day, but there's so much to see at the Royal British Columbia Museum, BC Experience, and the other museums that you could easily fill two days. This will also allow time for some shopping and visiting Craigdarroch Castle.

Sights to See

⓰ **Art Gallery of Greater Victoria.** Attached to an 1889 mansion, this modern building houses one of the largest collections of Chinese and Japanese artifacts in Canada. The Japanese garden between the buildings is home to the only authentic Shinto shrine in North America. The gallery, which is a few blocks west of Craigdarroch Castle, off Fort Street, displays a permanent exhibition of works by well-known Canadian artist Emily Carr and regularly changing exhibits of Asian and historical and contemporary Western art. The gallery also hosts major touring exhibitions. ✉ *1040 Moss St., Rockland* ☎ *250/384–4101* ⊕ *www.aggv. bc.ca* 🖃 *C$8* ○ *Mon.–Wed., Fri.–Sun. 10–5, Thurs. 10–9.*

⓫ **Bastion Square.** James Douglas, the former colonial governor for whom Douglas Street was named, chose this spot for the original Fort Victoria and Hudson's Bay Company trading post. Offices and restaurants occupy the old brick buildings and in summer the square comes alive with street performers and craft vendors. ✉ *Off Wharf St. at end of View St., Old Town.*

Ⓒ ⓨ **The BC Experience.** This new attraction, set, at this writing, to open in the spring of 2006, will occupy the former Crystal Garden Conservation Centre, a Victoria landmark that originally opened in 1925 as the largest saltwater swimming pool in the British Empire. Inside, hands-on displays about the different regions of B.C. will surround a massive three-dimensional map (the size of two football fields) of the province. Visitors can also explore the province's history, geography, and scenery via an H. G. Wells–style time machine, a high-definition movie screen, and other high-tech interactive displays. ✉ *713 Douglas St., Downtown* ☎ *No phone at press time.* ⊕ *www.bcexperience.info* 🖃 *C$12* ○ *May–Sept., daily 10–9; Oct.–Apr., daily 10–6.*

★ Ⓒ ⓺ **Beacon Hill Park.** The southern lawns and oceanside path of this 154-acre park have great views of the Olympic Mountains and the Strait of Juan de Fuca. Also here are ponds, jogging and walking paths, abundant flowers and gardens, a children's farmyard, a putting green, and a cricket pitch. The park is also home to Mile Zero of the Trans-Canada Highway and the world's largest freestanding totem pole. ✉ *East of Douglas St., south of Southgate St., Downtown* ☎ *250/361–0600 City of Victoria Parks Division, 250/381–2532 children's farmyard.*

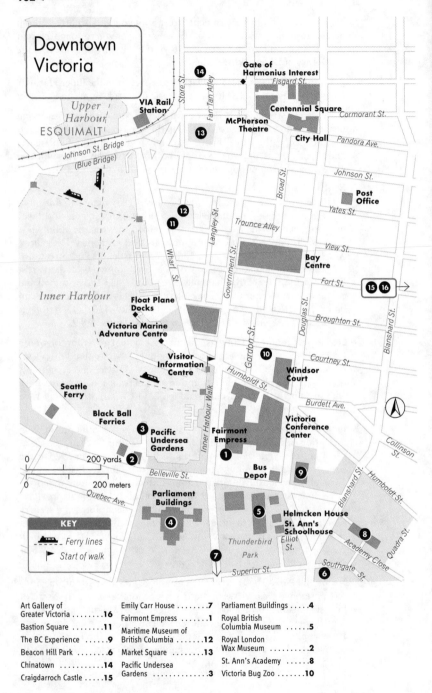

Downtown Victoria

Upper Harbour
ESQUIMALT

Johnson St. Bridge (Blue Bridge)

Inner Harbour

Store St.

VIA Rail Station

Fan Tan Alley

Gate of Harmonius Interest

Fisgard St.

Centennial Square

Cormorant St.

McPherson Theatre

City Hall

Pandora Ave.

Broad St.

Johnson St.

Post Office

Yates St.

Langley St.

Trounce Alley

View St.

Bay Centre

Wharf St.

Float Plane Docks

Victoria Marine Adventure Centre

Government St.

Fort St.

Gordon St.

Douglas St.

Broughton St.

Courtney St.

Windsor Court

Blanshard St.

Visitor Information Centre

Humboldt St.

Seattle Ferry

Black Ball Ferries

Inner Harbour Walk

Burdett Ave.

Victoria Conference Center

Collinson St.

Pacific Undersea Gardens

Fairmont Empress

Bus Depot

0   200 yards

0   200 meters

Belleville St.

Quebec Ave.

Helmcken House

St. Ann's Schoolhouse

Blanshard St.

Humboldt St.

KEY

🚢 Ferry lines
▶ Start of walk

Parliament Buildings

Thunderbird Park

Elliot St.

Academy Close

Quadra St.

Emily Carr House

Southgate St.

Superior St.

⑭ Chinatown. Chinese immigrants built much of the Canadian Pacific Railway in the 19th century, and their influence still marks the region. Victoria's Chinatown, founded in 1858, is the oldest and most intact such district in Canada. If you enter Chinatown from Government Street, you'll pass under the elaborate **Gate of Harmonious Interest,** made of Taiwanese ceramic tiles and decorative panels. Along Fisgard Street, merchants display paper lanterns, wicker baskets, and exotic produce. Mah-jongg, fan-tan, and dominoes were among the games of chance played on narrow **Fan Tan Alley.** Once the gambling and opium center of Chinatown, it's now lined with offbeat shops. Look for the alley on the south side of Fisgard Street between Nos. 545½ and 549½. ⊠ *Fisgard St. between Government and Store Sts., Chinatown.*

⑮ Craigdarroch Castle. This resplendent mansion was built as the home of one of British Columbia's wealthiest men, coal baron Robert Dunsmuir, who died in 1889, just a few months before the castle's completion. Converted into a museum depicting life in the late 1800s, the castle has ornate Victorian furnishings, stained-glass windows, carved woodwork (precut in Chicago for Dunsmuir and sent by rail), and a beautifully restored painted ceiling in the drawing room. A winding staircase climbs four floors to a ballroom and a tower overlooking Victoria. ⊠ *1050 Joan Crescent, Rockland* ☎ *250/592–5323* ⊕ *www.thecastle.ca* ☞ *C$10* ⊙ *Mid-June–Labor Day, daily 9–7; Labor Day–mid-June, daily 10–4:30.*

⑦ Emily Carr House. One of Canada's most celebrated artists and a respected writer, Emily Carr (1871–1945) was born and raised in this very proper wooden Victorian house before she abandoned her middle-class life to live in, and paint, the wilds of British Columbia. Carr's own descriptions, from her autobiography *Book of Small,* were used to restore the house. Displays of Carr's work alternate with shows by modern-day B.C. artists. ⊠ *207 Government St., James Bay* ☎ *250/383–5843* ⊕ *www.emilycarr.com* ☞ *C$5.35* ⊙ *May, June, and Sept., Tues.–Sat. 11–4; July and Aug., daily 11–4; Oct.–Apr. by arrangement or during special events.*

① Fairmont Empress. Opened in 1908 by the Canadian Pacific Railway, the Empress is one of the grand château-style hotels that grace many Canadian cities. Designed by Francis Rattenbury, who also designed the Parliament Buildings across the way, the Empress, with its solid Edwardian grandeur, has become a symbol of the city. The elements that made the hotel an attraction for travelers in the past—old-world architecture, ornate decor, and a commanding view of the Inner Harbour—are still here. The archives, a historical photo and cartoon display on the lower level, are open to the public. Nonguests can stop by the Empress for traditional afternoon tea (reservations are recommended, and the dress code calls for smart casual wear), meet for a curry under the tiger skin in the Bengal Room, enjoy a treatment at the hotel's Willow Stream spa, browse in the shops and galleries in the hotel's arcade, or sample the superb French-influenced cuisine in the Empress Room restaurant. ☾ **Miniature World** (☎ 250/385–9731), a display of doll-size dioramas, is on the Humboldt Street side of the complex; admission is C$9. ⊠ *721 Government St., entrance at Belleville and Government, Downtown*

☎ *250/384–8111, 250/389–2727 tea reservations* ⊕ *www.fairmont.com/ empress* ☜ *Free, afternoon tea C$55 July–Sept., C$30–C$40 Oct.–June.*

off the beaten path

FORT RODD HILL AND FISGARD LIGHTHOUSE NATIONAL HISTORIC SITES OF CANADA – This 1895 coast artillery fort and the oldest (and still functioning) lighthouse on Canada's west coast are about 15 km (9 mi) west of Victoria, off Highway 1A on the way to Sooke. ✉ *603 Fort Rodd Hill Rd., off Ocean Blvd., Colwood* ☎ *250/478– 5849* ⊕ *www.pc.gc.ca/fortroddhill* ☜ *C$4* ⊙ *Mar.–Oct., daily 10–5:30; Nov.–Feb., daily 9–4:30.*

HATLEY PARK NATIONAL HISTORIC SITE OF CANADA – Next door to Fort Rodd is Hatley Castle, the former estate of coal and railway baron James Dunsmuir and now part of the Royal Roads University campus. The 1908 castle is on 565 acres of beautifully landscaped grounds (including Italian, Japanese, and English rose gardens), which are open daily until dusk all year. Castle and garden tours are given daily year-round (call for times); a variety of workshops, from soap-making to treasure hunting are also offered. ✉ *2005 Sooke Rd., Colwood* ☎ *250/391–2666 or 866/241–0674* ⊕ *www.hatleypark.ca* ☜ *Garden only C$12; garden and castle tour C$16.*

☞ ⓬ **Maritime Museum of British Columbia.** The model ships, Royal Navy charts, photographs, uniforms, and ship bells at this museum, in Victoria's original courthouse, chronicle the province's seafaring history. Among the hand-built boats on display is the *Tilikum*, a dugout canoe that sailed from Victoria to England between 1901 and 1904. An 1899 hand-operated cage elevator, believed to be the oldest continuously operating lift in North America, ascends to the third floor, where the original 1888 vice-admiralty courtroom looks ready for a court-martial. ✉ *28 Bastion Sq., Old Town* ☎ *250/385–4222* ⊕ *www.mmbc.bc.ca* ☜ *C$8* ⊙ *Daily 9:30–4:30.*

⓭ **Market Square.** During the late 19th century, this three-level square, built like an old inn courtyard, provided everything a sailor, miner, or lumberjack could want. Restored to its original architectural, if not commercial character, it's a pedestrian-only, café- and boutique-lined hangout—now, as then, a great spot for people-watching. ✉ *560 Johnson St., Old Town* ☎ *250/386–2441.*

☞ ❸ **Pacific Undersea Gardens.** Wolf eels, red snapper, and the world's largest species of octopus are among the more than 5,000 varieties of local sea life at this kid-friendly attraction, sunk 15 feet beneath the waters of the Inner Harbour. Scuba divers run 20-minute shows several times a day. ✉ *490 Belleville St.* ☎ *250/382–5717* ⊕ *www.pacificunderseagardens. com* ☜ *C$8.50* ⊙ *Apr.–June, daily 9:30–6; July and Aug., daily 9–8:30; Sept.–Apr. daily 9:30–5.*

★ ❹ **Parliament Buildings.** These massive stone structures, designed by Francis Rattenbury and completed in 1898, dominate the Inner Harbour. Two statues flank the main entrance: one of Sir James Douglas, who chose the site where Victoria was built, and the other of Sir Matthew Baille

Begbie, the man in charge of law and order during the gold-rush era. Atop the central dome is a gilded statue of Captain George Vancouver, the first European to sail around Vancouver Island. A statue of Queen Victoria reigns over the front of the complex. More than 3,000 lights outline the buildings at night. The interior is lavishly done with stained-glass windows and murals depicting scenes from the province's history. When the legislature is in session, you can sit in the public gallery and watch British Columbia's democracy at work (custom has the opposing parties sitting 2½ sword lengths apart). Free, informative half-hour tours are obligatory on summer weekends (mid-May until Labor Day) and optional the rest of the time. ⊠ *501 Belleville St., Downtown* ☎ *250/387–3046* ⊕ *www.legis.gov.bc.ca* ⊠ *Free* ☉ *Mid-May–Labor Day, daily 9–5; Labor Day–mid-May, weekdays 9–5.*

off the beaten path

POINT ELLICE HOUSE – The O'Reilly family home, an 1860s Italianate villa overlooking the Upper Harbour, has been restored to its original splendor, with the largest collection of Victorian furnishings in western Canada. Tea and baked goods are served on the lawn. You can take an audio tour of the house, stroll in the gardens, or try your hand at croquet. Point Ellice House is a few minutes' drive north of downtown, but it's more fun to come by sea. (Victoria Harbour Ferries leave from a dock in front of the Fairmont Empress hotel.) ⊠ *2616 Pleasant St., Upper Harbour* ☎ *250/380–6506* ⊕ *www.heritage.gov.bc.ca* ⊠ *C$5, C$20 including tea* ☉ *May–Sept., daily 10–5; tea daily 11–4; some Christmas and Halloween programs.*

☾ ❺ **Royal British Columbia Museum.** This excellent museum, one of Victoria's leading attractions, traces several thousand years of British Columbian history. Exhibits include a genuine Kwakwaka'wakw big house (the builders retain rights to its ceremonial use) and an extensive collection of First Nations masks and other artifacts. The Living Land, Living Sea Gallery includes a climate-change exhibit, featuring thunder, lightning, and a massive Wooly Mammoth looming next to a wall of ice. In the History Gallery, a replica of Captain Vancouver's ship, the HMS *Discovery,* creaks convincingly, and a re-created frontier town comes to life with cobbled streets, silent movies, and the smells of home baking. Century Hall reviews British Columbia's 20th-century history, and an on-site IMAX theater shows *National Geographic* films on a six-story-high screen. Behind the museum, bordering Douglas Street, are three more interesting sites. **Thunderbird Park** is home to totem poles and Wawadit'la, the ceremonial house of Chief Nakapenkum (Mungo Martin). Next door is **Helmcken House** (⊠ 10 Elliot St., Downtown), one of B.C.'s oldest houses, erected in 1852 for pioneer doctor and statesman John Sebastian Helmcken. The house was not, at this writing, open to the public. Next to Helmcken House is **St. Ann's Schoolhouse,** one of British Columbia's oldest schools (you can view the interior through the door). ⊠ *675 Belleville St., Downtown* ☎ *250/356–7226 or 888/447-7977* ⊕ *www.royalbcmuseum.bc.ca* ⊠ *C$13.75, IMAX theater C$10.50, combination ticket C$21. Rates may be higher during special-exhibit periods* ☉ *Museum daily 9–5, theater daily 9–8; call for show times.*

Fodor'sChoice
★

2 Royal London Wax Museum. A collection of life-size wax figures resides in this elegant colonnaded building, once Victoria's steamship terminal. The 300-plus characters include members of the British royal family, famous Canadians, Hollywood stars, and some unfortunate souls in a Chamber of Horrors. ⊠ *470 Belleville St., Downtown* ☎ *250/388–4461* ⊕ *www.waxmuseum.bc.ca* ⊠ *C$10* ⊙ *May–Aug., daily 9–7:30; Sept.–Apr., daily 10–5.*

8 St. Ann's Academy. This former convent and school, founded in 1858, played a central role in British Columbia's pioneer life. The academy's little chapel—the first Roman Catholic cathedral in Victoria—has been restored to look just as it did in the 1920s. The 6-acre grounds, with their fruit trees and herb and flower gardens, are also being restored as historic landscapes. ⊠ *835 Humboldt St., Downtown* ☎ *250/953–8828* ⊕ *www. bcpcc.com/stanns* ⊠ *By donation* ⊙ *Gardens freely accessible. Chapel mid-May–mid-Oct., daily 10–4; mid-Oct.–mid-May, daily noon–4.*

10 Victoria Bug Zoo. Home to about 50 species of bugs, this offbeat, two-room minizoo houses the largest tropical insect collection in North America. You can even hold many of the varieties, which include walking sticks, scorpions, and centipedes. Staff members are on hand to dispense scientific information. ⊠ *631 Courtney St., Inner Harbour* ☎ *250/384–2847* ⊕ *www.bugzoo.bc.ca* ⊠ *C$7* ⊙ *July and Aug., daily 9:30–7:30; Sept.–June, daily 9:30–5:30.*

Visitor Information Centre. Get the lowdown on Victoria's attractions at this facility near the Inner Harbour. The staff can help with maps, theater and concert tickets, accommodation reservations, and outdoor-adventure day trips. ⊠ *812 Wharf St., Downtown* ☎ *250/953–2033* ⊕ *www.tourismvictoria.com* ⊙ *Mid-May–Labor Day, daily 8:30–6:30; Labor Day–mid-May, daily 9–5.*

Where to Eat

Cafés

¢–$ ✕ Willie's Bakery. Housed in a handsome Victorian building near Market Square, this bakery-café serves wholesome breakfasts, rich soups, delicious sandwiches made with house-baked bread, tasty baked treats, and house-made gelato. The brick patio with an outdoor fireplace and fountain is a great place to watch the world go by. ⊠ *537 Johnson St., Old Town* ☎ *250/381–8414* ⚠ *Reservations not accepted* ⊟ *MC, V* ⊙ *No dinner.*

Chinese

$–$$ ✕ Don Mee's. A large neon sign invites you inside this traditional Chinese restaurant, which has been in business since 1923. The entrées served in the expansive dining room include sweet-and-sour chicken, Peking duck, and ginger-fried beef. Dim sum is served at lunchtime. Reservations are not accepted for lunch. ⊠ *538 Fisgard St., Chinatown* ☎ *250/383–1032* ⊟ *AE, DC, MC, V.*

Contemporary

★ $$$$ ✕ Empress Room. Candlelight dances on tapestried walls beneath a carved mahogany ceiling, while a harpist plays at the Fairmont Empress hotel's flagship restaurant. The classically influenced Pacific Northwest menu, served as three-, four-, or five-course set menus, lists such imaginative locally inspired dishes as roasted loin of venison with spring vegetable ravioli, and rack of lamb with kalamata olive gnocchi. More than 800 labels make up the wine list. ☒ *Fairmont Empress, 721 Government St., Downtown* ☎ *250/389–2727* ☰ *AE, D, DC, MC, V* ☉ *Closed Jan. No lunch.*

★ **$$$–$$$$** ✕ **Camille's.** The menu at this long-established local favorite concentrates on fresh local products such as lamb, duck, and seafood; regional exotica, like game and ostrich, often appear, too. Highlights include lemon, ginger, and tiger-prawn bisque; citrus-and-coffee-marinated pork tenderloin; and local free-run venison. The setting, on the lower floor of a historic building in Bastion Square, is candlelit and romantic, with exposed brick, local art, low lights, soft music, and lots of intimate nooks and crannies. A 300-item wine list is one of the best on the island. ☒ *45 Bastion Sq., Old Town* ☎ *250/381–3433* ☰ *AE, MC, V* ☉ *Closed Mon. No lunch.*

$$$ ✕ **Cafe Brio.** A feast of local artwork on gold and burgundy walls cre-
Fodor'sChoice ates a warm glow at this bustling Italian-villa-style room. The menu,
★ described by the owners as "West Coast contemporary with a Tuscan hint," changes daily and uses local organic ingredients. Appetizers might include local mussels with saffron and olive tapenade, or a luscious risotto, perhaps with wild mushrooms and white truffles. Main dishes could be braised halibut, Cowichan Bay duck breast, or wild Spring salmon with hazelnut gnocchi. Handmade daily pastas and house-made charcuterie are also popular choices. ☒ *944 Fort St., Downtown* ☎ *250/383–0009 or 866/270–5461* ☰ *AE, MC, V* ☉ *No lunch.*

$$$ ✕ **Malahat Mountain Inn.** If you're heading up Highway 1, consider a stop at this roadhouse on the top of the Malahat hill about 30-minutes north of Victoria. It doesn't look like much from the highway, but inside, the view over Finlayson Arm and the Gulf Islands is magnificent. The scenery is especially striking from the big outdoor deck. The lunch menu lists such casual fare as burgers, quesadillas, and salads; dinner brings pasta, seafood, and meat dishes. Breakfast is served in summer. If you can't tear yourself away from the scenery, consider booking a room at the 10-room inn next door; it's run by the same people ($$$–$$$$). ☒ *265 Trans-Canada Hwy., Malahat* ☎ *250/478–1944* ☰ *AE, MC, V.*

$$–$$$ ✕ **Herald Street Caffe.** This lively art-filled bistro just north of Chinatown has been a local favorite for more than 20 years. A short but interesting lunch menu offers mix-and-match pastas, pizzas, and omelets, and such tasty sandwich options as softshell crab or baron of beef. Dinner brings classic Pacific Northwest fare, including maple-glazed salmon or hazelnut-crusted rack of lamb. The chef favors local, organic ingredients and makes almost everything, from the pastas to the desserts and even the ketchup, from scratch. ☒ *546 Herald St., Old Town* ☎ *250/ 381–1441* ☰ *AE, MC, V.*

French

★ **$$** ✕ **Brasserie L'école.** French country cooking shines at this informal Chinatown bistro. The historic room—once a schoolhouse for the Chinese community—evokes a timeless brasserie, from its white linens and patina-rich fir floors to the chalkboards above the slate bar listing the day's wines-by-the-glass. Sean Brennan, one of the city's better-known chefs, works with local farmers and fishers to source the best seasonal, local, and organic ingredients. The menu changes daily but lists such classic bistro fare as duck confit, steak frites, and mountain trout with brown butter, sage, and lemon. ⊠ *1715 Government St., Chinatown* ☎ *250/475–6260* ⊕ *www.lecole.ca* ⊟ *AE, MC, V* ☉ *Closed Sun. and Mon. No lunch.*

Greek

¢–$ ✕ **Eugene's.** Locals flock to this cafeteria-style eatery near Trounce Alley for great cheap eats. Souvlaki, in lamb, pork, chicken, and vegetarian versions, is the main event here, but the *spanakopita* (spinach pie), *kalamarakia* (deep-fried squid), and Greek salad are also worth a try. Aegean-blue walls, big archways, and Hellenic travel posters add atmosphere to the big bustling room. ⊠ *1280 Broad St., Downtown* ☎ *250/381–5456* ⌲ *Reservations not accepted* ⊟ *No credit cards* ☉ *No dinner Sun.*

Italian

$$–$$$ ✕ **Il Terrazzo.** A charming redbrick terrace edged with potted greenery and warmed by fireplaces and overhead heaters makes Il Terrazzo—tucked away off Waddington Alley near Market Square and not visible from the street—the locals' choice for romantic alfresco dining. The menu changes frequently, but starters might include mussels steamed with banana peppers, sun-dried tomatoes, cilantro, garlic, Asiago cheese, and cream. Main courses, such as the mustard-encrusted rack of lamb and osso buco with porcini mushrooms, come piping hot from the restaurant's wood oven. ⊠ *555 Johnson St., off Waddington Alley, Old Town* ☎ *250/361–0028* ⊟ *AE, DC, MC, V* ☉ *No lunch Sat. or Sun. Oct.–Apr.*

★ $$–$$$ ✕ **Zambri's.** The setting is a downtown strip mall, but inside is a lively trattoria worthy of a neighborhood in Rome. Lunch is casual: order at the counter from a daily-changing roster of pastas, soups, and hot hearty sandwiches (such as the hot meatball or Italian sausage). Dinner brings table service and a daily changing menu of such hearty fare as tagliolini with crab ragù and grappa, and roasted pork loin with salsa pizzaiola and polenta. An optional three-course set menu is good value. ⊠ *110–911 Yates St., Downtown* ☎ *250/360–1171* ⌲ *Reservations not accepted* ⊟ *AE, MC, V* ☉ *Closed Sun. and Mon.*

$–$$$ ✕ **Pagliacci's.** Long lines attest to the popularity of this lively New York–meets–Victoria–style trattoria where the marble-top tables are packed in tightly. Opened by Brooklyn's Siegel brothers in 1979, Pagliacci's is all showbiz, from the signed photos of the owners' movie-star friends plastering the walls to the live jazz playing several nights a week. The menu runs from the Mae West (finally a "veal" woman) to the Prawns Al Capone and includes about 20 pastas. "Pag's" is busy, crowded, and buckets of fun. ⊠ *1011 Broad St., Downtown* ☎ *250/386–1662* ⌲ *Reservations not accepted* ⊟ *AE, MC, V.*

Seafood

$$$–$$$$ ✕ **Blue Crab Bar and Grill.** Fresh daily seafood and expansive harbor views make this modern and airy restaurant a popular lunch and dinner spot. Signature dishes include herb-dusted Queen Charlotte black cod; scal-

lop and prawn sauté; and spring salmon with wild mushroom ravioli. Still, something tempting is usually on the long list of twice-daily blackboard specials. Desserts, made in-house, and a wine list that highlights British Columbia and California wines, round out the menu. The attached lounge area and patio, open until 10 PM nightly, have equally impressive views. Here you can choose from the dinner menu or opt for more casual, lower-price fare. ☒ *Coast Harbourside Hotel and Marina, 146 Kingston St., James Bay* ☏ *250/480–1999* ☰ *AE, D, DC, MC, V.*

$$$–$$$$ ✕ **The Marina Restaurant.** A prime spot for Sunday brunch, the Marina has a 180-degree view over Oak Bay. The extensive menu usually lists a variety of pastas, grills, and seafood entrées, such as grilled rare ahi tuna and slow-roasted B.C. spring salmon. There's also an evening sushi bar. Downstairs is a coffee bar with a patio overlooking the marina. ☒ *1327 Beach Dr., Oak Bay* ☏ *250/598–8555* ☰ *AE, MC, V.*

¢–$ ✕ **Barb's Place.** Funky Barb's, a tin-roofed take-out shack, floats on the quay where the fishing boats dock, west of the Inner Harbour off St. Lawrence St. Cod, halibut, haddock, salmon, oysters, burgers, and chowder are all prepared fresh on the premises. The picnic tables on the wharf provide a front-row view of interesting vessels, including a paddle wheeler, houseboats, and some vintage fishing boats. There's also a grassy park nearby. Ferries sail to Fisherman's Wharf from the Inner Harbour. ☒ *Fisherman's Wharf, St. Lawrence St., James Bay* ☏ *250/384–6515* ☰ *MC, V* ☺ *Closed Nov.–Feb.*

Spanish

$$ ✕ **The Tapa Bar.** Chef-owner team Armanda deTorres and Danno Lee have re-created the fun and flavors of a Spanish tapas bar in this little pedestrian-only lane off Government Street. Small flavorful dishes run from simple but tasty grilled vegetables to prawns in white wine, spicy mussels, open-faced sandwiches, thin crust pizzas, pastas, and hearty soups. A specialty is the Pollo Armanda: charbroiled boneless chicken with artichokes, sun-dried tomatoes, capers, lemon, and white wine. Lime- and cherry-color painted walls, exposed brick, distressed tile, and lively artwork create a casual interior; a wrought-iron balcony is a choice spot on a sunny day. Just need a snack? Tapas are served all afternoon and late into the evening. ☒ *620 Trounce Alley, Downtown* ☏ *250/383–0013* ☰ *AE, MC, V.*

Vegetarian

$–$$ ✕ **Re-Bar Modern Food.** Bright and casual, this kid-friendly café in Bastion Square is *the* place for vegetarians in Victoria; the almond burgers, enchiladas, decadent baked goodies, and big breakfasts keep omnivores happy, too. An extensive tea and fresh-juice selection shares space on the drinks list with espresso, microbrews, and British Columbia wines. ☒ *50 Bastion Sq., Old Town* ☏ *250/361–9223* ☰ *AE, DC, MC, V* ☺ *No dinner Sun.*

Afternoon Tea

Perhaps it's the city's British heritage, perhaps it's just a fun thing to do, but the tradition of afternoon tea lives on in Victoria. Many cafés will serve a tea, but the most popular and authentic places are clustered near the Inner Harbour and in the city's very British Oak Bay district, which you may hear described as being "behind the tweed curtain." A note about terminology: afternoon tea is a snack of tea, cakes, and sandwiches taken at about 4 PM. High tea is a hot meal eaten at dinnertime. The following places serve afternoon tea.

Victoria's best-known, most elaborate, and most expensive afternoon tea is served, as it has been since 1908, on bone china at antique tables in the chandelier and fern-draped tea lobby of the **Fairmont Empress Hotel** (⊠ 721 Government St., Downtown ☎ 250/389–2727). The tea is, of course, the hotel's own special blend, and the cakes, scones, tarts, and little crustless sandwiches are prepared by some of Victoria's finest pastry chefs. As you face the bill of C$55 per person in high season, remember that tea at the Empress is more than a snack. It was, historically, a way to keep civilization alive in this farthest outpost of the empire. Reservations are recommended.

Long-established and dripping with British memorabilia, the wood-beamed **Blethering Place** (⊠ 2250 Oak Bay Ave., Oak Bay ☎ 250/598–1413 or 888/598–1413) serves a tea of scones, Devonshire cream, fruit, sandwiches, cakes, tarts, and more between 11 AM and 7:30 PM. English breakfasts and roast dinners are also available and British-style musical evenings run weekends year-round. The cozy, lace-curtained **James Bay Tea Room** (⊠ 332 Menzies St. ☎ 250/382–8282) is a short walk from the Inner Harbour and serves full teas all day, starting at 7 AM. Breakfast and lunch are also available. Everything, including the jam, is homemade for the Scottish-style teas served in the **White Heather Tea Room** (⊠ 1885 Oak Bay Ave., Oak Bay ☎ 250/595–8020), a pretty place with big windows and white tablecloths. Lunch is also served.

Where to Stay

$$$$ 🏨 **Abigail's Hotel.** A Tudor-style inn built in 1930, Abigail's is within walking distance of downtown. The guest rooms are attractively furnished in an English Arts and Crafts style. Down comforters, together with whirlpool tubs and fireplaces in many rooms, add to the pampering. Six large rooms in the Coach House building are especially lavish, with whirlpool tubs, four-poster king beds, and wood-burning fireplaces. A three-course breakfast is served at a communal table, at tables for two, or on the patio; appetizers are served each evening in the library. ⊠ *906 McClure St., Downtown, V8V 3E7 ☎ 250/388–5363 or 800/561–6565 ⧉ 250/388–7787 ⊕ www.abigailshotel.com ➹ 23 rooms ⚘ IDD phones, some refrigerators, some in-room VCRs, Wi-Fi, library, shop, dry cleaning, laundry service, concierge, free parking; no TV in some rooms, no kids under 10, no smoking ⊟ AE, MC, V ⊠◉ BP.*

$$$$ 🏨 **The Aerie.** The breathtaking view of Finlayson Arm and the Gulf Is-
Fodor'sChoice   lands persuaded owner Maria Schuster to build her Mediterranean-style
★   villa complex on this hilltop, north of Victoria. Rooms in the three buildings vary, but all have lavish decor and most boast a patio or balcony, fireplace, and whirlpool tub. Six large suites in the Villa Cielo, set 300 feet up the hill from the main resort, are especially lush, with rich fabrics, dark woods, and sweeping views. In the view-blessed dining room

the top-notch cuisine relies almost exclusively on local ingredients. The chef incorporates organic products and heritage produce varieties into the à la carte, vegetarian, and multicourse tasting menus. ⊠ *600 Ebedora La., Box 108, Malahat V0R 2L0* ☎ *250/743–7115 or 800/518–1933* 🖷 *250/743–4766* ⊕ *www.aerie.bc.ca* ⇆ *27 rooms, 8 suites* ⚐ *Restaurant, room service, some in-room hot tubs, minibars, cable TV, in-room data ports, Wi-Fi, tennis court, indoor pool, exercise equipment, some hot tubs, sauna, spa, lounge, laundry service, Internet room, business services, meeting rooms, helipad, free parking; no kids under 12, no smoking* ☰ *AE, DC, MC, V* ⏺◯⏺ *BP.*

$$$$ ▦ **The Fairmont Empress.** Opened in 1908, this harborside château and city landmark has aged gracefully. Its sympathetically restored Edwardian decor and top-notch service recall a more gracious age. Rooms vary in size and layout (the hotel has 96 different room configurations) but most are tastefully lush, with rich fabrics, duvets, butter-color walls, and rosewood furniture. Many of those facing Government Street have front-row views of the Inner Harbour. Rooms in the turret are especially romantic. Accessed by a private elevator, these smallish concierge-floor hideaways have Jacuzzi tubs, and many have harbor views. ⊠ *721 Government St., Downtown, V8W 1W5* ☎ *250/384–8111 or 888/705–2500* 🖷 *250/381–5959* ⊕ *www.fairmont.com/empress* ⇆ *436 rooms, 41 suites* ⚐ *3 restaurants, room service, IDD phones, some fans, some in-room safes, refrigerators, cable TV with movies and video games, some in-room broadband, in-room data ports, Wi-Fi, indoor pool, wading pool, gym, hot tub, sauna, spa, lounge, shops, babysitting, dry cleaning, laundry service, concierge, concierge floor, business services, convention center, parking (fee), some pets allowed (fee), no-smoking floors; no a/c in some rooms* ☰ *AE, D, DC, MC, V.*

$$$$ ✕▦ **Marriott Victoria Inner Harbour.** Sweeping city and harbor views through floor-to-ceiling windows, a great location, and such thoughtful details as microfiber robes and windows that open are draws at Victoria's newest full-service hotel, opened in 2004 a block east of the Inner Harbour. The big bright guest rooms have a summery green-and-cinnamon palette, triple-sheeted beds with duvets, and marble bathroom floors; many have balconies. Suites verge on decadent, with lush fabrics, baroque touches, and plasma-screen TVs. One of the city's top chefs sources fresh, local fare for the on-site Fire & Water Fish and Chophouse ($$$). ⊠ *728 Humboldt St., V8W 3Z5* ☎ *250/480–3800 or 877/333–8338* 🖷 *250/480–3838* ⊕ *www.marriottvictoria.com* ⇆ *228 rooms, 8 suites* ⚐ *Restaurant, room service, in-room safes, minibars, cable TV, in-room broadband, Wi-Fi, indoor pool, gym, hot tub, massage, steam room, lounge, shop, babysitting, dry cleaning, laundry facilities, laundry service, concierge, concierge floor, business services, meeting rooms, parking (fee), some pets allowed (fee), no smoking floors* ☰ *AE, D, DC, MC, V.*

$$$–$$$$ ▦ **Beaconsfield Inn.** This 1905 registered historic building four blocks from the Inner Harbour is one of Victoria's most faithfully restored Edwardian mansions. Though the rooms and suites all have antique furniture, mahogany floors, stained-glass windows, Ralph Lauren fabrics, and period details, each has a unique look; one room even includes an

Edwardian wooden canopied tub. Full English breakfasts and afternoon tea and sherry in the conservatory or around the library fire complete the English country-manor ambience. ✉ *998 Humboldt St., Downtown, V8V 2Z8* ☎ *250/384–4044 or 888/884–4044* 🖶 *250/384–4052* 🌐 *www. beaconsfieldinn.com* 🛏 *5 rooms, 4 suites* 🔥 *Fans, Wi-Fi, library, dry cleaning, laundry service, free parking; no a/c, no room phones, no room TVs, no kids under 12, no smoking* ⊟ *AE, MC, V* ⦿❙ *BP.*

$$$–$$$$ ✕🖳 **Delta Victoria Ocean Pointe Resort and Spa.** Across the Johnson Street Bridge from downtown Victoria, and easily reached by foot-passenger ferry, this waterfront property is packed with facilities. The two-story lobby and half of its guest rooms have romantic views of the Inner Harbour and the lights of the Parliament Buildings across the water. Rooms are spacious and airy, with tall windows and rosewood furniture; the apartment-size suites have kitchenettes and separate living and dining areas. Check-in treats for kids, easy-access parking for families, free or half-price kids meals, and evening story time make this a good choice for families. The hotel's flagship restaurant, Lure, offers fresh local seafood, expansive harbor views, and a waterside terrace. ✉ *45 Songhees Rd., Vic West, V9A 6T3* ☎ *250/360–2999 or 800/667–4677* 🖶 *250/360–1041* 🌐 *www.deltahotels.com/prov/p_british.html* 🛏 *236 rooms, 6 suites* 🔥 *Restaurant, room service, IDD phones, some kitchenettes, minibars, cable TV with movies and video games, in-room broadband, Wi-Fi, 2 tennis courts, indoor pool, gym, hair salon, hot tub, sauna, spa, racquetball, squash, lounge, shop, babysitting, dry cleaning, laundry service, concierge, concierge floor, business services, meeting rooms, parking (fee), some pets allowed (fee), no-smoking floors* ⊟ *AE, D, DC, MC, V.*

$$$–$$$$ 🖳 **A Haterleigh Heritage Inn.** Lead- and stained-glass windows and ornate plasterwork on 11-foot ceilings transport you to a more gracious time at this 1901 mansion two blocks from the Inner Harbour. The Victorian-theme guest rooms have whirlpool tubs or the original claw-foot tubs, high ceilings, and duvets. The Secret Garden room, with its mountain-view balcony and oval whirlpool tub, is a romantic option, as is the Day Dreams suite, with its king bed, wicker seating area, and double whirlpool tub. Breakfasts include homemade breads, fresh fruit, and elaborate entrées; sherry is served in the guest lounge each afternoon. ✉ *243 Kingston St., James Bay, V8V 1V5* ☎ *250/384–9995 or 866/ 234–2244* 🖶 *250/384–1935* 🌐 *www.haterleigh.com* 🛏 *5 rooms, 2 suites* 🔥 *Fans, Wi-Fi, free parking; no a/c, no room phones, no room TVs, no kids under 10, no smoking* ⊟ *MC, V* ⦿❙ *BP.*

$$$–$$$$ 🖳 **Hotel Grand Pacific.** Designed according to the principles of Feng Shui, this modern Inner Harbour hotel is steps from the Seattle ferry terminal and a stone's throw from Victoria's key sights. Muted colors and rosewood furniture adorn the spacious, modern rooms and suites. All rooms have balconies, many have expansive harbor views, and several are fully wheelchair accessible. The on-site adventure center can arrange whale-watching charters. ✉ *463 Belleville St., James Bay, V8V 1X3* ☎ *250/386–0450 or 800/663–7550* 🖶 *250/380–4475* 🌐 *www. hotelgrandpacific.com* 🛏 *268 rooms, 40 suites* 🔥 *2 restaurants, coffee shop, room service, in-room safes, minibars, cable TV with movies and video games, in-room broadband, Wi-Fi, indoor pool, wading pool,*

health club, hot tub, sauna, spa, steam room, racquetball, squash, lounge, piano, shop, babysitting, dry cleaning, laundry service, concierge, Internet room, business services, meeting rooms, parking (fee), some pets allowed (fee), no-smoking floors ⊟ AE, D, DC, MC, V.

$$$–$$$$ 🏨 **Prior House Bed & Breakfast Inn.** In a beautifully restored 1912 manor home on a quiet street near Craigdarroch Castle, this B&B has a pretty garden, a guest library, two parlors, antique furniture, lead-glass windows, and oak paneling. All guest rooms have fireplaces; some have air-jet massage tubs and private balconies. Two garden-level suites each have a private entrance and sleep four. A chef prepares the lavish breakfasts and elaborate afternoon teas, which are included in the rates. ⊠ *620 St. Charles St., Rockland, V8S 3N7* ☎ *250/592–8847 or 877/924–3300* 🖷 *250/592–8223* ⊕ *www.priorhouse.com* 🛏 *3 rooms, 3 suites* ♨ *Fans, microwaves, refrigerators, cable TV, in-room VCRs, library, laundry service, meeting room, free parking; no a/c, no room phones, no kids under 10, no smoking ⊟ MC, V* ❧❘ *BP.*

$$–$$$$ 🏨 **Swans Suite Hotel.** This 1913 former warehouse in Victoria's old town is one of the city's most attractive boutique hotels. The one- and two-bedroom suites boast 11-foot ceilings, loft bedrooms, full kitchens, and pieces from the late owner's extensive Pacific Northwest art collection; most suites can sleep six. The lavish 3,000-square-foot penthouse suite has a private roof top hot tub; more art fills the brewpub on the main floor. ⊠ *506 Pandora Ave., Old Town, V8W 1N6* ☎ *250/361–3310 or 800/668–7926* 🖷 *250/361–3491* ⊕ *www.swanshotel.com* 🛏 *31 suites* ♨ *Restaurant, room service, kitchens, cable TV with movies, some in-room VCRs, in-room broadband, in-room data ports, Wi-Fi, pub, wine shop, babysitting, dry cleaning, laundry facilities, laundry service, meeting rooms, parking (fee); no smoking ⊟ AE, D, DC, MC, V.*

$$$ 🏨 **Coast Harbourside Hotel and Marina.** West of the Inner Harbour and on the water, the Coast Harbourside is handy to downtown but removed from the traffic on Government Street. The attitude is friendly, the decor modern but soothing. The rooms, in peach or blue with rosewood furniture, all have lean out balconies (suites have full balconies) and many rooms have striking harbor views. Fishing and whale-watching charters as well as the harbor ferries stop at the hotel's marina, and there's a free downtown shuttle. The on-site Blue Crab Bar and Grill ($$$–$$$$) is a popular dining spot. ⊠ *146 Kingston St., James Bay, V8V 1V4* ☎ *250/360–1211 or 800/663–1144* 🖷 *250/360–1418* ⊕ *www.coasthotels.com* 🛏 *126 rooms, 6 suites* ♨ *Restaurant, room service, IDD phones, minibars, cable TV with movies and video games, some in-room DVDs, some in-room VCRs, in-room broadband, Wi-Fi, indoor-outdoor pool, gym, hot tub, sauna, marina, lounge, babysitting, dry cleaning, laundry service, concierge, meeting rooms, free parking, some pets allowed (fee); no smoking. ⊟ AE, D, DC, MC, V.*

★ $$$ 🏨 **Fairholme Manor.** Original art, Viennese antiques, and dramatic decor shine in this lavish, 1885 Italianate mansion. Surrounded by an acre of garden in the Rockland district a mile from the Inner Harbour, the Fairholme has an open, airy feel in its spacious, high-ceiling rooms. The suites are massive—about 900 square feet each—and most have a king bed, a view, and a fireplace. The Olympic Grand Suite boasts a lavish chandelier and private ocean-view deck; the two-bedroom Rose Garden suite has a kitchen and private deck. Elaborate breakfasts are served at tables for two by the fireplace in the dining room or on the porch. ⊠ *638 Rockland Pl., Rockland V8S 3R2* ☎ *250/598–3240 or 877/511–3322* 🖶 *250/598–3299* 🌐 *www.fairholmemanor.com* 🛏 *1 room, 5 suites* 🛆 *Some kitchens, refrigerators, cable TV, in-room VCRs, in-room data ports, Wi-Fi, massage, free parking; no a/c, no kids, no smoking* 🟰 *AE, MC, V* ⦿❘ *BP.*

$$$ 🏨 **Spinnakers Guesthouse.** Three delightful houses make up the accommodations at this B&B—run by the owner of the popular Spinnakers Gastro Brewpub. A villa-style house has four suites that surround an ivy-draped courtyard. Suites have private entrances and are decorated with Asian antiques, Balinese teak butlers, and other objects gathered during the owner's world travels. The two other houses are beautifully renovated Victorian homes, decorated with local art and English and Welsh antiques. Most rooms have fireplaces and whirlpool tubs. ⊠ *308 Catherine St., Vic West, V9A 3S8* ☎ *250/386–2739 or 877/838–2739* 🖶 *250/384–3246* 🌐 *www.spinnakers.com* 🛏 *6 rooms, 5 suites* 🛆 *Restaurant, fans, some kitchens, some cable TV, in-room data ports, pub, free parking, some pets allowed (fee); no a/c, no TV in some rooms, no smoking* 🟰 *AE, DC, MC, V* ⦿❘ *CP.*

$$–$$$ 🏨 **Abbeymoore Manor Bed & Breakfast Inn.** This 1912 mansion has the wide verandas, dark wainscoting, and high ceilings of its era, but the attitude is informal, from the helpful hosts to the free snacks and coffee on tap all day. Two one-bedroom, ground-level suites have modern decor and kitchens; these welcome pets and children. Five adults-only upper level rooms charm with such period details as claw-foot tubs or sleigh beds, verandas or antique-tile fireplaces. The Penthouse Suite has a full kitchen and private entrance. Multicourse breakfasts are served family style or at tables for two in the sunroom. ⊠ *1470 Rockland Ave., Rockland V8S 1W2* ☎ *250/370–1470 or 888/801–1811* 🌐 *www. abbeymoore.com* 🛏 *5 rooms, 3 suites* 🛆 *Some kitchens, some in-room VCRs, some in-room DVDs, Wi-Fi, massage, Internet room, free parking, some pets allowed (fee); no phones in some rooms, no TV in some rooms, no smoking* 🟰 *MC, V* ⦿❘ *BP.*

$$ 🏨 **Chateau Victoria Hotel & Suites.** Wonderful views from the upper-floor suites and rooftop restaurant are a plus at this good value, centrally located 19-story hotel. The guest rooms are modern and airy, with duvets and a contemporary plum and silver color scheme. The apartment-size suites are a good choice for families: all have balconies and sitting areas, and most have kitchenettes or full kitchens. A full range of in-room spa services and a bike storage room are also available. ⊠ *740 Burdett Ave., Downtown, V8W 1B2* ☎ *250/382–4221 or 800/663–5891* 🖶 *250/380–1950* 🌐 *www.chateauvictoria.com* 🛏 *59 rooms, 118 suites* 🛆 *2 restaurants, room service, IDD phones, in-room safes, some kitchens, some kitchenettes, some refrigerators, cable TV with movies and video games, in-room broadband, indoor pool, gym, hot tub, massage, 2 bars, babysitting, dry cleaning, laundry service, concierge, Internet room, business services, meeting rooms, free parking, some pets allowed (fee), no-smoking floors* 🟰 *AE, D, DC, MC, V.*

$ ▦ **Craigmyle Guest House.** This Edwardian manor near Craigdarroch Castle, a mile from the city center, is Victoria's oldest B&B. The four-story house has a variety of rooms, some with original furniture and claw-foot tubs and most with offbeat combinations of patterned wallpaper and floral bedspreads. All have private baths, though a few are across the hall from the room. A small garden, a guest kitchen, a big comfy common room, and some units that sleep four make this a good choice for families. ⊠ *1037 Craigdarroch Rd., V8S 2A5* ☎ *250/595–5411 or 888/595–5411* 🖷 *250/370–5276* ⊕ *www.bctravel.com/craigmyle* ➷ *16 rooms, 1 suite* ⌂ *Free parking; no a/c, no room phones, no room TVs, no smoking* ☲ *AE, MC, V* ⧖ *BP.*

¢ ▦ **Hostelling International Victoria.** This clean, secure hostel, in a restored historic building, is in the thick of things near the waterfront and Market Square. Accommodations include private rooms with shared baths as well as beds in men's, women's, and coed dorms. Among the amenities are a game room, TV lounge, private lockers, bike storage, a shared kitchen, and loads of travel information for your trip. Free city tours and by-donation guided hikes leave from here, too. Bedding and towels are supplied, and reception is staffed 24 hours a day. ⊠ *516 Yates St., Old Town, V8W 1K8* ☎ *250/385–4511 or 888/883–0099* 🖷 *250/385–3232* ⊕ *www.hihostels.ca* ➷ *110 beds in 10 single-sex and coed dorms, 5 private rooms (2–8 people) without bath* ⌂ *Laundry facilities, Internet; no a/c, no room phones, no room TVs, no smoking* ☲ *MC, V.*

Nightlife & the Arts

For entertainment listings, pick up a free copy of *Monday Magazine* (it comes out every Thursday), or call the **Talking Super Pages** (☎ 250/953–9000).

The Arts

MUSIC The **Victoria Jazz Society** (☎ 250/388–4423 ⊕ www.vicjazz.bc.ca) organizes the annual JazzFest International in late June.

The **Victoria Symphony** (☎ 250/385–6515) plays in **the Royal Theatre** (⊠ 805 Broughton St., Downtown ☎ 250/386–6121) and at the **University Centre Auditorium** (⊠ Finnerty Rd., University of Victoria Campus ☎ 250/721–8480). Watch for **Symphony Splash** on the first Sunday in August, when the Victoria Symphony plays a free concert from a barge in the Inner Harbour.

OPERA **Pacific Opera Victoria** (☎ 250/385–0222) performs three productions a year at the Royal Theatre.

THEATER An old church houses the **Belfry Theatre** (⊠ 1291 Gladstone Ave., Fernwood ☎ 250/385–6815 ⊕ www.belfry.bc.ca), where a resident company specializes in contemporary Canadian dramas. The **Langham Court Theatre** (⊠ 805 Langham Ct., Rockland ☎ 250/384–2142 ⊕ www.langhamcourttheatre.bc.ca), one of Canada's oldest community theaters, stages the works of internationally known playwrights between September and June. **McPherson Playhouse** (⊠ 3 Centennial Sq. ☎ 250/386–6121 ⊕www.rmts.bc.ca) hosts touring theater and dance companies. University of Victoria students stage productions on campus at the

Phoenix Theatre (⊠ Off Gordon Head Rd. ☎ 250/721–8000 ⊕ www. phoenixtheatre.ca).

Nightlife

Victoria's nightlife is low key and casual, with many wonderful pubs, but a limited choice of nightclubs. Pubs offer a casual, convivial atmosphere for lunch, dinner, or an afternoon pint, often with a view, and an excellent selection of beer. The pubs listed here all serve food and many brew their own beer. Nightclubs attract a young crowd and most close by 2 AM. A dress code (no jeans or sneakers) may be enforced, but otherwise, dress is casual. Patrons must be 19 or older to enter a bar or pub in British Columbia, but many pubs have a separate restaurant section open to all ages. Smoking is banned indoors in all Victoria pubs, bars, and nightclubs.

BARS & CLUBS Deep leather sofas and a Bengal tiger skin help to re-create the days of British Raj at the **Bengal Lounge** in the Fairmont Empress Hotel. Martinis and a curry buffet are the draws through the week. On Friday and Saturday nights a jazz combo takes the stage. Filling a two-story former bank building on Victoria's main shopping strip, **Irish Times** (⊠ 1200 Government St. ☎ 250/383–7775) offers fish-and-chips, shepherd's pie, and Irish stew, as well as stout on tap and live Celtic music every night. The **Strathcona Hotel** (⊠ 919 Douglas St., Downtown ☎ 250/383–7137) is something of an entertainment complex, with a restaurant, a nightclub, and seven different bars, including a sports bar and a hillbilly-theme bar—not to mention beach volleyball played on the roof in summer. Blues, jazz, Top 40, and live bands twice a week draw an over-25 crowd to the attractive **Upstairs Cabaret** (⊠ 15 Bastion Sq., Old Town ☎ 250/385–5483).

BREWPUBS The patio at the **Canoe Brewpub** (⊠ 450 Swift St., Old Town ☎ 250/361–1940) looks over the Gorge. Inside, the former power station has been stylishly redone, with high ceilings, exposed brick and beams, a wide range of in-house brews, top-notch bar snacks, and a restaurant that welcomes children. Chic and arty **Hugo's Brewhouse** (⊠ 625 Courtney St., Downtown ☎ 250/920–4844) serves lunch, dinner, and six of its own brews. This multipurpose spot is a pub by day, a lounge in the early evening, and a dance club at night. **Spinnakers Gastro Brewpub** (⊠ 308 Catherine St., Vic West ☎ 250/386–2739 or 877/838–2739) pours Victoria's longest menu of microbrews in an atmospheric setting, with a waterfront deck, a double-sided fireplace, and a multitude of cozy rooms filled with pub paraphernalia. Excellent pub grub and an all-ages in-house restaurant make this a popular eatery, too. **Swans Brewpub** (⊠ 1601 Store St., Old Town ☎ 250/361–3310) serves its own microbrews in a room decorated with Pacific Northwest art; musicians play Saturday through Thursday nights.

Sports & the Outdoors

Biking

Victoria is a bike-friendly town with more bicycle commuters than any other city in Canada. Helmets are required by law and are supplied with bike rentals. You can rent a bike at **Harbour Rentals** (✉450 Swift St. ☎250/ 995–1211 ⊕ www.greatpacificadventures.com).

The **Galloping Goose Regional Trail** (☎ 250/478–3344 ⊕ www.crd.bc.ca/ parks) links with the Lochside Regional Trail to create a 100-km (62-mi) car-free bike path from Sidney, through Victoria, to Sooke. **Cycletreks** (✉ 450 Swift St. ☎ 877/733–6722 or 250/386–2277 ⊕ www. cycletreks.com) rents bikes and runs bike tours of Victoria, the Gulf Islands, and various parts of Vancouver Island, including a vineyard tour.

Boating

The quiet upper section of Victoria's harbor, called the Gorge, is a popular boating spot. You can rent a kayak, canoe, motorboat, or rowboat at **Harbour Rentals** (✉ 450 Swift St. ☎ 250/995–1211 ⊕ www. greatpacificadventures.com).

You can book almost any kind of guided marine activity, including seaplane tours and fishing and kayaking expeditions, at the **Inner Harbour Centre** (✉ 950 Wharf St. ☎ 250/995–2211 or 800/575–6700).

Golf

You can golf year-round in Victoria.

One of the island's best courses is the new **Bear Mountain Golf & Country Club** (✉ 1376 Lynburne Pl. ☎ 866/391–6100 or 250/391–6100 ⊕www.bearmountaingolf.com), built near the top of an 1,100-foot mountain about 20 minutes north of Victoria. Designed by Jack Nicklaus and his son Steve, this course has an extra 19th par-3 hole built on a cliff ledge with striking views across the city. The 1,000-acre site is also home to a hotel, restaurant, and private housing. More accommodations, a spa and conference facility are planned for 2006.

Hiking

The **Galloping Goose Regional Trail** (☎ 250/478–3344 ⊕ www.crd.bc.ca/ parks), an old railroad track that's been reclaimed for walkers, cyclists, and equestrians, runs from downtown Victoria to just north of Sooke. It links with the Lochside Regional Trail to Sidney to create a continuous 100-km (62-mi) car-free route. **Goldstream Provincial Park** (☎ 250/ 478–9414 ⊕ wlapwww.gov.bc.ca/bcparks), 19 km (12 mi) northwest of Victoria on Highway 1 at Finlayson Arm Road, has an extensive trail system, old-growth forest, waterfalls, a salt marsh, and a river. Goldstream is a prime site for viewing bald eagles in December and January. **Swan Lake Christmas Hill Nature Sanctuary** (✉ 3873 Swan Lake Rd. ☎250/479– 0211 ⊕ www.swanlake.bc.ca), a few miles from downtown, has a 23-acre lake set in 150 acres of fields and wetlands. From the 2½-km (1½-mi) trail and floating boardwalk, birders can spot a variety of waterfowl and nesting birds year-round. For great views of Victoria, take the 2½-km (1½-mi) round-trip hike to the top of Christmas Hill. The sanctuary's Nature House is open weekdays 8:30–4 and weekends noon–4.

Island Adventure Tours (☎ 250/812–7103 or 866/812–7103 ⊕ www. islandadventuretours.com) offers six-hour guided coastal rain-forest hikes in East Sooke Regional Park, including hotel pick up in Victoria and a picnic lunch.

Whale-Watching

To see the pods of orcas and other species that travel in the waters around Vancouver Island, you can take charter-boat tours from Victoria.

Great Pacific Adventures (⊠ 450 Swift St. ☎ 250/386–2277 or 877/733–6722 ⊕ www.greatpacificadventures.com) operates tours year-round with both Zodiac (motor-powered inflatable boat) and covered vessels. A three-hour tour starts at C$79. **Ocean Explorations** (⊠ 602 Broughton St. ☎ 250/383–6722 or 888/442–6722 ⊕ www.oceanexplorations.com) conducts two-hour marine tours in winter and three-hour whale-watching trips in summer—all on Zodiacs. Tours cost C$85 in summer and C$59 in winter.

Shopping

Shopping in Victoria is easy: virtually everything can be found in the downtown area on or near Government Street stretching north from the Fairmont Empress hotel. Remember to save your receipts to receive a 7% GST tax refund from the Canadian government when you leave Canada; ask for a form at customs (many shops have the forms as well). Victoria stores specializing in English imports are plentiful, though Canadian-made goods are usually a better buy.

Shopping Districts & Malls

Victoria Bay Centre (⊠ 1 Victoria Bay Centre, at Government and Fort Sts., Downtown ☎ 250/952–5680), a department store and mall, has about 100 boutiques and restaurants. **Antique Row,** on Fort Street between Blanshard and Cook streets, is home to more than 60 antiques, curio, and collectibles shops. **Market Square** (⊠ 560 Johnson St., Old Town ☎ 250/386–2441) has everything from fudge, music, and comic books to jewelry, local art, and new-age accoutrements. High-end fashion boutiques and galleries line **Trounce Alley,** a pedestrian-only lane north of View Street between Broad and Government streets.

Specialty Stores

At **Artina's** (⊠ 1002 Government St., Downtown ☎ 250/386–7000 or 877/386–7700) you can find unusual Canadian-made jewelry—mostly handmade, one-of-a-kind pieces. The **Cowichan Trading Co., Ltd.** (⊠ 1328 Government St., Downtown ☎ 250/383–0321) sells First Nations jewelry, art, moccasins, and Cowichan Indian sweaters. **Hill's Native Art** (⊠ 1008 Government St., Downtown ☎ 250/385–3911) sells souvenirs and original West Coast First Nations art. As the name would suggest, **Irish Linen Stores** (⊠ 1019 Government St., Downtown ☎ 250/383–6812) stocks fine linen, lace, and hand-embroidered items. **Munro's Books** (⊠ 1108 Government St., Downtown ☎ 250/382–2464) in a beautifully restored 1909 building, is one of Canada's prettiest bookstores. If the British spirit of Victoria has you searching for fine teas, head to **Murchie's** (⊠ 1110 Government St., Downtown ☎ 250/383–3112) for a choice of 40 varieties, to sip here or take home, plus blended coffees, tarts, and cakes. Locally made chocolates are displayed in antique cases at **Roger's Chocolates** (⊠ 913 Government St. ☎ 250/384–7021). For exotic teas, aromatherapy remedies, and spa treatments (think green-tea facials) stop at the chic and multifaceted **Silk Road Aromatherapy & Tea Company & Spa** (⊠ 1624 Government St., Chinatown ☎ 250/704–2688). At **Starfish Glassworks** (⊠ 630 Yates St., Downtown ☎ 250/388–7827) you can watch glassblowers create original works.

Victoria A to Z

To research prices, get advice from other travelers, and book travel arrangements, visit www.fodors.com.

AIR TRAVEL TO & FROM VICTORIA

Victoria International Airport is served by Horizon, Pacific Coastal, and WestJet airlines. Air Canada and its regional service, Air Canada Jazz, provide frequent airport-to-airport service from Vancouver to Victoria. Flights take about 35 minutes.

West Coast Air and Harbour Air provide 35-minute harbor-to-harbor service (between downtown Vancouver and downtown Victoria) several times a day. West Coast Air also flies from Vancouver International Airport to downtown Victoria. Kenmore Air Harbor operates direct daily floatplane service from Seattle to Victoria's Inner Harbour. Helijet International has helicopter service from downtown Vancouver and Vancouver International Airport to downtown Victoria. The Vancouver heliport is near Vancouver's SeaBus terminal.

🛪 **Air Canada** ☎ 888/247–2262 ⊕ www.aircanada.ca. **Air Canada Jazz** ☎ 888/247–2262 ⊕ www.flyjazz.ca. **Harbour Air** ☎ 604/274–1277 or 800/665–0212 ⊕ www.harbour-air.com. **Helijet International** ☎ 800/665–4354 or 250/382–6222 ⊕ www.helijet.com. **Horizon Air** ☎ 800/547–9308 ⊕ www.horizonair.com. **Kenmore Air Harbor** ☎ 425/486–1257 or 800/543–9595 ⊕ www.kenmoreair.com. **Pacific Coastal Airlines** ☎ 250/655–6411 or 800/663–2872 ⊕ www.pacific-coastal.com. **West Coast Air** ☎ 604/606–6888 or 800/347–2222 ⊕ www.westcoastair.com. **WestJet Airlines** ☎ 800/538–5696 ⊕ www.westjet.com.

AIRPORTS & TRANSFERS

Victoria International Airport is 25 km (15 mi) north of downtown Victoria, off Highway 17.

🛪 Airport Information **Victoria International Airport** ⊠ 1640 Electra Blvd., off Hwy. 17, Sidney ☎ 250/953–7500 ⊕ www.victoriaairport.com.

AIRPORT
TRANSFER
To drive from the airport to downtown, take Highway 17 south. A taxi ride costs about C$40, plus tip. The Airporter bus service drops off passengers at most major hotels. The fare is C$15 one-way, C$29 round-trip. BC Transit bus number 70 runs four or five times a day from the airport to downtown Victoria. The one-way fare is $2.75.

🛪 Shuttle **Airporter** ☎ 250/386–2525 or 877/386–2525 ⊕ www.akalairporter.travel.bc.ca. **BC Transit** ☎ 250/382–6161 ⊕ www.bctransit.com.

BOAT & FERRY TRAVEL

BC Ferries operates daily service between Tsawwassen, about an hour south of Vancouver, and Swartz Bay, at the end of Highway 17 (the Patricia Bay Highway), about 30-minutes north of downtown Victoria. Sailing time is about 1½ hours. Peak-season weekend fares are C$10.75

per adult passenger and C$37 per vehicle each way. Lower rates apply midweek and in the off-season; higher rates apply for recreational and other oversize vehicles. Vehicle reservations on Vancouver–Victoria and Nanaimo routes are optional and cost C$15 to C$17.50 in addition to the fare. Reservations are recommended if you're traveling with a car on a summer weekend.

Cafeteria and buffet-style food is available on board, as are cabins (for an additional C$25). For an extra C$7, you can use the Quiet Lounge, which includes coffee, a snack, newspapers, and satellite Internet access.

Black Ball Transport operates the *MV Coho,* a car ferry, daily year-round between Victoria and Port Angeles, Washington.

The *Victoria Clipper* runs daily year-round passenger-only service between downtown Seattle and downtown Victoria. The round-trip fare from mid-May to late September is US$78 to US$118. Overnight packages are available. Washington State Ferries runs a car ferry daily between mid-March and late December from Anacortes, Washington, to Sidney, about 30 km (18 mi) north of Victoria.

Within Victoria, Victoria Harbour Ferries serve the Inner Harbour, with stops that include the Fairmont Empress, Chinatown, Point Ellice House, the Delta Victoria Ocean Pointe Resort, and Fisherman's Wharf. Fares start at C$4. Boats make the rounds every 12 to 20 minutes daily, year-round. If you're by the Inner Harbour at 10:45 on a Sunday morning in summer, you can catch the little ferries performing a water ballet—they gather together and do maneuvers set to classical music that's played over loudspeakers.

🚢 Boat & Ferry Information **BC Ferries** 🕾 250/386-3431, 888/223-3779 in B.C. ⊕ www.bcferries.com. **Black Ball Transport** 🕾 250/386-2202 or 360/457-4491 ⊕ www. ferrytovictoria.com. *Victoria Clipper* 🕾 206/448-5000 in Seattle, 250/382-8100 in Victoria, 800/888-2535 elsewhere ⊕ www.victoriaclipper.com. **Victoria Harbour Ferries** 🕾 250/708-0201 ⊕ www.victoriaharbourferry.com. **Washington State Ferries** 🕾 206/464-6400 or 888/808-7977 ⊕ www.wsdot.wa.gov/ferries.

BUS TRAVEL TO & FROM VICTORIA
Pacific Coach Lines operates daily, connecting service between Victoria and Vancouver using BC Ferries.

🚌 Bus Information **Pacific Coach Lines** 🕾 604/662-8074 in Vancouver, 250/385-4411 in Victoria, 800/661-1725 elsewhere ⊕ www.pacificcoach.com.

BUS TRAVEL WITHIN VICTORIA
BC Transit serves Victoria and the surrounding areas, including the Swartz Bay ferry terminal, Victoria International Airport, and Butchart Gardens. An all-day pass costs C$6.

🚌 Bus Information **BC Transit** 🕾 250/382-6161 ⊕ www.bctransit.com.

CAR RENTAL
🚗 Major Agencies **Avis** 🕾 250/386-8468. **Budget** 🕾 250/953-5300. **Enterprise** 🕾 250/475-6900. **National** 🕾 250/386-1213.
🚗 Local Agency **Island Rent-A-Car** 🕾 250/384-4881.

EMERGENCIES

☎ Emergency Services **Ambulance, fire, police** ☎ 911.

☎ Hospital **Victoria General Hospital** ✉ 1 Hospital Way, off Helmcken Rd. ☎ 250/727-4212.

☎ Late-Night Pharmacy **Shopper's Drug Mart** ✉ Town and Country Shopping Centre, 3575 Douglas St. ☎ 250/475-7572 is open until midnight every night.

LODGING

Reservations for lodging can be made through Hello BC.

☎ Reservation Services **Hello BC** ☎ 800/435-5622 ⊕ www.hellobc.com.

TAXIS

☎ Taxi Company **Empress Taxi** ☎ 250/381-2222.

TOURS

BOAT TOURS   The best way to see the sights of the Inner Harbour is by Victoria Harbour Ferries; 45-minute harbor tours are C$16.

☎ Fees & Schedules **Victoria Harbour Ferries** ☎ 250/708-0201 ⊕ www.victoriaharbourferry.com.

BUS TOURS   Gray Line double-decker bus tours visit the city center, Chinatown, Antique Row, Oak Bay, and Beacon Hill Park; a combination tour includes Butchart Gardens.

☎ Fees & Schedules **Gray Line** ☎ 250/388-5248 or 800/663-8390 ⊕ www.graylinewest.com.

CARRIAGE TOURS   Tally-Ho Sightseeing and Victoria Carriage Tours operate horse-drawn tours of the city. Both tours leave from the corner of Belleville and Menzies streets, near the Parliament buildings.

☎ Fees & Schedules **Tally-Ho Sightseeing** ☎ 250/383-5067 or 866/383-5067 ⊕ www.tallyhotours.com. **Victoria Carriage Tours** ☎ 877/663-2207 or 250/383-2207 ⊕ www.victoriacarriage.com.

WALKING TOURS   The Architectural Institute of British Columbia conducts walking tours of Victoria's historic neighborhoods for C$5 during July and August. Victorian Garden Tours offers guided walks through some of the city's more interesting private gardens. Fees start at C$35 per person and transportation to the garden is provided.

☎ Fees & Schedules **Architectural Institute of British Columbia** ☎ 800/667-0753 Ext. 333, 604/683-8588 Ext. 333 Vancouver office ⊕ www.aibc.ca. **Victorian Garden Tours** ☎ 250/380-2797 ⊕ www.victoriangardentours.com.

VISITOR INFORMATION

☎ Tourist Information **Hello BC** ☎ 800/435-5622 ⊕ www.hellobc.com. **Tourism Victoria** ✉ 812 Wharf St. ☎ 250/953-2033 or 800/663-3883 ⊕ www.tourismvictoria.com.

VANCOUVER ISLAND

The largest island on Canada's west coast, Vancouver Island stretches 564 km (350 mi) from Victoria in the south to Cape Scott in the north. A ridge of mountains, blanketed in spruce, cedar, and Douglas fir, crowns the island's center, providing opportunities for skiing, climbing, and hiking. Outside Victoria and Nanaimo, most towns on the island are so small as to be dwarfed by the surrounding wilderness. However, many have a unique charm, from pretty Victorian Chemainus to such isolated fishing villages as Bamfield and growing ecotourism centers, including Tofino.

Sooke

17 *42 km (26 mi) west of Victoria on Hwy. 14.*

The village of Sooke provides a peaceful seaside escape, with rugged beaches, hiking trails through the surrounding rain forest, and views of Washington's Olympic Mountains across the Strait of Juan de Fuca. **East Sooke Regional Park,** 7 km (4 mi) east of Sooke on the south side of Sooke Harbour, has more than 3,500 acres of beaches, hiking trails, and wild-flower-dotted meadows. A popular hiking and biking route, the **Galloping Goose Regional Trail** (☎ 250/478–3344) is a former railway line that runs all the way to Victoria. The **Sooke Potholes Provincial Park** (⊠ End of Sooke River Rd., off Hwy. 14) has a series of swimming holes by the Sooke River. **Whiffen Spit,** a natural breakwater about a mile long, makes a scenic walk with great bird-watching. It's at the end of Whiffen Spit Road, west of the village.

The **Sooke Region Museum and Visitor Information Centre** (⊠ 2070 Phillips Rd., off Hwy. 14 ☎ 250/642–6351) displays First Nations crafts and artifacts from 19th-century Sooke. It's open daily 9 to 5, May to October; Tuesday through Sunday 9 to 5 the rest of the year.

off the beaten path

★

JUAN DE FUCA PROVINCIAL PARK – This park between Jordan River and Port Renfrew has campsites and a long series of beaches, including Botanical Beach, which has amazing tidal pools. The **Juan de Fuca Marine Trail** is a tough 47-km (30-mi) hike set up as an alternative to the overly popular West Coast Trail, which begins at China Beach, west of the Jordan River. There are three other trailheads, each with a parking lot: Sombrio Beach, Parkinson Creek, and Botanical Beach (which is 5 km [3 mi] southeast of Port Renfrew). *⊠ Off Hwy. 14, between Jordan River (southeast end) and Port Renfrew (northwest end) ☎ 800/689–9025 camping reservations ⊕ www.discovercamping.ca camping reservations.*

Where to Stay & Eat

★ **$$$** ✕ **Markus' Wharfside Restaurant.** Two art-filled rooms, one with a fireplace, and a small patio overlook Sooke Harbour from this former fisherman's cottage. The European-trained chef-owner makes the most of the local wild seafood and organic produce, with such made-from-scratch dishes as zucchini and cilantro bisque, halibut fillet with a black pepper and lemon butter sauce, and grilled lamb sirloin with peppered balsamic glaze. *⊠ 1831 Maple Ave. S ☎ 250/642–3596 ═ MC, V ⊙ Closed Mon. in July and Aug. Closed Sun. and Mon. Sept.–June. No lunch.*

$–$$ ✕ **Seventeen Mile House.** This 1894 roadhouse is a study in island architecture at the end of the 19th century. It's a good place for pub fare, beer, or fresh local seafood on the road between Sooke and Victoria. *⊠ 5126 Sooke Rd. ☎ 250/642–5942 ═ MC, V.*

$$$$
Fodor'sChoice
★
✕⛶ **Sooke Harbour House.** This 1929 oceanfront inn is home to one of Canada's finest dining rooms. Much of the produce for the daily menus ($$$$) is grown in the inn's pretty seaside garden, the seafood is just-caught fresh, and the wine cellar is among the country's best. The guest rooms, each with a sitting area and fireplace and most with Japanese soaking tubs on private ocean-view decks, are individually decorated with pieces from the owners' vast local art collection. Breakfast is delivered to your room and rates include a picnic lunch—except in the quiet season (mid-October to the end of April) when only a continental breakfast is served Sunday through Thursday. A full range of in-room spa services is also available. ⊠ *1528 Whiffen Spit Rd., V0S 1N0* ☎ *250/642–3421 or 800/889–9688* 📠 *250/642–6988* ⊕ *www.sookeharbourhouse.com* 📨 *28 rooms* ⟷ *Restaurant, room service, IDD phones, refrigerators, massage, bicycles, boccie, croquet, lounge, piano, shop, dry cleaning, laundry service, concierge, business services, meeting rooms, some pets allowed (fee); no a/c, no room TVs, no smoking* ☰ *AE, DC, MC, V* ☾ *Call for weekday closures Dec.–Feb.* �℺ *BP.*

$$–$$$
✕⛶ **Point No Point Resort.** Here's a place for your inner Robinson Crusoe. Twenty-five cabins sit on the edge of a cliff overlooking a mile of private beach, Juan de Fuca Strait, and the Olympic Mountains. The one- and two-bedroom cabins, in single, duplex, and quad units, range from the original 1952 log cabins, to high-ceiling modern cottages. Every unit has a kitchen, a fireplace or woodstove, a water view, and a deck; most have private water-view hot tubs. The lodge's view-blessed restaurant ($$$) serves lunch, afternoon tea, and dinner, with a focus on organic, local fare. Each table has a pair of binoculars for spotting whales and ships at sea. ⊠ *10829 West Coast Rd., 24 km (15 mi) west of Sooke, V0S 1N0* ☎ *250/646–2020* 📠 *250/646–2294* ⊕ *www.pointnopoint.com* 📨 *25 cabins* ⟷ *Restaurant, massage, beach, hiking, shuffleboard, babysitting, laundry service, some pets allowed (fee); no a/c, no room phones, no room TVs, no smoking* ☰ *MC, V* ☾ *Restaurant closed for dinner Mon. and Tues., and weekdays in Jan.*

$–$$
⛶ **Markham House Bed & Breakfast.** The owners make you feel welcome in this Tudor-style house set amid extensive gardens that include a trout pond, a stream, a golf pitching range, a hot tub in a gazebo, and walking trails. The bedrooms are decorated with family pieces and feather beds. The Garden Suite, which has a double Jacuzzi, and the English Country Room are spacious; the Morningside Room is cozy and its bathroom is adjacent to the room. All rooms have fireplaces. Tucked away in the woods is the Honeysuckle Cottage. Its private deck has a barbecue and a hot tub, and a kitchenette is inside—but breakfast (which is delicious) can be delivered to the door. Kids and pets are welcome in the cottage only. ⊠ *1775 Connie Rd., off Hwy. 14 (8 km [5 mi] east of Sooke), Victoria V9C 4C2* ☎ *250/642–7542 or 888/256–6888* 📠 *250/642–7538* ⊕ *www.markhamhouse.com* 📨 *2 rooms, 1 suite, 1 cottage* ⟷ *Some cable TV, in-room DVD/VCRs, Wi-Fi, outdoor hot tub, massage, bocce, croquet, horseshoes, laundry service, Internet room; no a/c, no room phones, no smoking* ☰ *AE, D, DC, MC, V* ℺ *BP.*

Sidney & the Saanich Peninsula

⑱ *30 km (18 mi) north of Victoria on Hwy. 17.*

Home to the B.C. and Washington State ferry terminals as well as the Victoria International Airport, the Saanich Peninsula, with its rolling green hills and small family farms, is the first section of Vancouver Island that most visitors see. Although it's tempting to head straight for Victoria, 25 minutes to the south, there are many reasons to linger here. Sidney-by-the-Sea, the main town on the peninsula, is a quiet seaside spot with so many bookstores it's known as Canada's only book town.

Fodor'sChoice The peninsula's best-known site is **Butchart Gardens.** Originally a pri-
★ vate estate and still family-run, this stunning 55-acre garden has been drawing visitors since it was planted in a limestone quarry in 1904. The site's Japanese, Italian, rose, and sunken gardens grow 700 varieties of flowers in a setting that's beautiful year-round. From mid-June to mid-September, the gardens are illuminated at night, and musicians and other entertainers perform in the afternoons and evenings. In July and August, fireworks light the sky over the gardens on Saturday nights. Also on the premises are a seed and gift shop, two restaurants, and a coffee shop. You can indulge in a gelato, cappuccino, or pastry in the Italian garden, or enjoy a traditional English afternoon tea in the dining room. ☒ *800 Benvenuto Ave., Brentwood Bay* ☎ *250/652–5256 or 866/652–4422* ⊕ *www.butchartgardens.com* ✉ *Mid-June–late Sept. C$22, discounted rates rest of yr* ☉ *Mid-June–Labor Day, daily 9 AM–10:30 PM; Sept.–mid-June, daily 9 AM–dusk; call for exact times.*

☾ At the **Centre of the Universe,** the public face of the Dominion Astrophysical Observatory, you can see great views of Victoria and the night sky through a 1.8 meter telescope, interactive astronomical exhibits, and planetarium shows. ☒ *5071 W. Saanich Rd., Victoria* ☎ *250/363–8262* ⊕ *www.hia.nrc.ca/cu* ☉ *Mid-May–Sept., daily 1 PM–11 PM; Apr.–mid-May, Sept., Sun.–Fri. 10–6, Sat. 10 AM–11 PM; Oct., Sun.–Thurs., 10–6, Fri.–Sat., 10 AM–11 PM; Nov.–Mar., Tues.–Sat. 10–4:30* ☉ *Closed for one week over Christmas.*

The Saanich Peninsula, with the Cowichan Valley to the west, is also a developing wine region, with several wineries open for tours and tastings. At **Church & State Wines** (☒ 1445 Benvenuto Ave., Brentwood Bay ☎ 250/652–2671 ⊕ www.churchandstatewines.com) you can enjoy a meal on the veranda or picnic on the lawn. The family-run **Marley Farm Winery** (☒ 1831D Mount Newton Cross Rd., Saanichton ☎ 250/652–8677) makes kiwi and other fruit wines.

Between May 15 and September 30, a foot passenger ferry (C$11)
☾ makes the half-hour run to **Sidney Spit** a long stretch of beach on Sidney Island, and part of the Gulf Islands National Park Reserve (☎ 250/474–1336 camping reservations, 250/474–5145 ferry information, 250/654–4000 park information). The ferry leaves hourly from Beacon Wharf at the end of Beacon Avenue in Sidney.

To view the Gulf Islands National Park by kayak, contact **Island Adventure Tours** (☎ 250/812–7103 or 866/812–7103 ⊕ www.islandadventuretours.

com). Their four-hour kayak tours of some of the park's many islands leave from Sidney's Van Isle Marina; the cost is C$75 per person. Six-hour trips, at C$125, include a picnic lunch. They also rent kayaks and offer lessons, and will pick you up at your hotel in Victoria or Sidney.

If you're heading north on Vancouver Island, consider taking a 25-minute shortcut on the **Mill Bay Ferry,** operated by BC Ferries (☎ 250/386–3431 or 888/223–3779 ⊕ www.bcferries.com), which sails between Brentwood Bay on the Saanich Peninsula and Mill Bay, just south of Duncan.

need a break? Not everyone loves ferry food. An option, if you're heading to or from a ferry at the Swartz Bay terminal, is to duck into the **Stonehouse Pub** (⊠ 2215 Canoe Cove Rd. ☎ 250/656–3498) for a pint or a home-cooked meal. The tiny stone pub with garden looks like something you'd find in rural England.

Where to Stay & Eat

★ **$$$–$$$$** ✕ **Dock 503 Waterfront Café.** Perched on a pier overlooking Van Isle Marina, this pretty blue-and-gold room is the place for fresh local cuisine. Chef Simon Manvell works with nearby farmers and fishers to source the best organic produce, wild salmon, regional seafood, and free-run meat for his seasonal menu and daily fresh sheet. Try the sockeye salmon spring rolls or grilled local oysters, followed by slow-roasted duck breast, miso-glazed halibut cheeks, or fennel and cumin crusted ahi tuna. Everything, including the bread, desserts, sorbets, and ice cream, is made in-house, from scratch. You can dine alfresco on the pier in fine weather. ⊠ 2320 Harbour Rd. ☎ 250/656–0828 ⊟ AE, MC, V.

$$$$ ✕🏠 **Brentwood Bay Lodge & Spa.** All rooms and suites at this modern,
Fodor'sChoice cedar-sided boutique resort have private, waterview decks or balconies,
★ gas fireplaces, hand-made furniture, and original local art. Slate-lined bathrooms have jetted tubs, multihead showers, and shuttered windows to let you see the ocean from the tub. This seaside resort is handy to Butchart Gardens (a five-minute hop on the resort's water taxi) and to local wineries. You can even indulge in wine-based treatments in the lavish spa. The ocean-view restaurant, casual marine pub, and on-site café serve locally raised fare. Marine ecocruises, kayak tours, and even underwater film-making classes are among the many distractions. A gym is planned for 2006. ⊠ 849 Verdier Ave., Brentwood Bay V8M 1C5 ☎ 250/544–2079 or 888/544–2079 🖶 250/544–2069 ⊕ www. brentwoodbaylodge.com ➥ 30 rooms, 3 suites 🔧 Restaurant, coffee shop, grocery, patisserie, room service, IDD phones, in-room safes, some in-room hot tubs, minibars, cable TV, in-room DVD, in-room broadband, Wi-Fi, pool, outdoor hot tub, sauna, spa, steam room, dive shop, boating, marina, fishing, pub, wine shop, shop, dry cleaning, laundry facilities, laundry service, concierge, business services, meeting rooms; no smoking ⊟ AE, MC, V ⟨◯⟩ BP.

$$–$$$$ ✕🏠 **Miraloma on the Cove.** Natural fabrics, an earth-tone palette, and art inspired by nature create a comfortable West Coast vibe in the roomy studio, one-, and two-bedroom suites at this getaway set among bayside gardens half a mile from Sidney-by-the-Sea. All units have kitchens or kitchenettes, deep soaker tubs, duvets, heated slate bathroom floors, and ocean or garden views; many have gas fireplaces and all but two have balconies. You can join winery tours, whale-watching trips and other adventures here and dine at housed in a historic mansion on-site. ☒ 2326 Harbour Rd., V8L 2P8 ☎ 250/656–6622 or 877/956–6622 🖷 250/656–6212 ⊕ www.miraloma.ca ➬ 9 rooms, 13 suites ⚓ IDD phones, cable TV, in-room DVDs, some in-room DVD/VCRs, in-room broadband, gym, outdoor hot tub, massage, sauna, boating, mountain bikes, croquet, shop, babysitting, dry cleaning, laundry facilities, laundry service, meeting rooms, free parking, some pets allowed (fee); no smoking ⊟ AE, DC, MC, V ⊚ CP.

$$–$$$ 🏨 **Beacon Inn at Sidney.** Each guest room in this Edwardian-style (though newly built) boutique hotel is sumptuous with velvet, brocade, and raw silk drapes and bedspreads, cherrywood furnishings, and duvet-topped feather beds. Some rooms have sleigh or canopy beds and most have a gas fireplace and an extra-large jetted or soaker tub. Breakfast is served at tables for two in the dining room or on the sunny patio. The three-story inn is on a quiet side street, walking distance from the Washington State Ferry terminal and the shops and cafés of Sidney-by-the-Sea. ☒ 9724 3rd. St., Sidney-by-the-Sea V8L 3A2 ☎ 250/655–3288 or 877/420–5499 ⊕ www.beaconinns.com ➬ 8 rooms, 1 suite ⚓ Refrigerator, microwave, cable TV, in-room VCR, Wi-Fi, free parking; no room phones, no kids under 12, no smoking. ⊟ DC, MC, V ⊚ BP.

Duncan

⑲ 60 km (37 mi) north of Victoria on Trans-Canada Hwy., or Hwy. 1.

Duncan is nicknamed the City of Totems for the many totem poles that dot the small community. Although Duncan looks a little drab from the highway, the surrounding Cowichan Valley is a bucolic region dotted with artists' studios and small wineries, many of which give tours, tastings, and entertainment.

The **Cowichan Valley Museum** has some interesting historic exhibits in a still-functioning 1912 train station. Between May and September, free walking tours of the totems leave hourly from the south end of the train station building. ☒ 130 Canada Ave. ☎ 250/746–6612, 250/715–1700 tours ☒ C$2 ⊙ June–Sept., Mon.–Sat. 10–4; Oct.–May, Wed.–Fri. 11–4, Sat. 1–4.

You can see how traditional cider is made at **Merridale Ciderworks** (☒ 1230 Merridale Rd., Cobble Hill ☎ 250/743–4293 or 800/998–9908 ⊕ www.merridalecider.com), B.C.'s only traditional English cidery. Lunches and weekend dinners of local fare are served in the cider house or on the vineyard-view veranda.

☾ The **Quw'utsun' Cultural and Conference Centre,** covering 6 acres on the banks of the Cowichan River, is one of Canada's leading First Nations cultural and educational facilities. You can see the work of some of the Northwest's most renowned artists in a lofty longhouse-style gallery, learn about the history of the Cowichan people from a multimedia show, and sample traditional foods at the Riverwalk Café. You can also watch carvers at work on the riverbank. Crafts demonstrations and performances take place in summer. The gift shop sells, among other items, hand-knit Cowichan sweaters, for which the region is known. ⊠ *200 Cowichan Way* ☎ *250/746–8119 or 877/746–8119* ⊕ *www.quwutsun.ca* ✉ *Mar.–May C$11, June–Sept. C$13, Oct.–Feb. C$7* ⊙ *Daily 9–5.*

☺ The **British Columbia Forest Discovery Centre** spans some 100 acres, combining indoor and outdoor forestry-related exhibits, including a 1930s-era logging camp, and a historic train that takes visitors around the site. Interpretive trails through the forest lead to trees as much as 600 years old. ⊠ *2892 Drinkwater Rd., Trans-Canada Hwy.* ☎ *250/715–1113* ⊕ *www.bcforestmuseum.com* ✉ *C$9* ⊙ *Easter–mid-May and Sept.–mid-Oct., daily 10–4; mid-May–Labor day, daily, 10–6.*

off the beaten path

COWICHAN BAY – About 9 km (5 mi) southeast of Duncan (take Cowichan Bay Road off Highway 1), this funky little town of houseboats and houses built on pilings over the ocean's edge, has cafés, craft studios, and B&Bs lining the waterfront. The **Cowichan Bay Maritime Centre** (⊠ 1761 Cowichan Bay Rd. ☎ 250/746–4955) has old dive suits, model boats, and other maritime-related displays set up along a pier. There's also a First Nations art studio and boat-building workshop here.

At **Pacific Northwest Raptors,** a conservation center about 10-minutes northeast of Duncan, you can learn about the ancient art of falconry and see owls, hawks, falcons, and eagles in natural settings. Free-flying bird demonstrations are held at noon and at 3 PM each day; you can also join a trainer on a brief falconry course. ⊠ *1877 Herd Rd.* ☎ *250/746–0372* ⊕ *www.pnwraptors.com* ✉ *C$7* ⊙ *Apr.–Oct., Thurs.–Tues. 11–4:30.*

Where to Stay & Eat

$$–$$$ ✕ **Vinoteca on the Vineyard.** This 1903 farmhouse with its wide veranda is the centerpiece of the Vigneti Zanatta vineyard. Try the chef's Italian-influenced, locally sourced cuisine together with the vineyard's own wines. The menu changes frequently, but popular lunch items include crab and shrimp cakes and a luscious pasta carbonara. Dinner could start with yam and garlic soup or roast-beet salad with honey-goat cheese, followed by a seafood medley or duck breast with port reduction. ⊠ *5039 Marshall Rd., 5 km (3 mi) southwest of Duncan* ☎ *250/709–2279* ⬟ *Reservations essential* ⊟ *MC, V* ⊙ *Closed Mon. and Tues., Jan. and Feb.*

$$ 🏨 **Fairburn Farm Culinary Retreat & Guesthouse.** This 1884 manor on 130 pastoral acres is the centerpiece of a family-run farm, water-buffalo dairy, and cooking school. Three meadow-view rooms are freshly decorated with Italian linens, deep rich colors, original woodwork, and local art. The more simply furnished two-bedroom cottage is a good choice for families. A wide veranda, meadows, a mile of creek, and trails through the surrounding woods provide plenty of space to unwind. Rooms, with homegrown breakfasts, are available anytime, but on Saturday guests can join in a farmers' market shopping trip, a cooking class, and lavish lunch. On Sunday, there's room for 28 at a four-hour Italian-style lunch on the veranda. ⊠ *3310 Jackson Rd., V9L 6N7* ☎ *250/746–4637* ⊟ *250/746–4317* ⊕ *www.fairburnfarm.bc.ca* ⇲ *3 rooms, 1 cottage*

    ♿ *Piano, Wi-Fi; no a/c, no room phones, no room TVs, no smoking*
🍴 *MC, V* 🍽 *BP.*

Chemainus

20 *25 km (16 mi) north of Duncan.*

Chemainus is known for the bold epic murals that decorate its townscape, as well as for its beautifully restored Victorian homes. Once dependent on the lumber industry, the small community began to revitalize itself in the early 1980s when its mill closed down. Since then the town has brought in international artists to paint more than 30 murals depicting local historical events around town. Footprints on the sidewalk lead you on a self-guided tour of the murals. Restaurants, shops, tearooms, coffee bars, art galleries, horse-and-carriage tours, several B&Bs, and antiques dealers have helped to create one of the prettiest towns on Vancouver Island. The **Chemainus Theatre** (✉ 9737 Chemainus Rd. ☎ 250/246–9820 or 800/565–7738) presents family-oriented performances along with dinner.

Where to Stay

$$$$ 🏠 **Castlebury Cottage.** This medieval-theme two-suite cottage is a good place to act out your Camelot fantasies. Each suite has a fireplace, an onyx soaker tub, and a private entrance, but the upper-floor Camelot Suite is the most theatrical, with its purple velvet sofa, canopy bed, 17th-century church window, and suit of armor. A CD player and a kitchen are nods to the modern world. Stairs climb to a small Juliette balcony with views over the town and sea. Breakfast is delivered to your door and the proprietors can, with notice, arrange horse-and-carriage rides, theater evenings, and in-suite dinners. ✉ 9910 Croft St., V0R 1K1 ☎ 250/246–9228 or 866/246–9910 🖷 250/246–2909 ⊕ www. castleburycottage.com ⇄ 2 suites ♿ Microwaves, refrigerators, cable TV, in-room VCR (Camelot), in-room DVD (Sonnet), Wi-Fi, some pets allowed (fee); no kids under 8, no smoking 🍴 AE, MC, V 🍽 BP.

$–$$ 🏠 **Bird Song Cottage.** The whimsical white-and-lavender Victorian cottage, an easy walk from the beach and town, has been playfully decorated with antiques and collectibles, including a grand piano, a Celtic harp, and Victorian hats. A full breakfast (often with piano accompaniment) is served in a glassed-in sunporch. The Nightingale room has a private garden and a claw-foot tub, and the other two rooms have baths with showers; every room has a window seat. ✉ 9909 Maple St., V0R 1K1 ☎ 250/246–9910 or 866/246–9910 🖷 250/246–2909 ⊕ www. birdsongcottage.com ⇄ 3 rooms ♿ Cable TV, in-room DVD/VCR, Wi-Fi, piano, laundry service; no a/c, no room phones, no kids under 8, no smoking 🍴 AE, MC, V 🍽 BP.

Nanaimo

21 *25 km (16 mi) north of Chemainus, 110 km (68 mi) northwest of Victoria.*

Nanaimo, Vancouver Island's largest city after Victoria, is the primary commercial and transport link for the mid-island, with direct ferry service to the mainland. Though Nanaimo's many malls sprawl untidily to the north, the landscape to the south, in the regions of Cedar and Yellow Point and around the village of Ladysmith, remains pretty and rural.

Downtown Nanaimo's **Harbourside Walkway,** which starts at the foot of Bastion Street, is a pleasant shop- and café-lined stroll past visiting yachts and fishing boats. The round building overlooking the waterfront at the foot of Bastion Street is the **Bastion** (☎ 250/753–1821), an 1853 Hudson's Bay Company arsenal, one of the last of its kind in North America. The restored interior is open 10 to 4 daily, June 1 to Labor Day. Admission is C$1.

Re-created streets from Nanaimo's Old Town and Chinatown highlight the **Nanaimo District Museum** (⊠ 100 Cameron Rd. ☎ 250/753–1821 ⊕ www.nanaimo.museum.bc.ca/ndm), which also has exhibits on the local First Nations' culture and the region's coal-mining history, and a variety of interesting temporary exhibits. You can pick up maps here for self-guided heritage walks around town. Mid-May to Labor Day the museum is open 10 to 5 daily; the rest of the year it's open Tuesday through Saturday 10 to 5. Admission is C$2.

From the waterfront downtown, you can take a 10-minute ferry ride (C$7) to **Newcastle Island** (☎ 250/754–7893 ferries and camping, 250/755–1132 visitor center and restaurant ⊕ www.newcastleisland.ca), a car-free provincial park where you can camp, picnic, bike, walk trails leading past old mines and quarries, and catch glimpses of deer, rabbits, and eagles. The Pavilion, a 1931 dance hall on the island, is home to a visitor center and restaurant.

need a break?   From Nanaimo's boat basin on the waterfront downtown, you can catch the Protection Island Ferry (C$5), which drops passengers at the **Dinghy Dock** (☎ 250/753–2373 pub, 250/753–8244 ferry information), a floating marine pub popular with boaters. The pub serves seafood lunches and dinners daily year-round. Children are welcome in the restaurant section.

Where to Stay & Eat

$$–$$$ ╳ **Glow World Cuisine.** This 1893 former firehall with 20-foot-high ceilings, Gothic windows and bright primary colors is home to Nanaimo's most dramatic looking restaurant. The food is locally sourced, organic, and a little off-beat. A tapas menu ranges from wild mushroom and tarragon soup to the house specialty: tempura-fried oysters with basil risotto and white-chocolate sauce. Mains might be roast leg of venison with cocoa-cassis jus and truffle-olive tapenade, or wild salmon over potato croquettes with mirin-poached shiitake mushrooms and pickled red onions. Feeling really adventurous? Opt for a three- or five-course tasting menu and let the chef decide. The wine list includes good choices from the nearby Cowichan Valley. ⊠ 7 Victoria Rd. ☎ 250/741–8858 ▭ AE, MC, V ⊘ No lunch Sat.

★ $$–$$$ ╳ **Mahle House.** Much of the innovative Pacific Northwest cuisine served at this cozy 1904 farmhouse is raised in the restaurant's organic garden or in the neighborhood. The menu changes frequently, but highlights have included different versions of lamb, rabbit, venison, mussels, and salmon, as well as good vegetarian options. On Wednesday night, you can try the Adventure Dining Experience: for C$32 you get five courses chosen by the chef, and your dinner companions (up to a party of four) each get something different. Mahle House is about 12 km (7 mi) south of Nanaimo. ⊠ *2104 Hemer Rd., at Cedar Rd.* ☎ *250/722–3621* 🖷 *AE, MC, V* ☺ *Closed Mon., Tues., and 1st 2 wks in Jan. No lunch.*

$$–$$$ ✗ **Milano Café and Grill.** Botticelli prints, arias on the CD player, and a fountain playing beside a flower-draped patio bring a little bit of the Italian Riviera to this 1892 downtown house. The seafood is local, the salmon is wild, and the pasta, sauces, breads, desserts, and even ice cream are made from scratch by the Lebanese-Italian team in the kitchen. ⊠ *247 Milton St.* ☎ *250/740–1000* 🖷 *AE, DC, MC, V* ☺ *Closed Sun.*

$–$$ ✗ **Crow and Gate Neighbourhood Pub.** Set among lawns on a country road south of Nanaimo, this weathered building is probably the most authentic British-style pub in the province. Potpies, ploughmen's lunches, and roast beef with Yorkshire pudding appear on the menu, as do local oysters and both British and British Columbian brews. From Highway 1 between Ladysmith and Nanaimo, follow the signs for Yellow Point Lodge, then the signs for the pub. No one under 19 is admitted. ⊠ *2313 Yellow Point Rd., Ladysmith* ☎ *250/722–3731* ⚲ *Reservations not accepted* 🖷 *MC, V.*

¢–$$ ✗ **Gina's.** From the surfboard on the roof to the sequinned sombreros gracing the walls, this bright and cheerful, kid-friendly cantina looks like a beach shack, even if it's on a hill in the center of town. The nachos, burritos, tacos, and quesadillas are fresh, tasty, and on the mild side—they'll spice them up if you like. Reservations are accepted only for groups of six or more. ⊠ *47 Skinner St.* ☎ *250/753–5411* 🖷 *AE, DC, MC, V.*

$–$$$ 🏨 **Yellow Point Lodge.** Since the 1930s, this lodge, on 165 waterfront acres south of Nanaimo, has been a kind of adults-only summer camp. Everything's included, from the use of kayaks, bicycles, and tennis courts to the meals and snacks served communally in the dining room (rates are for two people). Accommodations range from comfortable lodge rooms to cozy cottages with bed frames made with logs, most with private baths. Some summer-only cabins share a bathhouse and don't have running water. ⊠ *3700 Yellow Point Rd., Ladysmith V9G 1E8* ☎ *250/245–7422* 🖷 *250/245–7411* ⊕ *www.yellowpointlodge.com* ➴ *9 lodge rooms, 25 rooms, 9 units in shared cabins, 12 private cabins* ⚲ *Dining room, some refrigerators, 2 tennis courts, saltwater pool, outdoor hot tub, massage, sauna, beach, boating, mountain bikes, badminton, boccie, croquet, hiking, horseshoes, Ping-Pong, volleyball, piano, meeting room; no a/c, no room phones, no room TVs, no kids under 14, no smoking* 🖷 *AE, MC, V* ⊙ *AP.*

$ 🏨 **Best Western Dorchester.** Once Nanaimo's opera house, this nicely restored 1889 downtown hotel overlooks the harbor. Public areas, including a clubby library with wing chairs, retain their original brass fixtures and wood trim. Guest rooms vary in size but are all freshly decorated with rich colors and rosewood furniture. Rates include passes to a nearby gym. ⊠ *70 Church St., V9R 5H4* ☎ *250/754–6835 or 800/661–2449*

≞ 250/754–2638 ⊕ www.dorchesternanaimo.com ↩ 56 rooms, 9 suites ⚷ Restaurant, some refrigerators, cable TV with movies, some in-room broadband, hair salon, lobby lounge, library, shops, dry cleaning, laundry service, meeting rooms, free parking, some pets allowed (fee), no-smoking floors; no a/c in some rooms ⊟ AE, DC, MC, V.

Sports & the Outdoors

DIVING & SNORKELLING
The waters off Nanaimo offer some of the most varied and spectacular temperate-water diving in the world, especially in winter when the water is clearest. **Ocean Explorers Diving** (☎ 250/753–2055 or 800/233–4145 ⊕ www.oceanexplorersdiving.com) offers dive charters, equipment, and an option to go snorkeling with harbor seals.

KAYAKING
Kayak rentals and one- to six-day guided sea-kayak expeditions are operated by **Wild Heart Adventure Tours** (⊠ 1560 Brebber Rd., Nanaimo V9X 1P4 ☎ 250/722–3683 or 877/722–3683 ⊕ www.kayakbc.com). All trips are suitable for beginners.

Gabriola Island

3½ nautical mi (20-minute ferry ride) east of Nanaimo.

You can stay overnight on rustic, rural Gabriola Island, about a 20-minute ferry ride from Nanaimo. The small island, where about 4,000 people live full time, has beaches, parks, campgrounds, several B&Bs, two marinas, three pubs, and a small shopping area near the ferry terminal. A number of artists' studios are open to the public. The island is also known for its prehistoric petroglyphs and delightful coastal rock formations. **BC Ferries** (☎ 250/386–3431, 888/223–3779 in B.C.) runs car and passenger service from Nanaimo.

Port Alberni

 80 km (50 mi) northwest of Nanaimo, 195 km (121 mi) northwest of Victoria.

Port Alberni, a forest industry town, is a stopover on the way to Ucluelet and Tofino on Vancouver Island's west coast. The salmon-rich waters here attract anglers. The town's old industrial waterfront, at the foot of Argyle Street, has been revitalized into **Alberni Harbour Quay**, an attractive waterfront shopping area, which is also home to the town's historic train station and the pier for Lady Rose Marine Services and a year-round Saturday morning farmers' market.

The **Alberni Valley Museum** (⊠ 4255 Wallace St. ☎ 250/723–2181 ⊕ www.alberniheritage.com) displays First Nations cultural exhibits as well as local and industrial history and a folk-art collection. It's open Monday to Saturday 10–5, with late hours (until 8) on Thursday; admission is by donation.

You can see maritime-related exhibits and watch deep-sea vessels loading at the **Maritime Discovery Centre** (⊠ Harbour Quay Marina, Harbour Rd. ☎ 250/723–6164) in a lighthouse-style building on a pier. It's open late June to Labor Day, daily 10 to 5; admission is by donation.

A 1929 Baldwin Steam Locomotive leaves twice daily Thursday through Monday from late June to Labor Day from the historic 1912 railway station at the foot of Argyle Street for a scenic 35-minute ride to the **McLean Mill National Historic Site** (⊠ 5633 Smith Rd., off Beaver Creek Rd. ☎ 250/723–1376 ⊕ www.alberniheritage.com). The restored 1925 lumber camp and operating steam sawmill includes bunkhouses, a cook-house, a blacksmith's forge, and much of the original steam-driven sawmill equipment. A theater troupe performs a daily stage show and leads tours through the forested site. There's also a café and gift shop. The site is open 10 to 4:30 daily from late June to Labor Day (though with no stage show or mill demonstrations on Tuesday and Wednesday). Admission is C$11.50, or C$26 including the round-trip train trip. The site is also open, but without the show, mill demonstrations, or train from mid-May to late June and in September; rates are reduced at these times. You can bike or hike 8½ km (5 mi) to the mill from town along the **Log Train Trail,** a 25 km (15 mi) decommissioned logging railbed through the forest. The Visitor Infocentre (☎ 250/724–6535) has maps.

You can see local art exhibits at the **Rollin Art Centre** (⊠ 3061 8th Ave. ☎ 250/724–3412), a 1914 house surrounded by gardens. It's open Tuesday through Saturday 11 to 4. Admission is free. From Port Alberni, you can take a breathtaking 4½-hour trip aboard the *Lady Rose,* a Scottish ship built in 1937, to Bamfield. It's run by **Lady Rose Marine Services** (☎ 250/723–8313, 800/663–7192 reservations Apr.–Sept. ⊕ www.ladyrosemarine.com). The boat leaves Argyle Pier at the foot of Argyle St. (⊠ 5425 Argyle St.) at 8 AM Tuesday, Thursday, and Saturday year-round, with additional Friday and Sunday sailings in July and August. The round-trip fare is C$50. Or you can take the M. V. *Francis Barkley,* which sails to the Broken Group Islands (C$50 round-trip) and Ucluelet (C$55 round-trip). It leaves Argyle Pier at 8 AM Monday, Wednesday, and Friday between early June and late September. The company also operates the rustic **Sechart Whaling Station Lodge** (from C$140 for two per night, including meals), a kayaking base adjacent to the Broken Group Islands.

About 13 km (8 mi) west of town on Highway 4 is **Sproat Lake Provincial Park** (☎ 800/689–9025 camping reservations), with swimming, camping, and trails leading to ancient petroglyphs. Sproat Lake is also home to the only two Martin Mars water bombers still in existence. Originally World War II troop carriers, they are now used to fight forest fires.

Where to Stay

$$ 🏨 **Cedar Wood Lodge Bed & Breakfast Inn.** This modern cedar-sided lodge is on 2 acres of gardens on the road to Tofino. The rooms, most of which can sleep four, are decorated in rich greens and burgundies, with attractive art deco furniture, gas fireplaces, and air-massage tubs. The comfortable lounge has a pool table and leather couches set around a fireplace and French doors opening onto the garden. ⊠ *5895 River Rd., Hwy. 4, V9Y 6Z5* ☎ *250/724–6800 or 877/314–6800* 🖷 *250/724–6887* ⊕ *www.cedarwood.bc.ca* ⤴ *8 rooms* ⚭ *IDD phones, fans, cable TV, in-room broadband, Wi-Fi, fishing, billiards, meeting rooms; no a/c, no smoking* ⊟ *AE, MC, V* ⦿ *CP.*

Sports & the Outdoors

KAYAKING & **Alberni Outpost** (✉ 5161 River Rd., Hwy. 4 ☎ 250/723–2212 or 800/
CANOEING 325–3921 ⊕ www.albernioutpost.com) rents kayaks and runs guided
day paddles on Sproat Lake and Alberni Inlet and multiday trips to the
Broken Group Islands in the Pacific Rim National Park Reserve.

Bamfield

㉓ *100 km (62 mi) southwest of Port Alberni by gravel road.*

Bamfield, a remote community of about 500, is one of the last of British
Columbia's boardwalk fishing villages. It's built on either side of Bamfield Inlet: East Bamfield can be reached by sea or by logging road from
Port Alberni or Lake Cowichan; West Bamfield, across the inlet, is accessible only by boat or water taxi.

As a base for salmon fishing, boating trips to the Broken Group Islands,
and hikes along the West Coast Trail of the Pacific Rim National Park
Reserve, the town is well equipped to handle overnight visitors. If you
want to avoid traveling on the unpaved roads, and the logging trucks,
which kick up gravel and dust, take the **Lady Rose** (☎ 250/723–8313 or
800/663–7192), a ferryboat that travels from Port Alberni to Bamfied.

Ucluelet

㉔ *100 km (62 mi) west of Port Alberni, 295 km (183 mi) northwest of
Victoria.*

Ucluelet, which in the Nuu-chah-nulth First Nations language means
"people with a safe landing place," is, along with Bamfield and Tofino,
one of the towns serving the Pacific Rim National Park Reserve. Ucluelet
is less visited than Tofino and has a more relaxed pace. Despite a growing number of craft shops and B&Bs, it still feels more like a fishing village than an ecotourism retreat.

As in Tofino, whale-watching is another main draw, though visitors also
come in the off-season to watch the dramatic winter storms that pound
the coast here.

Various charter companies take boats to greet the 20,000 gray whales
that pass close to Ucluelet on their migration to the Bering Sea every
March and April. Some gray whales remain in the area year-round. The
Pacific Rim Whale Festival (☎ 250/726–7742 ⊕ www.island.net/~whalef)
is an event (here and in Tofino) that welcomes the whales each spring.

Ucluelet is the starting point for the **Wild Pacific Trail** (⊕ www.
wildpacifictrail.com), a path that winds along the coast and through the
rain forest. Eventually it will link Ucluelet to the Pacific Rim National
Park Reserve. At this writing two sections were complete. A 2½-km (1½-
mi) loop starts at **He-Tin-Kis Park** off Peninsula Road and can also be
reached from the **Amphitrite Point Lighthouse** at the end of Coast
Guard Road. Another 4-km (2½-mi) stretch starts at **Big Beach** at the
end of Matterson Road.

Where to Stay & Eat

$–$$ ✕ **Matterson House.** In a tiny 1931 cottage with seven tables and an outdoor deck in summer, husband-and-wife team Sandy and Jennifer Clark serve up generous portions of seafood, burgers, pasta, and filling standards such as prime rib and veal cutlets. It's simple food, prepared well with fresh local ingredients; everything, including soups, desserts, and the wonderful bread, is homemade. The wine list has local island wines unavailable elsewhere and worth trying. Matterson House is also a good breakfast stop. ⊠ *1682 Peninsula Rd.* ☎ *250/726–2200* ⊟ *MC, V.*

★ $$$–$$$$ ✕⊡ **Tauca Lea by the Sea.** This all-suites, family-friendly, waterfront resort of blue-stained cedar lodges combines a variety of facilities with a respect for the natural surroundings. Handcrafted furniture and terracotta tiles decorate the spacious one- and two-bedroom suites, which also have fireplaces and ocean-view decks; many with private hot tubs. The spa provides rain-forest-inspired pampering treatments, and the marina-view Boat Basin restaurant ($$$–$$$$) serves contemporary Pacific Rim fare with fresh, local ingredients—some of it straight from the fishing boats. A boardwalk around the property leads to a sheltered viewpoint for spotting wildlife across the inlet. Ask about kayaking and surfing packages. ⊠ *1971 Harbour Crescent, Box 286, V0R 3A0* ☎ *250/726–4625 or 800/979–9303* 🖶 *250/726–4663* ⊕ *www.taucalearesort.com* ➲ *72 suites* ⚘ *Kitchens, cable TV, in-room data ports, Wi-Fi, lounge, shop, laundry facilities, concierge, meeting rooms, some pets allowed (fee); no a/c, no smoking* ⊟ *AE, DC, MC, V* ⚏ *CP.*

★ $$$$ ⊡ **Eagle Nook Wilderness Resort & Spa.** This soft adventure lodge on Barkley Sound is accessible only by sea or air. Choose from spacious water-view lodge rooms with step-out balconies or nicely appointed log cabins, each with a fireplace. Pacific Northwest cuisine is served by the grand stone fireplace in the dining room or alfresco. Hiking trails lace the woods, and you can indulge in a full range of spa services. Guided activities include fishing, kayaking, and helicopter tours. Two- to seven-night packages include flights to Tofino from Seattle or Vancouver, transportation to the lodge, a nature cruise, meals, and all nonguided activities. ⌂ *120 W. Dayton, Suite B6, Edmonds, WA 98020* ☎ *800/760–2777* 🖶 *425/771–4518* ⊕ *www.eaglenook.com* ➲ *23 rooms, 2 cabins* ⚘ *Restaurant, some kitchenettes, outdoor hot tub, sauna, dock, boating, billiards, lounge, library, Internet room, meeting room, helipad; no a/c, no room phones, no room TVs, no kids under 12, no smoking* ⊟ *AE, MC, V* ⊗ *Closed Oct.–May* ⚏ *AP.*

$$$–$$$$ ⊡ **A Snug Harbour Inn.** Set on a cliff above the Pacific, this couples-oriented B&B has some of the most dramatic views anywhere. The rooms, all with fireplaces, private balconies or decks, and whirlpool baths, are decorated in a highly individual style. The Lighthouse room winds up three levels for great views, the Valhalla has a nautical theme, and the Atlantis room is the largest with dramatic First Nations art and a Jacuzzi tub for two. Eagles nest nearby, and a staircase leads down to a rocky beach. Two rooms, one of which is wheelchair accessible, in a separate cottage have forest views. ⊠ *460 Marine Dr., Box 318, V0R 3A0* ☎ *250/726–2686 or 888/936–5222* 🖶 *250/726–2685* ⊕ *www.awesomeview.com* ➲ *6 rooms* ⚘ *Some refrigerators, Wi-Fi, outdoor* *hot tub, bicycles, some pets allowed (fee); no a/c, no room phones, no room TVs, no kids, no smoking* ☰ *MC, V* ⭤ *BP.*

$–$$$ ⌂ **Canadian Princess Resort.** You can book a cabin on this 1932 steam-powered survey ship moored at Ucluelet's marina. Though hardly opulent, the staterooms are comfortable, with one to four berths and shared bathrooms. The captain's cabin is a full suite with a private bath. The resort's shoreside rooms are bigger, if less atmospheric, with private entrances, contemporary furnishings, and patios or balconies; a few have fireplaces, and some are large enough to sleep six. Most guests come here to fish or whale-watch—the resort is home to the area's largest charter company. ✉ *1943 Peninsula Rd., Box 939, V0R 3A0* ☎ *250/726–7771 or 800/663–7090* 🖷 *250/726–7121* ⊕ *www.canadianprincess.com* ⥽ *46 shoreside rooms, 27 shipboard cabins without bath, 1 suite* ⌂ *Restaurant, cable TV, lounge, pub, shop, meeting rooms; no a/c, no room phones, no TV in some rooms, no smoking* ☰ *AE, DC, MC, V* ⊗ *Closed mid-Sept.–mid-Mar.*

Sports & the Outdoors

ECOTOURS A great way to learn about the area's natural history and ecosystems is on a guided walk or hike with **Long Beach Nature** (☎ 250/726–7099 ⊕ www.oceansedge.bc.ca). Led by a biologist and former chief naturalist at Pacific Rim National Park, half- and full-day outings range from easy to challenging and include hikes through old-growth rain forest, beach and headland hiking, and storm watching during fall and winter. For a chauffeured four-wheel-drive tour of the backcountry, including the Clayoquot Biosphere Reserve, contact **RainCoast Back Road Adventures** (☎ 250/726–7625 ⊕ www.raincoastadventures.com).

FISHING The **Canadian Princess Resort** (✉ 1943 Peninsula Rd. ☎ 250/726–7771 or 800/663–7090 ⊕ www.canadianprincess.com) has 10 comfortable fishing and whale-watching boats with heated cabins and bathrooms. The relatively inexpensive charters appeal to groups and families. **Island West Fishing Resort** (✉ Foot of Bay St. ☎ 250/726–7515 ⊕ www.islandwestresort.com) specializes in fishing charters and also has accommodations, an RV park, boat moorage, and floatplane sightseeing tours in the Ucluelet area.

KAYAKING Experienced guides with **Majestic Ocean Kayaking** (✉ 1167 Helen Rd. ☎ 250/726–2868 or 800/889–7644 ⊕ www.oceankayaking.com) can take you out to explore the clear waters surrounding the Broken Group Islands.

WHALE- **Jamie's Whaling Station** (✉ 168 Fraser La., on waterfront promenade
WATCHING ☎ 250/726–7444 or 877/726–7444 ⊕ www.jamies.com) offers guaranteed sightings, so if you don't see a whale on your first trip, you can take another tour at no charge. You can book a whole range of adventures here including surfing, kayaking, four-wheel drive trips, and hot-spring tours. **Subtidal Adventures** (✉ 1950 Peninsula Rd. ☎ 250/726–7336 or 877/444–1134 ⊕ www.subtidaladventures.com) specializes in whale-watching and nature tours to the Broken Group Islands; there's a choice of a Zodiac (a motorized inflatable boat) or a 36-foot former coast-guard rescue boat.

Tofino

㉕ *42 km (26 mi) northwest of Ucluelet, 337 km (209 mi) northwest of Victoria.*

The end of the road makes a great stage—and Tofino is certainly that. On a narrow peninsula just beyond the north end of the Pacific Rim National Park Reserve, this is as far west as you can go on Vancouver Island by paved road. One look at the pounding Pacific surf at Chesterman Beach and the old-growth forest along the shoreline convinces many people that they've reached not just the end of the road but the end of the Earth.

Tofino's 1,400 or so permanent residents host about a million visitors every year, but they have made what could have been a tourist trap into a funky little town with several art galleries, good restaurants, and plenty of opportunity to get out to the surrounding wilds. Reservations are highly recommended any time of year.

Boats and floatplanes provide access to the surrounding roadless wilderness. The most popular day trip is to **Hot Springs Cove**, where you can soak in natural rock pools. On **Meares Island**, an easy 20-minute boardwalk trail leads to trees up to 1,600 years old. On **Flores Island**, a challenging five-hour hike called Walk on the Wild Side leads through the old growth.

At the **Tofino Botanical Gardens** (✉ 1084 Pacific Rim Hwy. ☎ 250/725–1220 ⊕ www.tofinobotanicalgardens.com) trails wind through displays of indigenous plant life. The 12-acre waterfront site about 2 km (1 mi) south of the village on the Pacific Rim Highway is open 9 to dusk daily, and the C$10 admission is good for three days.

Where to Stay & Eat

$$–$$$ ✕ **RainCoast Café.** Minimalist and candlelighted with peekaboo sea views, this tiny village-center restaurant shines with Asian takes on local seafood and great vegetarian options. For starters, consider the Pacific sweet-water oysters with smoked chili-lime crème fraiche, or the mussels and clams in sweet coconut broth. Main courses might be a delicious hot-and-sweet pad thai made with local seafood, organic Muscovy duck breast with blackberry sauce, or a rich *roghan josh*—lamb shank slow roasted in a traditional north Indian–almond sauce. You can catch live music here on Tuesday nights. ✉ *101–120 4th St.* ☎ *250/725–2215* ▭ *AE, MC, V* ☉ *No lunch.*

$$–$$$ ✕ **The Schooner on Second.** You can't miss this 1940s red-clapboard building in central Tofino—it's the one with the schooner sticking out the back; the bow of the boat takes up a chunk of the cozy rooms. The seafood-oriented menu changes frequently, but try, if it's available, the halibut Bawden Bay, which is a halibut fillet stuffed with Brie, crab, pine nuts, and shrimp in an apple-peppercorn brandy sauce. The Schooner is also popular with locals and tourists alike for its hearty breakfasts and lunchtime sandwiches, burgers, and pastas. ✉ *331 Campbell St.* ☎ *250/725–3444* ▭ *AE, MC, V.*

$$–$$$ ✕ **Shelter Restaurant.** From the outside, this seafood spot looks like an overgrown fishing shack; the interior, with its leather seats, vaulted ceiling and convivial bar, achieves rustic and hip at the same time—much like Tofino itself. The fare is, for the most part, organic, local, and in-season, with a seafood focus. Starters include local Dungeness crab fritters, organic greens from a nearby farm, or fries with smoked paprika mayonnaise. Bouillabaisse, clam linguini, prosciutto-wrapped halibut, and wild salmon are popular mains. In the off-season watch for unusual catches like skate, rockfish, or ling cod. ⊠ *601 Campbell St.* ☎ *250/725–3353* ▤ *AE, DC, MC, V* ⊘ *No lunch.*

$$ ✕ **Sobo in the Garden.** Local artwork and lush garden views are the background to a frequently changing menu of local, seasonal, and organic fare at this little café in the Tofino Botanical Gardens. The name, short for "sophisticated bohemian" sums up the style here: a classically trained chef offering casual fare influenced by international street food. Tapas might be halibut cheeks or sushi rice pockets. Mains range from cedar plank wild salmon to mushroom enchiladas. A catering truck on-site is open 11 AM to 5 PM daily for high-end takeout food, including the chefs legendary fish tacos. ⊠ *1084 Pacific Rim Hwy., Hwy. 4* ☎ *250/725–2341* ▤ *AE, MC, V* ⊘ *No lunch in café. Closed Tues. and Wed.*

★ $$$$ ✕▥ **Long Beach Lodge Resort.** Dramatic First Nations art, a tall granite fireplace, and expansive views of the crashing surf define the striking great room at this luxury lodge, which overlooks the long stretch of sand at Cox Bay. Throughout the lodge and cabins are handcrafted furniture, exposed fir beams, soothing earth tones, and such artful details as handwoven-kelp amenities baskets. Accommodations include comfortable lodge rooms and two-bedroom cottages. The chef uses fresh, local, organic ingredients whenever possible for the lunch and dinner menus ($$$$), for the shared plates served in the great room, and even for the picnic lunches. ⊠ *1441 Pacific Rim Hwy., Box 897, V0R 2Z0* ☎ *250/725–2442 or 877/844–7873* ⊟ *250/725–2402* ⊕ *www.longbeachlodgeresort.com* ⇝ *41 rooms, 20 cottages* ⊘ *Restaurant, some in-room hot tubs (in cottages), some kitchens (in cottages), cable TV, in-room DVDs, in-room data ports, lounge, meeting room, some pets allowed (fee); no a/c, no smoking* ▤ *AE, MC, V* ⊦◉⊧ *CP.*

$$$$ ✕▥ **The Wickaninnish Inn.** On a rocky promontory above Chesterman **Fodor'sChoice** Beach, with open ocean on three sides and old-growth forest as a backdrop, sits this cedar-sided inn. Every room has an ocean or beach view,
★ balcony, oversize soaker tub, and fireplace; the Ancient Cedars Spa offers hot-stone massages, Polynesian treatments, and couples massages in oceanfront treatment rooms; yoga classes run daily. The glass-enclosed Pointe Restaurant ($$$$) has views of the crashing surf and is renowned for its Pacific Northwest cuisine; chef Andrew Springett makes the most of such local delicacies as oysters, gooseneck barnacles, wild mushrooms, Dungeness crab, and Pacific salmon. ⊠ *Osprey La., at Chesterman Beach, Box 250, V0R 2Z0* ☎ *250/725–3100 or 800/333–4604* ⊟ *250/725–3110* ⊕ *www.wickinn.com* ⇝ *64 rooms, 11 suites* ⊘ *Restaurant, room service, IDD phones, in-room safes, some kitchens, minibars, microwaves, cable TV, in-room DVD, in-room broadband, gym, spa, steam room, beach, mountain bikes, lounge, library, shop, babysitting,*

laundry service, concierge, business services, meeting rooms, some pets allowed (fee); no a/c, no smoking ⊟ *AE, DC, MC, V.*

$$ ✕▦ **Inn at Tough City.** Vintage advertising paraphernalia and First Nations art create a fun and funky look at this harborside inn. The name is derived from Tofino's old nickname, from the days before roads, when life was rough here. It certainly isn't anymore: the guest rooms have bold colors, stained-glass windows, hardwood floors, antiques, decks or balconies, and down duvets. Several have striking views over Tofino Harbour and Clayoquot Sound, fireplaces, and soaking tubs. The hotel's water-view restaurant, Tough City Sushi ($$–$$$), uses fresh local seafood for its sushi and Pacific Northwest fare. ⊠ *350 Main St., Box 8, V0R 2Z0* ☎ *250/725–2021 or 877/725–2021* 🖷 *250/725–2088* ⊕ *www.toughcity.com* ⌨ *8 rooms* ⚭ *Restaurant, IDD phones, cable TV, bar; no a/c, no smoking* ⊟ *AE, MC, V.*

$$$$ ▦ **Clayoquot Wilderness Resorts & Spa.** This two-part wilderness retreat includes a floating lodge moored next to a landscape of private lakes, ancient forests and a natural waterfall-fed pool, in Quait Bay, about 30 minutes by boat from Tofino. Part two is the resort's Wilderness Outpost on the banks of the pristine Bedwell River, where luxurious tents, complete with antiques, and woodstoves are fashioned after the Rockefellers' summer camp. Three, four, and seven night packages include everything from meals, drinks, and spa services to whale-watching, canoeing, kayaking, sailing, day trips to outlying islands, and even airfare from Vancouver. Day packages at the lodge's spa are also available. ⊡ *Box 130, V0R 2Z0* ☎ *250/726–8235 or 888/333–5405* 🖷 *250/726–8558* ⊕ *www.wildretreat.com* ⌨ *16 rooms, 10 tents* ⚭ *Restaurant lodge only, room service lodge only, gym lodge only, outdoor hot tubs, sauna, spa, dock lodge only, boating, fishing, mountain bikes, hiking, horseback riding, lounge lodge only, shop lodge only, business services lodge only, meeting rooms lodge only; no a/c, no room phones, no room TVs, no smoking* ⊟ *AE, MC, V* ☉ *Closed Nov.–Apr.* ⦿⧉ *AP.*

★ $–$$$$ ▦ **Middle Beach Lodge.** This longtime favorite, set on a bluff over a mile of private beach, has several options: serene, adults-only phone- and TV-free rooms in the Lodge at the Beach; ocean-view rooms and suites, most with kitchenettes, at the Headlands; and self-contained cabins, some with hot tubs, suitable for families. The decor throughout defines West Coast rustic elegance, with recycled timbers, woodsy colors, and a smattering of antiques. Each lodge has an expansive common room with a floor-to-ceiling stone fireplace and far-reaching ocean views. ⊠ *400 MacKenzie Beach Rd., Box 100, V0R 2Z0* ☎ *250/725–2900* 🖷 *250/725–2901* ⊕ *www.middlebeach.com* ⌨ *35 rooms, 10 suites, 19 cabins* ⚭ *Restaurant, some kitchenettes, cable TV, some in-room DVD/VCRs, some in-room data ports, gym, outdoor hot tub, massage, sauna, Ping-Pong, lounge, shop, babysitting, laundry facilities, business services, meeting rooms, some pets allowed (fee); no a/c, no phones in some rooms, no TV in some rooms, no smoking* ⊟ *AE, MC, V* ☉ *Restaurant closed Sun.–Thurs. Sept.–June. No lunch* ⦿⧉ *CP.*

★ ¢ ▦ **Whalers on the Point Guesthouse.** With its hardwood floors, harbor-view picture windows, and big stone fireplace, this modern seaside hostel looks more like an upscale lodge than a backpackers' haven. It also has pretty much everything a budget traveler could want: a game room and TV lounge, a shared kitchen and living room, even surfboard storage. Accommodation is available in private rooms with shared bathrooms, family rooms (for four) with private bathrooms, and four-bed dorm rooms with shared bathrooms. Advance reservations are highly recommended. ⊠ *81 West St., Box 296, V0R 2Z0* ☎ *250/725–3443* 🖷 *250/725–3463* ⊕ *www. tofinohostel.com* ↩*7 rooms, 11 dorm rooms* ⚅*Dining room, Wi-Fi, sauna, billiards, recreation room, laundry facilities, Internet room; no a/c, no room phones, no room TVs, no smoking* ☰*MC, V.*

Sports & the Outdoors

FISHING **Chinook Charters** (⊠ 331 Main St. ☎ 250/725–3431) leads fishing charters in the area. **Weigh West Marine Resort Adventure Centre** (☎ 250/ 725–3277 or 800/665–8922 ⊕ www.weighwest.com) operates a marina and conducts fishing charters, including saltwater fly-fishing. The outfitter can also arrange accommodation, meals, and guides as well as kayaking, whale-watching, hot-springs tours, and surfing trips.

FLIGHTSEEING **Tofino Air** (☎ 250/725–4454 or 866/486–3247) runs 20-minute flightseeing tours over outlying forests and beaches, flights to Hot Springs Cove, trips to the lakes and glaciers of Strathcona Provincial Park and flights to Cougar Annie's Garden—a century old wilderness homestead, once the home of the eponymous legendary local character.

KAYAKING **Remote Passages** (⊠ 71 Wharf St. ☎ 250/725–3330 or 800/666–9833 ⊕ www.remotepassages.com) has easy guided paddles in sheltered waters; no experience is necessary. **Tofino Sea-Kayaking Company** (⊠ 320 Main St. ☎ 250/725–4222 or 800/863–4664 ⊕ www.tofino-kayaking. com) rents kayaks, runs a kayaking school, and offers day and multiday wilderness kayaking trips. No experience is necessary.

SURFING Tofino, despite the chilling waters, is a popular place to surf. You can rent boards and other gear at **Storm, the Tofino Surf Shop** (⊠ 444 Campbell St. ☎ 250/725–3344). **Inner Rhythm Surf Camp** (☎ 250/726–2211 or 877/393–7873 ⊕ www.innerrhythm.ca) has lessons, rentals, surf camps, and surf tours to remote beaches. For surfing lessons at all levels, contact the **Pacific Surf School** (⊠ 430 Campbell St. ☎ 250/725–2155 or 888/777–9961 ⊕ www.pacificsurfschool.com). **Surf Sister** (⊠ 1180 Pacific Rim Hwy. ☎ 250/725–4456 or 877/724–7873 ⊕ www.surfsister. com) teaches women-only and coed surfing lessons.

WHALE-
WATCHING &
MARINE
EXCURSIONS In March and April, an estimated 20,000 gray whales migrate along the coast here; resident grays can be seen anytime between March and October. In addition, humpback whales, sea otters, orca, bears, and other wildlife are increasingly seen in the area. Most whale-watching operators lead excursions along the coast and to the region's outlying islands, including Meares Island, Flores Island, and Hot Springs Cove. Services range from no-frills water-taxi drop-off to tours with experienced guides; prices vary accordingly.

Jamie's Whaling Station & Adventure Centre (⊠ 606 Campbell St. ☎ 250/ 725–3919 or 800/667–9913 ⊕ www.jamies.com) is one of the most established whale-watching operators on the coast. It has both Zodiacs and more comfortable covered 65-foot tour boats. You can book a whole range of adventures here, including kayaking, 4X4 tours, Meares Island trips, and surf lessons. **Remote Passages Marine Excursions** (✉ 71 Wharf St. ☎ 250/725–3330 or 800/666–9833 ⊕ www.remotepassages.com), a well-established operator, runs whale-watching, bear-watching, and other wildlife-viewing trips with an ecological and educational focus using both Zodiacs and covered boats. **Sea Trek Tours and Expeditions** (☎ 250/725–4412 or 800/811–9155 ⊕ www.seatrektours.bc.ca) operates whale- and bear-watching and harbor tours as well as day trips to Hot Springs Cove and Meares Island and glass-bottom-boat tours. With **Tla-ook Cultural Adventures** (☎ 250/725–2656 or 877/942–2663 ⊕ www.tlaook.com) you can paddle a traditional Nuu-chah-nulth dugout canoe with a First Nations Guide.

The **Whale Centre** (✉ 411 Campbell St. ☎ 250/725–2132 or 888/474–2288 ⊕ www.tofinowhalecentre.com) has a maritime museum with a 40-foot whale skeleton you can study while waiting for your boat.

Shopping

In a traditional longhouse, the magnificent **Eagle Aerie Gallery** (✉ 350 Campbell St. ☎ 250/725–3235) houses a collection of prints, paintings, and carvings by the renowned artist Roy Henry Vickers. **House of Himwitsa** (✉ 300 Main St. ☎ 250/725–2017 or 800/899–1947) sells First Nations crafts, jewelry, and clothing. The complex also has a seafood restaurant and lodge rooms. Photographs, paintings, carvings, pottery, and jewelry by local artists are available at **Reflecting Spirit Gallery** (✉ 411 Campbell St. ☎ 250/725–2472). **Wildside Booksellers** (✉ 320 Main St. ☎ 250/725–4222) has an extensive selection of books and kites and houses an espresso bar.

Pacific Rim National Park Reserve

❷ *105 km (63 mi) west of Port Alberni, 9 km (5 mi) south of Tofino.*

Fodor's Choice
★

This national park has some of Canada's most stunning coastal and rain-forest scenery, abundant wildlife, and a unique marine environment. It comprises three separate units—Long Beach, the Broken Group Islands, and the West Coast Trail—for a combined area of 123,431 acres, and stretches 130 km (81 mi) along Vancouver Island's west coast. The **Pacific Rim Visitor Centre** located at the Tofino-Ucluelet junction on Highway 4 (☎ 250/726–4212) is open daily mid-March to mid-October 9 to 5. Park-use fees apply in all sections of the park.

The **Long Beach** unit gets its name from a 16-km (10-mi) strip of hard-packed sand strewn with driftwood, shells, and the occasional Japanese glass fishing float. Long Beach is the most accessible part of the park and can get busy in summer. People come in the off-season to watch winter storms and to see migrating whales in early spring. A C$10 daily group pass, available from dispensers in the parking lots, is required for each private vehicle and includes admission to the Wickaninnish Interpretive Centre and all park interpretive programs, including shows at the Green Point campground theater. You can camp on a bluff above Long Beach at **Green Point Campground** (✉ Off Hwy. 4 just north of Tofino-Ucluelet junction ☎ 877/737–3783 ⊕ www.pccamping.ca) between mid-March and mid-October. Walk-in sites, in the woods and on the beach, are issued on a first-come, first-served basis and fill quickly. Drive-in sites (with no RV hookups) can be reserved by phone or through the Web site. A theater at the campground runs films and interpretive programs about park ecology and history.

A first stop for many Pacific Rim National Park visitors, the **Wickaninnish Interpretive Centre** (⊠ Hwy. 4 ☎ 250/726–4701 center, 250/726–7706 restaurant) is on the ocean's edge about 16 km (10 mi) north of Ucluelet. It's a great place to learn about the wilderness; theater programs and exhibits provide information about the park's marine ecology and rainforest environment. Open daily mid-March to mid-October 10 to 6, the center is also a good lunch stop—it was originally an inn, and its restaurant still serves up hearty seafood lunches and dinners.

The 100-plus islands of the **Broken Group Islands** archipelago can be reached only by boat. The islands and their clear waters are alive with sea lions, seals, and whales. The inner waters are good for kayaking. Guided kayak and charter-boat tours are available from Ucluelet, Bamfield, and Port Alberni. Camping is limited to designated sites and costs C$8 per person per night. The sites are rustic and available on a first-come, first-served basis.

The third element of the park, the **West Coast Trail,** runs along the coast from Bamfield to Port Renfrew. This extremely rugged 75-km (47-mi) trail is for experienced hikers. It can be traveled only on foot, takes an average of six days to complete, and is open from May 1 to September 30. A quota system helps the park manage the number of hikers on the trail, and reservations are recommended between mid-June and mid-September, although some spaces are available on a first-come, first-served basis at each end of the trail during this time. A number of fees apply: C$25 for a reservation, C$90 for a hiker's permit, and C$28 for two ferry crossings. Reservations can be made up to three months in advance via Hello BC (☎ 800/435–5622) from March through September. ⬧ *Box 280, Ucluelet V0R 3A0* ☎ *250/726–7721* 🖨 *250/726–4720* ⊕ *www.pc.gc.ca/pacificrim.*

Parksville

㉗ *47 km (29 mi) east of Port Alberni, 38 km (24 mi) northwest of Nanaimo, 72 km (45 mi) southeast of Courtenay, 154 km (95 mi) north of Victoria.*

The resort and retirement town of Parksville marks the start of the Oceanside Route, or Highway 19A, which winds along the coast to Courtenay, through woods and past sandy beaches and small seaside settlements. If you're in a hurry you can travel north on the faster, newer Inland Highway (Highway 19).

☾ Forest trails lead to thundering waterfalls at **Englishman River Falls Provincial Park** (⊠ Errington Rd., Exit 51 off Hwy. 19 ☎ 800/689–9025 camping reservations ⊕ www.discovercamping.ca), 13 km (8 mi) south-
☾ west of Parksville. At **Rathtrevor Beach Provincial Park** (⊠ Off Hwy. 19A ☎ 800/689–9025 camping reservations ⊕ www.discovercamping.ca),

2 km (1 mi) south of Parksville, high tide brings ashore the warmest ocean water in British Columbia.

COOMBS – If you're traveling from Parksville to Port Alberni, it's worth taking the quieter Highway 4A past this odd little village, best known for its cluster of antiques and curio shops and the goats grazing on the grass-covered roof of its Old Country Market.

BUTTERFLY WORLD – Worth a stop is Butterfly World where you can wander through an atrium filled with hundreds of free-flying butterflies. Admission is C$8.75 in summer, with discounts other months. ☒ *1080 Winchester Rd., Hwy. 4A* ☎ *250/248–7026* ⊕ *www.nature-world.com/tropical.html* ☯ *mid-Mar.–Apr., daily 10-4; May–Sept., daily 10–5.*

Where to Stay

★ **$$–$$$$** 🏨 **Tigh-Na-Mara Seaside Spa, Resort & Conference Centre.** A 2,500-square-foot mineral bath, complete with waterfall and grottolike setting, is the centerpiece of this beachside spa resort. Twenty-two forested seaside acres also include a long, sandy beach, and loads of kids activities. At the log-construction lodge high over the water, all units have fireplaces and decks with ocean views. Several studio, and one- and two-bedroom cabins in the woods don't have water views but do have kitchens and fireplaces. Pets (fee) are permitted in the off-season. ☒ *1095 E. Island Hwy., Hwy. 19A, V9P 2E5* ☎ *250/248–2072 or 800/663-7373* 🖷 *250/248–4140* ⊕ *www.tigh-na-mara.com* ☞ *88 rooms, 72 suites, 33 cabins* ♺ *Restaurant, IDD phones, some kitchens, microwaves, refrigerators, cable TV with movies and video games, in-room broadband, tennis court, indoor pool, hair salon, steam room, boating, bicycles, badminton, basketball, boccie, croquet, horseshoes, Ping-Pong, volleyball, lounge, shop, babysitting, children's programs (ages 4–16), laundry facilities, concierge (summer only), business services, meeting rooms; no a/c, no smoking* ▤ *AE, DC, MC, V.*

Sports & the Outdoors

With six ocean- and mountain-view courses in the area, Parksville is a major year-round golf destination. **Fairwinds Golf & Country Club** (☒ 3730 Fairwinds Dr., Nanoose Bay ☎ 250/468–7666 or 888/781–2777 ⊕ www.fairwinds.bc.ca) is a par-71, 18-hole course. **Morningstar International Golf Course** (☒ 525 Lowry's Rd. ☎ 250/248–8161 or 800/567–1320 ⊕ www.morningstar.bc.ca) is a par-72, 18-hole course.

The peaks and watersheds inland from Qualicum Beach and Parksville create an environment so distinct the area has been declared a U.N. Biosphere Reserve (the Mount Arrowsmith Biosphere Reserve). Two provincial parks, both along Highway 4 en route to Port Alberni and the west coast, provide a taste of this unique ecosystem. At **Little Qualicum Falls Provincial Park** (☎ 800/689–9025 camping reservations), 15 km (9 mi) west of Qualicum Beach, Cameron Lake empties into Little Qualicum River over a series of waterfalls, and hiking trails lace the woods. The campground is popular with families. At **Cathedral Grove** in MacMillan Provincial Park, 20 km (12 mi) west of Qualicum Beach, walking trails lead past Douglas fir trees and western red cedars, some as many as 800 years old. Their remarkable height creates a spiritual effect, as though you were gazing at a cathedral ceiling.

Qualicum Beach

28 *10 km (6 mi) north of Parksville.*

Qualicum Beach's long stretch of sand has attracted vacationers for more than a century. The pedestrian-friendly village, on a hill above the sea, is full of interesting shops and cafés. From Qualicum Beach, Highway 4 travels to the island's west coast.

The **Old School House Arts Centre** (⊠ 122 Fern Rd. W ☎ 250/752–6133) shows and sells the work of local artists. At **Milner Gardens and Woodland** (⊠ 2179 W. Island Hwy., Hwy. 19A ☎ 250/752–6153 ⊕ www. milnergardens.org) a 1930s tea plantation–style house and 10 acres of gardens, surrounded by woodlands, are set on a bluff above the sea. The gardens are open May to mid-October, daily 10 to 5 admission is C$10.

Guided and self-guided spelunking tours for all levels are conducted year-round at **Horne Lake Caves Provincial Park** (☎ 250/757–8687 information, 250/248–7829 tour reservations ⊕ www.hornelake.com). Prices start at C$15 for a 1½-hour family-oriented tour; reservations are recommended in summer and required in winter. There's also a campsite at the park. The park turnoff is about 11 km (7 mi) north of Qualicum Beach off Highway 19 or 19A. From the turnoff, the park is another 15 km (9 mi) along a gravel road.

Pheasant Glen Golf Resort (⊠ 1025 Qualicum Rd. ☎ 250/752–8786 or 877/407–4653) is a challenging 6,600 yard, par 72 championship course with water in play on 9 holes and over 50 bunkers. Also on-site are a golf academy and a high-tech driving range. Accommodation is planned for late 2006.

Where to Stay & Eat

$–$$ ✕ **The Beach House Café.** European, Asian, and Canadian dishes highlight this casual, kid-friendly seaside restaurant, where spaetzle and schnitzel share menu space with Thai satay and West Coast bouillabaisse. A local favorite, though, is roast duckling in blackberry sauce. Sandwiches, burgers, pasta, and pizza fill the lunch menu. Both the beachfront deck and the two-tiered interior have ocean views. ⊠ 2775 W. Island Hwy., Hwy. 19A ☎ 250/752–9626 ☰ MC, V ☉ Closed Jan.

$$–$$$ ▣ **Ships Point Inn.** Six themed rooms, from the colonial Bombay room to the Mediterranean Rafael room fill this century old home 20 km (12 mi) north of Qualicum Bay. Canopy beds, antiques, and lush color schemes make each room unique; seaside gardens include a waterfront walkway and a hot tub in an ocean-view gazebo. The kitchen, deck, sitting room, and several guest rooms also take in sweeping ocean and mountain views. Three rooms in another building on-site are planned for 2006. The hosts will also provide evening meals by prior arrangement. ⊠ 7584

Ships Point Rd., Station 39-C18, Fanny Bay, V0R 1W0 ☏ *250/335–1004 or 877/742–1004* 🖷 *250/335–1014* ⊕ *www.shipspointinn.com* ⇝ *6 rooms* ⌂ *Outdoor hot tub, Internet room; no a/c, no room phones, no room TVs, no kids under 12, no smoking* ⊟ *AE, MC, V* ⎢⊙⎢ *BP.*

---

en route

Between Qualicum Beach and the twin cities of Courtenay and Comox is tiny Buckley Bay, where BC Ferries leave for **Denman Island**, with connecting service to **Hornby Island.** Both these pretty rural islands have crafts shops, cafés, walking trails, and accommodations. Hornby is best known for its long, sandy beaches.

Courtenay

㉙ *220 km (136 mi) northwest of Victoria, 17 nautical mi west of Powell River, 57 km (34 mi) northwest of Qualicum Beach.*

This friendly town makes a good base to enjoy the area's wealth of outdoor activities, including golf, hiking, and skiing at nearby Mount Washington Alpine Resort. Ferries to Powell River on the mainland sail from Little River, 6 km (4 mi) north of Courtenay.

Dinosaur fans should love the **Courtenay and District Museum and Paleontology Centre** (⊠ 207 4th St. ☏ 250/334–0686 ⊕ www. courtenaymuseum.ca), one of British Columbia's leading paleontology centers. It's home to the reconstructed skeleton of a 35-foot elasmosaur—a dinosaur-era sea creature found in the Comox Valley—and a 13-foot mosasaur skeleton. It also has some interesting First Nations and pioneer artifacts and arranges fossil-hunting day trips in the area. Admission is C$3. The museum is open daily 10 to 5 mid-May to Labor Day and, during the other months, Tuesday through Saturday 10 to 5.

---

off the beaten path

COMOX – East of Courtenay about 6 km (4 mi) is the twin town of Comox, which also serves as a base for Mt. Washington skiers. It's best known as the home to Canadian Forces Base Comox, an air-force base. Ferries to Powell River on the mainland leave from Little River, 6 km (4 mi) north of Comox.

FILBERG HERITAGE LODGE AND PARK – At the Filberg Heritage Lodge and Park you can stroll around 9 acres of beautifully landscaped waterfront grounds and tour the rustic 1929 lodge. The lodge is open 11 to 5 daily June through August, and weekends in May and September. In summer a petting zoo and seaside teahouse are also open. Admission to the gardens, which are open 8 AM to dusk all year, is free; lodge admission is C$2. ⊠ *61 Filberg Rd.* ☏ *250/339–2715* ⊕ *www.filberg.com.*

COMOX AIR FORCE MUSEUM – The Comox Air Force Museum, at Canadian Forces Base Comox in Lazo, about 1 km (1/2 mi) north of Comox, has a collection of air-force memorabilia and historic aircraft in the nearby airpark. The museum is open daily 10 to 4. The airpark is open daily 10 to 4 May through October only. Admission is by donation. ☏ *250/339–8162* ⊕ *www.comoxairforcemuseum.ca.*

Where to Stay & Eat

$-$$$ ✕ **Old House Restaurant.** This riverside restaurant set among gardens provides casual dining in a restored 1938 house with cedar beams, four stone fireplaces, and a patio for dining. People flock here for the West Coast home-style cuisine—sandwiches and salads at lunch; seafood, steaks, and pastas, along with more innovative dishes (house-aged beef tenderloin, Moroccan pork, Fanny Bay oysters) at dinner—and the fresh daily specials. Everything, including breads and desserts, is made in-house. ⊠ *1760 Riverside La.* ☎ *250/338–5406* ▤ *AE, DC, MC, V.*

$-$$ ✕ **The Atlas Café.** A vintage map of South America lends an exotic feel to this casual town-center café and local gathering place. The wholesome menu appeals to a globe-trotting clientele: nori rolls, falafel, Greek spinach pie, pastas, and vegan dishes appear along with an evening fresh sheet featuring local bounty. The dining room and attached martini bar serve the full menu until 10 PM, and crowds gather at breakfast for huevos rancheros and eggs benny. ⊠ *250 6th St.* ☎ *250/338–9838* ▤ *MC, V* ☽ *No dinner Mon. Closed last 2 wks of Jan.*

★ $$-$$$$ ✕▥ **Kingfisher Oceanside Resort & Spa.** A circuit of massaging waterfalls and mineral pools, called The Pacific Mist Hydropath, is the centerpiece of this low-key spa retreat 7 km (4½ mi) south of Courtenay. Beauty treatments, aromatherapy, and massage are all available. Dinner in the ocean-view restaurant ($$-$$$) might include fennel-crusted halibut with mango and chive butter, lamb shank with curried yogurt marinade, or wild salmon from the fresh sheet. Halibut and chips, wraps, salads, and local Fanny Bay oysters make this a good lunch stop as well. Folk art, sea shells, and soft earth and sea tones warm the beachfront suites, which all have balconies or patios, kitchens, gas fireplaces, and expansive ocean views. Lower-price rooms, set a little farther back from the water, also have views and balconies, and some have kitchenettes. ⊠ *4330 Island Hwy. S, V9N 9R9* ☎ *250/338–1323 or 800/663–7929* ▤ *250/338–0058* ⊕ *www.kingfisherspa.com* ☞ *28 rooms, 36 suites* ♧ *Restaurant, room service, IDD phones, some in-room safes, some kitchens, some kitchenettes, refrigerators, cable TV with movies, in-room DVC/VCRs, some in-room broadband, some in-room data ports, Wi-Fi, tennis court, indoor-outdoor pool, fitness classes, gym, outdoor hot tub, sauna, spa, steam room, mountain bikes, boccie, croquet, lounge, shop, babysitting, dry cleaning, laundry service, concierge, meeting rooms, some pets allowed (fee); no a/c in some rooms, no smoking* ▤ *AE, D, DC, MC, V.*

$ ▥ **Greystone Manor.** About 3 km (2 mi) south of Courtenay, this 1918 house has a lovingly tended 1½-acre English garden and views over Comox Bay, where seals are often visible. Inside, the original hardwood floors and period furnishings make things cozy. Two of the prettily decorated rooms have baths with showers; the third has a claw-foot tub in a room across the hall. ⊠ *4014 Haas Rd., V9N 9T4* ☎ *250/338–1422 or 866/338–1422* ⊕ *www.greystonemanorbb.com* ☞ *3 rooms* ♧ *Hiking, piano; no a/c, no room phones, no room TVs, no kids under 12, no smoking* ▤ *MC, V* ▥ *BP.*

Sports & the Outdoors

GOLF The 18-hole, par-72 course at the **Crown Isle Resort & Golf Commur˙** (⊠ 399 Clubhouse Dr., off Ryan Rd. ☎ 250/703–5050 or 888/33ᵖ

⊕ www.crownisle.com) is, at 7,024 yards, the longest course on Vancouver Island. You can stay here, too, in one of the lavish fairway-view rooms, suites, or kitchen-equipped villas. The clubhouse has a sweeping Titanic-style double staircase, classic-car museum, steak house, pub, and gym.

SKIING **Mount Washington Alpine Resort** (☎ 250/338–1386, 888/231–1499 lodging reservations ⊕ www.mountwashington.ca), 30 km (18 mi) from Courtenay via Strathcona Parkway, the island's largest ski area, receives some of North America's biggest snow falls—an average of nine meters (30 feet) each year. It boasts 60 downhill runs, a 1,657-foot vertical drop, five chairlifts, three surface lifts, and an elevation of 5,200 feet. The resort also has 55 km (33 mi) of track-set cross-country trails, 20 km (12 mi) of snowshoe trails, two snowboard parks, a half pipe (for snowboarding), snow-tubing chutes, and a natural luge track. In summer there are miles of alpine hiking and mountain-bike trails accessible by chairlift, as well as a disc-golf course, ATV tours, fly-fishing, and horseback riding. The resort has a good selection of restaurants, shops, and accommodations.

Campbell River

③ *50 km (31 mi) north of Courtenay, 155 km (96 mi) northwest of Nanaimo, 270 km (167 mi) northwest of Victoria.*

Campbell River draws people who want to fish; some of the biggest salmon ever caught on a line have been landed just off the coast here. Cutthroat trout are also plentiful in the river. Other recreational activities include kayaking, whale-watching, and diving in Discovery Passage, where a battleship was sunk for diving purposes. Ferries leave Campbell River for Quadra and Cortes islands, both popular fishing destinations.

You can rent fishing tackle and try your luck at the 600-foot-long **Discovery Pier** (✉ 655 Island Hwy. ☎ 250/286–6199). Or you could just buy some fish-and-chips at the concession. It's the real thing—made with fresh local halibut and wrapped in newspaper.

Haig-Brown Heritage Site (✉ 2250 Campbell River Rd. ☎ 250/286–6646 ⊕ www.haig-brown.bc.ca), the preserved home of conservationist and writer Roderick Haig-Brown, is set in a riverside garden surrounded by 20 acres of trail-laced woods. The grounds are open daily and admission is free; call ahead if you'd like to arrange a tour of the house. B&B rooms (C$85) are available year-round.

The **Campbell River Maritime Heritage Centre** (✉ 621 Island Hwy. ☎ 250/286–3161 ⊕ www.bcp45.org) has a large range of marine artifacts and displays about the town's maritime history. It's also home to BCP 45, the little fishing boat that long graced the Canadian $5 bill. Admission is by donation; it's open 9 to 5, Monday to Friday; ½-hour tours run between 1 and 3 PM.

On a hill overlooking the sea, the **Museum at Campbell River** (✉ 470 Island Hwy. ☎ 250/287–3103 ⊕ www.crmuseum.ca ✆ C$6 ☉ Mid-May–Sept., Mon.–Sat. 10–5, Sun. noon–5; Oct.–mid-May, Tues.–Sun.

noon–5) has great views, an excellent collection of First Nations arti-facts, and some intriguing historical exhibits, including a re-created pi-oneer cabin and floathouse, and a dramatic audiovisual retelling of a First Nations legend.

Where to Stay

$$–$$$$ ✕▦ **Painter's Lodge Holiday & Fishing Resort.** John Wayne and his fish-ing buddies came to this waterfront lodge to catch salmon in the 1940s and '50s. The attractive, refurbished cedar buildings still draw anglers; the resort's fleet of Boston Whalers runs fishing and nature cruises. The bar in the pub is upholstered with salmon leather, but accommodations are more subdued, with maple furniture, pastel bedspreads, and historic photos. The rooms, suites, and one- to three-bedroom cabins all have balconies or patios. Some have fireplaces and whirlpool baths and many are on two levels. The resort's ocean-view restaurant ($$–$$$) serves fresh seafood (naturally), and the resort's free water taxi runs to Painter's sister property, April Point Resort & Spa on Quadra Island, where you can dine, kayak, indulge in spa treatments, or explore biking and hik-ing trails. ⊠ *1625 McDonald Rd., V9W 5C1* ☎ *250/286–1102 or 800/663–7090* 🖶 *250/286–0158* ⊕ *www.obmg.com* ➳ *87 rooms, 3 suites, 4 cabins* ☖ *Restaurant, picnic area, some fans, in-room data ports, some kitchenettes, some refrigerators, cable TV, some in-room VCRs, 2 tennis courts, pool, exercise equipment, 2 outdoor hot tubs, billiards, lounge, pub, shop, babysitting, playground, dry cleaning, laundry ser-vice, business services, meeting rooms, airport shuttle, no-smoking rooms; no a/c* ➭ *AE, DC, MC, V* ⊘ *Closed mid-Oct.–mid-Mar.*

Shopping

Housed in a modern longhouse-style building, the **Wei Wai Kum House of Treasures** (⊠ 1370 Island Hwy., in Discovery Harbour Centre mall ☎ 250/286–1440) has an excellent collection of local First Nations masks, jewelry, and artwork. Attached to the gallery is the **Gildas Box of Treasures Theatre** (☎ 250/287–7310), where dance troupes perform in summer.

Quadra Island

㉛ *10 minutes by ferry from Campbell River.*

Quadra is a thickly forested island, rich with wildlife and laced with hik-ing trails. It's also home to a thriving arts community—the Campbell River Visitor Information Centre has maps of the studios and galleries that are open to the public. At low tide you can spot ancient petroglyphs along the shore at the south end of the island. BC Ferries (⇨ Vancou-ver Island A to Z) runs car ferries here from Campbell River, or you can hop the free foot-passenger ferry run by Painter's Lodge.

Rebecca Spit Provincial Park has pretty pebble beaches and picnic areas.

Where to Stay & Eat

$$–$$$ ✕▦ **April Point Resort & Spa.** You can try whale- and bear-watching, kayak-ing, fishing, hiking, and biking at this family-oriented, waterfront eco-tourism resort. Pine furniture and forest-green fabric enrich the roomy

lodge rooms and suites. Many rooms have fireplaces, and the three- and four-bedroom guesthouses each have a kitchen, fireplace, hot tub, and sundeck. The window-lined restaurant ($$–$$$) is a scenic place to enjoy fresh seafood. The Japanese-theme Spa at April Point offers a full range of Aveda treatments and the resort's free water taxi takes you to the tennis courts, pool, and hot tubs at Painter's Lodge in Campbell River. ✉ *900 April Point Rd., Box 248, Campbell River V9W 4Z9* ☎ *250/285–2222 or 800/663–7090* 🖷 *250/285–2411* ⊕ *www.aprilpoint.com* ⇋ *43 rooms, 6 cabins, 6 guesthouses* ⚐ *Restaurant, picnic area, some fans, some kitchenettes, some refrigerators, cable TV, spa, boating, marina, mountain bikes, boccie, croquet, lounge, pub, shop, babysitting, laundry facilities, laundry service, business services, meeting rooms, helipad, some pets allowed (fee); no air-conditioning, no room phones, no smoking* ☰ *AE, DC, MC, V* ⊗ *Closed Oct.–Apr.*

$$ ✕▣ **Tsa-Kwa-Luten Lodge.** Set on a bluff amid acres of forest, this lodge, operated by the Cape Mudge First Nations band, has a foyer built in the style of a longhouse and comfortable rooms with Kwagiulth art, balconies, and ocean views. Three two-bedroom beachfront cottages have gas fireplaces, whirlpool tubs, kitchenettes, and private verandas. A four-bedroom guesthouse is great for groups. You can kayak, bike, hike, fish, take a whale- or bear-watching cruise, and even try archery here. The restaurant ($$–$$$) serves traditional Kwagiulth cuisine such as cedar-baked salmon and venison stew. ✉ *1 Lighthouse Rd., Box 460, Quathiaski Cove V0P 1N0* ☎ *250/285–2042 or 800/665–7745* 🖷 *250/285–2532* ⊕ *www.capemudgeresort.com* ⇋ *30 rooms, 4 cottages* ⚐ *Restaurant, IDD phones, some kitchenettes, in-room data ports, exercise equipment, outdoor hot tub, massage, sauna, dock, mountain bikes, boccie, bar, lounge, shop, laundry service, business services, meeting rooms; no a/c, no room TVs, no smoking* ☰ *AE, DC, MC, V* ⊗ *Closed Oct.–Apr.*

Strathcona Provincial Park

★ ㉜ *40 km (25 mi) west of Campbell River.*

The largest provincial park on Vancouver Island, Strathcona Provincial Park encompasses **Mt. Golden Hinde,** at 7,220 feet the island's highest mountain, and **Della Falls,** one of Canada's highest waterfalls, reaching 1,440 feet. This strikingly scenic wilderness park's lakes and 161 campsites attract summer canoeists, hikers, anglers, and campers. The main access is by Highway 28 from Campbell River; Mt. Washington ski area, next to the park, can be reached by roads out of Courtenay. ☎ *800/689–9025 camping reservations* ⊕ *www.discovercamping.ca.*

Where to Stay

$–$$ ▣ **Strathcona Park Lodge and Outdoor Education Centre.** One of Canada's foremost outdoor education centers, this lakefront resort on the outskirts of Strathcona Provincial Park is a great place for kids and adults to try their hand at rock climbing, canoeing, kayaking and more. Family-run and kid-friendly, the resort has comfortable cottages and lodge rooms (some with shared baths), wholesome meals served buffet style in the rustic Whale Room or à la carte in the Canoe Club Café, and striking views of the snowcapped mountains behind Upper Campbell Lake. The activities are optional but hard to resist: the guides here are renowned for their patience and skill. ⊠ *40 km (24 mi) west of Campbell River on Hwy. 28, Box 2160, Campbell River V9W 5C5* ☎ *250/286–3122* 🖶 *250/286–6010* ⊕ *www.strathcona.bc.ca* 🛏 *39 rooms, 10 cottages, larger buildings available for groups* ♻ *Restaurant, cafeteria, picnic area, some kitchens, some kitchenettes, lake, massage, sauna, beach, dock, boating, basketball, hiking, volleyball, lounge, shop, laundry facilities, meeting rooms; no a/c, no room phones, no room TVs, no smoking* 🖃 *MC, V* ☉ *Canoe Club restaurant closed Sept.–June, Whale Room cafeteria closed mid-Nov.–Feb., lounge closed Sept.–June.*

Telegraph Cove

★ ㉝ *182 km (109 mi) northwest of Campbell River, 56 km (34 mi) southeast of Port Hardy, 16 km (10 mi) off Hwy. 19, partly by gravel road.*

Fishing villages built on pilings over the water were once a common sight on Canada's west coast. Telegraph Cove, with its row of brightly painted shops and houses connected by a boardwalk, is one of the last still standing. It's now home to a pub and restaurant, a general store, a marina, and several wildlife-watching and kayaking outfitters. You can see the skeleton of a 60-foot fin whale and other natural artifacts at the **Bones Project,** an interpretive center on the boardwalk. Accommodation options include a campground, a small hotel, and cabins run by **Telegraph Cove Resorts** (☎ 250/928–3131 or 800/200–4665 ⊕ www.telegraphcoveresort.com).

WHALE-WATCHING Telegraph Cove overlooks Johnstone Strait, one of the best places in the province to see orca, or killer, whales especially during the salmon runs of July, August, and September. Between late May and mid-October, **Stubbs Island Whale Watching** (☎ 250/928–3185 or 800/665–3066 ⊕ www.stubbs-island.com), on the boardwalk, runs 3½-hour whale-watching trips on its two 60-foot vessels. A naturalist accompanies the tours, and the boats are equipped with hydrophones for listening to the whales. Reservations are required.

off the beaten path

U'MISTA CULTURAL CENTRE – From Port McNeill, 26 km (16 mi) north of Telegraph Cove, a 40-minute ferry ride takes you to Alert Bay, where you can see the First Nations artifacts housed at this center. ⊠ *1 Front St., Alert Bay* ☎ *250/974–5403* ⊕ *www.umista.org.*

Thirty minutes by ferry from Port McNeill is **SOINTULA –** on Malcolm Island, which was founded in the early 1900s by a Finnish Utopian community. Three cooperatives founded by the commune are still operating. The village also has accommodations, camping, restaurants and a marina.

Port Hardy

③④ *238 km (148 mi) northwest of Campbell River, 499 km (309 mi) northwest of Victoria, 274 nautical mi southeast of Prince Rupert.*

Port Hardy is the departure and arrival point for BC Ferries' year-round trips through the scenic Inside Passage to and from Prince Rupert, the coastal port serving the Queen Charlotte Islands and southeast Alaska. In summer ferries sail from Port Hardy to Bella Coola and other small communities along British Columbia's mid-coast. Port Hardy can be crowded in summer, so book your accommodations early. Ferry reservations for the trip between Port Hardy and Prince Rupert or Bella Coola should also be made well in advance. **North Island Transportation** (☎ 250/949–6300) runs a shuttle bus between most Port Hardy hotels and the ferry terminal, which is 10 km (6 mi) from town. The fare is C$6.50.

off the beaten path

CAPE SCOTT PROVINCIAL PARK – At the northern tip of Vancouver Island and 67 km (42 mi) north of Port Hardy by gravel road is a wilderness camping region suitable for well-equipped and experienced hikers. It's home to coastal rain forest, salt marshes, sea stacks, and beautiful long sandy beaches. Hikers are drawn here to tackle the new 50 km (31 mi) North Coast Trail which, with the adjoining Cape Scott trail, creates 77 km (48 mi) of rugged coastal hiking. ⊕ *wlapwww.gov.bc.ca/bcparks or www.northernvancouverislandtrailssociety.com.*

Where to Stay

$$ 🏨 **Quarterdeck Inn and Marine Resort.** Most rooms have water views at this hotel on Port Hardy's waterfront. The rooms are bright and spacious with pastel decor. Two rooms have fireplaces and whirlpool tubs. A variety of outdoor activities, wildlife viewing, and First Nations cultural tours can be arranged from the hotel, which is a 10-minute drive from the ferry terminal. ⊠ *6555 Hardy Bay Rd., Box 910, V0N 2P0* ☎ *250/902–0455 or 877/902–0459* 🖷 *250/902–0454* ⊕ *www.quarterdeckresort.net* 🛏 *39 rooms, 1 suite* ☖ *Restaurant, IDD phones, some kitchenettes, cable TV, some in-room VCRs, in-room broadband, exercise equipment, outdoor hot tub, marina, pub, laundry facilities, business services, meeting rooms, some pets allowed (fee), no-smoking floor; no a/c* ▤ *AE, D, DC, MC, V* ◎ *CP.*

$–$$ 🏨 **Glen Lyon Inn.** You can often spot eagles scouting the water for fish to prey on from this modern hotel next to the marina on Hardy Bay. All rooms have full ocean views, most have balconies and two high-end rooms have king beds, Jacuzzi tubs, a bar, and a fireplace. Diving, wildlife viewing, and chartered fishing can be arranged from here, as well as freezing and storing your catch. The hotel is a 10-minute drive from the ferry terminal. ⊠ *6435 Hardy Bay Rd., Box 103, V0N 2P0* ☎ *250/949–7115 or 877/949–7115* 🖷 *250/949–7415* ⊕ *www.glenlyoninn.com* 🛏 *44 rooms* ☖ *Restaurant, IDD phones, some kitchenettes, some microwaves, some refrigerators, cable TV, Wi-Fi, exercise equipment, pub, laundry facilities, Internet room, meeting room, some pets allowed (fee), no-smoking floors* ▤ *AE, MC, V.*

Vancouver Island A to Z

To research prices, get advice from other travelers, and book travel arrangements, visit www.fodors.com.

AIR TRAVEL

Air Canada Jazz serves the larger towns on Vancouver Island. Baxter Aviation links Vancouver to Nanaimo by seaplane. Kenmore Air Harbor runs daily direct seaplane flights from Seattle to Victoria year-round and has summer service from Seattle to Nanaimo, Campbell River, Quadra Island, and other North Island and Inside Passage destinations. Sonic Blue Airways links Tofino with Vancouver. Northwest Seaplanes operates scheduled summer floatplane service from Seattle to Campbell River, and charter service to most northern Vancouver Island destinations.

Airlines & Contacts **Air Canada Jazz** ☎ 888/247-2262 ⊕ www.flyjazz.ca. **Baxter Aviation** ☎ 250/754-1066 or 800/661-5599 ⊕ www.baxterair.com. **Kenmore Air Harbor** ☎ 425/486-1257 or 800/543-9595 ⊕ www.kenmoreair.com. **Sonic Blue Airways** ☎ 604/278-1608 or 800/228-6608 ⊕ www.sonicblueair.com. **Northwest Seaplanes** ☎ 425/277-1590 or 800/690-0086 ⊕ www.nwseaplanes.com.

AIRPORTS

Vancouver Island is served by Victoria International Airport. Otherwise, there are domestic airports in or near many towns on the island, including Campbell River, Comox, and Nanaimo. Tofino and Port Hardy have airports that don't have phones. Smaller communities without airports are served by floatplanes.

Airport Information **Campbell River Airport** ✉ 1-2000 Jubilee Pkwy., Campbell River ☎ 250/923-5012. **Comox Valley Airport** ✉ Canadian Forces Base Comox ☎ 250/897-3123. **Nanaimo Airport** ✉ 3350 Spitfire Rd., Cassidy ☎ 250/245-2157.

BOAT & FERRY TRAVEL

BC Ferries has frequent, year-round passenger and vehicle service to Vancouver Island: a 1½-hour crossing from Tsawwassen (about an hour's drive south of Vancouver) to Swartz Bay (a 30-minute drive north of Victoria); a two-hour crossing from Tsawwassen to Duke Point, 15 km (9 mi) south of Nanaimo; and a 1½-hour crossing from Horseshoe Bay (a 30-minute drive north of Vancouver) to Departure Bay, 3 km (2 mi) north of Nanaimo. Vehicle reservations can be made for any of these routes; a C$15 reservation fee applies if you book more than a week ahead of time. The fee is C$17.50 for reservations within a week of sailing.

BC Ferries also has year-round passenger and vehicle service to most of the inhabited islands off Vancouver Island's east coast and links Comox with Powell River on the Sunshine Coast, though reservations cannot be made for this route. In addition, BC Ferries links Port Hardy, on the northern tip of Vancouver Island, with Bella Coola, Prince Rupert, and other towns along British Columbia's Inside Passage. Vehicle reservations are essential on these routes.

Lady Rose Marine Services takes passengers on packet freighters from Port Alberni to Vancouver Island's west coast. The M. V. *Lady Rose* makes the 4½-hour trip to Bamfield on Tuesday, Thursday, and Saturday year-round, with additional Friday and Sunday sailings in July and August. The round-trip fare is C$50. The M. V. *Francis Barkley* sails from Port Alberni to the Broken Group Islands and Ucluelet on Monday, Wednesday, and Friday between early June and late September. The round-trip fare is C$55 to Ucluelet, C$50 to the Broken Group Islands.

The M. V. *Uchuck*, a 100-passenger coastal packet freighter, sails from Gold River, 100 km (62 mi) west of Campbell River at the end of Highway 28, to a number of isolated west-coast settlements. Day trips (C$60 per person) and overnight trips (C$335–C$395 for two including one night at a B&B) are available all year. Reservations are essential.

HarbourLynx runs direct, high-speed, foot-passenger-only service between downtown Nanaimo and downtown Vancouver. The trip takes 80 minutes and costs C$25 plus tax each way.

🚢 Boat & Ferry Information **BC Ferries** ☎ 250/386-3431, 888/223-3779 in B.C. ⊕ www.bcferries.com. **HarbourLynx** ☎ 866/206-5969, 250/753-4443 in Nanaimo, 604/688-5465 in Vancouver ⊕ www.harbourlynx.com. **Lady Rose Marine Services** ☎ 250/723-8313, 800/663-7192 reservations Apr.–Sept. ⊕ www.ladyrosemarine.com. **M. V. *Uchuck*** ☎ 250/283-2515 or 250/283-2325 ⊕ www.mvuchuck.com.

BUS TRAVEL

Gray Line of Victoria provides bus service to most towns on Vancouver Island. From Vancouver, Greyhound serves Nanaimo and Pacific Coach Lines serves Victoria. The Tofino Bus has daily, year-round service from Victoria, and from Nanaimo's Departure Bay ferry terminal and HarbourLynx terminal, to Port Alberni, Tofino, and Ucluelet. One-way fares are C$35 from Nanaimo, C$53 from Victoria.

🚌 Bus Information **Gray Line of Victoria** ☎ 250/385-4411 or 800/318-0818 ⊕ www. graylinewest.com. **Greyhound** ☎ 604/482-8747 or 800/661-8747 ⊕ www.greyhound. ca. **Pacific Coach Lines** ☎ 250/385-4411 or 800/661-1725 ⊕ www.pacificcoach.com. **Tofino Bus** ☎ 250/725-2871 or 866/986-3466 ⊕ www.tofinobus.com.

CAR RENTAL

Most major agencies, including Avis, Budget, Hertz, and National Tilden, serve towns throughout Vancouver Island.

CAR TRAVEL

Major roads on Vancouver Island, and most secondary roads, are paved and well engineered. Many wilderness and park-access roads are unpaved. Inquire locally about logging activity before using logging or forest-service roads.

Highway 17 connects the Swartz Bay ferry terminal on the Saanich Peninsula with downtown Victoria. The Trans-Canada Highway (Highway 1) runs from Victoria to Nanaimo. The Island Highway (Highway 19) connects Nanaimo to Port Hardy. (Highway 19A, the old road, runs parallel as far as Campbell River. It's a slower, seaside option.) Highway 14 connects Victoria to Sooke and Port Renfrew on the west coast. Highway 4 crosses the island from Parksville to Tofino and Pacific Rim National Park Reserve.

EMERGENCIES

⚡ **Ambulance, fire, poison control, police** ☎ 911.

LODGING

Reservations for lodging anywhere in the province can be made through Hello BC's reservation service. From March through October the provincial government also runs Discover Camping, a toll-free Campground Reservation Line.

⚡ **Reservation Services Discover Camping** ☎ 800/689-9025 ⊕ www.discovercamping. ca. **Hello BC** ☎ 800/435-5622 ⊕ www.hellobc.com.

SPORTS & THE OUTDOORS

FISHING
Separate licenses are required for saltwater and freshwater fishing in British Columbia. Both are available at sporting-goods stores, government-agency offices, and most fishing lodges and charter-boat companies in the province. A one-day license for nonresidents costs about C$20 for freshwater fishing, C$7.50 for saltwater fishing. Additional fees apply to salmon fishing. For information about saltwater-fishing regulations, contact Fisheries and Oceans Canada, or pick up a free *Sport Fishing Guide,* available at most tourist-information centers or from Hello BC.

⚡ **Fisheries and Oceans Canada** ☎ 604/666-2828 ⊕ www.pac.dfo-mpo.gc.ca. **Hello BC** ☎ 800/435-5622 ⊕ www.hellobc.com.

GOLF
Vancouver Island's mild climate allows most golf courses to stay open all year. Summer greens fees range from C$50 to C$125. Golf Central provides a transportation and booking service for golfers on Vancouver Island. For advance tee-time bookings at courses in Victoria or Parksville, you can try Last Minute Golf.

⚡ **Golf Central** ☎ 250/380-4653 or 866/380-4653 ⊕ www.golfcentraltours.com. **Last Minute Golf** ☎ 604/878-1833 or 800/684-6344 ⊕ www.lastminutegolfbc.com.

HIKING
Ecosummer Expeditions has guided hiking trips along the West Coast trail. For parks information, visit B.C. Parks' Web site. For information and reservations about the West Coast Trail, contact Hello BC.

⚡ **B.C. Parks** ☎ No phone ⊕ wlapwww.gov.bc.ca/bcparks. **Ecosummer Expeditions** ☎ 250/674-0102 or 800/465-8884 ⊕ www.ecosummer.com. **Hello BC** ☎ 800/435-5622 ⊕ www.hellobc.com

KAYAKING
Several companies conduct multiday sea-kayaking trips to the coastal areas of Vancouver Island. Some of the excursions are suitable for beginners, and many trips provide an excellent chance to view orcas. Ecosummer Expeditions runs multiday paddles to Johnstone Strait. Gabriola Cycle and Kayak has sea-kayaking trips to the Broken Group Islands and other areas off the west coast of Vancouver Island. Ocean West Expeditions has three- to six-day paddling, camping, and orca-watching trips in Johnstone Strait. Majestic Ocean Kayaking offers guided half-day harbor tours, day trips, and multiday camping trips to the Broken Group Islands in the Pacific Rim National Park Reserve. Island Adventure Tours runs three-day, mothership-supported paddles through the Broken Group Islands in the Pacific Rim National Park Reserve. Nights are spent in a Bamfield lodge. With Mothership Adventures you can sea kayak

into remote areas of Johnstone Strait, using the *Columbia III,* a comfortable vintage 68-foot vessel as a floating base camp.

F **Ecosummer Expeditions** ☎ 250/674-0102 or 800/465-8884 ⊕ www.ecosummer. com. **Gabriola Cycle and Kayak** ☎ 250/247-8277 ⊕ www.gck.ca. **Island Adventure Tours** ✉ ☎ 250/812-7103 or 866/812-7103 ⊕ www.islandadventuretours.com. **Majestic Ocean Kayaking** ☎ 250/726-2868 or 800/889-7644 ⊕ www.oceankayaking.com. **Mothership Adventures** ☎ 250/202-3229 or 888/833-8887 ⊕ www. mothershipadventures.com. **Ocean West Expeditions** ☎ 250/362-7599 or 604/688-5770 ⊕ www.ocean-west.com.

TRAIN TRAVEL
VIA Rail operates the Malahat service, a small-gauge train that runs daily between Victoria, Chemainus, Nanaimo, and Courtenay.

F Fees & Schedules **VIA Rail** ☎ 888/842-7245 ⊕ www.viarail.ca.

VISITOR INFORMATION
F Tourist Information **Bamfield Chamber of Commerce** ☎ 250/728-3006 ⊕ www. bamfieldchamber.com. **Campbell River Visitor Info Centre** ✉ 1235 Shoppers Row Campbell River ☎ 250/287-4636 or 866/830-1113 ⊕ www.visitorinfo.incampbellriver. com. **Comox Valley Visitor Infocentre** ✉ 2040 Cliffe Ave., Courtenay ☎ 250/334-3234 or 888/357-4471 ⊕ www.comox-valley-tourism.ca. The **Duncan-Cowichan Visitor Infocentre** ✉ 381 Trans-Canada Hwy., Duncan ☎ 888/303-3337 or 250/746-4636 ⊕ www. duncancc.bc.ca. **Hello BC** ☎ 800/435-5622 ⊕ www.hellobc.com. **Nanaimo Visitor InfoCentre** ✉ 2290 Bowen Rd., Nanaimo ☎ 250/756-0106 or 800/663-7337 ⊕ www. tourismnanaimo.com. **Port Alberni Tourist Infocentre** ✉ 2533 Redford St., off Hwy. 4, Port Alberni ☎ 250/724-6535 ⊕ www.avcoc.com. **Port Hardy Visitor Information Centre** ✉ 7250 Market St., Port Hardy ☎ 250/949-7622 ⊕ www.ph-chamber.bc.ca. **Qualicum Beach Visitor Info Centre** ✉ 2711 W. Island Hwy., Qualicum Beach ☎ 250/ 752-9532 ⊕ www.qualicum.bc.ca. **Saanich Peninsula Visitor InfoCentre** ✉ 10382 Patricia Bay Hwy., Hwy. 17, Sidney ☎ 250/656-0525. **Sooke Visitor Information Centre** ✉ 2070 Phillips Rd., off Hwy. 14, Sooke ☎ 250/642-6351 ⊕ www.sookenet.com. **Tofino Visitor Info Centre** ✉ 1426 Pacific Rim Hwy., Tofino ☎ 250/725-3414 ⊕ www. tofinobc.org. **Tourism Vancouver Island** ✉ 203-335 Wesley St., Nanaimo V9R 2T5 ☎ 250/ 754-3500 ⊕ www.islands.bc.ca.

British Columbia

3

WORD OF MOUTH

"Whistler . . . SO much to do, and so nice! We go every year now. Usually in January. No rain, and the mountain is so high that you can usually ski ABOVE the clouds and rain if it happens to be a wet day."   —Stephanie_in_Canada

"I have to speak up for the Okanagan Valley, especially if you're with kids. The swimming is fantastic and the hiking is unbeatable. . . . The whole area is stunningly beautiful. Kelowna, the biggest town, has restaurants, shopping, and fun parks for young people who have tired of too much scenery. . . . Summerland and Penticton and the towns around Lake Okanagan are wonderful and welcoming. The fresh fruit and local fish are unbeatable, as is the camping . . ."   —LJ

By Sue
Kernaghan
and Chris
McBeath

BRITISH COLUMBIA'S MAINLAND harbors untouched forests, snow-capped peaks, powder skiing, and world-class fishing—a wealth of out-door action and beauty. The citizens are similarly diverse with descendants of original Native American peoples, British, European, and Asian set-tlers, as well as immigrants from all other corners of the earth.

As Canada's third-largest province (Québec and Ontario are bigger), British Columbia occupies almost 10% of Canada's total area, stretch-ing from the Pacific Ocean eastward to the province of Alberta and from the U.S. border north to the Yukon and Northwest Territories. It spans almost 1 million square km (about 360,000 square mi), making it larger than every American state except Alaska.

With most of the population clustered in Vancouver and Victoria, those who venture farther afield have plenty of room to explore. Two hours north of Vancouver is the popular resort town of Whistler, with North America's two biggest ski mountains. The Okanagan Valley in the east, replete with lakes and vineyards, is famous for its wines. Near Vancouver is the Sunshine Coast with its secluded fjords, and the Gulf Islands, both popular vacation spots for B.C. residents. To the north lies the Cariboo-Chilcotin region, beyond which you'll discover vast wilderness areas of mountainous and forested terrain; to the east are the foothills of the spec-tacular Rockies and a host of even more outdoor adventures.

Exploring British Columbia

Most of the population huddles in the Lower Mainland, a region in and around Vancouver in B.C.'s southwest corner. Beyond the Lower Main-land, three highways climb over the Coast Mountains to the rolling high plateau that forms the central interior. To the north lie the ranchlands of the Cariboo and, beyond that, the province's vast, sparsely inhabited north-ern half. To the east are the Okanagan and Shuswap valleys, home to the fruit- and wine-growing region and the lake district. Farther east are the mountainous Kootenays and the foothills of the Rockies.

The southernmost stretch of coastline just north of Vancouver, called the Sunshine Coast, is popular with boaters, artists, and summer vaca-tioners. Farther north is a roadless, fjord-cut wilderness leading to the mist-shrouded Haida Gwaii, or Queen Charlotte Islands, home to the Haida people and to old-growth forest. Just west of Vancouver, in the Strait of Georgia, are the gentler, more pastoral Gulf Islands, which have long attracted escapists of every kind.

The North Coast and the Queen Charlotte Islands can be wet year-round. The interior is drier, with greater extremes, including hot summers and reliably snowy winters. Temperatures here drop below freezing in win-ter and sometimes reach 90°F in summer.

When you travel by car, remember that more than three-quarters of British Columbia is mountainous terrain. Forest roads cut across the craggy hill-sides, which though fun to explore in an all-terrain vehicle are also pretty remote and should be traveled with caution. Many areas, including the North Coast, have no roads at all and are accessible only by air or sea.

British Columbia is about the size of Western Europe, with as much geographical variety yet with substantially fewer roads. The good news is that many great sights, stunning scenery, and even wilderness lie within a few days' tour of Vancouver or the U.S. border.

Numbers in the text correspond to numbers in the margin and on the British Columbia map.

If you have 3 days

Take a ferry for a brief tour of the Sunshine Coast: **Gibsons Landing ①**, **Sechelt ②**, **Powell River ③**, and **Lund ④**. An alternative is to take a ferry to one of the Gulf Islands—🚗**Galiano ⑤**, 🚗**Mayne ⑥**, **Pender ⑦**, and 🚗 **Salt Spring ⑧** are the most popular—and stay at a romantic country inn.

Another option is to take the Coast Mountain Circle tour, where you'll find no shortage of stunning mountain and ocean scenery: drive north from Vancouver along the Sea to Sky Highway to 🚗 **Squamish ⑩** and the resort town of 🚗 **Whistler ⑪**, then over the scenic Duffy Lake Road to the gold-rush town of **Lillooet ⑫**. You can return to Vancouver through the steep gorges of the Fraser Canyon, with stops at Hell's Gate on the Fraser River near **Hope ⑬** and at 🚗 **Harrison Hot Springs ⑭**.

If you have 6 days

A longer trip allows time to explore the interior. Start with a one- or two-day trip over the mountains via 🚗 **Whistler ⑪** and **Lillooet ⑫**, through the dramatic scenery of the Fraser Canyon, or by the quicker—but still scenic, with its mountains and lakes—Coquihalla Highway. On Days 3 through 5, loop through the High Country and the Okanagan Valley. You can make stops in 🚗 **Kamloops ⑮** to fish or tour the Secwepemc Native Heritage Museum; in **Vernon ⑰** to visit the mountain resort at Silver Star; or in 🚗 **Kelowna ⑱**, **Summerland & Peachland ⑲**, 🚗 **Penticton ⑳**, or 🚗 **Osoyoos ㉑** to relax at a beach or tour a vineyard. Any of these towns is fine for an overnight stay.

About the Restaurants
Although Vancouver and Victoria have British Columbia's most varied and cosmopolitan cuisine, smaller communities, particularly Whistler, and several fine inns have defined an excellence in local cuisine. Regional fare includes seafood, lamb, organic produce, and increasingly good wine. Attire is generally casual, and nearly all restaurants as well as many bars and pubs ban smoking indoors.

About the Hotels
Accommodations range from bed-and-breakfasts and rustic cabins to deluxe chain hotels, country inns, and remote fishing lodges. The cities have an abundance of lodgings, but outside the major centers, especially in summer, it's a good idea to reserve ahead, even for campsites. In winter, many backcountry resorts close, and city hotels drop prices by as

much as 50%. Most small inns and B&Bs ban smoking indoors; almost all hotels have no-smoking rooms.

WHAT IT COSTS in Canadian dollars				
$$$$	**$$$**	**$$**	**$**	**¢**
RESTAURANTS over $30	$21–$30	$13–$20	$8–$12	under $8
HOTELS over $250	$176–$250	$126–$175	$75–$125	under $75

Restaurant prices are for a main course at dinner, not including 7% GST and 10% liquor tax. Hotel prices are for two people in a standard double room in high season, excluding 10% provincial accommodation tax, service charge, and 7% GST.

Timing

The Gulf Islands and Sunshine Coast are enjoyable anytime, but there are fewer ferries and more rain between October and April, and many tourist facilities close in winter. The interior—the Cariboo, High Country, Okanagan and Kootenays—can be tough to reach in winter, but more ski resorts are making it worth the effort. Spring and fall, with their blossoms and harvest and wine festivals, are attractive, peaceful travel seasons; summer is a great time for most of the interior, although the Okanagan can get hot and crowded in July and August.

SUNSHINE COAST

The stretch of mainland coast north of Vancouver, backed by mountains and accessible only by sea or air, is so deeply cut with fjords that it looks and feels like an island—or, rather, two islands. The lower Sunshine Coast is popular with artists, writers, and Vancouver weekenders. The upper Sunshine Coast, a ferry ride across Jervis Inlet, is wild and densely forested. Highway 101, the one paved road running the length of the coast, forms the last (or the first) 139 km (86 mi) of the Pan-American Highway, connecting the village of Lund, British Columbia, to Puerto Montt, Chile, 24,000 km (15,020 mi) away.

The coast is sunnier than the more exposed coastline to the north (hence its name), and its many provincial parks, marinas, lakes, and walking trails are popular with outdoorspeople and families, though not, as yet, with mass tourism or luxury-resort developers. The relaxed lifestyle has attracted many artists and craftspeople to the area; to visit their studios, pick up a free *Purple Banner Tour* map (after the banners that fly when a studio is open) from any Sunshine Coast tourist-info office.

Gibsons Landing

❶ *5 km (3 mi) plus 12 nautical mi northwest of Vancouver.*

The first stop on the Sunshine Coast, 5 km (3 mi) north of the Langdale ferry terminal, Gibsons Landing (often just called Gibsons) is an attractive seaside town that's best known as the location of *The Beachcombers*, a syndicated, long-running Canadian TV show about life on the B.C. coast. **Molly's Reach** (✉ Molly's La. ☎ 604/886–9710), a waterfront café built as a set for the show, still serves fish-and-chips and TV memories.

3

Canoeing & Kayaking

The Inside Passage, the Strait of Georgia, and the other island-dotted straits and sounds that border the mainland provide fairly protected sea-going from Washington State to the Alaskan border, with numerous marine parks to explore along the way. Two favorites for canoeing are the Powell Forest Canoe Route, an 80-km (50-mi) circuit of seven lakes, and Bowron Lake Park, in the Cariboo region.

First Nations Culture

Interest in the British Columbia's Native culture is enjoying a renaissance. First Nations groups such as the Kwakwaka'wakw, Haida, Nisga'a and Coast Salish have occupied the land for some 12,000 years, and you can see their rich heritage throughout the region in art galleries, restaurants, and cultural centers as well as at ceremonial potlances and in re-created villages. Northern B.C. and the Queen Charlotte Islands have the best examples, including totems, ancient villages, and museum collections of some of the province's finest First Nations artifacts.

Fishing

Miles of coastline and thousands of lakes, rivers, and streams bring more than 750,000 anglers to British Columbia each year. The province's waters hold 74 species of fish (25 of them sport fish), including chinook salmon and rainbow trout.

Golf

British Columbia has more than 230 golf courses, and the number is growing. The topography tends to be mountainous and forested, and many courses have fine views as well as challenging approaches to greens.

Hiking

Virtually all the provincial parks have fine hiking-trail networks, and many ski resorts keep their chairlifts running throughout the summer to help hikers and mountain bikers reach trails. Heli-hiking is also very popular; helicopters deliver you to alpine meadows and verdant mountaintops.

Rafting

A wide range of rafting trips are available on the many beautiful rivers lacing British Columbia, including the Chilcotin, Fraser, Thompson, Skeena, and Tatshenshini. You can choose between an adrenaline-rich white-water route or a scenic float suitable for photographers and families.

Skiing & Snowboarding

With more than half the province higher than 4,200 feet above sea level, more than 60 resorts have downhill skiing and snowboarding facilities. Most of them also offer groomed cross-country (Nordic) ski trails, and many of the provincial parks have cross-country trails as well. The resorts are easy to get to, as several have shuttles from the nearest airport.

The **Sunshine Coast Museum and Archives** (⊠ 716 Winn Rd. ☎ 604/886–8232 ⊕ www.sunshinecoastmuseum.ca) has an eclectic collection of pioneer artifacts, rare butterflies, and exhibits showcasing the region's seafaring history. It's open Tuesday through Saturday 10:30–4:30; donations are suggested.

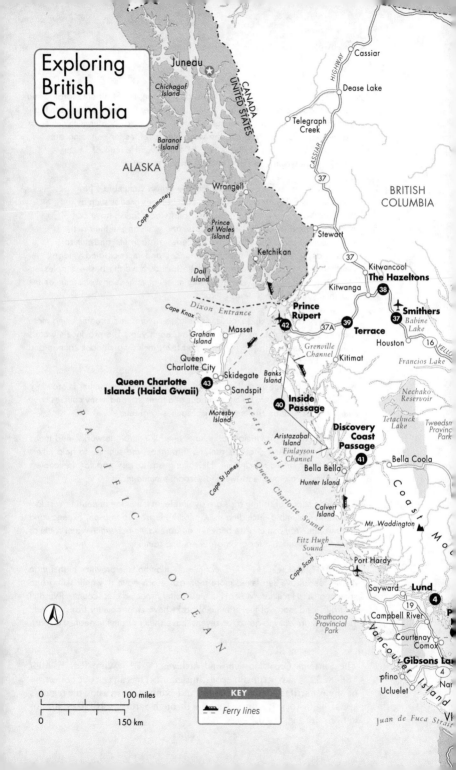

Exploring British Columbia

Juneau

Chichagof Island

Baranof Island

ALASKA

Wrangell

Cape Ommaney

Prince of Wales Island

Ketchikan

Dall Island

Cape Knox

Dixon Entrance

Masset

Graham Island

Queen Charlotte City

Skidegate

Sandspit

Queen Charlotte Islands (Haida Gwaii) 43

Moresby Island

Cape St James

P A C I F I C   O C E A N

0 — 100 miles
0 — 150 km

CANADA
UNITED STATES

Cassiar

HIGHWAY

Dease Lake

Telegraph Creek

CASSIAR

Stewart

37

Kitwancool

The Hazeltons

Kitwanga

37

BRITISH COLUMBIA

38 ✈ **Smithers**

Babine Lake

37 ✈

Houston

16 YELLO

Prince Rupert 42

37A

39 **Terrace**

Grenville Channel

Kitimat

Francios Lake

Nechako Reservoir

Banks Island

40 **Inside Passage**

Discovery Coast Passage

Aristazabal Island

Finlayson Channel

Bella Bella

41

Bella Coola

Hunter Island

Tetachuck Lake

Tweedsn Provinc Park

Hecate Strait

Queen Charlotte Sound

Calvert Island

Mt. Waddington

Fitz Hugh Sound

Cape Scott

Port Hardy ✈

Sayward

Lund

4

Coast Mou

Strathcona Provincial Park

Campbell River

19

Courtenay Comox

Gibsons La

Vancouver Island

pfino

Ucluelet

4

Nar

VI

Juan de Fuca Strait

KEY

🚢 *Ferry lines*

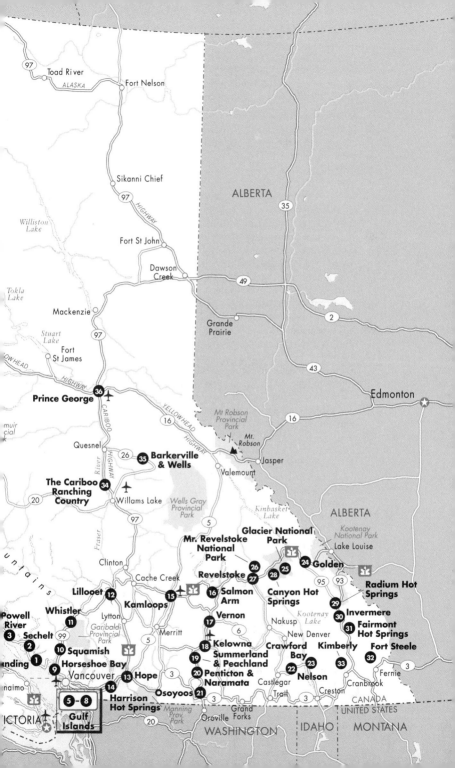

About 15 minutes north of Gibsons on Highway 101 is the delightful village of **Roberts Creek,** where the buildings date to the 1930s and the ambience recalls the 1960s. There's a public beach a short stroll from the village and seaside camping at **Roberts Creek Provincial Park.**

Where to Stay & Eat

$–$$$ ✗ **Gumboot Restaurant.** This wisteria-draped cottage in Roberts Creek is now under the management that has made the Gumboot Café such a destination treat. The menu specials change frequently, although you can always find delicious made-from-scratch soups; ethnic, organic items such as buffalo burgers and rice bowls; and a good vegetarian selection. The outdoor patios create a casual, cozy ambience. Many guests enjoy strolling down to the beach between courses. ✉ *1041 Roberts Creek Rd., Roberts Creek* ☎ *604/885–4216* ▭ *MC, V* ☺ *No dinner Oct.–Apr.*

¢–$$ ✗ **Gumboot Garden Café.** This funky, kid-friendly village-center café is such an area institution that the sign outside simply reads CAFÉ. The home-baked breads, pizzas, deli-choices, and desserts feature, where possible, local and organic ingredients. There's a patio, woodstove, flower-stuffed gum boots (rubber boots) by the door, and a warm atmosphere that makes it tempting to just hang out. ✉ *1057 Roberts Creek Rd., Roberts Creek* ☎ *604/885–4216* ▭ *MC, V* ☺ *No dinner Sun.–Thurs.*

$$–$$$ ✗▥ **Bonniebrook Lodge.** This seaside lodge, 5 km (3 mi) north of Gibsons, is a romantic spot. Rooms and suites in the original 1922 building and in the 1998 addition are attractive, with custom pine furniture, a woodsy green color scheme, fireplaces, and whirlpool tubs for two. Chez Philippe, a fine French restaurant ($$–$$$), is open to the public for dinner, serving such dishes as rack of lamb in a seven-grain crust, and grilled scallops and prawns with a saffron-cream sauce. The C$32 four-course set menu is an excellent value. ✉*1532 Oceanbeach Esplanade, R.R. 5, V0N 1V5* ☎ *604/886–2887 or 877/290–9916, 604/886–2188 dinner reservations* 🖷 *604/886–8853* ⊕ *www.bonniebrook.com* ↻ *5 rooms, 2 suites,* ⚴ *Restaurant, fans, refrigerators, cable TV, in-room VCRs; no a/c, no smoking* ▭ *AE, DC, MC, V* ☺ *Restaurant closed Mon.–Thurs. mid-Sept.–mid-May. No lunch. Lodge and restaurant closed Jan.* ⦿ *BP.*

$$–$$$ ▥ **Country Cottage Bed & Breakfast.** Loragene and Philip Gaulin have lovingly decorated two private cottages on their 2-acre farm. Tiny, romantic Rose Cottage has a woodstove and an antique sideboard. Cedar Lodge, the farm's former barn, is a feast of woodsy Canadiana—from its stone fireplace to its handmade furniture. Rates include breakfast, delivered to your room, and afternoon tea. ✉ *1183 Roberts Creek Rd., Box 183, Roberts Creek V0N 2W0* ☎ *604/885–7448* ⊕ *www. countrycottagebb.ca* ↻ *2 cottages* ⚴ *Kitchens, some pets allowed; no room phones, no a/c in some rooms, no room TVs, no kids, no smoking* ▭ *No credit cards* ⦿ *BP.*

Sports & the Outdoors

Sunshine Coast Golf & Country Club (✉ 3206 Hwy. 101, Roberts Creek ☎ 604/885–9212 or 800/667–5022) is an 18-hole, par-71 course with tree-lined fairways and mountain and ocean views. Greens fees are C$40–C$45.

Shopping

More than 100 local artists show their wares at **Gift of the Eagle Gallery** (✉ 689 Gibsons Way ☎ 604/886–4899), where you can can find everything from contemporary and native-carved silver jewelry to pottery, stone carvings, and masks.

Sechelt

② *37 km (23 mi) plus 12 nautical mi northwest of Vancouver.*

Sechelt, the largest town on the lower Sunshine Coast, is home to many artists and writers as well as a strong First Nations community, the Sechelt Nation. If you're in Sechelt in mid-August, you can catch readings by internationally acclaimed Canadian writers at the **Sunshine Coast Festival of the Written Arts** (✉ 5511 Shorncliffe Ave., Sechelt V0N 3A1 ☎ 604/885–9631 or 800/565–9631 ⊕ www.writersfestival.ca), held at Sechelt's Rockwood Centre.

House of Hewhiwus (✉ 5555 Hwy. 101 ☎ 604/885–8991) includes a small First Nations museum, performance space for local dancers and aboriginal storytellers, and a gift shop–art gallery. **Porpoise Bay Provincial Park** (☎ 604/898–3678, 800/689–9025 camping reservations ⊕ www.discovercamping.ca), north of Sechelt on Sechelt Inlet, is a wonderful destination for summer fun, including hiking trails, and a sandy swimming beach.

The coast's best scenery is to the north of Sechelt, around and beyond the little marinas of Madiera Park, Garden Bay, and Irvine's Landing, collectively known as Pender Harbour. Here Highway 101 winds past forests, mountains, and a confusion of freshwater lakes and ocean inlets. In summer **Slow Cat Ferries** (☎ 604/741–3796) runs 1½-hour boat tours of the area.

A dramatic natural sight is at **Skookumchuk Narrows Provincial Park** (✉ Egmont Rd. off Hwy. 101 ☎ 604/898–3678), 5 km (3 mi) inland from the Earls Cove ferry terminal and 45 km (28 mi) northwest of Sechelt. You can walk through the forest for 4 km (2½ mi) to a viewpoint where, at the turn of the tide, seawater churning through the narrow channel creates thrilling tidal rapids. Tide tables are posted at the trailhead.

Princess Louisa Inlet is an 8-km- (5-mi)-long narrow fjord at the top of Jervis Inlet; more than 60 waterfalls tumble down its steep, rugged walls. The fjord is accessible only by boat or floatplane. The *Malibu Princess* (☎ 604/883–2003 ⊕ www.malibuyachts.com), a 200-passenger tour boat, makes day trips to Princess Louisa Inlet from the Malibu Landing in Egmont; the fare is C$80 and the ship makes about 12 sailings during its June–mid-September season; call ahead for precise dates. **Sunshine Coast Tours** (☎ 604/883–2280 or 800/870–9055 ⊕ www.sunshinecoasttours.bc.ca) also runs boat tours to Princess Louisa Inlet daily June to September. The cost is C$99.

Where to Stay & Eat

★ $$–$$$ ✗ **Blue Heron Inn** This charming dinner-only restaurant is on the lower level of a family home on the shore of Porpoise Bay. The dining room is elegant, filled with fresh flowers and local artwork, and has very romantic views. House specialties include seafood such as live Dungeness crab and West Coast bouillabaisse, and smoked items ranging from duck to trout. ⊠ *5521 Delta Rd., Sechelt* ☎ *604/885–3847 or 800/818–8977* ▤ *AE, MC, V* ⊗ *Closed Mon. and Tues.*

$–$$ ✕ **The Old Boot Eatery.** Upbeat jazz, mismatched furniture, and a Wild West mural create a fun atmosphere at this town-center local favorite. Twenty different pastas range from simple spaghetti with meat sauce to elaborate creations such as linguine with tiger prawns and Italian sausage. The bread, pasta sauces, and thin-crust pizza are all made from scratch. Half orders and a kids' menu make this a good choice for families. ⊠ *5530 Wharf St. Plaza, Sechelt* ☎ *604/885–2727* ▤ *AE, MC, V* ⊗ *Closed Sun.*

$$–$$$ ✕▥ **Ruby Lake Resort.** The Cogrossi family from Milan chose this lake-
Fodor'sChoice   side resort and 90-acre ecoparadise as the place to serve the area's best
★   Italian home cooking ($–$$$$). Homegrown organic produce highlights seafood, pasta, and vegetarian dishes, served in the woodsy restaurant or on the patio. A floating footbridge leads to five spacious duplex cottages, all with private entrances and pine furniture. The two suites are especially romantic: each has a woodstove, soaker tub, and a lakeside deck with sunset views. The tents come with four-poster beds and decks. In spring 2005 the resort added an amphitheater and a health spa. ⊠ *Hwy. 101, R.R. 1, Site 20, C25, Madeira Park V0N 2H0* ☎ *604/883–2269 or 800/717–6611* 🖷 *604/883–3602* ⊕ *www.rubylakeresort. com* ⇨ *10 cottages, 2 suites, 4 deluxe tents* ⚹ *Restaurant, some kitchens, some kitchenettes, refrigerators, cable TV, lake, massage, dock, boating, hiking, bar, meeting room; no room phones, no TV in some rooms, no smoking* ▤ *MC, V* ⊗ *Restaurant closed late Dec.–mid-Mar.; Mon.–Thurs. No lunch* ⊠◎ *CP.*

★ $–$$ ✕▥ **West Coast Wilderness Lodge.** Set on 10 acres of temperate rain forest, this eco-oriented lodge puts soft adventure on your doorstep. The main hall, built largely from heritage materials, has floor-to-ceiling windows and wraparound decks overlooking majestic fjords, islands, and mountain ranges. Five cozy, minilodges accommodate up to 16 people. The restaurant ($$–$$$) is airy with a huge stone fireplace and serves such dishes as barbecue salmon, penne with fresh basil and brie, and Thai mango vermicelli. Rates include all meals and a range of activities such as kayaking, rock climbing, hiking, and relaxing in the small spa. Meal-only, cabin-only, and activity-only options are available. ⊠ *6570 Maple Rd., Egmont V0N 1N0* ☎ *604/883–3667 or 877/988–3838* 🖷 *604/883–3604* ⊕ *www.wcwl.com* ⇨ *20 rooms* ⚹ *Restaurant, some refrigerators, hot tub, massage, sauna, dock, boating, hiking, lounge, recreation room, meeting room; no room phones, no smoking* ▤ *MC, V* ⊠◎ *FAP.*

$$$ ▥ **Wildflowers Bed & Breakfast.** Two serene, Asian-style studio cottages overlook a meadow in the woods. Each is large and comfortable, with its own fireplace, extra-deep bathtub, and porch. The decor, from the four-poster canopy beds to the adobe mantels and touches of Balinese art, is delightfully eclectic but never cluttered. ⊠ *5813 Brooks Rd., Halfmoon Bay V0N 3A0* ☎ *604/885–7346* 🖷 *604/885–7242* ⊕ *www.*

wildflowers-bb.com ✏ *2 rooms* ⚷ *Fans, microwaves, refrigerators, cable TV, in-room VCRs, outdoor hot tub, massage, laundry service; no a/c, no room phones, no kids, no smoking* ☰ *MC, V* ❚⦿❚ *BP.*

Sports & the Outdoors

Pender Harbour and the Sechelt Inlet are spectacular cold-water diving spots, especially in winter, when the water is clearest. An artificial reef has been formed by a scuttled navy ship off Kunechin Point in Sechelt Inlet. **Suncoast Diving and Water Sports** (✉ 5643 Wharf St. ☏ 604/740–8006 or 866/740–8006 ⊕ www.suncoastdiving.com) is a PADI five-star dive center. A one-day dive charter with two dives is C$110–C$125 per person. Based at pretty Halfmoon Bay, 15 minutes north of Sechelt, **Halfmoon Sea Kayaks** (☏ 604/885–2948 ⊕ www.halfmoonseakayaks.com) has rentals, tours, and lessons. **Pedals and Paddles** (✉ 5794 Naylor Rd. ☏ 866/884–6440 or 604/885–6440 ⊕ www.pedalspaddles.com) conducts easy paddling day trips and lessons for beginners as well as overnight excursions to provincial park campsites. For mountain-bike rentals and tours, check out **On the Edge Biking** (✉ 5642 Cowrie St. ☏ 604/885–4888 ⊕ www.ontheedgebiking.com).

Powell River

❸ *70 km (43 mi) plus 12 nautical mi by ferry northwest of Sechelt, 121 km (75 mi) plus 12½ nautical mi northwest of Vancouver, 17 nautical mi (80-min ferry ride) east across Strait of Georgia from Comox on Vancouver Island.*

The main town on the Upper Sunshine Coast, Powell River, was established around a pulp-and-paper mill in 1912, and the forestry industry remains a strong presence in the area. Renowned as a year-round salmon-fishing destination, Powell River has 30 regional lakes with exceptional trout fishing and is a popular scuba-diving destination. The town has several B&Bs, restaurants, and parks with oceanfront camping and RV hookups. The Powell River Townsite, 3 km (2 mi) north of town, is one of the province's oldest functioning mill towns and a national historic site.

Where to Stay & Eat

$–$$ ✕ **Shingle Mill Pub.** Stunning views over Powell Lake and a deck are the draws at this friendly local pub just north of Powell River. Pub fare— fish-and-chips, sandwiches, and burgers—predominates, but the menu also lists steak, salmon, and halibut dishes. Kids are welcome in the bistro section, which also has water views. ✉ *6233 Powell Pl., off Hwy. 101* ☏ *604/483–3545* ⚷ *Reservations not accepted* ☰ *AE, MC, V.*

¢–$ 🏛 **Old Court House Inn.** This 1939 Tudor-style building, next to the pulp mill in the historic town site was Powell River's original courthouse. Private rooms are decorated in an early-20th-century style; some have antiques. A shuttle picks you up from the bus station, airport, or the Westview (Comox) ferry terminal for C$8. ✉ *6243 Walnut St., V8A 4K4* ☏ *604/483–4000 or 877/483–4777* 🖷 *604/483–4089* ⊕ *www. oldcourthouseinn.ca* ✏ *9 rooms, 7 with bath* ⚷ *Kitchen, some refrigerators, cable TV, Wi-Fi, piano, laundry facilities; no a/c, no room phones, no smoking* ☰ *MC, V.*

Sports & the Outdoors

HIKING & BIKING   The Inland Lake Site and Trail System, 12 km (8 mi) inland from Powell River, is a 13-km-long (8-mi-long) hiking and biking lakeside trail that's wheelchair accessible. Hikers can also try the Sunshine Coast Trail, which runs 180 km (112 mi) from Sarah Point, north of Lund, to Saltery Bay.

SCUBA DIVING   Sunken ships, red coral, wolf eels, enormous octopi, and—especially in winter—uncommonly clear water make Powell River one of Canada's leading scuba-diving spots. A popular attraction is the *Emerald Princess,* a 9-foot bronze mermaid statue in 60 feet of water off Saltery Bay Provincial Park. **Alpha Dive Services** (⌧ 7013 Thunder Bay St. ☎ 604/ 485–6939 ⊕ www.divepowellriver.com) has dive charters, gear rental, guiding services, and instruction. A one-day dive charter is C$90 per person and includes two dives and tanks and weights.

Lund

❹ *28 km (17 mi) north of Powell River.*

Founded by the Swedish Thulin brothers in 1889, the historic seaside village of Lund marks the end (or start) of the Pan-American Highway. Lund is the nearest village to **Desolation Sound,** a major draw for boaters and kayakers. A water taxi runs from Lund to **Savary Island,** nicknamed the South Pacific of the North for its rolling dunes and white-sand beaches.

Where to Stay & Eat

★ $–$$$ ✕ **The Laughing Oyster.** Every seat in this pretty restaurant 10 minutes from Lund has a stunning view over Okeover Arm. Although the menu lists vegetarian, beef, lamb, and poultry dishes, the focus here is seafood. The house specialty, Laughing Oysters, are steamed, shucked, and broiled with artichokes, olives, sun-dried tomatoes, hot peppers, and feta cheese. The deck is a local hot spot; boaters can tie up at the dock in front. ⌧ *10052 Malaspina Rd.* ☎ *604/483–9775* ▤ *AE, MC, V* ☉ *Closed Sun.–Tues., Nov.–Apr.*

$$–$$$ ⌂ **Desolation Resort.** Tree-house-like chalets perch high above Okeover
FodorʼsChoice   Arm at this isolated retreat 10 minutes from Lund. The one-, two-, and
★   three-bedroom units, handcrafted in local woods and set on stilts for the best views, have large decks and big picture windows; some have electric fireplaces, and all have showers rather than bathtubs. This is a good base to explore the scenic reaches of Desolation Sound: you can rent powerboats, kayaks, or canoes here or take a tour in the resort's 33-foot cabin cruiser. ⌧ *2694 Dawson Rd., C-36, Malaspina Rd., R. R. 2, Powell River V8A 4Z3* ☎ *604/483–3592 or 800/399–3592* ⎙ *604/ 483–7942* ⊕ *www.desolationresort.com* ⇆ *5 chalets, 4 suites* ☖ *Some in-room hot tubs, kitchens, dock, hiking, laundry facilities; no a/c in some rooms, no room phones, no room TVs, no smoking* ▤ *AE, MC, V.*

$–$$ ⌂ **Lund Hotel.** This three-story seaside hotel with its dormer windows and wraparound veranda dates to 1905. The rooms have simple, modern decor; some have balconies, and those in a newer extension have motel-style private entrances. On-site are a post office, a sea-view restaurant and pub, a general store, and a diving and kayaking outfitter.

✉ 1436 Hwy. 101, Box 158, Lund V0N 2G0 ☎ 604/414–0474 or 877/ 569–3999 🖷 604/414–0476 ⊕ www.lundhotel.com ⇥ 27 rooms ⚘ Restaurant, some refrigerators, in-room VCRs, outdoor hot tub, dive shop, boating, marina, fishing, pub, shops, laundry facilities, Internet room, business services, meeting rooms, some pets allowed; no smoking ▤ AE, MC, V.

Sports & the Outdoors

Rockfish Kayaks (✉ Lund Hotel, 1436 Hwy. 101 ☎ 604/414–9355) has rentals and runs guided paddles in summer, including all-inclusive, multiple day excursions. **Powell River Sea Kayaks** (✉ 10676 Crowther Rd., off Malaspina Rd., off Hwy. 101, 5 km [3 km] south of Lund ☎ 604/ 483–2160) provides lessons, rentals, and tours into Desolation Sound year-round. A one-day kayak rental is C$33–C$41 and a six-hour guided kayak tour is C$99, including lunch.

Cultural Tours

Artesia Tours (☎ 604/886–7300 or 800/690–7887 ⊕ www.suncoastarts. com/artesiatours.html) is a nonprofit organization that promotes the ecological and cultural heritage of the Sunshine Coast such as rain-forest hikes, regional foods and wines, and the Sliammon First Nations.

THE GULF ISLANDS

Of the hundreds of islands sprinkled across the Georgia Strait between Vancouver Island and the mainland, the most popular and accessible are Galiano, Mayne, Pender, and Salt Spring. A temperate climate (warmer than Vancouver's and with half the rainfall), shell beaches, rolling pastures, and virgin forests are common to all, but each island has its unique flavor. Marine birds are numerous, and there's unusual vegetation such as arbutus trees (also known as madrones, a leafy evergreen with red peeling bark) and Garry oaks.

These islands are rustic but not undiscovered. Writers, artists, and craftspeople as well as weekend cottagers and retirees from Vancouver and Victoria take full advantage of them. Make hotel reservations for summer stays. If you're bringing a car from the B.C. mainland, ferry reservations are highly recommended; for busier sailings, they're required.

Galiano Island

❺ *20 nautical mi (1 to 2 hrs by ferry due to interisland stops) from Swartz Bay (32 km [20 mi] north of Victoria), 13 nautical mi (a 50-min ferry ride) from Tsawwassen (39 km [24 mi] south of Vancouver).*

Galiano's 26-km-long (16-mi-long), unbroken eastern shore is perfect for leisurely walks, and the numerous coves and inlets along its western coast make it a prime area for kayaking. Biological studies show that the straits between Vancouver Island and the B.C. mainland are home to North America's greatest variety of marine life. The frigid waters have superb visibility; Alcala Point, Porlier Pass, and Active Pass are top scuba-diving locations.

Galiano also has miles of trails through Douglas-fir forest that beg exploration on foot or by bike. Hikers can climb to the top of Mt. Galiano for a view of the Olympic Mountains in Washington or trek the length of Bodega Ridge. The best spots for picnics, bird-watching, and views of Active Pass and the surrounding islands are Bluffs Park and Bellhouse Park. Anglers head to the point at Bellhouse Park to spin cast for salmon from shore, or they go by boat to Porlier Pass and Trincomali Channel.

★ ☾ **Montague Harbour Provincial Marine Park** (✉ Montague Park Rd., off Montague Rd. ☎ 800/689–9025 camping reservations ⊕ www. discovercamping.ca) has walk-in and drive-in campsites and a long shell beach famed for its sunset views. You can rent a kayak or scooter or take a boat tour at **Montague Harbour Marina** (✉ Montague Park Rd., just east of park ☎ 250/539–5733 marina, 250/539–2442 kayak rentals, 250/539–3443 scooter rentals, 250/539–2278 boat tours). **Newfie Bill's** (☎ 250/539–9942) at the marina serves burgers, salads and seafood on its heated outdoor deck May through October.

> **need a break?** The **Hummingbird Inn Pub** (✉ 47 Sturdies Bay Rd. ☎ 250/539–5472) is a friendly local hangout, with live music on summer weekends. Also in summer, the pub runs a free shuttle bus to the Montague Harbour Marina and campsite.

Where to Stay & Eat

$$$$ ✕⌂ **Galiano Oceanfront Inn & Spa.** Lawns and gardens reach down to the water's edge from this cedar-sided West Coast–style inn. Rooms have a lush Mediterranean feel, with wood-burning fireplaces, balconies or patios, jetted or soaker tubs, and sweeping views of Active Pass. The oceanfront restaurant ($$$$) serves locally caught seafood and organic produce; entrées include sandalwood-smoked wild coho salmon and truffle-crusted rack of lamb. In summer you can dine alfresco or enjoy a drink at Galiano's only seaside lounge. The resort's spa is one of the most lavish on the islands. ✉ 134 Madrona Dr., Box S24-C47, Galiano Island V0N 1P0 ☎ 250/539–3388 or 877/530–3939 ☐ 250/539–3338 ⊕ www.galianoinn.com ⇗ 10 rooms ♻ Minibars, Wi-Fi, outdoor hot tub, spa, steam room, lounge, wine shop, Internet room, meeting room; no a/c, no room TVs, no smoking ☐ MC, V ☉ Closed Jan. ⃝ BP.

$$–$$$ ✕⌂ **Woodstone Country Inn.** This serene inn lies between a forest and a meadow for some fantastic bird-watching. Tall windows bring the pastoral setting into spacious bedrooms decorated with antiques, hand-stenciled walls, and lush designer fabrics. All guest quarters have fireplaces; most have patios and oversize tubs. The elegant Wisteria Dining Room ($$$$) serves four-course meals of French-influenced Pacific Northwest fare, such as sweet corn and fennel soup, or herb-crusted rack of lamb; reservations are required. Afternoon tea is included in the rates. ✉ 743 Georgeson Bay Rd., R.R. 1, V0N 1P0 ☎ 250/539–2022 or 888/339–2022 ☐ 250/539–5198 ⊕ www.woodstoneinn.com ⇗ 12 rooms ♻ Restaurant, lounge, piano, meeting room; no a/c, no room phones, no room TVs, no kids under 12, no smoking ☐ AE, MC, V ☉ Closed Dec. and Jan. ⃝ BP.

$$–$$$ 🛏 **Bellhouse Inn.** This seaside inn, modeled on an English manor house, blends 19th-century antiques, such as the 1860 farmhouse table where breakfast is served, with modern amenities. The Kingfisher Room has a whirlpool tub and a balcony with a full water view. The Eagle Room also has a balcony, with a forest and ocean view, as well as an extra-deep tub and the original hardwood floor. You can spot whales and eagles through the picture windows in the lounge or join the owner on his 43-foot sailboat. Morning tea and coffee is delivered to your room. ✉ *29 Farmhouse Rd., V0N 1P0* ☎ *250/539–5667 or 800/970–7464* 🖷 *250/ 539–5316* ⊕ *www.bellhouseinn.com* ⇆ *3 rooms* ⌂ *Beach, croquet; no a/c, no room phones, no room TVs, no kids under 16, no smoking* ☰ *MC, V* ﹗◯﹗ *BP.*

Sports & the Outdoors

BIKING Bike rentals are available from **Galiano Bicycle** (✉ 36 Burrill Rd. ☎ 250/ 539–9906), within walking distance of the Sturdies Bay ferry terminal. **Galiano Mopeds** (☎ 250/539–3443), at Montague Harbour, rents bikes from May to September.

FISHING **Sporades Tours** (☎ 250/539–2278 ⊕ www.galianoisland.com/ sporadestours), based at Montague Harbour Marina, runs fishing and sightseeing charters. Tours are for a minimum of three hours, at C$120 an hour for up to seven people.

GOLF The **Galiano Golf and Country Club** (✉ 24 St. Andrew Crescent ☎ 250/ 539–5533 or 877/909–7888) is a 9-hole, par-32 course in a forest clearing. The clubhouse is open summer only; an honor box for greens fees operates the rest of the year.

KAYAKING **Gulf Islands Kayaking** (✉ Montague Harbour Marina, Montague Harbour Rd. ☎ 250/539–2442 ⊕ www.seakayak.ca) has equipment rentals and guided kayak tours (three hours C$45, six hours C$75).

Mayne Island

❻ *28 nautical mi from Swartz Bay (32 km [20 mi] north of Victoria), 22 nautical mi from Tsawwassen (39 km [24 mi] south of Vancouver).*

Middens of clam and oyster shells are evidence that tiny Mayne Island—only 21 square km (8 square mi)—was inhabited as early as 5,000 years ago. It later became the stopover point for miners headed from Victoria to the gold fields of the Fraser River and Barkerville. By the mid-1800s it was the communal center of the inhabited Gulf Islands, with the first school, post office, police lockup, church, and hotel. Farm tracts and orchards, established in the 1930s and 1940s and worked by Japanese farmers until their internment in World War II, still thrive here. Mayne's mild hills and wonderful scenery make it great territory for a vigorous bike ride.

A 45-minute hike up **Mt. Parke** leads to the island's highest point and a stunning view of the mainland and other gulf islands.

The village of Miners Bay is home to **Plumper Pass Lockup** (✉ 433 Fernhill Rd. ☎ No phone), built in 1896 as a jail but now a minuscule museum (open July 1 to Labor Day, hours vary free) chronicling the island's history. After touring the Plumper Pass Lockup, consider stopping for a drink on the seaside deck at the **Springwater Lodge** (✉ 400 Fernhill Rd., Miners Bay ☎ 250/539–5521), one of the province's oldest hotels. Saturday, between July and mid-October, check out the **Farmers' Market** outside the Miners Bay Agricultural Hall. Open 10 to 1, it sells produce and crafts while local musicians entertain shoppers.

Built entirely by volunteers, the 1-acre **Japanese Garden** at Dinner Bay Park honors the island's early Japanese settlers. It's about ½ mi (1 km) south of the Village Bay ferry terminal. Admission is free.

From Miners Bay head north on Georgina Point Road to **St. Mary Magdalene Church,** a pretty chapel built in 1898. Active Pass Lighthouse, at the end of Georgina Point Road, is part of **Georgina Point Heritage Park.** Built in 1885, it still signals ships into the busy waterway. The grassy

★ ☕ grounds are great for picnicking. **Bennett Bay Park,** part of the Gulf Islands National Park Reserve, has walking trails, one of the island's most scenic beaches, and some lovely picnic areas. There's a wide, sandy beach at **Piggot Bay,** making it ideal for family fun as well as kayakers in search of a safe launch. At **Campbell Bay,** a pebble beach beckons beachcombers with shallow (and therefore warmer) waters. Tidal pools abound at both alongside resident seals and the odd sea otter.

Where to Stay & Eat

★ $$$–$$$$ ✕▥ **Oceanwood Country Inn.** This Tudor-style house on 10 forested acres overlooks Navy Channel and has English country decor throughout. Fireplaces, airjet tubs, and French doors leading to private oceanview decks are available in several rooms. Some rooms boast Japanese soaking tubs. The waterfront restaurant ($$$$) serves four-course table d'hôte dinners of outstanding regional cuisine. The menu changes daily, but highlights include slow-roasted wild salmon with Dijon caper sauce, and rosemary-smoked leg of Mayne Island lamb. Room rates include afternoon tea and breakfast. ✉ 630 Dinner Bay Rd., Mayne Island V0N 2J0 ☎ 250/539–5074 or 866/539–5074 🖷 250/539–3002 ⊕ www. oceanwood.com ➵ 12 rooms ⚘ Restaurant, outdoor hot tub, sauna, bicycles, library, meeting room; no a/c, no room phones, no room TVs, no kids under 16, no smoking ▤ MC, V ☯ Closed Nov.–mid-Mar. ⧉ BP.

$$–$$$ ▥ **A Coachhouse on Oyster Bay.** This waterfront house, built in the style of an early-20th-century carriage house, has lovely ocean views. Rooms are elegant, with bold colors, hardwood floors, private entrances, gas fireplaces, and views of Oyster Bay. The Landau Room has a four-poster bed with an ocean view and a private hot tub on a seaside deck. You can swim in the warm bay next to the property; watch seals, eagles, and whales from the shoreside gazebo; or soak in a hot tub on the ocean's edge. ✉ 511 Bayview Dr., Mayne Island V0N 2J0 ☎ 250/539–3368 or 888/629–6322 🖷 250/539–3355 ⊕ www.acoachhouse.com ➵ 3 rooms ⚘ Outdoor hot tub, beach, mountain bikes, piano; no a/c, no room phones, no room TVs, no kids, no smoking ▤ AE, MC, V ⧉ BP.

Sports & the Outdoors

Island Charters (☎ 250/539–5040) operates half- and full-day trips on a crewed 33-foot sailboat. Half-day trips are C$155 for two people; full-day trips are C$180. At **Mayne Island Kayak, Canoe, and Bicycle Rentals** (⊠411 Fernhill Rd., Miners Bay ☎250/539–5599 ⊕www.maynekayak. com), kayak day rentals start at C$25 for 2 hours, C$50 for 24 hours.

Pender Island

❼ A few miles north of the U.S. border, Pender is actually two islands: North Pender and South Pender, divided by a canal and linked by a one-lane bridge. Most of the population of about 2,000 cluster on North Pender, whereas South Pender is largely forested and undeveloped.

★ Both islands host sections of the **Gulf Islands National Park Reserve** (☎ 250/654–4000 ⊕ www.pc.gc.ca/pn-np/bc/gulf/). On South Pender a steep trail leads to the 244 meter (800 foot) summit of **Mount Norman** with its expansive ocean and island views. Trails start at Ainslie Road, Canal Road, and the Beaumont section of the park. The beach and backcountry campsites at South Pender's **Beaumont** can be reached by boat or by a 40-minute hike from the islands' connecting bridge. Also on South Pender a decommissioned road leads to **Greenburn Lake.** At **Roesland** on North Pender trails lead to a freshwater lake and to an islet connected by a bridge. You can camp on North Pender at the drive-in **Prior Centennial Campground.**

Even outside the park, the Penders are blessed with beaches, boasting over 30 public beach-access points. The small pebble beach at **Gowlland Point Park,** at the end of Gowlland Point Road on South Pender, is one of the prettiest on the islands, with views across to Washington State. The sandy beach at **Mortimer Spit** is a sheltered spot for swimming and kayaking; it's near the bridge linking the two islands.

There's no town on either island, but you can find groceries and other basics at North Pender's Driftwood Centre. Watch for small craft shops, studios and galleries throughout the islands.

need a
break?

You can refuel before catching the ferry at the **Stand** (⊠ Otter Bay Ferry terminal, end of Otter Bay Rd. ☎ 250/629–3292) a rustic take-out shack at the Otter Bay ferry terminal. The burgers—whether beef, venison, oyster or veggie—are enormous, messy, and delicious.

Where to Stay & Eat

★ $$$$ ✕⊡ **Poets Cove Resort & Spa.** One of the Gulf Islands' most luxurious developments fills a secluded cove on South Pender. A nautical-theme lodge and a scattering of two- and three-bedroom cottages overlook a marina and a forest-framed cove. All units have fireplaces, duvets, and heated bathroom floors and most have decks or balconies with stunning ocean views. The restaurant ($$$–$$$$), serves top-notch Pacific Northwest fare, whereas the lounge offers high-end pub meals. A waterfall tumbles over a steam grotto outside the lavish spa. The resort's activity center offers guided hikes, vineyard tours, deep-sea fishing, and scuba lessons. ⊠ 9801 Spalding Rd., V0N 2M3 ☎ 250/629–2100 or 888/512–7638 ⊟ 250/629–3212 ⊕ www.poetscove.com ↝ 22 rooms, 15 cottages, 9 villas ⚴ Restaurant, grocery, IDD phones, some in-room

*hot tubs, some kitchens, cable TV, some in-room DVDs, in-room broad-
band, 2 tennis courts, 2 pools, gym, 2 outdoor hot tubs, spa, boating,
marina, fishing, mountain bikes, hiking, pub, shop, children's programs
(ages 5–14), dry cleaning, laundry facilities, laundry service, concierge,
meeting rooms, some pets allowed (fee); no smoking.* ▤ *AE, MC, V.*

Salt Spring Island

❽ *28 nautical mi from Swartz Bay (32 km [20 mi] north of Victoria), 22
nautical mi from Tsawwassen (39 km [24 mi] south of Vancouver).*

With its wealth of studios, galleries, restaurants, and B&Bs, Salt Spring
is the most developed, and most visited, of the Gulf Islands. It boasts
the only town in the archipelago (Ganges) and, although it can get busy
on summer weekends, has not yet lost its relaxed rural feel. Outside of
Ganges, the rolling landscape is home to small organic farms (including two wineries), forested hills, quiet white-shell beaches, and several
swimming lakes.

What really sets Salt Spring apart is its undisputed status as a "little arts
town." Island residents include hundreds of artists, writers, craftspeople, and musicians, many of whom open their studios to visitors. To visit
local artists in their studios, pick up a free **Studio Tour** map from the Visitor Information Centre in Ganges.

Ganges, a seaside village about 6 km (4 mi) from the Long Harbour ferry
terminal, is the main commercial center for Salt Spring Island's 11,000
residents. It has several boutiques, galleries, and restaurants.

★ Locals and visitors flock to Ganges on summer Saturdays for the **Salt
Spring Island Saturday Market** (☎ 250/537–4448 ⊕ www.saltspringmarket.
com), held in Centennial Park every Saturday April through October.
Everything sold at this colorful outdoor market is made or grown on
the island; the array and quality of crafts, food and produce is dazzling.

At the south end of Salt Spring Island, where the ferries from Victoria
arrive, is the tiny village of **Fulford,** which has a restaurant, a café, a kayaking and bike-rental outlet, and several offbeat boutiques. Ferries from
Crofton, on Vancouver Island, arrive on the west side of Salt Spring Island at **Vesuvius,** an even smaller community with a restaurant, an old-
fashioned general store, a swimming beach, and crafts studios.

Near the center of Salt Spring Island, the summit of **Mt. Maxwell Provincial Park** (⊠ Mt. Maxwell Rd., off Fulford–Ganges Rd.) has spectacular views of south Salt Spring, Vancouver Island, and other Gulf Islands.
The last portion of the drive is steep, winding, and unpaved.

★ ♻ **Ruckle Provincial Park** (⊠ Beaver Point Rd. ☎ 250/539–2115 or 877/559–
2115 ⊕ www.bcparks.ca) is the site of an 1872 homestead and extensive fields still farmed by the Ruckle family. The park also has several
small sandy beaches, and 8 km (5 mi) of trails winding through forests
and along the coast. Walk-in campsites on a grassy, seaside field are available on a first-come first-served basis.

Salt Spring Island

Salt Spring, along with neighboring Vancouver and Saturna islands, is part of British Columbia's burgeoning wine country. The island's two vineyards are side-by-side, on the main road between Ganges and Fulford. **Garry Oaks Winery** (✉ 1880 Fulford-Ganges Rd. ☎ 250/653–4687 ⊕ www.garryoakswine.com) is open for tastings daily noon to 5, May through October; tours are offered by appointment. There's also a meditative labyrinth and a loft room where you can spend the night. **Salt Spring Vineyards** (✉ 151 Lee Rd., off 1700 block Fulford-Ganges Rd ☎ 250/653–9463 ⊕ www.saltspringvineyards.com) offers tastings, daily noon to 5, June through September. There's also a small B&B onsite. You can spend a day visiting island wineries, cheese-makers, chocolate-makers, farms, and studios with **Island Gourmet Safaris** (☎ 250/537–4118 ⊕ www.islandgourmetsafaris.com).

The **Ganges Faerie Mini Shuttle** (☎ 250/537–6758 or 250/538–9007 ⊕ www.gangesfaerie.com) offers shuttle service between the ferry terminals and Ganges, Ruckle Park, and the island's north end.

The tiny *Queen of de Nile* passenger ferry runs from Ganges Marina to Ganges town center. A water taxi runs to Mayne and Galiano islands. Cabs, rental cars, bike and scooter rentals are also available on the island.

Where to Stay & Eat

★ **$$$–$$$$** ✕ **House Piccolo.** Piccolo Lyytikainen, the Finnish-born chef-owner of this tiny restaurant, serves beautifully prepared and presented European cuisine. Creations include Scandinavian-influenced dishes such as B.C. venison with a rowan- and juniper-berry demi-glace and charbroiled filet of beef with gorgonzola sauce. For dessert the vodka-moistened lingonberry crepes are hard to resist. The 250-item wine list includes many hard-to-find vintages. The indoor tables are cozy and candlelighted; the outdoor patio is a pleasant summer dining spot. ⊠ *108 Hereford Ave., Ganges* ☎ *250/537–1844* 🖃 *MC, V* ☉ *No lunch.*

$–$$ ✕ **Raven Street Café.** This little north-end café, which doubles as the only grocery store for miles, serves a creative host of dishes. Pizza and burgers, chicken paella, seafood gumbo, wood-fired mussels, and beer-baked cioppino emerge fresh from the wood-fired oven at surprisingly low prices. The café is near the Fernwood dock, about 15 minutes north of Ganges. ⊠ *321 Fernwood Rd.* ☎ *250/537–2273* ⌂ *Reservations not accepted* 🖃 *AE, DC, MC, V* ☉ *Closed Mon. Oct.–Apr.*

$ ✕ **Tree House Café.** Hearty, wholesome, and homemade sandwiches, wraps, quesadillas, burgers, and smoothies draw locals to these two funky cafés. At the Ganges location, seating is outside under a spreading plum tree and local musicians play every night in summer. Treehouse South, at the Fulford ferry terminal, has indoor seating and a patio, both with ocean views. ⊠ *106 Purvis La., next to Mouat's Trading Company, Ganges* ☎ *250/537–5379* ⊠ *2921 Fulford-Ganges Rd., Fulford* ☎ *250/653–4833* ⌂ *Evening reservations not accepted at Ganges* 🖃 *DC, MC, V* ☉ *No dinner Sept.–mid-May at Ganges.*

$$$$ ✕🖽 **Hastings House.** The centerpiece of this 25-acre seaside estate is a
Fodor'sChoice 1930 country house, built in the style of an 16th-century Sussex manor.
★ Guest quarters, which are in the manor, in renovated historic outbuildings, and in a newer addition overlooking Ganges Harbour, are decorated in an English-country style, with antiques, locally crafted woodwork, and fireplaces or woodstoves. Three- or five-course prix-fixe dinners in the manor house are open to the public ($$$$; reservations essential). The excellent cuisine includes local lamb, seafood, and herbs and produce from the inn's gardens. The spa gives facials, manicures, and massages. ⊠ *160 Upper Ganges Rd., V8K 2S2* ☎ *250/537–2362 or 800/661–9255* 🖷 *250/537–5333* ⊕ *www.hastingshouse. com* ⇋ *3 rooms, 14 suites, 1 guesthouse* ⌂ *Restaurant, IDD phones, minibars, some in-room broadband, in-room data ports, spa, mountain bikes, boccie, croquet, shop, dry cleaning, laundry service, business services, meeting rooms; no a/c in some rooms, no room TVs, no kids under 16, no smoking* 🖃 *AE, MC, V* ☉ *Closed mid-Nov.–mid-Mar.* ❍⊙ *BP.*

$$$–$$$$ 🖽 **Anne's Oceanfront Hideaway.** On a steep seaside slope 6 km (4 mi) north of the Vesuvius ferry terminal, this modern home has a cozy library, a sitting room, an elevator, and two verandas. Every room has a hydromassage tub; three have balconies. The Douglas Fir and Garry Oak rooms have the best views. Luxurious amenities—morning coffee brought to your door, robes, and fresh flowers in the rooms—make this a comfortable place to unwind. One room is wheelchair accessible. A lavish four-course breakfast is served. ⊠ *168 Simson Rd., V8K 1E2* ☎ *250/*

537–0851 or 888/474–2663 ≞ 250/537–0861 ⊕ www.annesoceanfront. com ➷ 4 rooms ♿ IDD phones, refrigerators, massage, library, laundry facilities, Internet room; no room TVs, no kids, no smoking ⊟ AE, MC, V ⎮○⎮ BP.

Nightlife & the Arts

To find out what's happening and who's playing, see the local weekly, the *Driftwood,* or contact the visitor-information center.

You can catch a live music show or a play at **ArtSpring** (✉ 100 Jackson Ave. ☎ 250/537–2102 or 866/537–2102), a theater and gallery complex in Ganges. The **Treehouse Café** (✉ 106 Purvis La. ☎ 250/537–5379), next to Mouat's Trading Company, hosts local musicians throughout the summer.

Sports & the Outdoors

For information about hiking trails and beach access, pick up a copy of the "Salt Spring Out-of-Doors Map" at the visitor-information center.

BIKING You can rent bikes at **Salt Spring Kayak and Cycle** (✉ 2923 Fulford-Ganges Rd., Fulford ☎ 250/653–4222 or 866/341–0007 ⊕ www. saltspringkayaking.com) near the Fulford ferry terminal. Charges are C$30 for the first day, C$15 a day for subsequent days, or C$15 for two hours. They'll deliver bikes to any island location for an extra C$15.

BOATING **Island Escapades** (✉ 163 Fulford-Ganges Rd., Ganges ☎ 250/537–2537 or 888/529–2567 ⊕ www.islandescapades.com) has guided kayaking (C$40–C$115 for two to six hours; the longer tour includes a three-course dinner on the beach) and sailing trips (C$50 per person for three or four hours). **Salt Spring Kayak and Cycle** (✉ 2923 Fulford-Ganges Rd., Fulford ☎ 250/653–4222 or 866/341–0007 ⊕ www.saltspringkayaking. com) rents kayaks and provides lessons and trips. Guided day paddles are C$50 (C$30 for two hours at sunset). It delivers kayaks as well as bikes to any island location. **Salt Spring Marine Rentals** (✉ On Ganges Harbour off Upper Ganges Rd. ☎ 250/537–5464 ⊕ www.saltspring. com/rentals) rents powerboats for C$110 a day. Here's where to arrange fishing, sailing, and sightseeing charters. They also rent scooters (C$70 a day) and cars (starting at C$50 a day). **Sea Otter Kayaking** (✉ 149 Lower Ganges Rd., on Ganges Harbour at foot of Rainbow Rd., Ganges ☎ 250/537–5678 or 877/537–5678 ⊕ www.seaotterkayaking.com) provides kayak sales, rentals, lessons, and tours. A two-hour introductory lesson is C$40. The company also leads sailing charters, and multiday kayaking and sailing trips around the Gulf Islands.

GOLF **Blackburn Meadows Golf Club** (✉ 269 Blackburn Rd. ☎ 250/537–1707 ⊕ www.blackburnmeadows.com) borders a lake. Its 9 holes (C$16; C$26 for 18 holes) offer you the chance to play Canada's first organic golf course. At **Hart Memorial Disc Golf Course** (✉ End of Seaview Ave., in Mouat Park Ganges) players aim Frisbee-like discs to hit a series of 18 targets. It's free (you can pick up a disc at Ganges's toy or hardware store). **Salt Spring Island Golf and Country Club** (✉ 805 Lower Ganges Rd. ☎ 250/537–2121 ⊕ www.saltspringgolf.com) is a pleasant 9-hole course (C$20; C$32 for 18 holes) with a restaurant in the clubhouse.

HIKING   **Island Escapades** (✉ 163 Fulford-Ganges Rd., Ganges ☎ 250/537–2537 or 888/529–2567 ⊕ www.islandescapades.com) organizes guided shoreline and mountain hikes and rock-climbing expeditions on Salt Spring. A three-hour hike costs about C$30; outdoor rock climbing (with equipment supplied) is C$65. It also runs wilderness camps and outdoor adventure programs for children and teens and mountaineering trips to Vancouver Island.

HORSEBACK   You can take small group trail rides with **Salt Spring Guided Rides**
RIDING   (☎ 250/537–5761). Reservations are necessary. The cost is C$35 (cash only) an hour.

SWIMMING   St. Mary Lake, on North End Road, and Cusheon Lake, south of Ganges, are your best bets for warm-water swimming.

Shopping

Ganges's Mahon Hall is the site of **ArtCraft**, a summer-long sale of works by more than 200 local artisans. Salt Spring's biggest arts-and-crafts gallery, **Coastal Currents Gallery** (✉ 133 Hereford Ave., Ganges ☎ 250/537–0070), sells assorted crafts from all over British Columbia. For some intriguing First Nations and local works, check out **Thunderbird Gallery** (✉ Grace Point Sq. ☎ 250/537–8448 or 877/537–8448).

COAST MOUNTAIN CIRCLE

The drive into the Coast Mountains from Vancouver is a stunning sampler of mainland British Columbia. It follows the Sea to Sky Highway (Highway 99) past fjordlike Howe Sound, the town of Squamish, and Whistler Resort, and then continues on a quiet back road to the gold-rush town of Lillooet. From Lillooet you can continue into the High Country or return to Vancouver on highways 12 and 1 through the gorges of the Fraser Canyon, stopping for a soak at Harrison Hot Springs on the way. This is a scenic two- to three-day drive; the roads are good but are best avoided in snow, particularly if you plan to travel past Whistler.

Horseshoe Bay

🌀 *20 km (12 mi) north of Vancouver, 100 km (62 mi) south of Whistler.*

Tucked into a cove under the Coast Mountains, this small community is the ferry hub for boats to Nanaimo on Vancouver Island, Langdale on the Sunshine Coast, and tiny Bowen Island, a rural retreat 20 minutes across the sound that has pubs, B&Bs, crafts shops, and even a winery. Near Horseshoe Bay, off Marine Drive, is **Whytecliff Park,** with a swimming beach, picnic sites, and a rocky little island that's connected to the mainland at low tide.

From Horseshoe Bay, the Sea to Sky Highway (Highway 99) becomes one of British Columbia's most scenic roads, climbing into the mountains along the edge of Howe Sound. Most people on this winding road are eager to reach the resort town of Whistler, and traffic can be heavy. A number of sights along the way are worth a stop.

The **B.C. Museum of Mining** was once the British Empire's largest copper mine. It's now a national historic site. There's an underground train and knowledgeable staff give guided tours and provide a chance to pan for gold. In winter these activities are considerably cut back, as is the entrance fee. The museum is about an hour north of Vancouver. ⊠ *Hwy. 99, Britannia Beach* ☎ *604/896–2233 or 800/896–4044* ⊕ *www.bcmuseumofmining.org* ☑ *C$15* ☉ *May–mid-Oct., daily 9–5; late Oct.–Apr., 9–4:30.*

About 42 km (25 mi) north of Horseshoe Bay is **Shannon Falls,** which at 1,099 feet is six times higher than Niagara Falls and Canada's third-highest waterfall. You can see it from the highway or follow a short trail through the woods for a closer look.

Between mid-May and the end of October **Ocean West Expeditions** (☎ 250/362–7599 year-round, 604/688–5770 summer only ⊕ www.ocean-west.com) rents kayaks and offers lessons and tours from Lions Bay, just past Horseshoe Bay.

Squamish

❿ *67 km (42 mi) north of Vancouver, 58 km (36 mi) south of Whistler.*

Squamish, or "mother of the wind" in Coast Salish, has long languished in the shadow of Whistler Resort up the highway. Outdoors enthusiasts have, however, discovered its possibilities. The big winds that gave the area its name make it an excellent windsurfing spot. Diving in Howe Sound, kayaking, and hiking are also draws. The rock face of the **Stawamus Chief** soars 2,139 feet from the edge of Highway 99 and is the world's second-largest freestanding granite monolith (after the Rock of Gibraltar). It attracts all levels of rock climbers to its more than 200 routes.

Between November and February the world's largest concentrations of bald eagles gather at the **Brackendale Eagles' Park** (⊠ Government Rd., off Hwy. 99, Brackendale ☎ No phone), about 7 km (4 mi) north of Squamish. The park is open dawn to dusk; admission is free. You can watch the eagles from the banks of the Squamish River, off Government Road in Brackendale, or from a raft on the Cheakamus River. The **Brackendale Eagle Festival** (☎ 604/898–3333 Brackendale Art Gallery for information), held in January, is a growing part of an annual eagle count, which in 1994 set the record at 3,766. Festival activities include art exhibits, a photo contest, concerts, and guided ecoexcursions.

The **West Coast Railway Heritage Park,** about a 10-minute drive north of downtown Squamish, has more than 60 pieces of vintage rolling stock. You can ride a mini-train around the site, climb on a caboose, and stroll through a restored 1890 first-class business car—the sort that railway barons rode—as well as a 1905 colonists' car that carried settlers to the prairies in minimal comfort. The park is home to the famed Royal Hudson steam engine that used to run between North Vancouver and Squamish. There's a gift shop and archives in a 1915-style station house. ⊠ *39645 Government Rd.* ☎ *604/898–9336* ⊕ *www.wcra.org* ☑ *C$10* ☉ *Daily 10–5.*

Where to Stay & Eat

$–$$ ✕ **The Roadhouse Restaurant.** A fixture on Highway 99 since the 1970s, this wood-panel roadhouse across from Shannon Falls serves breakfasts, lunches, and dinners of updated comfort food, huge burgers, and Pacific Northwest cuisine. The menu changes seasonally, but highlights have included baby-back ribs with honey-apple glaze and grilled spring salmon with sun-dried cranberry cream. Most of the seats inside and on the patio have great views of the mountains and the falls. ⊠ *Hwy. 99, 5 km (3 mi) south of Squamish, Klahanie* ☎ 604/892-5312 ▭ *MC, V.*

$ ✕▥ **Howe Sound Inn & Brewing Company.** This cedar inn near Squamish town center covers all the bases. The fireplace in the cozy post-and-beam brewpub is a great place to relax after a day of hiking or rafting. You can also watch climbers tackling Stawamus Chief from the pub's patio or take a brewery tour. The rustic yet elegant North Beach Lounge and Grill ($–$$) serves Pacific Northwest cuisine alongside pastas, thin crust pizzas, and fresh goods from the in-house bakery (try the ale-and-cheddar bread). The rooms upstairs have furniture made of reclaimed fir; most have striking views of Stawamus Chief or the Tantalus Mountains. ⊠ *37801 Cleveland Ave., Box 978, V0N 3G0* ☎ 604/892-2603 or 800/919-2537 ▤ *604/892-2631* ⊕ *www.howesound.com* ⟲ *20 rooms* ♨ *Restaurant, cable TV, in-room data ports, sauna, billiards, pub, business services, meeting rooms; no smoking* ▭ *AE, MC, V.*

$$$–$$$$ ▥ **Nu-Salya Bed & Breakfast Guest Chalet.** One of the most beautiful alpine B&Bs in Canada, the chalet provides a peaceful respite from the bustle of nearby Squamish and Whistler. Flared logs, river rock, and creative landscaping enhance the exterior. The Great Room houses a 40-foot high river-rock fireplace and owners Bill and Sue McComish's Native art collection. Rooms are adorned with original oil paintings, Native American art, and reproduction Colonial log furniture. Expansive windows throughout provide breathtaking fjord and mountain views. ⊠ *2014 Glacier Heights Pl., 17 km (10 mi) north of Squamish, off Hwy. 99, Box 927 Garibaldi Highlands V0N 1T0* ☎ 604/898-3039 or 877/604-9005 ▤ *604/898-3039* ⊕ *www.nusalya.com* ⟲ *3 rooms* ♨ *Fans, in-room VCRs, outdoor hot tub, fishing, mountain bikes, hiking, lounge, piano, Internet room, Wi-Fi; no a/c, no kids, no smoking* ▭*MC, V* ⦿*BP.*

$ ▥ **Sunwolf Outdoor Centre.** A highlight of this former fishing lodge on the Cheakamus River, 10 km (6 mi) north of Squamish, is its rafting center. It specializes in Class IV (fast-moving rapids) white-water trips but also offers peaceful floats on slow-moving water. Sunwolf's cabins, tucked in the woods on the 5½-acre property, are attractive and modern, with fir floors, four-poster beds, handcrafted pine furniture, gas fireplaces, and vaulted ceilings. The cozy lodge has fireplaces and an outdoor deck. In December and January this is a prime spot for viewing bald eagles. ⊠ *70002 Squamish Valley Rd., 4 km (2½ mi) off Hwy. 99, Box 244, Brackendale V0N 1H0* ☎ 604/898-1537 or 877/806-8046 ▤ 604/898-1634 ⊕ *www.sunwolf.net* ⟲ *10 cabins* ♨ *Café, fans, some kitchenettes, outdoor hot tub, fishing, mountain bikes, badminton, croquet, horseshoes, volleyball, meeting rooms, some pets allowed (fee); no a/c, no room TVs, no smoking* ▭ *MC, V.*

Sports & the Outdoors

Squamish is a major rock-climbing destination and a popular spot for hiking, diving, trail riding, sailing, rafting, and kayaking. The **Canadian Outback Adventure Company** (☎604/921–7250 or 800/565–8735 ⊕www. canadianoutback.com) runs a variety of rafting day trips in the area, including eagle rafting trips on the Cheakamus River (C$99 for two hours) and an easygoing trip for families (from C$139). For airplane or helicopter flightseeing tours over glaciers, including landings and picnics on the ice, or other helicopter-based adventures, contact **Glacier Air Tours** (☎ 604/898–9016 or 800/265–0088 ⊕ www.glacierair.com). **Sea to Sky Stables** (⊠Paradise Valley Rd., about 3 km [2 mi] off Hwy. 99 ☎604/ 898–3934 or 866/898–3934 ⊕www.seatoskystables.com) leads trail rides for all levels year-round. Guided rides start at about C$40 an hour, C$69 for two hours. The company also has river rafting, ATV tours, kayaking, and guided hikes; you can stay overnight in chuck wagons or a tepee.

GOLF   The challenging 18-hole, par-72 course at **Furry Creek Golf and Country Club** (⊠ Hwy. 99, Furry Creek ☎ 604/922–9576 or 888/922–9462 ⊙Mar.–late Oct.), south of Squamish, has striking ocean views and greens fees of about C$109, including a mandatory cart. The **Squamish Valley Golf & Country Club** (⊠ 2458 Mamquam Rd. ☎ 604/898–9691 or 888/ 349–3688) is an 18-hole, par-72 course close to town. Greens fees are about C$60.

en route   Between Squamish and Whistler on Highway 99 lies Brandywine Falls Provincial Park and the 231-foot-high **Brandywine Falls.** A short trail through the woods takes you to a viewing platform and if you cross the bridge over the creek, a 10-minute walk takes you to a clearing right beside the tumbling water.

Whistler

⑪   *120 km (74 mi) north of Vancouver, 58 km (36 mi) north of Squamish.*

Fodor'sChoice   Whistler and Blackcomb mountains, part of Whistler Resort, which will
★   host the 2010 Olympic and Paralympic Winter Games, are consistently ranked among North America's top ski destinations. Between them they have the largest ski area and two longest vertical drops on the continent, as well as one of the world's most advanced lift systems. The ski-in, ski-out village has enough shops, restaurants, nightlife, and other activities that it's easy to fill a vacation without ever hitting the slopes. In winter the resort buzzes with skiers and snowboarders from all over the world. In summer the pace relaxes as the focus shifts to cycling, hiking, golfing, and boating around Whistler Valley, although heli-skiers will still find snow. Whistler's Mountain Bike Park is quickly becoming a top summer draw, in large part because every year it introduces ever more innovative jump-infested trails.

At the base of the mountains are Whistler Village, Village North (also called Marketplace), and Upper Village—a rapidly expanding, interconnected community of lodgings, restaurants, pubs, and boutiques. Locals refer to the entire area as Whistler Village. With dozens of hotels and condos within a five-minute walk of the mountains, the site is always bustling. Another village center, called Whistler Creek, is developing along Highway 99 a couple of miles to the south.

Whistler Village is a pedestrians-only community. Anywhere you want to go within the resort is within a few minutes' walk, and parking lots are just outside the village (although as a hotel guest, you may have access to underground parking). The bases of Whistler and Blackcomb mountains are also just at the village edge; in fact, you can ski right into the lower level of the Fairmont Chateau Whistler Hotel.

Where to Eat

$$$$ ✕ **Bearfoot Bistro.** The cutesy name belies the elegance of this acclaimed bistro. The 75-seat dining room has a warm Latin feel with tall leather chairs, open kitchen, and live jazz nightly. The multicourse set menus (C$90–C$225) change frequently but have featured dishes such as marinated duck foie gras, wild arctic caribou, and herb-crusted striped bass. The adjacent wine bar serves casual French bistro fare ($$–$$$). Diners in either section can sample from the highly rated 1,600-label wine cellar. ⊠ *4121 Village Green* ☏ *604/932–3433* ▤ *AE, D, DC, MC, V* ☺ *No lunch.*

$$$–$$$$ ✕ **Après Restaurant.** This 50-seat wine bar with modern art and comfy leather chairs is one of the funkiest and most romantic in British Columbia. More than 50 wines by the glass are available as are flights for appropriate pairing. The food is sensational with lots of regional specialties such as Cowichan Bay duck and Queen Charlotte Island sable fish. From June through November, the restaurant runs *après gastronomique*, a five-night, six-day cooking school where you can learn all manner of trade secrets from award-winning master chef Eric Vernice. ⊠ *103–4338 Main St.* ☏ *604/935–0200* ▤ *AE, DC, MC, V* ☺ *Closed Sun. and Mon. No lunch Tues.–Sat.*

★ **$$$–$$$$** ✕ **Araxi.** Golden walls, terra-cotta tiles, antiques, and original artwork create a vibrant backdrop for the French-influenced Pacific Northwest cuisine here. Local farmers grow produce exclusively for Araxi's chef, who also makes good use of cheese, game, and fish from the province. Breads and pastries are made in-house each morning. The menu changes seasonally, but dishes have included Fraser Valley rabbit and alder-smoked B.C. arctic char with saffron and oyster-mushroom sauce. The multitier seafood tower is a must-try for seafoodies who love to graze and share. Wine lovers, take note: there's a 13,000-bottle inventory and three sommeliers. A heated patio is open in summer, and the lounge, with a low-price bar menu ($), is a popular après-ski spot. ⊠ *4222 Village Sq.* ☏ *604/932–4540* ⌖ *Reservations essential* ▤ *AE, DC, MC, V* ☺ *No lunch Oct.–May.*

$$$–$$$$ ✕ **La Rúa.** Reddish flagstone floors and sponge-painted walls, a wine cellar behind a wrought-iron door, modern oil paintings, and sconce lighting give La Rúa an intimate, Mediterranean ambience. Favorites from the continental menu include charred rare tuna, loin of fallow deer, seafood tagliolini, and rack of lamb. ⊠ *4557 Blackcomb Way* ☏ *604/932–5011* ▤ *AE, DC, MC, V* ☺ *No lunch.*

$$$–$$$$ ✕ **Rim Rock Café.** About 2 mi south of the Village, this restaurant is a local favorite as much for its cozy, unpretentious ambience (complete with stone fireplace) as for its great seafood. If deciding on only one item is hard, why not go for the samplers: the Rim Rock Trio combines sea bass in an almond-ginger crust, grilled prawns, and rare ahi tuna marinated in soya, sake, and mirin. If you want a booth or a coveted table near the fireplace, make a reservation. The café closes for roughly a month every fall, so call ahead. ⊠ *2117 Whistler Rd.* ☎ *604/932–5565 or 877/ 932–5589* ▤ *AE, DC, MC, V* ⊘ *No lunch.*

$$$–$$$$ ✕ **Val d'Isère.** Chef-owner Roland Pfaff satisfies a skier's craving for fine French food with traditional dishes from his native Alsace and with Gallic takes on Canadian produce. Specialties include caramelized duck à l'orange, and veal tenderloin with Vancouver Island morel-mushroom sauce. In summer the large patio overlooking the Town Plaza is great for people-watching. ⊠ *Bear Lodge, Town Plaza, 4314 Main St.* ☎ *604/ 932–4666* ▤ *AE, DC, MC, V* ⊘ *No lunch Nov.–May.*

$$–$$$$ ✕ **Quattro at Whistler.** Vancouverites who've enjoyed the Corsi family's central Italian fare at their city restaurants flock here for warming après-ski meals. The *L'Abbufata*, a five-course Roman feast (C$60), comes on family-size platters meant for sharing. Other popular dishes include spaghetti pescatore, pistachio-crusted sea bass, and shaved beef tenderloin. The seasonal three-course menu is a good deal. Dark woods, fireplaces, and an open kitchen create a relaxing ambience. Nine hundred wine varieties and an impressive grappa selection fill the cellar. ⊠ *4319 Main St.* ☎ *604/905–4844* ▤ *AE, DC, MC, V* ⊘ *No lunch.*

$–$$ ✕ **Pasta Lupino.** Fresh pasta at tiny prices draws hungry skiers to this little Whistler Marketplace trattoria. You can mix and match from a choice of pastas of the day with homemade alfredo, Bolognese, or fresh basil and plum tomato sauce or dig into one of the house specialties: lasagna, ravioli, and spaghettini with meatballs. Vegetarian pastas, homemade soups and sauces, decadent desserts, beer, and wine are also available. The eight tables fill up quickly, but there's always takeout. ⊠ *121–4368 Main St., next to 7-Eleven* ☎ *604/905–0400* ⌕ *Reservations not accepted* ▤ *MC, V.*

Where to Stay

Price categories are based on January-to-April ski-season rates; prices can be higher during Christmas and spring break, but considerably lower in summer. Many properties require minimum stays, especially during the Christmas season. Also, Whistler Village has some serious nightlife. If peace and quiet are important to you, ask for a room away from the main pedestrian thoroughfares or stay in one of the residential neighborhoods outside the village. Expect to pay C$18 to C$20 for overnight parking at hotels in the village; accommodations outside the village don't normally charge for parking.

You can book lodgings, including B&Bs, pensions, and hundreds of time-share condos, through **Whistler Central Reservations** (☎ 604/932–4222, 604/664–5625 in Vancouver, 800/944–7853 in U.S. and Canada ⊕ www. tourismwhistler.com). You can also request accommodation information for the 2010 Olympics on the Web site.

$$$$ ⊞ **Fairmont Château Whistler Resort.** This family-friendly fortress, just steps
FodorśChoice from the Blackcomb ski lifts, is a self-contained, ski-in, ski-out resort-
★ within-a-resort, with its own shopping arcade, golf course, and an impressive spa with exotic Asian and ayurvedic treatments. The lobby is
filled with rustic Canadiana, handmade Mennonite rugs, overstuffed sofas,
and a grand fireplace. Standard rooms are comfortably furnished and
of average size, decorated in burgundies and turquoises, and most have
mountain views. Rooms and suites on the Entrée Gold floors have fireplaces, whirlpool tubs, and their own concierge and private lounge. Ski
and bike storage are convenient. The resort's Wildflower Restaurant serves
fine Pacific Northwest fare against stunning mountain views. ⊠ *4599
Château Blvd., V0N 1B4* ☎ *604/938–8000 or 800/606–8244* ⊜ *604/
938–2099* ⊕ *www.fairmont.com* ➳ *500 rooms, 56 suites* △ *2 restaurants, room service, in-room safes, minibars, cable TV with movies and
video games, in-room broadband, Wi-Fi, 18-hole golf course, 3 tennis
courts, 2 pools (1 indoor-outdoor), gym, health club, hair salon, 4 hot
tubs (1 indoor), sauna, spa, steam room, ski shop, ski storage, lobby
lounge, shops, babysitting, children's programs (ages 5–12), dry cleaning, laundry facilities, concierge, concierge floor, business services, convention center, parking (fee), some pets allowed (fee), no-smoking rooms,
no-smoking floors* ⊟ *AE, D, DC, MC, V.*

$$$$ ⊞ **Four Seasons Resort Whistler.** Opened in June 2004, this plush nine-
story hotel gives alpine chic a new twist with warm earth-tones and wood
interiors, big leather chairs beside the fireplace, and amazingly spacious
rooms. Its restaurant has a bistro feel and is focused around a central
fire pit. The luxurious spa has become a destination in itself with its 15
treatment rooms and wide range of massages. Child-friendly amenities
include children's programs and pint-size bath robes. ⊠ *Upper Village,
4591 Blackcomb Way V0N 1B4* ☎ *604/935–3400 or 888/935–2460*
⊜ *604/935–3455* ⊕ *www.fourseasons.com* ➳ *269 studios and suites,
3 townhomes* △ *Restaurant, room service, in-roof safes, cable TV with
movies and video games, in-room DVD, in-room broadband, Wi-Fi, pool,
gym, spa, steam room, lounge, children's programs (ages 13 and under),
concierge, business services, parking (fee), no-smoking rooms.* ⊟ *AE,
D, DC, MC, V.*

$$$$ ⊞ **Hilton Whistler Resort.** A wealth of facilities highlight this family-
friendly resort complex, scheduled to open in December 2005, at the
base of the Whistler and Blackcomb gondolas. Attractively decorated
rooms are so large that most can easily accommodate four people.
Many have fireplaces, whirlpool baths, and balconies; some suites have
saunas. An on-site health club and spa has a variety of soothing post-
ski treatments, including acupressure and stone therapy. ⊠ *4050 Whistler
Way, V0N 1B4* ☎ *604/932–1982 or 800/445–8667* ⊜ *604/932–7332*
⊕ *www.hilton.com* ➳ *264 rooms, 24 suites* △ *Restaurant, room service, in-room safes, in-room hot tubs, some kitchens, minibars, cable
TV with movies and video games, in-room broadband, Wi-Fi, 2 tennis
courts, pool, gym, health club, hair salon, outdoor hot tubs, massage,
sauna, spa, steam room, billiards, ski shop, ski storage, bar, sports bar,
piano, shops, babysitting, children's programs (ages 4–12), dry cleaning, laundry facilities, laundry service, concierge, business services,*

meeting rooms, parking (fee), some pets allowed (fee), no-smoking rooms, no-smoking floors ☰ *AE, DC, MC, V.*

$$$$ 🏨 **Pan Pacific Whistler Mountainside** This eight-story lodge is steps from the Whistler and Blackcomb gondolas. Guest quarters include studios with pull-down queen beds or one- and two-bedroom suites. All units have balconies, gas fireplaces, and floor-to-ceiling windows that make the most of the mountain or valley views. Rich colors, cherry wood, and granite make the rooms sleek and modern. In the evening excellent Irish cuisine is served and you can hear traditional music in the Dubh Linn Gate Pub downstairs. ⊠ *4320 Sundial Crescent, V0N 1B4* ☎ *604/ 905–2999 or 888/905–9995* 🖷 *604/905–2995* ⊕ *www.panpacific.com* ⬦ *76 suites, 45 studios* ♨ *Room service, in-room safes, kitchens, cable TV with movies and video games, in-room broadband, Wi-Fi, pool, gym, hair salon, 2 outdoor hot tubs, massage, steam room, ski shop, ski storage, pub, shops, dry cleaning, laundry facilities, laundry service, meeting rooms, parking (fee); no smoking* ☰ *AE, DC, MC, V.*

$$$$ 🏨 **Pan Pacific Whistler Village Centre.** Opened in summer 2005, adjacent to its sister property, this all-suite, full-service boutique hotel is steps away from the slopes and village activity. A full-buffet breakfast and evening hors d'oeuvres are served in the Pacific Lounge, open to guests throughout the day for complimentary nonalcoholic drinks. The outdoor patio has terrific mountain vistas. Suites come in one- to three-bedroom configurations, and have fully equipped kitchens, gas fireplaces, balconies, soaker tubs, and expansive view windows. ⊠ *4299 Blackcomb Way, V0N 1B4* ☎ *604/905–2999 or 888/905–9995* 🖷 *604/905–2995* ⊕ *www. panpacific.com* ⬦ *82 rooms* ♨ *Room service, in-roof safes, kitchens, cable TV with movies and video games, in-room broadband, Wi-Fi, indoor pool, gym, hot tub, sauna, lounge, ski storage, dry clearning, laundry service, business services, meeting rooms, parking (fee); no smoking* ☰ *AE, DC, MC, V* ⦿ *BP.*

$$$$ 🏨 **Summit Lodge & Spa.** Service is gracious and attentive at this friendly boutique hotel, which is also one of Whistler's best values within the luxury range of hotels. Tucked in a quiet part of the village, the spacious rooms here are beautifully decorated with soft neutrals, custommade cherrywood furnishings, original art, granite countertops, and such details as aromatherapy toiletries. All units have balconies and fireplaces. A shuttle whisks guests to the nearby slopes. The lodge's full-service spa is among Whistler's most exotic with its Javanese theme and royal heritage treatments. It claims to be North America's only authentic Indonesian-style spa. ⊠ *4359 Main St., V0N 1B4* ☎ *604/932–2778 or 888/913–8811* 🖷 *604/932–2716* ⊕ *www.summitlodge.com* ⬦ *75 rooms, 6 suites* ♨ *Kitchenettes, cable TV, in-room VCRs, in-room data ports, pool, exercise equipment, outdoor hot tub, sauna, spa, ski storage, dry cleaning, laundry facilities, laundry service, concierge, business services, meeting rooms, parking (fee), some pets allowed (fee), no-smoking floors* ☰ *MC, V* ⦿ *CP.*

★ **$$$$** 🏨 **Westin Resort & Spa.** This luxury hotel has a prime location on the edge of the village. Stone, slate, pine, and cedar are used throughout the two-story lobby. The rooms are chic and cozy, with moss-green and rust color schemes, gas fireplaces, extra-deep tubs, and exceptionally comfortable beds. The 1,400-square-foot, split-level suites are great for families: each has a full kitchen and a loft bedroom with a whirlpool tub. The hotel's large restaurant has an open kitchen and fantastic over-size windows. The spa, with 25 treatment rooms and a mountain-view lounge, has facials, body wraps, and holistic therapies such as herbol-ogy and acupuncture. ⊠ *4090 Whistler Way, V0N 1B4* ☎ *604/905–5000 or 888/634–5577* ☒ *604/905–5589* ⊕ *www.westinwhistler.net* ⤳ *204 rooms, 215 suites* ⌕ *Restaurant, room service, in-room safes, some kitchens, cable TV with movies and video games, in-room broad-band, Wi-Fi, golf privileges, indoor-outdoor pool, health club, hot tubs, massage, sauna, spa, steam room, ski shop, ski storage, bar, shops, babysitting, children's programs (ages 18 months–12 yrs), dry cleaning, laundry facilities, laundry service, concierge, business services, meeting rooms, parking (fee); no smoking* ⊟ *AE, D, DC, MC, V.*

$$$–$$$$ 🖭 **Delta Whistler Village Suites.** Gold-color walls, light-pine furniture, Navajo-pattern sofas, and desert-theme art create a warm Southwest look at this family-friendly hotel near the Whistler Conference Centre. The apartment-size studio and one- and two-bedroom suites have fully equipped kitchens, fireplaces, balconies—even an en-suite washer and dryer. The cozy studio suites have kitchenettes. The spa offers a full range of services and exotic body massages. ⊠ *4308 Main St., V0N 1B4* ☎ *604/905–3987 or 888/299–3987, 604/966–0888 spa* ☒ *604/938–6335* ⊕ *www.deltahotels.com/whistler* ⤳ *225 suites* ⌕ *2 restaurants, room service, in-room hot tubs, some kitchens, some kitchenettes, cable TV with movies and video games, in-room data ports, indoor-outdoor pool, gym, outdoor hot tubs, massage, sauna, steam room, bicycles, ski shop, ski storage, bar, nightclub, shops, babysitting, children's pro-grams (ages 4–12), dry cleaning, laundry facilities, laundry service, con-cierge, business services, meeting rooms, parking (fee), some pets allowed (fee), no-smoking floors* ⊟ *AE, DC, MC, V.*

★ $$–$$$$ 🖭 **Durlacher Hof.** Custom woodwork, exposed ceiling beams, a *kache-lofen* (farmhouse fireplace-oven), and antler chandeliers hung over fir benches and tables exemplify the rustic Tyrolean theme of this inn, a few minutes' walk from the village. The bedrooms are adorned in Ralph Lauren and have custom-crafted furniture; most have balconies. Two top-floor rooms are very spacious and have such amenities as whirlpool tubs; smaller rooms have showers rather than tubs. Rates include a hearty European breakfast and afternoon tea; dinner is served occasionally. Suit-able for longer stays, a self-contained deluxe suite on the ground floor commands a price of up to C$499. ⊠ *7055 Nesters Rd., V0N 1B7* ☎ *604/932–1924 or 877/932–1924* ☒ *604/938–1980* ⊕ *www.durlacherhof. com* ⤳ *8 rooms* ⌕ *Fans, outdoor hot tub, massage, sauna, ski storage, piano, free parking; no a/c, no room phones, no room TVs, no smok-ing* ⊟ *MC, V* ⑩ *BP.*

$$$ 🖭 **Edgewater Lodge.** This cedar lodge lies along glacier-fed Green Lake on 45 acres of private forested land, about 3 km (2 mi) north of the vil-lage. The rooms and suites are big, with a woodsy sage-green color scheme, private entrances, and window seats set before expansive water and moun-tain views. The restaurant is a romantic retreat that serves Pacific cui-sine including seafood, pasta, steak, and venison. Whistler Outdoor

Experience runs an activity center here, providing guests and nonguests fishing, hiking, canoeing, kayaking, and trail rides in summer and snowshoeing, sleigh rides, and cross-country skiing in winter. ⊠ *8841 Hwy. 99, Box 369, V0N 1B0* ☎ *604/932–0688 or 888/870–9065* 🖷 *604/932– 0686* ⊕ *www.edgewater-lodge.com* ⌁ *6 rooms, 6 suites* ⏦ *Restaurant, fans, cable TV, Wi-Fi in some rooms, outdoor hot tub, boating, fishing, hiking, cross-country skiing, sleigh rides, bar, meeting room, free parking, some pets allowed (fee); no a/c, no smoking* ⊟ *AE, MC, V* ⍯ *CP.*

¢ 🖾 **Hostelling International Whistler.** One of the nicest hostels in Canada is also the area's cheapest sleep. Beds in men's or women's four-bunk dorms, a shared kitchen, and a game room make up the basic accommodations. It's 7 km (4 mi) by road, or 4 km (2½ mi) by footpath, from the village. About five buses a day serve the hostel from Whistler Village. ⊠ *5678 Alta Lake Rd., V0N 1B5* ☎ *604/932–5492* 🖷 *604/932– 4687* ⊕ *www.hihostels.ca* ⌁ *28 beds in 7 dorms, 1 4-bed private room (no bath)* ⏦ *Kitchen, kitchenettes, lake, sauna, dock, boating, bicycles, ski storage, piano, Internet room, free parking; no room phones, no room TVs, no smoking* ⊟ *MC, V.*

Nightlife & the Arts

For a small mountain village, Whistler has a surprisingly good choice of nightlife, most of it in the pedestrian-oriented village and within walking distance of the hotels and ski slopes. Most of the pubs, clubs, and bars are open year-round. Dance clubs are open until 2 AM Monday–Saturday and until 1 AM on Sunday (be prepared to line up on weekends); pubs close around 1 AM, midnight on Sunday. Most nightspots serve food, which is often good value compared with that of Whistler's pricey restaurants, and many of them either ban smoking or have large no-smoking areas. You have to be at least 19 to enter bars or nightclubs, though many pubs have restaurant sections open to all. For entertainment listings, pick up Whistler's weekly news magazine, the *Pique.*

BARS & PUBS **Black's Pub.** Here you'll find Whistler's largest selection of whiskeys (more than 40 varieties) and 99 beers from around the world. The adjoining restaurant is reasonably priced, offering mainly pizzas and pastas. ⊠ *4270 Mountain Sq.* ☎ *604/932–6945.*

BrewHouse. This place brews six of its own ales and lagers in a big woodsy building with fireplaces, pool tables, seven 27-inch TVs, and a patio. Brewery tours are offered Thursday and Saturday afternoons; the attached restaurant (open to minors) is a good place for casual meals. ⊠ *4355 Blackcomb Way* ☎ *604/905–2739.*

Citta'. The village-center patio is consistently touted as the best outdoor patio–it's *the* hot spot for people-watching and microbrew sipping. The place attracts a ton of late-night partiers. ⊠ *Whistler Village Sq.* ☎ *604/ 932–4177.*

Dubh Linn Gate Pub. As its name implies, this place has an Irish theme with original decor that was actually transported all the way from the old country. The staff pours a decent pint of Guinness and serves good Irish food. Those under 19 are welcome in the restaurant section. ⊠ *Pan Pacific Hotel, 4320 Sundial Crescent* ☎ *604/905–4047.*

DANCE CLUBS   **Buffalo Bill's Bar & Grill.** The DJs here play mainstream music for an over-25 crowd, and well-known bands jam once or twice a month. ✉ *1–4122 Village Green* ☏ *604/932–6613.*

Down Under. With its house, hip-hop, and theme nights, and occasional live bands, Down Under is geared to the young and hip. ✉ *Whistler Village Sq.* ☏ *604/932–1904.*

Garfinkle's. One of Whistler's largest clubs hosts live rock and roll, hip-hop, funk, and jazz. It's a hangout for the young and a high point (literally) on any Whistler trip. ✉ *1–4308 Main St.* ☏ *604/932–2323.*

Moe Joes. Its hot, central location makes this a perennial favorite. Theme nights appeal to a diverse crowd from Reggae Monday to Country Thursday. ✉ *4115 Golfers Approach* ☏ *604/935–1152.*

Tommy Africa's. Here international guest DJs play alternative and progressive dance music. The trademark shooters (rapidly consumed shot glasses of undiluted alcoholic concoctions) make for a lively crowd. ✉ *4216 Gateway Dr.* ☏ *604/932–6090.*

FILM & THEATER   **Maurice Young Millennium Place.** You can catch theatrical, dance, live music, and other performances here. The facility also has arts, child care, and teen centers, as well as drop-in bridge, yoga, and dance classes. Ecumenical church services are held here Sunday morning. ✉ *4335 Blackcomb Way* ☏ *604/935–8410.*

Rainbow Theatre. In the Whistler Conference Centre, this theater shows first-run movies twice nightly for C$5 per person (C$3 Tuesday). ✉ *4010 Whistler Way* ☏ *604/932–2422.*

Sports & the Outdoors

Adjacent to the Whistler area is the 78,000-acre **Garibaldi Provincial Park** (✉ Off Hwy. 99 ☏ 604/898–3678), with dense mountainous forests splashed with hospitable lakes and streams.

The best first stop for any Whistler outdoor activity is the **Whistler Activity and Information Center** (✉ 4010 Whistler Way ☏ 604/932–2394 or 604/938–2769) in the conference center at the edge of the village, where you can book activities; pick up hiking, biking, and cross-country skiing trail maps; and find out about equipment rentals.

BIKING & HIKING   The 28-km (45-mi) paved, car-free Valley Trail links the village to lakeside beaches and scenic picnic spots. For more challenging routes, ski lifts whisk hikers and bikers up to the alpine, where marked trails are graded by difficulty. The Peak Chair operates in summer to take hikers to the top of 7,160-foot-high Whistler.

You can rent bikes, arrange for repairs, or book a bike tour at **Fanatyk Co. Ski and Cycle** (✉ 6–4433 Sundial Pl. ☏ 604/938–9452). Bike rentals are available in summer at the **Whistler Gondola Base** (✉ 3434 Blackcomb Way ☏ 604/905–2252). **Whistler Outdoor Experience** (✉ Edgewater Outdoor Centre, 8841 Hwy. 99 ☏ 604/932–3389 or 877/386–1888 ⊕ www.whistleroutdoor.com) leads guided hikes and mountain-bike tours.

CANOPY TOURS &   **Ziptrek Ecotours** (✉ 4282 Mountain Sq. ☏ 604/935–0001 or 866/935–
ZIPLINE TOURS   0001 ⊕ www.ziptrek.com) offers two of the newest year-round adventures around Whistler: zip trekking and canopy tours. There are 2½-

hour adventures along five progressively higher and longer ziplines (one measures 1,100 feet) between Whistler and Blackcomb Mountains, as well as a canopy walk through old-growth treetops via a spectacular network of suspension bridges, boardwalks, and trails. **Skyline at Cougar Mountain** (☎ 604/932–4086 ⊕ www.cougarmountain.ca) is set to open six ziplines in 2005.

BOATING   Canoe and kayak rentals are available at Alta Lake at both Lakeside Park and Wayside Park. A spot that's perfect for canoeing is the River of Golden Dreams, which connects Alta Lake with Green Lake.

The **Canadian Outback Adventure Company** (☎ 604/921–7250 or 800/565–8735 ⊕ www.canadianoutback.com) leads river-rafting trips in the area, including an easygoing trip for families. For guided canoeing and kayaking trips as well as sailing and fishing, call **Whistler Outdoor Experience** (✉ 8841 Hwy. 99 ☎ 604/932–3389 or 877/386–1888 ⊕ www.whistleroutdoor.com) at the Edgewater Outdoor Centre on Green Lake. **Whistler River Adventures** (☎ 604/932–3532 or 888/932–3532 ⊕ www.whistlerriver.com) has both river-rafting and jet-boating trips on rivers near Whistler.

CROSS-COUNTRY SKIING   The meandering trail around the Whistler Golf Course from the village is an ideal beginners' route. The 28 km (17 mi) of track-set trails that wind around scenic Lost Lake, Chateau Whistler Golf Course, the Nicklaus North Golf Course, and Green Lake include routes suitable for all levels; 4 km (2½ mi) of trails around Lost Lake are lighted for night skiing from 4 to 10 each evening. **Whistler Outdoor Experience** (✉ Edgewater Outdoor Centre, 8841 Hwy. 99 ☎ 604/932–3389 or 877/386–1888) organizes cross-country ski treks.

DOWNHILL SKIING & SNOWBOARDING   **Blackcomb and Whistler mountains** (☎ 604/932–3434 or 800/766–0449 ⊕ www.whistlerblackcomb.com) receive an average of 360 inches of snow a year. The regular season is the longest in Canada, with lifts operating from late November to early June. If that's not enough, Blackcomb's Horstman Glacier is open June to early August for summer glacier skiing. The mountains' statistics are impressive: the resort covers 7,071 acres of skiable terrain in 12 alpine bowls and on three glaciers; it has more than 200 marked trails and is served by the continent's most advanced high-speed lift system. Blackcomb has a 5,280-foot vertical drop, North America's longest, and a top elevation of 7,494 feet. Whistler's drop comes in second at 5,020 feet, and its top elevation is 7,160 feet.

For a primer on the ski facilities, drop by the resort's free Whistler Welcome Night, held at 6:30 every Sunday evening during ski season at the base of the village gondolas. First-timers at Whistler, whether beginners or experienced skiers or snowboarders, may want to try Ski or Ride Esprit. Run by the resort, these three- to four-day programs combine ski or snowboarding lessons, après-ski activities, and an insider's guide to the mountains.

The **Mountain Adventure Centre** (✉ Pan Pacific Lodge, 4320 Sundial Crescent ☎ 604/905–2295) rents high-performance gear and lets you swap equipment during the day. It also has two alpine locations, one in the Fairmont Chateau Whistler and another at Blackcomb Day Lodge. **Whistler/Blackcomb Ski and Snowboard School** (⌧ 4545 Blackcomb Way ☎ 604/932–3434 or 800/766–0449) has lessons for skiers of all levels. Equipment rentals are available at the **Whistler/Blackcomb Hi Performance Rentals** (⌧ 3434 Blackcomb Way ☎ 604/905–2252), at the Whistler gondola base, and at several outlets in the village.

FISHING All five of the lakes around Whistler are stocked with trout. The guides at **Cougar Mountain Adventures** (⌧ 36–4314 Main St. ☎ 604/932–3474) can take you fly-fishing or spinning in the lakes and rivers around Whistler. Gear is supplied. **Whistler River Adventures** (⌧ Whistler Village Gondola Bldg., 4165 Springs La. ☎ 604/932–3532 or 888/932–3532 ⊕ www.whistlerriver.com) conducts guided trips on rivers in the area. The staff takes care of everything: equipment, guides, transportation.

GOLF Golf season runs from May through October; greens fees range from C$159 to C$210. The **Big Sky Golf and Country Club** (☎ 604/894–6106 or 800/668–7900 ⊕ www.bigskygolf.com) is an 18-hole, par-72 course, in Pemberton, 30 minutes north of Whistler. **Chateau Whistler Golf Club** (⌧ 4612 Blackcomb Way ☎ 604/938–2092 or 877/938–2092) has an excellent 18-hole, par-72 course designed by Robert Trent Jones Jr. The **Nicklaus North Golf Course** (⌧ 8080 Nicklaus North Blvd. ☎ 604/938–9898 or 800/386–9898) is a challenging 18-hole, par-71 course designed by Jack Nicklaus. Arnold Palmer designed the 18-hole, par-72 championship course at the **Whistler Golf Club** (⌧ 4010 Whistler Way ☎ 604/932–4544 or 800/376–1777).

HELI-SKIING **Whistler Heli-Skiing** (⌧ 3-4241 Village Stroll ☎ 604/932–4105 or 888/435–4754 ⊕ www.whistlerheliskiing.com) has helicopter-accessed guided day trips with three or more glacier runs for intermediate to expert skiers. The cost starts at C$640 per person.

HORSEBACK RIDING **Whistler Outdoor Experience** (⌧ Edgewater Outdoor Centre, 8841 Hwy. 99 ☎ 604/932–3389 or 877/386–1888 ⊕ www.whistleroutdoor.com) on Green Lake runs trail rides (starting a C$45 for a one-hour ride) for kids and adults.

SNOWMOBILING, SNOWSHOEING & SLEIGH OR SLED RIDES **Blackcomb Snowmobiles** (☎604/932–8484 ⊕www.blackcombsnowmobile. com) runs guided snowmobile trips into the backcountry (from C$119 for two hours). The company has outlets at the Fairmont Chateau Whistler and the Hilton Whistler Resort. **Cougar Mountain Wilderness Adventures** (⌧ 36–4314 Main St. ☎ 604/932–4086 or 888/297–2222 ⊕ www.cougarmountain.ca) has dogsled trips (from C$140 for 2½ hours) as well as snowmobiling and snowshoeing tours. In summer, dog sleds are equipped with wheels are run like chariots. **Outdoor Adventures@Whistler** (⌧ Timberline Lodge, 4205 Village Sq. ☎ 604/932–0647 ⊕ www.adventureswhistler.com) can take you for walks in the deep powder on snowshoes (from C$69 for 1½ hours). The company also runs ATV excursions in summer (C$109 for two hours). **Whistler Outdoor Experience** (⌧ Edgewater Outdoor Centre, 8841 Hwy. 99 ☎ 604/932–3389 or 877/386–1888 ⊕ www.whistleroutdoor.com) runs romantic horse-drawn sleigh rides (from C$49), including sleigh rides with dinner at a lakefront restaurant, as well as snowshoeing trips.

SPORTS COMPLEX **Meadow Park Sports Centre** (⊠ 8107 Camino Dr. ☎ 604/935–7529), about 6 km (4 mi) north of Whistler Village, has a six-lane indoor pool, children's wading pool, ice-skating rink, hot tub, sauna, steam room, gym, aerobics studio, and two squash courts. Day passes are C$9; family passes are C$18.

Shopping

Whistler has almost 200 stores, including chain and designer outlets, art galleries, gift shops, and, of course, outdoor-clothing and ski shops. Most are clustered in the pedestrian-only Whistler Village Centre; more can be found a short stroll away in Village North, Upper Village, and in the shopping concourses of the major hotels. Many goods reflect the tastes (and budgets) of the international moneyed set that vacations here, though savvy shoppers can get good deals on ski gear in spring and on summer clothing in fall.

Almost anything you buy in British Columbia is subject to a Canada-wide 7% Goods and Services Tax (GST) and a 7% Provincial Sales Tax (PST), and these are added at the register. If you aren't a Canadian resident, you can reclaim the GST on goods you take out of the country. **Global GST Refund Services** (⊠ 4299 B Mountain Sq. ☎ 604/905–4977) can give you an immediate refund.

ART GALLERIES **Adele-campbell Fine Art Gallery** has paintings and sculptures by both established and up-and-coming B.C. artists (many with wildlife and wilderness themes), including several affordable pieces. ⊠ *Hilton Whistler Resort, 4050 Whistler Way* ☎ *604/938–0887.* **Black Tusk Gallery** displays Northwest Coast native art, including limited-edition silk-screen prints, and traditional crafts such as masks, paddles, bowls, jewelry, and totem poles. ⊠ *108–4293 Mountain Sq., Hilton Whistler Resort* ☎ *604/905–5540.* **Plaza Galleries** showcases the painting efforts of Hollywood stars Tony Curtis, Anthony Quinn, and Red Skelton, as well as works by British Columbian visual artists such as Robert Bateman. ⊠ *Whistler Town Plaza, 22–4314 Main St.* ☎ *604/938–6233.* **Whistler Art Galleries** has sculpture, painting, and glassworks by Canadian artists at two outlets: the Hilton Whistler Resort and the Westin Resort & Spa. ⊠ *Hilton Whistler Resort, 4050 Whistler Way* ☎ *604/938–3001* ⊠ *Westin Resort & Spa, 4090 Whistler Way* ☎ *604/935–3999.*

CLOTHING **Amos and Andes** sells handmade sweaters and dresses in offbeat designs. ⊠ *2–4321 Village Gate Blvd.* ☎ *604/932–7202.* **Helly Hansen** sells its own brand of Norwegian-made skiing, boarding, and other outdoor wear. ⊠ *Westin Resort & Spa, 115–4090 Whistler Way* ☎ *604/932–0142.* **Horstman Trading Co.** specializes in ski togs and accessories, including a good selection of Bogner, Tsunami, and other high-fashion gear. ⊠ *The Four Seasons Resort, 4545 Blackcomb Way* ☎ *604/938–7746* ⊠ *Westin Resort & Spa, 4090 Whistler Way* ☎ *604/905–2203.* **Open Country** stocks casual designs for men and women by La Cost, Jack Lipson, Kenneth Cole, Michael Kors, Tommy Hilfiger, and others. ⊠ *Fairmont Chateau Whistler Resort, 4599 Chateau Blvd.* ☎ *604/938–9268.* **Roots,** the Canadian-owned enterprise known for its sweatshirts and cozy casuals, is something of a fixture in Whistler, especially now that it outfits both the Canadian and American Olympic teams. ⊠ *4229 Village Stroll* ☎ *604/938–0058.*

Can-Ski, operated by Whistler-Blackcomb Resort, has four locations with a good selection of brand-name ski gear, clothes, and accessories. The staff also offers custom boot fitting and repairs. ⊠ *Crystal Lodge, Whistler Village* ☎ *604/938–7755* ⊠ *Deer Lodge, Town Plaza* ☎ *604/ 938–7432* ⊠ *Glacier Lodge, Upper Village* ☎ *604/938–7744* ⊠ *Creekside (winters only)* ☎ *604/905–2160.* **Fanatyk Co. Ski and Cycle** sells skis, boots, and custom boots in winter. In summer the shop specializes in top-of-the-line mountain bikes as well as bike rentals, repairs, and tours. ⊠ *6–4433 Sundial Pl.* ☎ *604/938–9455, 604/938–9452 rentals.* **Showcase Snowboards** supplies gear to the growing number of snowboarders at Whistler. ⊠ *Sundial Hotel, 4340 Sundial Crescent* ☎ *604/938–7519.* **Snowcovers Sports** carries brand-name ski equipment and outerwear in winter; in summer it carries high-end bikes and cycling gear. ⊠ *126–4340 Lorimer Rd.* ☎ *604/905–4100.*

In addition to the many terrific hotel spas that have arrived on the Whistler scene in the past few years, **Solarice Wellness Centre & Spa** is worth a visit for its drop-in yoga, Pilates, tai chi, and meditation classes. The center also offers a mix of Eastern and Western spa treatments as well as Chinese Medicine (acupuncture, Tui Na massage, and others), and Naturopathic therapies. ⊠ *202–4230 Gateway Dr.* ☎ *604/935–1222* ⊕ *www. solarice.com.*

Lillooet

⑫ *131 km (81 mi) northeast of Whistler.*

Beyond Whistler, Highway 99 is much less traveled as it passes lakes and glaciers, past the town of Pemberton, through the Mount Currie First Nations reserve, and over the mountains to Lillooet.

The arid gullies and Wild West landscape around Lillooet may come as a surprise after the greenery of the coast and mountains. During the 1850s and 1860s this was Mile Zero of the Cariboo Wagon Road, which took prospectors to the gold fields. There are several motels in Lillooet and a number of historic sites.

Hope

⑬ *153 km (95 mi) south of Lillooet, 150 km (93 mi) east of Vancouver.*

Hope is the only sizable town on Highway 1 between Vancouver and the province's interior; it's also the point where the scenery changes suddenly from the steep gorges of the Fraser Canyon to the wide, flat farmland of the Fraser Valley. If you're traveling into the interior from Vancouver you have a choice of three routes here: Highway 1 through the Fraser Canyon, the Coquihalla (Highway 5), and Highway 3. Highway 1, the Trans-Canada Highway, follows the Fraser River as it cuts through the Coast Mountains to the High Country; the deepest, most dramatic cut is the 38-km (24-mi) gorge between Yale and Boston Bar, north of Hope, where the road clings to the hillside high above the water.

Highway 5 is a fast, high-altitude toll road with awesome mountain scenery, and Highway 3 is a quiet back road that winds through Manning Park. Note, however, that it can get congested with slow-moving RVs with few places to pass.

You can find plenty of facilities for overnight stays in Hope, nicknamed the Chainsaw Carving Capital for its 30 giant wooden sculptures scattered around downtown. The Fraser and Thompson rivers north of town are popular rafting centers; several operators are based in Lytton and Yale.

At the **Coquihalla Canyon Provincial Park** 6 km (4 mi) northeast of Hope off Highway 5, you can walk through the abandoned Othello-Quintette tunnels of the old Kettle Valley Railway. Still regarded as one of the world's greatest engineering feats, they provide spectacular views of the Coquihalla Canyon. The tunnels are open dawn to dusk April through mid-October, weather permitting. The **Hope Visitor Info Centre** (☎ 604/869–2021) has information.

At **Hell's Gate,** about 55 km (33 mi) north of Hope on Highway 1, an aerial gondola (cable car) carries you across the foaming canyon waters. The thrilling descent provides a good view of the fishways, where millions of sockeye salmon fight their way upriver to spawning grounds. At the far side of the river, you can find displays on the life cycle of the salmon, a fudge factory, ice-cream parlor, general store, and restaurant. ⊠ *Hwy. 1, 10 km (6 mi) south of Boston Bar* ☎ *604/867–9277* ⊕ *www. hellsgateairtram.com* 🚠 *Cable car C$11* ⊙ *Mid-Apr.–mid-May and Sept., daily 10–4; mid-May–Aug., daily 9:30–5:30.*

en route Following Highway 3 east to Princeton and Penticton, you pass through **Manning Provincial Park,** which has campgrounds, hiking trails, swimming, boating, and trail rides, in addition to downhill and cross-country skiing in winter.

Where to Stay

C ¢–$$$ 🏨 **Manning Park Resort.** A year-round family holiday spot since the 1970s, this lodge still makes a handy stopover on the long drive to the interior. Though updated with modern amenities, the resort retains its old-fashioned camp feel, from the bear-shape house posts to the snowshoes dangling from the restaurant ceiling. The food is surprisingly good and the restaurant makes for a good break if you're traveling Highway 3. There's biking, hiking, snowshoeing, snowboarding, and downhill and cross-country skiing. Accommodations are a mix of lodge rooms kitchen-equipped cabins for up to 10 people; rustic, low-price chalets that can sleep up to 16; and campsites. ⊠ *64 km (38 mi) east of Hope on Hwy. 3* 🏠 *Box 1480, Hope V0X 1L0* ☎ *250/840–8822 or 800/330–3321* 🖶 *604/840–8848* ⊕ *www.manningparkresort.com* 🛏 *41 rooms, 35 cabins* ⑁ *Restaurant, café, some kitchens, microwaves, refrigerators, cable TV with movies, in-room data ports, 2 tennis courts, gym, hot tub, sauna, steam room, boating, mountain bikes, basketball, billiards, boccie, croquet, horseshoes, Ping-Pong, volleyball, ski shop, lounge, pub, piano, recreation room, shop, playground, laundry facilities, business services, meeting rooms, some pets allowed (fee)* 🚬 *AE, MC, V.*

Harrison Hot Springs

⑭ *128 km (79 mi) northeast of Vancouver.*

The small resort community of Harrison Hot Springs lies at the southern tip of picturesque Harrison Lake, off Highway 7 in the Fraser Valley. Mountains surround the 64-km-long (40-mi-long) lake, which is ringed by pretty beaches. Besides the hot springs, boating, windsurfing, and swimming are popular here. In summer the region hosts a number of agricultural fairs and festivals, including the World Championship Sand Sculpture Competition.

A striking 200-foot-high waterfall is the main attraction at **Bridal Veil Falls Provincial Park** (⌧ Off Hwy. 1, about 15 km [9 mi] southeast of Harrison Hot Springs ☎ 604/582–5200 ⊕ www.bcparks.ca), open dawn to dusk. A short path through the forest leads to a viewing platform and the surrounding area is popular with campers.

The **Harrison Public Pool,** across from the beach in Harrison Hot Springs Resort & Spa, is an indoor hot-springs-fed pool. ⌧ *224 Esplanade* ☎ *604/796–2244* ⌧ *C$8.50* ☺ *Daily 9–9.*

☺ **Kilby Historic Store and Farm,** a 20-minute drive west of Harrison Hot Springs, re-creates a rural B.C. store and farm of the 1920s with farm animals, some original buildings, some replicas, and 1920s-style home cooking in the Harrison River Restaurant. ⌧ *215 Kilby Rd., off Hwy. 7, Harrison Mills* ☎ *604/796–9576* ⊕ *www.kilby.ca* ⌧ *C$7* ☺ *May–Oct., daily 11–5; call for off-season hrs.*

Minter Gardens, 8 km (5 mi) southwest of Harrison Hot Springs, is a 32-acre site with 11 beautifully presented theme gardens including rose, lake, and stream, as well as a fragrance garden for the blind and an English-style evergreen maze. There's also a good restaurant and casual café on-site. ⌧ *Exit 135 off Hwy. 1, 52892 Bunker Rd., Rosedale* ☎ *604/794–7191 or 888/646–8377* ⊕ *www.mintergardens.com* ⌧ *C$12* ☺ *Apr. and Oct., daily 10–5; May and Sept., daily 9–5:30; June, daily 9–6; July and Aug., daily 9–7.*

Where to Stay & Eat

★ **$$$–$$$$** ✕⌧ **Rowena's Inn on the River.** Built on a 160-acre parcel of land deeded by Queen Victoria, this English-style manor is an ancestral family home, refurbished as an elegant, upscale inn. Sepia-tone photos and family heirlooms add to the inn's historic charm. All rooms are comfortable with overstuffed beds, soft pillows, and antique furnishings. The forest cabins provide ultimate privacy with cozy fireplaces and spa-style bathrooms. Rates include English breakfast. Dinners ($$$) highlight regional fare such as savory chicken in an apple-based gravy and prime rib with a blue-cheese sauce. The **Sandpiper Golf Club** (☎ 877/796–1001) is next door. ⌧ *14282 Moris Valley Rd., Harrison Mills V0M 1L0* ☎ *604/796–0234 or 800/661–5108* 🖷 *604/796–0280* ⊕ *www.rowenasinn.com* 🛏 *5 rooms, 4 cottages* ⚿ *Restaurant, golf course, outdoor pool, hot tub, boating, fishing, bicycle, hiking, lounge, piano, meeting room; no a/c in some units, no room phones, no room TVs, no smoking* ⍔ *BP* ⊟ *AE, MC, V.*

$$–$$$$ ✕⊡ **Harrison Hot Springs Resort & Spa.** A fixture on Harrison Lake since 1926, the hotel has a full-service spa, several hot-springs-fed pools, a children's water park, and a marina with water sports such as sturgeon-fishing charters, canoeing, kayaking, waterskiing, and lake cruises. Golfing is nearby. Most of the contemporary-looking rooms (many have been recently refurbished) have patios or balconies; those on the north side have views over the lake and nearby glacier-topped mountains. The Copper Room Restaurant ($$–$$$) serves beautifully prepared, locally sourced Continental cuisine and a dance band Tuesday through Saturday nights. ⊠ *100 Esplanade, V0M 1K0* ☎ *604/796–2244 or 800/663–2266* 📠 *604/796–3682* ⊕ *www.harrisonresort.com* ⤴ *323 rooms, 11 cottages* ⌂ *2 restaurants, café, room service, cable TV with movies, some in-room broadband, 2 tennis courts, 5 pools (2 indoor), wading pool, gym, 2 outdoor hot tubs, saunas, steam room, spa, hair salon, boating, bicycles, volleyball, bar, shops, playground, dry cleaning, laundry service, concierge, Internet room, convention center, some pets allowed (fee), no-smoking floor* ▭ *AE, D, DC, MC, V.*

Sports & the Outdoors

The **Hemlock Valley Resort** (⊠ Hemlock Valley Rd., off Hwy. 7, Agassiz ☎ 604/797–4411, 800/665–7080 snow report), 40 km (24 mi) northwest of Harrison Hot Springs, is a family-oriented ski resort with three chairlifts, 35 runs, and a vertical rise of 1,200 feet. You can also try cross-country skiing and snow tubing here.

> **en route** From Harrison Hot Springs two routes lead back to Vancouver. Highway 7 is a scenic back road along the north side of the Fraser River. Highway 1 is the faster, main highway. On Highway 1 you pass the turnoff to **Fort Langley National Historic Site of Canada,** a restored 1850s Hudson's Bay trading post, is about an hour west of Harrison Hot Springs. Costumed guides demonstrate woodworking, blacksmithing, and other fur-trade activities, and you can try your hand at gold panning. The nearby village of Fort Langley retains a 19th-century charm with plenty of galleries and bookstores to browse through. ⊠ *23433 Mavis Ave., Fort Langley* ☎ *604/513–4777* ⊕ *www.parkscanada.gc.ca/langley* 🎫 *C$6* ⊙ *Mar.–Oct., daily 10–5.*

HIGH COUNTRY & THE OKANAGAN VALLEY

South-central British Columbia (often simply called the "interior" by Vancouverites) encompasses the high arid plateau between the Coast Mountains on the west and the Monashees on the east. The Okanagan, five hours east of Vancouver by car or one hour by air, contains the interior's largest concentration of people. The region's sandy lake beaches and hot, dry climate have long made it a family-holiday magnet for Vancouverites and Albertans, and rooms and campsites can be hard to come by in summer.

The Okanagan Valley is the fruit-growing capital of Canada and a major wine-producing area. Many of the region's almost 60 wineries are in scenic spots, and they welcome visitors with tastings, tours, and restaurants.

The Wine Museum in Kelowna and the British Columbia Wine Information Centre in Penticton can help you create a winery tour and can provide details about annual wine festivals. In addition, 25 golf courses and several ski resorts draw sports people to the region year-round.

Throughout the Okanagan you can see depictions of a smiling green lizard that looks a bit like the Loch Ness Monster without the tartan cap. This is Ogopogo, a harmless, shy, and probably mythical creature said to live in Okanagan Lake.

Kamloops

⓯ *355 km (220 mi) northeast of Vancouver, 163 km (101 mi) northwest of Kelowna.*

Virtually all roads meet at Kamloops, High Country's sprawling transport hub. From here, highways fan out to Vancouver, the Okanagan, the Cariboo, and Jasper in the Rockies. Kamloops is also the closest town to such guest ranches as Douglas Lake (the largest working cattle ranch in Canada) and Sun Peaks, one of the province's leading ski resorts.

The **Kamloops Museum and Archives** has extensive and regularly changing displays about the area's human and natural history. ⊠ *207 Seymour St.* ☎ *250/828–3576* ⊕ *www.city.kamloops.bc.ca/parks/* ⊠ *By donation* ⊙ *Tues.–Sat. 9:30–4:30.*

Art lovers shouldn't overlook the **Kamloops Art Gallery,** which, although small, has an extensive permanent collection of contemporary and local art. ⊠ *465 Victoria St.* ☎ *250/828–3543* ⊕ *www.kag.bc.ca* ⊠ *C$5* ⊙ *Mon.–Wed. and Fri. 10–5, Thurs. 10–9, weekends noon–4.*

British Columbia has more species diversity than any other province in Canada, which the **Kamloops Wildlife Park** is trying to preserve. Although most are local and endangered animals such as antelope, grizzly bears, and bison, there are still one or two anomalies like the Siberian tiger, which make this refuge their home. In summer a miniature train runs around the property, and a playground and splash park invite youngsters. ⊠ *Hwy. 1, 15 km (9 mi) east of Kamloops* ☎ *250/573–3242* ⊕ *www.bczoo.org* ⊠ *C$9, lower rates in off-season* ⊙ *Sept.–June, daily 8–4:30; July and Aug., daily 8–8:30.*

The **Secwepemc Museum and Heritage Park,** a reconstructed village on a traditional gathering site, interprets the culture and lifestyle of the Secwepemc (Shuswap) people, who have lived in this area for thousands of years. Displays in the 12-acre parklike setting include a replica winter pit-house village, a summer lodge, and ethnobotanical gardens showcasing plants used by the Secwepemc. There's also a wildlife marsh, and the museum holds recorded oral history, photographs, and artifacts. Local First Nations artwork is sold at the gift shop. ⊠ *202–355 Yellowhead Hwy., Hwy. 5* ☎ *250/828–9801* ⊕ *www.secwepemc.org* ⊠ *June–Labor Day C$6, Labor Day–May C$5* ⊙ *June–Labor Day, daily 8:30–4:30; Labor Day–May, weekdays 8:30–4:30.*

Take a ride with the **Kamloops Heritage Railway,** and enjoy an 11 km (7 mi) round-trip through the surrounding countryside, over trestle bridges and past historical sights. Pulled by the restored steam locomotive 2141 "Spirit of Kamloops," you can ride in either open-air hayrack cars or a 1930s heritage coach. Trains run Friday through Monday in summer, with special theme excursions at Halloween and Christmas. Daylong trips are also offered. Call for schedules. ⊠ *510 Lorne St.* ☎ *250/374–2141* ⊕ *www.kamrail.com* ☜ *C$14* ⊙ *May–Sept., Fri.–Mon.*

As an offshoot to its highly successful ginseng operation, Sunmore Healthtech has recently opened **The Sunmore Ginseng Spa**—a surprising destination to find in cowboy country. The spa's spacious and elegant decor incorporates Feng Shui elements throughout and each treatment room is themed to a different culture. It offers a full range of traditional and ginseng-based therapies. The spa also houses a teahouse where tea is served with traditional Asian ceremony alongside first-class cuisine. Be sure to include a visit to the Ginseng information center and showroom. ⊠ *925 McGill Pl.* ☎ *250/372–2814 spa, 250/374–3027 showroom* ⊕ *www.sunmore.com.*

> off the
> beaten
> path

WELLS GRAY PROVINCIAL PARK – This vast and diverse wilderness area has great canoeing, fishing, and hiking. About 120 km (74 mi) north of Kamloops on Highway 5 is Clearwater, the major access point to Wells Gray. There's a visitor-information center at the junction of Highway 5 and the Clearwater Valley Road. ☎ *250/674–2646* ⊕ *www.bcparks.ca.*

Where to Stay & Eat

$$$–$$$$ ✕⊡ **Stump Lake Guest Ranch.** Abounding with lakes, grasslands, rolling hills, forests, creeks and rocky outcrops, Nicola Valley provides a scenic backdrop for this working cattle ranch. Inside its timber-frame main lodge, however, it feels more like a resort. Rooms, some adjoining, are bright and airy with hardwood floors and a traditional country-style decor. The cottages, which are funky conversions of a chicken coop and other historic outbuildings, are equally deluxe. Rates include all meals, two horseback rides daily, and full use of ranch facilities and activity equipment. Two-night minimum stays are required; three-night stays during holiday periods. ⌂ *Box 29, off Hwy. 5A, 30 km (18 mi) south of Kamloops, 20 km (12 mi), V2C 5K3* ☎ *250/372–1215 or 877/677–1215* ☐ *250/372–1256* ⊕ *www.stumplake.com* ⌫ *6 rooms, 4 cottages* ⌂ *Dining room, lake, spa, dock, boating, fishing, mountain bikes, billiards, hiking, horseback riding, horseshoes, lounge, recreation room; no a/c, fans, room TVs, in-room VCRs, no room phones, no smoking* ⊟ *MC, V* ⊙ *Closed Nov.–Apr.* ⊠| *AP.*

¢–$$ ✕⊡ **Quilchena Hotel & Resort.** Movie stars and outlaws have stayed at this 1908 inn on the grounds of a working cattle ranch, 75 km (45 mi) south of Kamloops. The hotel has a Victoriana-meets–Wild West ambience, with 19th-century antiques, original woodwork, an elegant parlor, and a saloon with a lovingly preserved bullet hole behind the bar. The Ladies' Parlour Room has a private sunporch, and Jack's Room (where Jack Nicholson stayed while filming in the area) has views of the lake across the road. Every room has a pedestal wash sink and some have a shared bath and shower down the hall. A two-bedroom ranch house is also available. The restaurant ($$$) is worth a trip for the local venison or the filet mignon. ⊠ *Hwy. 5A, Quilchena V0E 2R0, 20 km (12 mi) north of Merritt* ☎ *250/378–2611* 🖶 *250/378–6091* ⊕ *www. quilchena.com* 🛏 *16 rooms, 6 with bath* ⚐ *Restaurant, coffee shop, fans, 9-hole golf course, tennis court, lake, dock, billiards, boccie, hiking, horseback riding, horseshoes, pub, piano, shop, meeting rooms, airstrip; no a/c, fans, no room phones, no room TVs, no smoking* ▭ *AE, MC, V* ⊘ *Closed mid-Oct.–mid-Apr.*

$–$$$ ⊞ **Plaza Heritage Hotel.** Built in 1927 as the province's premier hotel, this six-story Spanish mission–style boutique hotel in the heart of Kamloops has been restored to its original look; rooms have a period feel with reproduction pine and wicker furniture and 1930s fixtures. The elevator is funky small and slow as molasses. ⊠ *405 Victoria St., V2C 2A9* ☎ *250/377–8075 or 877/977–5292* 🖶 *250/377–8076* ⊕ *www. plazaheritagehotel.com* 🛏 *66 rooms* ⚐ *Restaurant, room service, in-room data ports, some refrigerators, cable TV, hair salon, wine shop, Internet, business services, meeting rooms, no-smoking floors* ▭ *AE, DC, MC, V.*

$–$$ ⊞ **Helmcken Falls Lodge.** At the entrance to Wells Gray Park, this hand-hewn, intimate lodge was originally built in 1949. Now refurbished with contemporary comforts in an historical setting, accommodation is housed in three log buildings, including a refurbished 1922 Trapper's Cabin (available only in summer). Whatever the choice, all rooms are comfortably furnished and come with extra-long double beds, a balcony, or patio. The dining room has a rustic feel and serves hearty, North American fare. The lodge is an ideal base for exploring Wells Gray and indulging in myriad outdoor activities. Also available are 7 tent and 17 RV campsites. ⊠ *Box 239, off Hwy. 5, on Clearwater Valley Rd., 161 km (100 mi) north of Kamloops, Clearwater V0E 1N0* ☎ *250/674–3657* 🖶 *250/674–2971* ⊕ *www.helmckenfalls.com* 🛏 *21 rooms* ⚐ *Dining room, 9-hole golf course, boating, fishing, mountain bikes, hiking, horseback riding, cross-country skiing, lounge; no room phones, no room TVs, no smoking, no a/c* ▭ *MC, V* ⊘ *Closed Nov.*

Sports & the Outdoors

GOLF **Rivershore Golf Links** (⊠ 330 Rivershore Dr. ☎ 250/573–4622) is an 18-hole, par-72 course designed by Robert Trent Jones Sr. It's about 20 km (12 mi) east of Kamloops on Highway 1. Greens fees are C$55 on weekdays, C$60 on weekends. **Sun Peaks Resort** (⊠ 1280 Alpine Rd., Sun Peaks ☎ 250/578–5484 or 800/807–3257 ⊕ www.sunpeaksresort. com) has expanded its Graham Cooke–designed course to 18 holes that wind their way in and around McGilvray Creek and between thick pine and spruce forests. Watch for wildlife. Greens fees are C$52 weekdays and C$57 weekends.

SKIING With a 2,891-foot vertical drop, 3,408 skiable acres on three mountains, lots of sunshine, powder snow, and a 2,500-foot-long snowboard park, **Sun Peaks Resort** (⊠ 1280 Alpine Rd., Sun Peaks ☎ 250/578–5484 or 800/807–3257 ⊕ www.sunpeaksresort.com), 53 km (33 mi) north of Kamloops, is one of B.C.'s leading ski resorts. The compact Tyrolean-theme village has a number of ski-in, ski-out hotels; several restaurants; and an 18-hole golf course. Ski facilities include 114 downhill runs (the longest is 8 km [5 mi]), 5 chairlifts, and 20 km (12 mi) of groomed and tracked cross-country trails. A lift ticket is about C$56. This family-friendly resort also offers a ski school, day care, snowshoeing, dogsledding, snowmobiling, and sleigh rides. In summer visitors come for trail riding, canoeing, and lift-accessed hiking and mountain biking in wildflower-strewn meadows.

Salmon Arm

🔟 *108 km (67 mi) east of Kamloops, 106 km (66 mi) north of Kelowna.*

Salmon Arm is the commercial center of the Shuswap (named for Shuswap Lake), a greener and less-visited region than the Okanagan to the south. From Sicamous, 27 km (16 mi) northeast of Salmon Arm, you can take a two- to six-hour summer (May to October) trip on Shuswap Lake on the **Phoebe Anne** (✉ 117 Finlayson St., Sicamous ☎ 250/836–2220 ⊕ www.narrowsvillage.com), a 40-passenger paddle wheeler. Prices are C$15 for an introductory ride and C$50 for either a BBQ-lunch cruise or a dinner cruise. You can also rent kayaks and canoes here.

R. J. Haney Heritage Park and Museum. This 40-acre open-air museum re-creates an early-20th-century North Okanagan village. Most of the buildings, which include a log gas station, a fire hall, a school (where a Miss Hellpenny teaches visiting school classes in a 1914 style), and a manor house, are originals. A 3-km (2-mi) nature trail winds around the site. A tearoom on-site serves lunches, and a theater troupe performs outdoor dinner theater three times a week in July and August. Tickets are C$18. ✉ *751 Hwy. 97B, off Hwy. 1, 5 km (3 mi) south of Salmon Arm* ☎ *250/832–5243* ⊕ *www.salmonarmmuseum.org* 🈯 *Site by donation, house tours C$2* ⊗ *Mid-May–mid-June, Wed.–Sun. 10–5; mid-June–Aug., daily 10–5; Sept., weekdays 10–5.*

Roderick Haig-Brown Provincial Park (✉ Off Hwy. 1 at Squilax ☎ No phone ⊕ www.bcparks.ca) is where thousands of salmon come to spawn in the Adams River in late September and October. The best views are in the channel near the parking lot. The park is about 40 km (25 mi) northwest of Salmon Arm.

Located 2 km (1 mi) west of Sorrento, **Crannog Ales** (✉ 706 Elson Rd. ☎ 250/675–6847) is a certified organic, microbrewery that supplies its award-winning ales to some of the poshest restaurants in the province. The sampling room is a treat for those with hops in their heart. Call ahead for appointment.

Where to Stay & Eat

$–$$$ ✕🏨 **Quaaout Lodge Resort.** This modern three-story hotel, with its 40-foot-high lobby shaped like a traditional First Nations winter home, provides the chance to experience the culture of interior native peoples. Some of the large, well-appointed rooms have log furniture, gas fireplaces, and two-person whirlpool baths under windows overlooking the lake. The restaurant ($$–$$$) serves First Nations–influenced fare such as rainbow trout stuffed with blueberries or Bird in Clay, a house specialty. The grounds house a ceremonial sweat lodge and a reconstructed *kekuli,* or winter shelter where you can enjoy evenings of traditional storytelling, as well as a sandy beach and trails through hundreds of forested acres. Construction has started on a golf course, expected to open in late 2006. The hotel is 43 km (27 mi) northwest of Salmon Arm. ⊠ *Little Shuswap Rd. off Hwy. 1, Box 1215, Chase V0E 1M0* ☎ *250/679–3090 or 800/663–4303* 🖷 *250/679–3039* ⊕ *www.quaaout.com* 🗪 *72 rooms* ♿ *Restaurant, room service, some refrigerators, indoor pool, gym, hot tub, steam room, dock, boating, mountain bikes, bar, shop, babysitting, playground, laundry facilities, business services, meeting rooms, some pets allowed (fee), no-smoking floors* ▤ *AE, MC, V.*

Sports & the Outdoors

Sicamous on Shuswap Lake is a mecca for houseboat vacationers. **Waterway Houseboats** (⊠ Box 69, 113 Weddup St., Sicamous ☎ 250/836–2505 or 877/928–3792 ⊕ www.waterwayhouseboats.com) rents luxurious houseboats (C$3,500–C$6,500 a week), many with hot tubs, waterslides, and fireplaces. They sleep up to 24. Three- and four-day rentals are available; rates are lower in early spring and fall. **Twin Anchors** (⊠ 101 Martin St., Sicamous ☎ 250/836–2450 or 800/663–4026 ⊕ www.twinanchors.com) has a range of fully equipped houseboats that can accommodate 8 to 22 people and rent for C$3,000–C$8,000 per week in July and August; all have hot tubs.

Adams River Rafting (⊠ 3843 Squilax Anglemont Hwy., Scotch Creek ☎ 250/955–2447 or 888/440–7238 ⊕ www.adamsriverrafting.com) runs white-water rafting adventures May through mid July. Tickets are C$58.

en route Between Salmon Arm and Vernon lies Armstrong, an agricultural community whose claim to fame is its cheeses. The **Village Cheese Company** and factory (⊠ 3475 Smith Dr. ☎ 250/546–8659) is easy to find beneath the giant clock tower, and a fun place to stop for cheese, ice cream, or a soda. The village also has a small museum, as well as a turn-of-the-20th-century **The Olde Schoolhouse** where tea is served in summer. (☎ 250/546–9190).

Vernon

⑰ *117 km (73 mi) southeast of Kamloops.*

Vernon's star attractions include the all-season, gaslight-era-theme village resort atop Silver Star Mountain, and the lakes that border the city limits.

Although Lake Okanagan lies to the south, and Swan Lake to the north, it's the westerly **Kalamalka Lake Provincial Park** (⊠ Kidston Rd.) that steals the show. Pristine and protected, this "lake of 1,000 colors" is popular for its warm-water beaches, hiking trails, and some of the most scenic viewpoints in the region.

The 50-acre **Historic O'Keefe Ranch** provides a window on 19th-century cattle-ranch life. Among the many original and restored ranch buildings are the O'Keefe mansion, a church, and a general store. In August, Cowboy Theatre presents two outdoor shows nightly (C$22). There's also a restaurant and a gift shop on-site. ⊠ *9380 Hwy. 97, 12 km (8 mi) north of Vernon* ☎ *250/542–7868* ⊕ *www.okeeferanch.bc.ca* ⊠ *C$8* ⊘ *May–mid-Oct., daily 9–5; tours by appointment rest of yr.*

Sports & the Outdoors

GOLF **Predator Ridge Golf Resort** (⊠ 301 Village Centre Pl. ☎ 250/542–3436 or 888/578–6688 ⊕ www.predatorridge.com) is a 27-hole facility, with a par-36 on each 9. The course is the focal point to a full-service resort, comprising 51 luxurious golf cottages, 75 lodge suites, an Aveda spa, a fitness center, tennis court, hot tubs, and 4 swimming pools. Greens fees for 18 holes are C$145 with a cart, C$105 without a cart. It's about 15 km (9 mi) south of Vernon on Highway 97.

SKIING **Silver Star Mountain Resort** (⊠ Silver Star Rd., Silver Star Mountain ☎ 250/542–0224, 800/663–4431 reservations ⊕ www.skisilverstar. com), 22 km (13 mi) northeast of Vernon, has six chairlifts and two T-bars, a vertical drop of 2,500 feet, 108 runs on 2,725 skiable acres, and night skiing. A one-day lift ticket is C$64. The resort also has 70 km (44 mi) of groomed, track-set cross-country trails; two half pipes for boarders; snow tubing, snowmobile, or snowshoe tours; and sleigh rides, skating, and dogsledding. Day care and free ski tours are available at this friendly resort, and hiking and mountain-biking trails open in summer. The Victorian-style village has several ski-in, ski-out hotels and lodges, restaurants, an Aveda spa and shops, many of which are open all year.

Kelowna

⓲ *46 km (29 mi) south of Vernon, 68 km (42 mi) north of Penticton.*

The largest town in the Okanagan Valley, Kelowna (population nearing 100,000), on the edge of Okanagan Lake, makes a good base for exploring the region's beaches, ski hills, wineries, and golf courses. Although its edges are looking untidily urban these days, the town still has an attractive, walkable core and a restful beachside park. It's also at the heart of British Columbia's wine and fruit-growing district. The **Wine Museum**, set in an historic packing house, has wine-making exhibits and daily wine tastings as well as a wine shop and information about touring local wineries. ⊠ *1304 Ellis St.* ☎ *250/868–0441* ⊕ *www. kelownamuseum.ca* ⊠ *By donation* ⊘ *Mon.–Sat. 10–5, Sun. noon–5.*

The **British Columbia Orchard Industry Museum** (⊠ 1304 Ellis St. ☎ 250/763–0433), in the same building as the Wine Museum, has displays about the area's other critical industry.

The **Father Pandosy Mission**, the first European settlement in central British Columbia, was founded here by Oblate missionaries in 1859. The 4-acre site has three original mission buildings made of logs (including a tiny chapel) as well as a farmhouse and settler's cabin. The buildings, furnished to look as they did in the late 19th century, are open for viewing. ⊠ *3685 Benvoulin Rd.* ☎ *250/860–8369* ⊠ *C$2* ⊘ *Mid-Mar.–mid-Oct., daily 9–5; weather permitting the rest of yr.*

The **Kelowna Art Gallery** (✉ 1315 Water St. ☎ 250/762–2226) is an elegant public art gallery with a variety of local and international exhibits. ✉ *1315 Water St.* ☎ *250/762–2226* 🖅 *C$4* ⊙ *Tues.–Sat. 10–5, Thurs. 10–9, Sun. 1–4.*

For many Canadians the Okanagan means apples, and much of the valley is still covered with orchards. One of the largest and oldest (dating from 1904) is the **Kelowna Land & Orchard Company,** which you can tour on foot or in a tractor-drawn covered wagon. The farm animals are a hit with kids. There's an excellent lake-view restaurant on-site that serves lunch and dinner (check out the chef's retail line of dressings and sauces, *Okanagan's Finest*), as well as an award-winning cider that turns Fuji, Braeburn, and Granny Smith apples into great-tasting ciders. ✉ *3002 Dunster Rd., 8 km (5 mi) east of Kelowna* ☎ *250/763–1091, 250/712–9404 restaurant reservations* ⊕ *www.k-l-o.com* 🖅 *Site free, tours C$5.25* ⊙ *Apr.–Dec., daily 9–5; tours May–Oct., daily at 11, 1, and 3.*

Elysium Garden is a 3-acre perennial oasis carved out of a lovely old apple orchard. Family run, almost as a labor of love, these carefully tended gardens are worth the scenic drive up the mountain for the views within the garden walls, and beyond to the mountains and pastoral countryside. ✉ *2834 Belgo Rd.* ☎ *250/491–1368* ⊕ *www.elysiumgardennursery. com* 🖅 *C$7.50* ⊙ *Apr.–early Oct., daily 9–5.*

WINERIES   Almost all of the region's wineries offer tastings and tours throughout the summer and during the Okanagan Wine Festivals held in April and October; several have restaurants and most also have wine shops open year-round. The Wine Museum can help you create a winery tour and can provide details about annual wine festivals. Several local operators will act as guides and designated drivers. Note that many wineries charge a nominal fee (C$2–C$5) for tastings.

Cedar Creek Estate Winery (✉ 5445 Lakeshore Rd. ☎ 250/764–8866 or 800/730–9463 ⊕ www.cedarcreek.bc.ca), south of Kelowna, has a scenic lakeside location with picnic areas and a new patio. Free tours are given daily mid-May to mid-October; call for times. Cedar Creek has a sister winery, Greata Ranch Vineyards, 9 km south of Peachland.

Atop a hill overlooking Okanagan Lake, **Mission Hill Family Estate** was built to look, as the owner describes it, like "a combination of monastery, Tuscan hill village, and French winery," complete with a vaulted cellar blasted from volcanic rock and a 12-story bell tower. Tours—vineyard, cellar, or landscape and architecture—include a video presentation and tastings (prices vary). Dinner, snacks, and wine by the glass are served on the terrace, which overlooks the vineyard and lake, and an outdoor amphitheater hosts music and theater events on summer evenings. ✉ *1730 Mission Hill Rd., Westbank* ☎ *250/768–7611 or 800/957–9911* ⊕ *www.missionhillwinery.com* 🖅 *Tours C$5–C$30* ⊙ *May–mid-Oct., weekdays 10–5; weekends 10–6; call for tour times.*

Quails' Gate Estate Winery (✉ 3303 Boucherie Rd. ☎ 250/769–4451 or 800/420–9463 ⊕ www.quailsgate.com), on the edge of Okanagan Lake, gives tours (C$5) daily from May to mid-October. It has a wine shop in a 19th-century log home and a just renovated patio restaurant (open for lunch and dinner May to mid-October) with views of the vineyard and lake.

Summerhill Estate Winery (✉ 4870 Chute Lake Rd. ☎ 250/764–8000 or 800/667–3538 ⊕ www.summerhill.bc.ca), south of Kelowna on the east side of the lake, is an organic producer best known for its sparkling and ice wines. What tends to startle visitors, though, is the four-story-high replica of the Great Pyramid at Cheops; it's used to age and store the wine. You can visit the wine shop, a preserved settler's cabin, and a re-created First Nations earth house. An on-site restaurant with a veranda overlooking Okanagan Lake serves lunch daily year-round and dinner daily in summer. Tours and tasting are free and are run year-round; call for times.

Where to Stay & Eat

\$\$–\$\$\$\$ ✕ **Fresco Restaurant.** Seasonally inspired, locally sourced contemporary cuisine is the theme at this downtown Kelowna restaurant. Chef-owner Rodney Butters, one of B.C.'s better-known chefs, prepares creative seafood dishes, such as his signature Dungeness crab cappuccino, and Asian, Italian, and other touches for his frequently changing menus. The decor is simple, with an open kitchen and exposed brick and beams revealing the historic building's architectural roots. ✉ *1560 Water St.* ☎ *250/868–8805* ⊟ *AE, MC, V* ⊘ *Closed Sun. and Mon., Oct.–May. No lunch.*

\$\$–\$\$\$ ✕ **Bouchons Bistro.** Lots of windows and crisp white-linen tablecloths give this restaurant a bright, French café ambience and the chalkboard specials and extensive menu offer regional fare with a French twist. Signature dishes include a mouthwatering bouillabaisse containing everything from fresh scallops, shrimp, salmon, halibut, and mussels; cassoulet of duck; smoked lamb chop; and Toulouse sausage over white navy beans. Save room for the dessert-taster featuring mouthfuls of five sweet options. The bistro is justifiably proud of its 800-bottle temperature-controlled wine cellar and three certified sommeliers. ✉ *105–1180 Sunset Dr.* ☎ *250/763–6595* ⊟ *AE, MC, V* ⊘ *Closed mid-Feb.–mid-Mar. No lunch.*

¢–\$\$ ✕ **Guisachan House Restaurant.** Once the summer home of Lord Aberdeen, a former governor general of Canada, this 1891 house on 2½ garden acres is now an attractive restaurant. White cane chairs, pink tablecloths, period furniture, and seating on the glassed-in veranda re-create a Victorian summertime ambience. Chef Georg Rieder, originally from Germany, delivers a lengthy menu that includes several varieties of schnitzel, risottos, pastas, and seafood as well as bison, local venison, and Asian-influenced dishes such as Szechuan pork tenderloin. A four-course lunch for less than C\$9 is an especially good value. ✉ *1060 Cameron Ave.* ☎ *250/862–9368* ⊟ *AE, MC, V* ⊘ *No dinner.*

\$\$\$–\$\$\$\$ ✕▣ **Manteo Resort Waterfront Hotel & Villas.** This striking Tuscan-looking resort sits on a sandy swimming beach on the shores on Okanagan Lake. All the water sports are here, from windsurfing to parasailing to waterskiing. Accommodation choices include rooms and suites—all with balconies—in the main building and two- and three-bedroom villas with full kitchens. The villas are especially attractive, with gas fireplaces, terra-cotta tiles, high ceilings, and patios. The restaurant, the Wild Apple Grill (\$\$–\$\$\$), serves Pacific Northwest cuisine inside and on its big lakeside patio. ⊠ *3766 Lakeshore Rd., V1W 3L4* ☎ *250/860–1031 or 800/ 445–5255* 🖶 *250/860–1041* ⊕ *www.manteo.com* 🛏 *48 rooms, 30 suites, 24 villas* ⚐ *Restaurant, coffee shop, room service, in-room data ports, in-room hot tubs, some kitchens, some refrigerators, cable TV, some in-room VCRs, putting green, tennis court, 3 pools (1 indoor), wading pool, gym, outdoor hot tubs, massage, sauna, spa, steam room, dock, jet skiing, mountain bikes, billiards, movie theater, lounge, cinema, babysitting, children's programs (ages 3–12), playground, dry cleaning, laundry service, meeting rooms; no smoking* ▭ *AE, DC, MC, V.*

$$$$ 🏨 **Grand Okanagan Resort.** On the shore of Okanagan Lake, this resort is a five-minute stroll from downtown Kelowna, though you may never have to leave the grounds because of all the amenities. Most standard rooms and suites are spacious, with balconies, sitting areas, and attractive modern decor (the north tower is newer than the south tower). About half the rooms have views over the lake and the surrounding hills. The two-bedroom waterfront condo suites are a good option for families: suites have two full baths, full kitchens, washer-dryers, gas fireplaces, and whirlpool baths. ⊠ *1310 Water St., V1Y 9P3* ☎ *250/763–4500 or 800/465–4651* 🖶 *250/763–4565* ⊕ *www.grandokanagan.com* 🛏 *261 rooms, 34 suites, 60 condominiums* ⚐ *3 restaurants, café, room service, in-room data ports, some in-room hot tubs, some kitchens, minibars, cable TV with movies, indoor pool, outdoor pool, gym, hair salon, hot tubs, sauna, spa, dock, boating, mountain bikes, lounge, pub, casino, shops, babysitting, dry cleaning, laundry service, concierge, concierge floor, Internet, business services, convention center, travel services, some pets allowed (fee), no-smoking floors* ▭ *AE, D, DC, MC, V.*

$$$–$$$$ 🏨 **Lake Okanagan Resort.** This self-contained, kid-friendly resort 25 km (15 mi) from Kelowna spreads across a mile of waterfront and 300 acres of mountainside on the west side of Okanagan Lake. The attractive modern units, decorated with rich colors and pine furniture, range from studio and one-bedroom suites in the main hotel to multiple-room villas for up to 18 people. Most have lake views and balconies or decks. Activities are plentiful, including lots of supervised kids' programs in July and August, and a resort shuttle that scoots you up and down the hillside. ⊠ *2751 Westside Rd., V1Z 3T1* ☎ *250/769–3511 or 800/663– 3273* 🖶 *250/769–6665* ⊕ *www.lakeokanagan.com* 🛏 *12 rooms, 105 suites, 12 villas* ⚐ *Restaurant, café, some in-room data ports, some kitchens, some kitchenettes, cable TV, 9-hole golf course, 7 tennis courts, 3 pools, gym, 3 hot tubs (2 indoor), massage, sauna, beach, boating, marina, waterskiing, badminton, basketball, billiards, hiking, horseback riding, horseshoes, Ping-Pong, volleyball, 2 bars, lounge, recreation room, video game room, shop, babysitting, children's programs (ages 4–16), playground, laundry facilities, business services, meeting rooms, no-smoking rooms* ▭ *AE, DC, MC, V.*

$ 🏨 **Apple Blossom B&B.** Set on the western slopes of the Okanagan Lake, this cheery B&B offers terrific views and genuine hospitality. A separate guest entrance opens to a comfy communal lounge where you have access to a large-screen TV and DVD, lots of local information, the Internet, and a small kitchenette. True to its namesake, an apple-theme permeates everything, especially at breakfast where apple motifs adorn linens and dishes. Food is tailored to guest preferences and yes, it might come decorated with an apple slice or two. If you're home by mid-evening, you'll also be offered a delicious evening dessert and coffee. ✉ *3582 Apple Way Blvd., Westbank V4T 1Y7* ☎ *250/768–1163 or 888/718–5064* 🖷 *250/768–7128* 🛏 *3 rooms* ♦ *Kitchenette, Internet, cable TV, lounge, mountain bikes; no kids* ▤ *AE, MC, V* ◯⦿ *BP.*

Sports & the Outdoors

BIKING & HIKING   Bikers and hikers can try the rail bed of the **Kettle Valley Railway** between Penticton and Kelowna. Sadly, some sections and trestle bridges were destroyed by forest fires so be sure you use up-to-date maps and information, available from the visitor's bureau in Kelowna.

GOLF   With four championship golf courses close to town, Kelowna is a major golf destination. **Gallagher's Canyon Golf and Country Club** (✉ 4320 Gallagher's Dr. W ☎ 250/861–4240 or 800/446–5322 ⊕ www.golfbc. com), about 15 km (9 mi) southeast of Kelowna, has an 18-hole, par-72 championship course and a 9-hole, par-32 course; greens fees for the 18-hole course are C$105 in high season. Surrounded by orchards (golfers can pick fruit as they play), **Harvest Golf Club** (✉ 2725 KLO Rd. ☎ 250/862–3103 or 800/257–8577 ⊕ www.harvestgolf.com) is an 18-hole, championship par-72 course. Greens fees in high season are C$102. The Harvest Dining Room, in the clubhouse, has lake views and is open to nongolfers for dinner. The **Okanagan Golf Club** (✉ 3200 Via Centrale ☎ 250/765–5955 or 800/446–5322 ⊕ www.golfbc.com) has two 18-hole, par-72 championship courses with Okanagan Valley views. The Quail Course is a challenging hillside course with tight tree-lined fairways; the newer Bear Course, designed by the Jack Nicklaus Group, is more forgiving. High-season greens fees are C$95 for either course.

SKIING   One of B.C.'s leading ski destinations, **Big White Ski Resort** (✉ Big White Rd., off Hwy. 33 about 1 hr southeast of Kelowna ☎ 250/765–8888 or 800/663–2772, 250/765–7669 snow reports ⊕ www.bigwhite.com) is an affordable, family-oriented resort with excellent day care and children's programs, a ski school, a good mix of more than 100 runs, and 13 up-to-date lifts, including a gondola and 4 high-speed quad chairs. Snow hosts take you out on the mountain for a half day at no charge. A one-day lift ticket is C$64. You can ski or walk anywhere in the compact village, which has several restaurants and a total of 10,000 beds in hotels, condos, B&Bs, and hostels. There are 2,565 acres of skiable terrain, a vertical drop of 2,550 feet, average annual snowfall of more than 24 feet, and night skiing five times a week. Three snowboard parks, 25 km (15 mi) of cross-country trails, snowmobiling, ice-skating, horse-drawn sleigh rides, Canada's largest snow-tubing park, and even dogsledding round out the resort's myriad options.

Summerland & Peachland

⑲ *Summerland is 52 km (31 mi) south of Kelowna, Peachland is 25 km (15 mi) southwest of Kelowna.*

Between Kelowna and Penticton, Highway 97 winds along the west side of Okanagan Lake, past vineyards, orchards, fruit stands, beaches, picnic sites, and some of the region's prettiest lake and hill scenery. In Summerland you can ride the historic **Kettle Valley Steam Railway** (✉ 18404 Bathville Rd., 7 km [4 mi] off Hwy. 97 ☎ 250/494–8422 or 877/494–8424 ⊕ www.kettlevalleyrail.org), which has trips along 10 km (6 mi) of the 1915 rail line between mid-May and mid-October for C$17. The year 2005 was the inaugural season for the restored 1912 steam locomotive; it was once the backup engine to the famed Royal Hudson. The train runs twice daily Saturday through Monday in May, June, September, and October and Thursday through Monday in July and August. Cyclists and hikers can purchase a one-way trip for C$13.

WINERIES **Hainle Vineyards Estate Winery** (✉ 5355 Trepanier Bench Rd., Peachland ☎ 250/767–2525 or 800/767–3109 ⊕ www.hainle.com), British Columbia's first organic winery and the first to make ice wines, is a small producer open for tastings (though not tours). The Amphora Bistro ($) has lake views and dishes that incorporate seasonal and organic ingredients. The bistro is open for lunch and dinner, daily year-round.

Tours are given daily from May until mid-October at **Sumac Ridge Estate Winery** (✉ 17403 Hwy. 97 N, Summerland ☎ 250/494–0451 ⊕ www.sumacridge.com), but you can taste or buy wines here all year. The C$5 tour fee comes off the price of any wine you buy. The Cellar Door Bistro ($$–$$$) serves Pacific Northwest cuisine using fresh, local, organic ingredients. It's open daily for lunch and dinner.

Penticton & Naramata

⓴ *16 km (10 mi) south of Summerland, 395 km (245 mi) east of Vancouver.*

Penticton, with its long, sandy beach backed by motels and cruising pickup trucks, is a nostalgia-inducing family-vacation spot. A growing city extends to the south, but the arid hills around town are full of orchards, vineyards, and small farms. The **S.S. Sicamous**, a 1914 paddle wheeler moored at the lakeside, is now a museum. ✉ *1099 Lakeshore Dr. W* ☎ *C$5* ⊙ *Mid-June–Labor Day, daily 9–9; Apr., May, and Sept., daily 9–6; Oct.–Mar., weekdays 10–4.*

The **British Columbia Wine Information Centre** (✉ 553 Railway St. ☎ 250/490–2006 ⊕ www.bcwineinfo.com) will help you plan a self-drive winery tour and can provide details about annual wine festivals, held in spring and fall. It also stocks more than 500 local wines.

Drive through Penticton's city-center to the east side of Okanagan Lake and you'll follow the Naramata Benchlands (⊕ www.discovernaramata.com) to picturesque—and sleepy—**Naramata Village** at the end of the road. The route is peppered with one winery after the other, so the seemingly short, 15-minute drive could take all afternoon.

NARAMATA **Lake Breeze Vineyards** (✉ 930 Sammet Rd., Naramata ☎ 250/496–5659)
WINERIES is one of the region's most attractively located wineries. Tastings are available but not tours, and the winery is open daily from mid-May to mid-October, from 10 to 5. The outdoor **Patio Restaurant** ($–$$) is open for lunch (weather permitting) between mid-June and mid-September.

Elephant Island Orchard Wines (⊠ 2730 Aikens Loop, Naramata ☎ 250/ 496–5522 ⊕ www.elephantislandwine.com) creates some delightful table and dessert wines from fruits such as pear, cherry, and black currant. Many of the recipes are generations old. **Red Rooster Winery** (⊠ 891 Naramata Rd., Naramata ☎ 250/492–2424 ⊕ www.redroosterwinery.com) is a stunning new winery with a spacious tasting room that showcases wine alongside the work of local artists; there's also a small gallery upstairs. For those who fantasize about owning a vineyard, Red Rooster has an Adopt A Row program (a row of 50 vines) with the guarantee of 12 bottles of wine.

Where to Stay & Eat

$$$$ ✕ **Country Squire.** Plan to spend the evening if you book a meal at this rambling country house in Naramata, 10 km (6 mi) north of Penticton. Diners are asked to choose one of seven or eight main courses when they reserve their table; the chef then designs a five-course meal around it. The options change each evening but may include various treatments of scallops, duck breast, veal, tiger prawns, and lamb. There's only one sitting per evening, so lingering over the meal—even taking a stroll along the lake between courses—is very much the thing to do. The same can be said for Sunday brunch. The wine cellar has hundreds of local and imported labels. ⊠ *3950 1st St., Naramata* ☎ *847/223–0121* ᐧ *Reservations essential* ⊟ *MC, V* ⊗ *Closed Mon.*

$$–$$$$ 🏨 **Penticton Lakeside Resort, Convention Centre and Casino.** On the shore of Okanagan Lake, this modern resort is within walking distance of Penticton's beachfront and town center. It has an elegant Italianate lobby and spacious rooms with modern decor, large balconies, and lake or mountain views. The facilities include a health club, a casino, a private beach, and a lakeside café. Magnum's restaurant ($$–$$$) serves Pacific Northwest cuisine and has lakeside seating. ⊠ *21 Lakeshore Dr. W, V2A 7M5* ☎ *250/493–8221 or 800/663–9400* 🖷 *250/493–0607* ⊕ *www.rpbhotels. com* ⇌ *197 rooms, 7 suites* ᐧ *2 restaurants, room service, in-room data ports, cable TV with movies and video games, indoor pool, health club, hair salon, hot tub, beach, dock, windsurfing, boating, jet skiing, parasailing, waterskiing, 2 bars, casino, shop, babysitting, dry cleaning, laundry service, Internet, convention center, some pets allowed (fee), no-smoking floors* ⊟ *AE, D, DC, MC, V*

$–$$$ 🏨 **God's Mountain Crest Chalet.** This adult-oriented Mediterranean-style villa sits on 115 acres of sunny hilltop overlooking Skaha Lake, 4 km (2½ mi) south of Penticton. The three common rooms are filled with European antiques, plush cushions, and theatrical props. The patio, poolside bar and gazebo, and several suites have expansive lake views. The Rooftop Queen room is fun and romantic: it has a fireplace, private hot tub, and four-poster bed with a shake roof, but the room itself is open to the stars. There's also an elaborate two-story penthouse suite. Group dinners for 10 or more require reservations. ⊠ *4898 Lakeside Rd., V2A 8W4* ☎🖷 *250/490–4800* ⊕ *www.godsmountain.com* ⇌ *5 rooms, 7 suites* ᐧ *Dining room, fans, some refrigerators, pool, hiking, shop, Internet, meeting room, helipad; no a/c, no room phones, no room TVs, no smoking* ⊟ *MC, V* ⊗ *Closed Nov.–Feb.* ⦿ *BP.*

Sports & the Outdoors

For downhill skiing, **Apex Mountain Resort** (⊠ Apex Mountain Rd., off Green Mountain Rd. ☎ 250/292–8222 or 877/777–2739 ⊕ www. apexresort.com) has 67 trails, 5 lifts, a vertical drop of 2,000 feet, and a peak elevation of 7,187 feet. The resort, known for its intimate ambience and soft powder snow, has night skiing as well as a terrain park and half pipe for boarders, a snow-tube park, an outdoor ice rink, a skating trail through the forest, and snowmobile tours. Summer brings lift-accessed hiking and mountain biking, along with trail rides and helicopter tours. Apex is 33 km (21 mi) west of Penticton. A one-day lift ticket is C\$52. The resort village has a full-service hotel, a stylish B&B, cabin, condos, restaurants, bars, shops, ski rentals, a ski school, and children's programs.

Osoyoos

㉑ *58 km (36 mi) south of Penticton.*

South of Penticton between the southern tip of Lake Okanagan and the U.S. border, Highway 97 runs along a chain of lakes: Skaha, Vaseaux, and Osoyoos, and through Canada's only desert. Although the sandy lakeshores can be crowded in summer, the hot, dry climate makes this a prime wine-producing area; several wineries run tours and tastings. For information on wine tours and tastings around B.C., contact the **British Columbia Wine Information Centre** (⊠ 553 Railway St. ☎ 250/490–2006) in Penticton. Accommodations are available in Osoyoos and other towns in the region.

The northern tip of the Great Basin Desert is home to flora and fauna found nowhere else in the country. You can learn more about the unique local ecology at the **Desert Centre**, where you can take a guided tour along a boardwalk desert trail. ⊠ *Rd. 146, off Hwy. 97, 4 km (3 mi) north of Osoyoos* ☎ *250/495–2470 or 877/899–0897* ⊕ *www.desert.org* ⊡ *C\$6, including tour* ☉ *Daily 9:30–3:30; guided tours at 10, noon, and 2.*

Just west of Osoyoos lies **The Nk'Mip Cellars,** North America's first aboriginal owned and operated winery. On a bench overlooking Osoyoos lake, this stunningly designed winery is one of the last tracts of natural desert land so the vineyards provide quite a scenic contrast. The cellars are part of a 112-acre master plan that the Osoyoos Indian Band is developing. Construction is well underway for **Desert & Heritage Centre,** (☎ 250/495–7901) a resort and medi-spa, and a golf course. ⊠ *1400 Rancher Creek Rd.* ☎ *250/495–2985* ⊕ *www.nkmipcellars.com* ☉ *May–Oct., daily 10–7.*

From the viewing tower and patio at **Burrowing Owl Estate Winery,** you get sweeping views of the vineyards and Osoyoos Lake. In 2003 the winery expanded its facilities to include a restaurant (\$\$–\$\$\$) where the winery's award-winning blends are paired with dishes like grilled albacore tuna, pan-baked guinea fowl, and skillet-roasted filet mignon. At the 25-foot tasting bar, donations (C\$2) for tastings are put toward the Burrowing Oil Recovery Society. A 10-room guesthouse is currently being built onsite, complete with pool and spa. ⊠ *100 Burrowing Owl Place Rd., Oliver*

☎ *250/498–0620 or 877/498–0620* ⊕ *www.burrowingowlwine.ca*
⊙ *May–Oct., daily 10–5.*

THE KOOTENAYS

Tucked between highways 1 and 3, and framed by the Monashee Mountains to the west and the Purcell Mountains to the east, the Kootenays are an idyllic backwater of mountains, lakes, natural hot springs, ghost towns, historic forts, Doukabour farmlands, and preserved Victorian villages. Kootenay Lake and Lower Arrow Lake define the region. A century ago this area was booming because of the discovery of silver in the hills, and with the prospectors came vestiges of European society: stately homes, an elegant paddle wheeler, and the town of Nelson—built in respectable Victorian brick. These days the Kootenays are filled with fine restaurants, historic country inns, and a wealth of opportunities for outdoor activities amid fantastic scenery.

Nelson

★ ㉒ *321 km (199 mi) east of Penticton, 657 km (407 mi) east of Vancouver.*

Bypassed a little by history, this laid-back city of 10,000, with its Victorian architecture and lake and mountain setting is one of British Columbia's prettiest towns. Nelson has a wealth of crafts shops and coffee bars, several B&Bs, three youth hostels, and a restored 1906 streetcar running along the lakeshore. The visitor center has self-guided walking or driving tours of many of the town's 355 historic buildings.

About 45 km (30 mi) north of Nelson is **Ainsworth Hot Springs Resort** (⊠ Hwy. 31, Ainsworth Hot Springs ☎ 250/229–4212 or 800/668–1171), where you can wade through a network of caves and plunge into hot-and-cold spring-fed pools. The resort has accommodation and a casual dining room. The hot springs are open daily 10 to 7 (C$7).

On the west side of Kootenay Lake, as you head north from Nelson on Highway 31, is the charming village of **Kaslo.** An 1898 stern-wheeler, the **S.S.** *Moyie* (☎ 250/353–2525), is moored on the lakeshore. Its cargo deck has been restored 1930s style, and the salon deck revisits the year 1898. The *Moyie,* is a National Historic Site, open 9:30 to 5, daily mid-May to mid-October. Admission is C$5.

If you head west from Kaslo on scenic, winding Highway 31A, you'll pass a number of 19th-century silver-mining towns. Most were abandoned when the ore ran out, but **Sandon,** off Highway 31A, is enjoying a resurgence as a historic site, with a handful of shops and an offbeat café. It's also home to Canada's oldest operating power plant; some of the equipment dates to 1890s.

Where to Stay & Eat

$$–$$$ ✕ **All Seasons Cafe.** Tucked into an alley between Baker and Victoria streets,
Fodor's Choice this former family cottage serves innovative cuisine that its owners have
★ dubbed (because people kept asking) Left Coast Inland Cuisine. In practice this means a seasonally changing menu that uses fresh, local, often

organic produce and lists lots of vegetarian creations. Among the good choices are rabbit pot pie with sauteed shallots; cumin-rubbed honey-braised lamb; and Silverking Tofu with sweet potato tart and asparagus. The flourless dark chocolate–espresso torte is a popular dessert. ⊠ *620 Herridge La.* ☎ *250/352–0101* ☰ *MC, V* ☯ *No lunch.*

★ **$$–$$$$** ⊞ **Blaylock's Resort & Health Spa.** The locals call this Tudor-style manor, Sleeping Beauty's Castle. Built in the 1930s and set on 13 acres of beautifully tended gardens, it feels like a fairy tale. Richly textured fabrics and period and antique furniture enhance such details as limestone fireplaces and hand-carved white-oak mantles. Rooms are spacious, and what they lack in decor they make up for in beds topped with goose-down comforters, cambric-cotton linens, and a 3-inch thick feather bed on top of the mattress (a European idea) that virtually guarantees a beauty sleep. The 900-square-foot master suite has a fireplace, an in-room TV, an adjoining sunroom, and an ensuite bathroom. All rooms have either lake or mountain views. In addition to massage and mainstream services, the spa offers a variety of holistic therapies. ⊠ *1679 Hwy. 3A, V1L 5R3* ☎ *250/825–2200 or 888/788–3613* ⊟ *250/825–4123* ⊕ *www. blaylock.ca* ⇋ *6 rooms, 1 suite* ₺ *Dining room, fans, tennis court, sauna, spa, steam room, billiards, boccie, croquet, hiking, 2 lounges, Internet; no a/c, no room phones, no room TVs, no smoking* ☰ *MC, V* ℸ○╎ *BP.*

$–$$ ⊞ **Inn the Garden B&B.** One block from Nelson's restaurants and shopping, this beautifully restored heritage home is adorned with plants, wicker, and antiques. You can relax in the sitting room, on the front porch, or the sunny back deck, and a full hot breakfast (the inn caters to special diets if necessary) is included in the rates. A two-bedroom suite has a kitchenette and private entrance. The three-bedroom guesthouse next door, with a full kitchen and private backyard, is a good choice for families. Ask about golf, ski, and spa packages. ⊠ *408 Victoria St., V1L 4K5* ☎ *250/352–3226 or 800/596–2337* ⊟ *250/352–3284* ⊕ *www. innthegarden.com* ⇋ *5 rooms, 3 with bath; 1 suite; 1 guesthouse* ₺ *Fans, kitchen, kitchenette; no room phones, no room TVs, no kids under 12, no smoking* ☰ *AE, MC, V* ℸ○╎ *BP.*

$–$$ ⊞ **Willow Point Lodge.** About 6 km (4 mi) north of Nelson, this three-story 1920 country inn with a broad, covered veranda is perched on 3½ acres of forested hillside. Four rooms have expansive views of Kootenay Lake and the Selkirk Mountains; the others overlook an extensive garden. A favorite is the Oak Room, with its large stone fireplace, red-velvet bed canopy, and private entrance. The Green Room has a private balcony, and the Kokanee Room has a detached bath. Rates include a lavish breakfast. Trails lead from the property to waterfalls nearby. ⊠ *2211 Taylor Dr., V1L 6K3* ☎ *250/825–9411 or 800/949–2211* ⊟ *250/825–3432* ⊕ *www.willowpointlodge.com* ⇋ *6 rooms* ₺ *Fans, outdoor hot tub, hiking, Internet; no a/c/, no room phones, no room TVs, no smoking* ☰ *MC, V* ℸ○╎ *BP.*

¢–$ ⊞ **Sweet Dreams Guesthouse.** New Denver, about 100 km (62 mi) northwest of Nelson, is in the mountains and a mecca for hikers and ecoenthusiasts, especially since the area boasts insect-free summers. This charming and unpretentious guesthouse has lovely lake views and a country-style decor—wicker furniture, floral duvets, and hardwood floors.

Dinner is a bonus and usually includes an ethnic twist, be it Greek, Thai, or even Japanese. Set menus are priced according to appetite (plates are C$15, platters are C$20) and always include a choice of chicken, fish, or vegetarian. ⊠ *702 Eldorado Ave., New Denver* ☎ *250/358–2415* 🖷 *250/358–2556* ⊕ *www.newdenverbc.com* 🛏 *5 rooms, 2 with bath* 🖔 *Fans, refrigerator; no a/c, no room phones, no room TVs, no smoking* 🖃 *MC, V* ¶◎ *BP.*

Sports & the Outdoors

HIKING **Kokanee Creek Provincial Park** (⊠ North of Nelson, off Hwy. 3A ☎ 250/852–4212, 800/689–9025 campground reservations) has lake swimming, walking trails, picnic sites, and drive-in camping, as well as nearby boat rentals. **Kokanee Glacier Provincial Park** (⊠ North of Nelson off Hwy. 3A ☎ 250/422–4200) is a backcountry park with hike-in campsites and extensive trail networks.

SKIING **Red Mountain Resorts** (⊠ 1000 Red Mountain Rd., Rossland ☎ 250/362–7384 or 800/663–0105 ⊕ www.ski-red.com), about an hour southwest of Nelson, spans two mountains and has 83 marked runs, 5 lifts, and a vertical drop of 2,900 feet as well as cross-country ski trails and heli- and Cat-skiing. Famed for its powder and tree skiing, the resort also has accommodations, ski rental, and ski lessons. A one-day lift ticket is C$52. **Whitewater Ski and Winter Resort** (⊠ Whitewater Ski Rd., off Hwy. 6 ☎ 250/354–4944 or 800/666–9420 ⊕ www.skiwhitewater.com), about 20-minutes south of Nelson, has 43 runs, 3 lifts, a 1,300-foot vertical drop, and plenty of powder skiing. Ski rentals and lessons are available, though the resort doesn't offer lodging. A one-day lift pass goes for C$44.

Crawford Bay

㉓ *40 km (25 mi) northeast of Nelson, including ferry ride.*

This peaceful backwater has pastoral scenery framed by snowcapped mountains. It's home to several artisans, including an ironworker and a glassblower, whose workshops are open to the public. On the east side of Kootenay Lake, Crawford Bay can be accessed by a scenic, 45-minute car ferry from Balfour, north of Nelson. By car it's off Highway 3 on Route 3A.

Where to Stay

$–$$ 🏨 **Wedgwood Manor.** Built for the daughter of the famous china magnate, this 1910 country manor with a wide veranda has an Edwardian charm. Rooms are elegant: two have whirlpool baths, and several have canopy beds and fine, original woodwork. Much of the 50-acre estate includes forested walking trails, and the Purcell Mountains form a striking backdrop to croquet games on the lawn. The house makes an atmospheric setting for the murder-mystery weekends held in the spring and fall. The hosts can also arrange golf packages. A one-bedroom summer cottage with a kitchen is also available. ⊠ *16002 Crawford Creek Rd., Box 135, V0B 1E0* ☎🖷 *250/227–9233 or 800/862–0022* ⊕ *www.wedgwoodcountryinn.com* 🛏 *6 rooms, 1 cottage* 🖔 *Fans, badminton, croquet, hiking; no a/c, no room phones, no room TVs, no kids under 3, no smoking* 🖃 *MC, V* ☉ *Main house closed mid-Oct.–Easter* ¶◎ *BP.*

Sports & the Outdoors

The 18-hole, par-72 **Kokanee Springs Golf Resort** (✉ 16082 Woolgar Rd.
☎ 250/227–9226 or 800/979–7999) has views of Kokanee Glacier, accommodations, and a restaurant. Greens fees are C$63 on weekdays
and C$65 on weekends.

THE BRITISH COLUMBIA ROCKIES

The national and provincial parks of the British Columbia Rockies are
a close match for the grandeur of Alberta's parks to the east. But the
parks in British Columbia are smaller, and most of the British Columbia
Rockies are not protected within park boundaries. This means that
fewer limitations are placed on activities like snowmobiling, heli-skiing,
or heli-hiking compared to elsewhere in the region.

"British Columbia Rockies" is in part a misnomer. The term is often used
to refer to the Columbia Mountains of southeastern British Columbia,
which flank the western slope of the Rockies but are not geologically a
part of the Rockies. The Columbias and the true Rockies are separated
by the broad valley of the Columbia River, known colloquially as the
Columbia River trench. Four separate ranges form the Columbias themselves. To the north are the Cariboos, west of Jasper and Mt. Robson
parks. Reaching south like three long talons from the Cariboos are (west
to east) the Monashees, the Selkirks, and the Purcells.

As the first ranges to capture storms moving from the west across the
plains of interior British Columbia, the Columbias get much more rain
and snow than the Rockies. In the Monashees, the westernmost of the
subranges, annual snowfalls can exceed 65 feet. This precipitation has
helped create the large, deep glaciers that add to the high-alpine beauty
of the Columbias. Lower down, the moist climate creates lusher forests
than those in the Rockies to the east. The deep snows in winter make
the Columbias a magnet for deep-powder and helicopter skiers.

Many of the towns of the British Columbia Rockies have grown around
the natural-resource industries. Only a relatively small portion of the
British Columbia Rockies is protected from development; as a result,
farming, mining, and lumbering are rather common in the accessible portions of these ranges. Poor commodity prices since the mid-1990s, however, have driven the mountain towns to look increasingly toward
tourism to help their economies. Although still no Banff or Jasper, many
of these towns have amenities for visitors, often at substantially lower
prices than in the Alberta Rockies.

Golden

 105 km (65 mi) north of Radium Hot Springs.

Little more than a truck stop in the early 1990s, Golden, a town of 4,000
residents that serves a regional population of about 7,000 people, today
has hotels, restaurants, and tour operators. Although the town retains
its role as an active service center for the lumber and trucking industries,
summer sightseeing from the 924-foot gondola ascent and alpine are a

big draw. Many fine alpine lodges, most offering hiking and cross-country skiing right out the door, dot the hills and mountains around Golden. You still have to scratch below the surface a bit to get past the industrial history of the town, but the effort will be rewarded with some hidden gems, minus the crowds found in the towns of the national parks.

Where to Stay & Eat

$$–$$$ ✕ **Eleven 22 Guest House Grill & Liquids.** Local artwork (for sale) adorns the walls of this early-20th-century house with numerous cozy dining rooms. The international menu lists appetizers such as hummus and nachos; entrées include pad thai, curried rice with crab, buffalo rib-eye steak, a daily pasta, and a daily fish special. The homemade breads are delectable. Garden seating is available in summer. ⊠ *1122 10th Ave. S, at Hwy. 95 and 12th St.* ☎ *250/344–2443* ⊕ *www.eleven22.ca* ▤ *MC, V* ☯ *Closed late Oct.–mid-Nov. and late Apr.–mid-May.*

$–$$$ ✕ **Kicking Horse Grill.** Dark brown wood dominates this rustic-yet-elegant restaurant with exposed log beams and walls. The cuisine of 18 different countries, including Greece, Japan, Spain, France, Thailand, and Indonesia gives the restaurant its motto: "taste the world," and also means the menu changes frequently. ⊠ *1105 9th St. S* ☎ *250/344–2330* ▤ *AE, MC, V.*

$$ ▦ **Kapristo Lodge.** The lodge is an oasis of pampering service 14 km (9 mi) south of Golden. Although the view 600 feet above the Columbia River valley is impressive enough, the Kapristo's real charm is an unabashed effort to spoil you. The rate includes breakfast; lunch, and dinner are extra and must be booked in advance—you should reserve well in advance for peak-season accommodation. Check out the tour packages that include various ecoadventures, as well as golf. ⊠ *1297 Campbell Rd., Box 90, V0A 1H0* ☎ *250/344–6048* 🖶 *250/344–6755* ⊕ *www. kapristolodge.com* ➝ *3 rooms, 3 suites* ⚒ *Dining room, lounge with TV, outdoor hot tub, massage, sauna, boating, fishing, mountain bikes, hiking, horseback riding, travel services, in-room fan; no a/c, no in-room TV* ▤ *MC, V* ❙⃝❙ *BP.*

$$ ▦ **Prestige Mountainside Resort.** Furnishings and amenities make this three-story motel the pick of the lot along Highway 1, just up the hill from the main part of town. Large rooms, queen-size beds, and high ceilings create a very spacious feeling. Ten rooms have kitchenettes, and the suites have whirlpool baths. Ask for a room overlooking town—there's no extra charge, the room faces away from the highway, and the view is far more pleasing. Rates drop by a third off-season. ⊠ *1049 Hwy. 1 N, Box 9, V0A 1H2* ☎ *250/344–7990* 🖶 *250/344–7902* ⊕ *www.prestigeinn. com* ➝ *82 rooms, 3 suites* ⚒ *Restaurants, some kitchenettes, indoor pool, health club, hot tub, lounge, meeting rooms* ▤ *AE, D, MC, V.*

Sports & the Outdoors

The gondola at the **Kicking Horse Mountain Resort** (⊠ Kicking Horse Mountain ☎ 866/754–5425 ⊕ www.kickinghorseresort.com), an all-season resort that is earning top kudos transports eight people per car on the 12-minute ride to the summit of Kicking Horse Mountain. There are 4 lifts and 78 ski runs ranging from beginner to expert. In summer you can take the gondola (C$17) to Canada's highest restaurant, Eagle's Eye

($$$–$$$$), or you can head to the top and zoom down on a mountain bike or sign up for an interpretive hike. There are more than 22 trails to enjoy as well as a grizzly bear wilderness refuge to visit. A gondola–grizzly refuge tour is C$20; with lunch it's C$30. Hours vary, so call ahead.

HIKING & SKIING **Golden Alpine Holidays** (☎ 250/344–7273 🖷 250/344–7274 ⊕ www.goldenalpineholidays.com) runs three- to seven-day alpine hiking and backcountry ski tours in the Selkirk Mountains, with accommodation in three backcountry mountain lodges near the tree line (expect propane lights, woodstoves, saunas, full kitchens, no running water or electricity, and outhouse toilets). You and your gear are helicoptered to the lodges. You can hire a guide and move between lodges or stay at a single lodge. Backcountry skiing season lasts from December through April; hiking is offered from early July to mid-September. **Purcell Heli-Ski/Hiking** (☎ 250/344–5410 or 877/435–4754) has one- to seven-day heli-skiing-and-snowboarding packages in the Purcell Mountains, with day use of a modern mountain lodge. Overnight accommodations are in Golden. Heli-skiing is available from December to mid-May, and there's also half- or full-day heli-hiking from mid-June to September.

RAFTING   There's excellent white-water rafting on the Kicking Horse River. Half-day excursions run about C$55 per person, full-day excursions about C$89 to C$110. Rafting season is generally May through September, but high-water conditions, especially in spring, may force cancelation of the wilder trips. **Alpine Rafting** (☎ 250/344–6778 or 888/599–5299) ⊕ www.alpinerafting.com) runs mild to extreme white-water trips on the Kicking Horse. **Glacier Raft Company** (☎ 250/344–6521 ⊕ www.glacierraft.com) specializes in extreme white water (Class IV) but also runs more serene trips for those of fainter heart. **Wet 'N' Wild Adventures** (☎ 250/344–6546 or 800/668–9119 ⊕ www.wetnwild.bc.ca) conducts moderate to wild half- and full-day trips on Kicking Horse white water.

SPORTING GEAR   **Selkirk Source for Sports** (✉ 504 9th Ave. N ☎ 250/344–2966) rents and sells bicycles, cross-country skis, kayaks, and canoes. It also has a large selection of sportswear and accessories. **Summit Cycle** (✉ 1007 11th Ave. ☎ 250/344–6600) rents bicycles.

Shopping

Canyon Creek Pottery (✉ 917 10th Ave. N ☎ 250/344–5678) sells pottery crafted on-site. You can visit the studio and see future gallery items being created. They are closed Sunday.

en route   The 105 km (65 mi) south from Golden to Radium Hot Springs, where Highway 93 joins Highway 95, is a pleasant drive, rambling along the rolling floodplain of the Columbia River. To the right are the river and the Purcell Mountains; more immediately to the left are the Rockies, although the major peaks are hidden by the ranges in the foreground. Resorts catering to RVs abound.

Glacier National Park

25 *58 km (36 mi) west of Golden, 45 km (28 mi) east of Revelstoke.*

Glacier National Park, not to be confused with the U.S. park of the same name in Montana, is known for rugged mountains and, not surprisingly, an abundance of glaciers (more than 400). The glaciers result not because of the exceptionally high elevation—although some peaks here do exceed 10,000 feet—but because of the high winter snowfalls in the park. Many of the glaciers can be seen from the highway, but to appreciate Glacier National Park fully, you must take to the trail.

At **Rogers Pass,** near the center of Glacier National Park along Highway 1, the heavy winter snowfalls made rail and road construction exceedingly difficult. Avalanches claimed the lives of hundreds of railway-construction workers in the early 1900s and continued to be a threat during highway construction in the 1950s.

Today, the Rogers Pass war against avalanches is both active and passive. Heavy artillery—105-millimeter howitzers—is used to trigger controlled avalanches before they build up to threaten truly dangerous slides. (If you're traveling in the backcountry, always be alert to unexploded howitzer shells that pose a potential hazard.) On the passive side, train tunnels and long snow sheds along the highway shield travelers from major slide paths.

The **Rogers Pass Centre** documents Glacier National Park's history and is well worth a visit even if you're not stopping long. Exhibits highlight the geology and wildlife of the park, and 30-minute movies focus on such subjects as avalanches and bears. ⊠ *Hwy. 1* ☎ *250/837–7500* 🖅 *Included in park pass* ☉ *May–mid-June and mid-Sept.–Oct., daily 9–5; mid-June–mid-Sept., daily 7:30 AM–8 PM; Nov., Thurs.–Mon. 9–5; Dec.–Apr., daily 7–5.*

Where to Stay

$$ 🏨 **Glacier Park Lodge.** The modern, two-story Best Western at the top of Rogers Pass is one of the best ski hotels in the country. The spacious, refurbished rooms are bright and cheery. The steep-sloping A-frame roof is a design concession to the heavy winter snows. The lodge accommodates travelers with its 24-hour service station and 24-hour cafeteria. Rates drop 40% off-season. The park's information center is nearby. ⊠ *The Summit, Rogers Pass, Glacier National Park, Hwy. 1, V0E 2S0* ☎ *250/837–2126 or 800/528–1234* 🖷 *250/837–2130* ⊕ *www. glacierparklodge.ca* ⇨ *50 rooms* ⚹ *Restaurant, cafeteria, lounge, heated outdoor pool, hot tub, sauna, shop* ⊟ *AE, D, DC, MC, V.*

Sports & the Outdoors

Several trails from the Illecillewaet Campground, a few miles west of the park's Rogers Pass Centre on Highway 1, make good day hikes. One of the best, although fairly strenuous, is the **Asulkan Valley Trail,** a 13-km (8-mi) loop that passes waterfalls and yields views of the Asulkan Glacier and three massifs—the Ramparts, the Dome, and Mt. Jupiter. A much easier hike is the 1½-km (1-mi) **Brook Trail** loop, which starts 6 km (4 mi) west of the Rogers Pass Centre and leads to views of the glaciers of Mt. Bonney.

Mount Revelstoke National Park

❷❻ *Eastern border 20 km (12 mi) west of Glacier National Park; western edge is by town of Revelstoke.*

This park on the western flanks of the Selkirks has smaller mountains than those in the Rockies to the east, and lusher vegetation, thanks to the additional rain and snow on the west-facing slopes. Conceived primarily as a day-use park, Mt. Revelstoke National Park covers 260 square km (100 square mi). Its main attraction is the 26-km (16-mi) **Meadows in the Sky Parkway** to the summit of Mt. Revelstoke, at 6,395 feet. As it climbs to the top, the parkway takes you through several different geographical zones, from alpine meadows to tundra. The paved road, which is generally open and snow-free from mid-July to late September, begins from Highway 1, 1½ km (1 mi) before the turnoff to the town of Revelstoke. This is a narrow road with many switchbacks, so trailers are not permitted. From the Balsam Lake parking lot, there's a free shuttle bus for the last 2 km (1 mi) to the summit area from 10 to 4:20. Several easy hikes from the Balsam parking lot meander past small lakes and have excellent views of the Selkirk and Monashee ranges.

Revelstoke

❷❼ *148 km (92 mi) west of Golden, on western edge of Mt. Revelstoke National Park.*

The pretty little town of Revelstoke has both summer and winter activities. The downtown district's spruced-up buildings from the late-19th-century house modern shops, restaurants, and businesses.

🖑 ❷❽ The two pools at **Canyon Hot Springs**, tucked between Mt. Revelstoke and Glacier national parks about 35 km (22 mi) east of Revelstoke, make a good rest stop. A 15,000-gallon hot pool is naturally heated to 42°C (108°F), and a 60,000-gallon pool is mixed with cool water to maintain a temperature of 32°C (90°F). They are open May through September. Log cabins—with private baths and kitchenettes—and camping are available. **Albert Canyon**, a ghost town that was the site of the original hot-springs complex built by railroad workers in the late 1800s, is a short distance south of the present facility, though little of it remains. ✉ *Off Hwy. 1* ☎ *250/837–2420* 💲 *C$6.50* ☉ *May–June and Sept., daily 9–9; July and Aug., daily 9 AM–10 PM.*

Where to Stay & Eat

$$–$$$ ✕ **One-Twelve.** Low cedar ceilings and an abundance of historic photos lend warmth to this restaurant in the Regent Inn. Fine seafood dishes compose about half the menu and include items such as B.C. salmon and East Coast lobster. Continental favorites such as chicken cordon bleu and beef brochette complete the choices. ✉ *112 1st St. E* ☎ *250/837–2107* ⚬ *Reservations essential* 🞸 *AE, MC, V.*

$$ 🏨 **Regent Inn.** Many styles mix at this Revelstoke landmark in the heart of downtown: colonial, with its brick-arcade facade; true Canadian, in its pine-trimmed lobby area and restaurant; and Scandinavian, in the angular, low-slung wood furnishings of the guest rooms. Rooms are on the large side but don't have spectacular views. The cozy microbrewery pub gets quite lively on weekends. ⊠ *112 1st St. E, Box 582, V0E 2S0* ☎ *250/837–2107 or 888/245–5523* 🖷 *250/837–9669* ⊕ *www. regentinn.com* ➷ *47 rooms* ♿ *Restaurant, gym, outdoor hot tub, sauna, pub* ▤ *AE, D, DC, MC, V* ⊖⦶ *CP.*

Sports & the Outdoors

BIKING **High Country Cycle & Sports** (⊠ 118 Mackenzie Ave. ☎ 250/814–0090) rents bicycles.

SKIING **Cat Powder Skiing,** at the Powder Springs ski area at Mount MacKenzie (☎ 800/991–4455 ⊕ www.catpowder.com), has ski runs for all levels. Day passes are C$28 to C$32. They also organize two- to five-day all-inclusive packages that run into the Selkirks and on the upper slopes of Mt. MacKenzie in Revelstoke. **Selkirk Tangiers Helicopter Skiing** (☎ 250/, 837–5378 or 800/663–7080 ⊕ www.selkirk-tangiers.com) runs three-, five-, and seven-day all-inclusive heli-skiing packages in the Selkirk and Monashee mountains near Revelstoke, with accommodations at the Coast Hill resort in town.

SNOWMOBILING **Revelstoke Snowmobile Tours** (☎ 250/837–5200 ⊕ www.revelstokecc. bc.ca/rst) offers half- and full-day tours in the Columbia Mountains that start at C$99 you can also rent snowmobiles here without a guide for C$185 a day.

Radium Hot Springs

㉙ *127 km (79 mi) southwest of Banff, 103 km (64 mi) south of Golden, at junction of Hwys. 93 and 95.*

Radium Hot Springs is little more than a service town for the busy highway traffic passing through, but the town makes a convenient access point for Kootenay National Park and has lower prices than the national parks.

♨ **Radium Hot Springs,** the springs that give the town its name, are the town's longest-standing attraction and the summer lifeblood for the numerous motels in the area. Two outdoor pools are tucked at the bottom of the spectacular Sinclair Canyon. The hot pool is maintained at 41°C (106°F); in a cooler pool, the hot mineral water is diluted to 28°C (82°F). Lockers, towels, and suits (period and modern) can be rented. The Pleaides day spa is earning a quality reputation for its massages and other treatments. ⊠ *Hwy. 93, 2 km (1 mi) northeast of Hwy. 95* ☎ *250/347–9485 or 800/767–1611* ⊕ *www.parkscanada.gc.ca/hotsprings* 💲 *C$6.50 per soak, C$9.75 for day pass* ⊙ *Hot pool: May–mid-Oct., daily 9 AM–11 PM; mid-Oct.–Apr., Fri. and Sat. noon–10. Cooler pool: schedule varies with weather.*

Where to Stay & Eat

$–$$$ ✕ **Old Salzburg Restaurant.** The staff here prepares quality food reflecting the pervasive Bavarian motif of the region yet avoids the greasiness so common in the many low-end Bavarian restaurants nearby. Choose from schnitzels, *spaetzle* (dumplings), and bratwurst, as well as chicken, beef, and lamb entrées. Steaks, seafood, and pastas are also available. ✉ *4943 Hwy. 93* ☎ *250/347–6553* ☟ *Reservations essential* ▭ *MC, V* ⊙ *No lunch mid-Sept.–mid-May.*

$–$$$ ☷ **Radium Resort.** Recreational facilities and activities bring this resort to life. Golf is the main attraction (packages are available), along with the proximity to the hot springs. Accommodations are in hotel rooms or one-, two-, or three-bedroom condo units. The rooms are modern, with hardwood furnishings and sponge-painted walls, and each has a sundeck, a mini-refrigerator, and a view overlooking the golf fairways. Condos have full kitchens. There's a small rate reduction off-season. ✉ *8100 Golf Course Rd., Box 310, V0A 1M0* ☎ *250/347–9311 or 800/ 667–6444* ☒ *250/347–6299* ⊕ *www.radiumresort.com* ↩ *90 rooms, 30 condo units* ☟ *Dining room, lounge, some kitchens, 18-hole golf course, 2 tennis courts, indoor pool, health club, hot tub, sauna, mountain bikes, racquetball, squash, cross-country skiing* ▭ *AE, D, MC, V.*

$–$$ ☷ **Chalet Europe.** This all-suite hotel sits on a crest above town, and all of the bright and modern suites have balconies with expansive views of the Columbia River valley. The best views are from the top floor, and some deluxe suites (some are pet-friendly) even come with telescopes to take full advantage of the vista. Rates drop by a third off-season. ✉ *5063 Madsen Rd., Box 456, V0A 1M0* ☎ *250/347–9305 or 888/ 428–9998* ☒ *250/347–9306* ⊕ *www.chaleteurope.com* ↩ *17 suites* ☟ *Kitchenettes, hot tub, sauna, Internet, recreation room, laundry facilities, some pets allowed; no a/c in some rooms* ▭ *AE, D, DC, MC, V* ⦿ *CP.*

Sports & the Outdoors

Radium Resort (✉ 8100 Golf Course Rd. ☎ 250/347–9311 or 800/667–6444 ⊕ www.radiumresort.com) has an 18-hole, par-69 golf course and an 18-hole, par-72 course.

Invermere

③⓪ *18 km (11 mi) south of Radium Hot Springs.*

Invermere, one of the many highway service towns in the British Columbia Rockies, is the central-access point for Windermere Lake, Panorama, and the Mountain Village resort area.

For summer water sports, **Windermere Lake**—actually an extra-wide stretch of the Columbia River—is popular among swimmers, boaters, and boardsailors. There's a good beach on the lake.

One of the best area museums is the **Windermere Valley Pioneer Museum,** which depicts the life of 19th-century settlers through artifacts and other memorabilia in eight pioneer buildings. ✉ 622 3rd St. ☎ 250/342–9769 ☒ C$2 ⊙ June, Tues.–Sat. 1–4, July–early Sept., Tues.–Sat. 10–4.

The **Pynelogs Cultural Centre** (✉ 1720 4th Ave., at Kinsmen Beach ☎ 250/ 342–4423) showcases and sells all types of local crafts: paintings, pottery, photographs, jewelry, and sculptures. There are occasional evening folk or jazz concerts.

Panorama Mountain Village is a year-round resort best known for skiing in winter. In summer, whether or not you're staying at the resort, you can take advantage of an excellent golf course, tennis courts, outdoor pools, waterslides, hiking and biking trails, and lift-accessed mountain biking. In either season, there are shops, restaurants, and activities in the village. ⊠ *Toby Creek Rd.* ☎ *250/342–6941 or 800/663–2929* ⊕ *www.panoramaresort.com.*

Where to Stay & Eat

$$–$$$$ ✕ **Toby Creek Dining Lounge.** The ski-lodge restaurant at the Panorama Mountain Village is an elegant fine-dining establishment. The menu showcases superior (Alberta beef) steaks, imaginative pastas, chicken, and seafood, but more adventurous diners may opt for the ostrich, pheasant, venison, caribou, or musk ox. ⊠ *Panorama Resort Rd., 18 km (11 mi) west of Invermere* ☎ *250/342–6941* ⚖ *Reservations essential* ▭ *AE, D, MC, V* ☉ *Closed Apr.–early Dec. No lunch.*

$$–$$$ ✕ **Strand's Old House Restaurant.** Strand's is a gem set amid the usual pizza and burger joints in Invermere. The renovated heritage home has five rooms that provide varied levels of coziness; in summer there's seating on a large outdoor patio, and a gazebo opens for additional seating in an attractive courtyard. A deliciously international menu includes dishes such as Thai shrimp salad, snails in garlic butter and red wine, lamb linguine, and a delicious Polynesian prawn and chicken dish. ⊠ *818 12th St.* ☎ *250/342–6344* ⚖ *Reservations essential* ▭ *AE, MC, V* ☉ *No lunch.*

$–$$$ ✕ **Black Forest Restaurant.** A Bavarian theme pervades the region, and this is a good place to sample the cuisine. Schnitzels are the specialty, but other options are smoked pork with sauerkraut, bratwurst, seafood, chicken, and steak. Save room for the elaborate cheesecake desserts. Exposed wood, Bavarian pottery, and big-game trophies decorate the interior, creating something of a cross between a hunting lodge and a Bavarian mountain chalet. ⊠ *540 Hwy. 93/95, 5 km (3 mi) west of town* ☎ *250/342–9417* ▭ *AE, DC, MC, V* ☉ *No lunch.*

$$ ⌂ **Best Western Invermere Inn.** There are few surprises at this location of the familiar hotel chain, although rooms are on the large side. The hotel is at a quiet end of the main shopping and dining area in town. It's the nearest major hotel to the town beach, but still about a mile away. Rates drop 20% off-season. ⊠ *1310 7th Ave., V0A 1K0* ☎ *250/342–9246 or 800/661–8911* 🖷 *250/342–6079* ⊕ *www.invermereinn.com* ⇰ *45 rooms* ☖ *Restaurant, health club, outdoor hot tub, lounge, wine shop, some pets allowed* ▭ *AE, D, MC, V.*

$ ⌂ **Panorama Mountain Village.** Accommodation is either in condo villas (many have fireplaces, patios, or balconies) that resemble part of a mountainside suburb or in a lodge at the base of the ski lift that has a college-dorm atmosphere. Depending on the season you can ski, hike, bike, or play golf or tennis. A water park has two large year-round outdoor heated pools, two hot tubs, and a 4,000-square-foot swimming pool. In summer the waterslides are open. Summer is still a slower season than winter, however, and some services may be reduced. Rates decrease by 25% off-season. ⊠ *Toby Creek Rd., V0A 1T0, 18 km (11*

mi) west of Invermere ☎ 250/342–6941 *or* 800/663–2929 🖷 250/
342–3395 ⊕ *www.panoramaresort.com* ⟿ *105 hotel rooms, 350 condo
units* ⌔ *5 restaurants, 2 cafeterias, 18-hole golf course, 8 tennis courts,
3 pools, 2 hot tubs, sauna, hiking, downhill skiing, 3 bars* ▭ *AE, D,
MC, V.*

Sports & the Outdoors

DOWNHILL **Panorama Mountain Village** (⊠ Toby Creek Rd. ☎ 800/663–2929 ⊕ www.
SKIING panoramaresort.com) has the second-highest lift-served vertical drop
(4,000 feet) in Canada; there are more than 100 runs, 2 terrain parks,
and 19 lifts. Lift rates are C$59.

GOLF **Greywolf at Panorama** (⊠ Toby Creek Rd. ☎ 800/663–2929 ⊕ www.
panoramaresort.com) has an 18-hole, par-72 course, which some consider the best in B.C. The 6 hole requires you to play across "Hopeful
Canyon" to a green perched above vertical rock cliffs. Greens fees are
C$99 to C$119.

HELI-SKIING **R. K. Heli-Ski** (☎ 250/342–3889 *or* 800/661–6060 ⊕ www.rkheliski.
com), based at the Panorama Mountain Village resort, has daily ski tours
in winter.

SPORTING GEAR **Columbia Cycle and Motorsports** (⊠ 375 Laurier St. ☎ 250/342–6164)
rents bicycles, snowboards, downhill and cross-country skis, and snowshoes. In summer **D. R. Sports** (⊠ 2755 13th St. ☎ 250/342–3517) rents
bikes for children and adults (hourly or daily) and snowboards in winter. **Invermere Sales & Rentals** (⊠ 403 7th Ave. ☎ 250/342–6336) sells
and rents canoes, boats, and personal watercraft.

Fairmont Hot Springs

③¹ *20 km (12 mi) south of Invermere, 94 km (58 mi) north of Fort Steele.*

Fairmont Hot Springs is named for the hot springs and the resort that
has sprouted around it. The "town" is little more than a service strip
along the highway, but turn in at the resort and things become more
impressive. Well, it *is* Canada's largest all-natural hot mineral springwater pool complex. The town is also close to Columbia Lake, popular with boaters and boardsailors. Golf is a growing attraction at several
fine courses in the area.

Where to Stay

⌔ **$$–$$$** ▦ ⚠ **Fairmont Hot Springs Resort.** The wide selection of activities—
from golf to heli-hiking—makes vacationing here feel somewhat like being
at camp, but the hot springs and the spa can't be overlooked. Inside the
attractive, low-slung bungalow-style structure, rooms are contemporary,
many with wood paneling; some are equipped with kitchens and have
balconies or patios. The 311-unit RV site is among the highest rated in
the Canadian Rockies. Golf, ski, and spa packages are available. Rates
decrease by 40% off-season. ⊠ *Hwy. 93/95, Box 10, V0B 1L0* ☎ *250/
345–6311, 800/663–4979 in Canada* 🖷 *250/345–6616* ⊕ *www.
fairmontresort.com* ⟿ *140 rooms, 311 RV sites* ⌔ *4 restaurants, snack
bar, 2 18-hole golf courses, 2 tennis courts, 4 pools, spa, bicycles, horseback riding, 2 lounges, airstrip* ▭ *AE, D, DC, MC, V.*

Sports & the Outdoors

Fairmont Hot Springs Resort (⌧ Hwy. 93/95 ☎ 250/345–6514 or 800/663–4979 ⊕ www.fairmontresort.com) has two 18-hole courses: a par-72 course at the resort and a par-71 course along the river in town, as well as a new 9-hole, par-3 "Creekside" course. There are several hiking trails, including a spectacular one that leads from the hot-springs waterfall into the canyon.

Fort Steele

㉜ *94 km (58 mi) south of Fairmont Hot Springs.*

Many German and Swiss immigrants who arrived in the late 19th century settled in Fort Steele and nearby Kimberley to work as miners and loggers. Southeastern British Columbia was not unlike the Tyrol region they had left. Later, a demand for experienced alpinists to guide and teach hikers, climbers, and skiers brought more settlers from the Alpine countries. Today, a Tyrolean influence is evident throughout southeastern British Columbia and schnitzels and fondues appear on menus as often as burgers and fries.

Fort Steele Heritage Town, a reconstructed 1890s boomtown consisting of more than 60 buildings, is a step back to the silver- and lead-mining days of the 1890s. Its theater, period tradespeople, barbershop, and dry-goods store exude the authenticity of a bygone era. Steam-train and wagon rides are available. There's enough here to hold the interest of children and adults alike for a half day or more. ⌧ 9851 Hwy. 93/95 ☎ 250/417–6000 🖷 250/489–2624 ⊕ *www.fortsteele.bc.ca* ✉ *Museum: May–Sept. C$9–C$12. Grounds: Oct.–Apr. free* ☉ *Museum: May–Sept., daily 9:30–8. Grounds: daily 9:30–dusk.*

Kimberley

㉝ *40 km (25 mi) west of Fort Steele, 98 km (61 mi) south of Fairmont Hot Springs.*

A cross between quaint and kitschy, Kimberley is another town in the area rich with Tyrolean character. The *Platzl* ("small plaza," in German) is a pedestrian mall of shops and restaurants modeled after a Bavarian village. Chalet-style buildings are as common here as log cabins are in the national parks. In summer Kimberley plays its alpine theme to the hilt: merchants dress up in lederhosen, gimmicks abound, and the promotion works. The Canadian Rockies are a popular destination for German tourists; Kimberley catches their attention, and sometimes there's as much German as English being spoken in the Platzl.

Where to Stay & Eat

$$–$$$ ✕ **Chef Bernard's Inn and Restaurant.** Eating in this small, homey store-front restaurant on the Kimberley pedestrian mall is like dining in someone's pantry. Packed into the shelves of the many small rooms in the dining area are the chef's collection of travel memorabilia—license plates, glass figurines, and much more, including a model train that runs on the ceiling in the restaurant. If things aren't too busy, don't be surprised to see cheery chef Bernard out front in the Platzl, wooing customers inside. The international menu ranges from German and Thai to Cajun. Homemade desserts are always popular. There's also an inn upstairs. ⊠ *170 Spokane St.* ☎ *250/427–4820 or 800/905–8338* ⌂ *Reservations essential* ▤ *D, DC, MC, V.*

★ **$$$–$$$$** 🏨 **Lizard Creek Lodge at Fernie Alpine Resort.** This log-beam, mountain lodge exudes comfort and luxury, complete with ski-in, ski-out access to the resort's Elk Quad chair. Accommodations range from intimate studio suites to family-oriented two-bedroom units with a loft, and come with full kitchens, a gas fireplace, and private balconies. The main dining room serves up gourmet fare such as roasted duck breast with pear-ginger chutney and coffee-scented merlot sauce, and rack of lamb in a hazelnut-orange crust, whereas the Great Room offers more casual fare. Winter activities include nearby skiing, snowshoeing, and sledding; summer offers tennis, golf, hiking, and fishing. Rates are higher in the holiday season and in peak-time February. ⊠ *5346 Highline Dr., Fernie V0B 1M1* ☎ *250/423–2058 or 877/228–1948* 🖶 *250/423–2057* ⊕ *www.lizardcreek.com* ➯ *99 rooms* ⌂ *Restaurant, kitchens, in-room VCRs, outdoor heated pool, health club, hot tub, spa, steam room, meeting rooms; no smoking* ▤ *AE, MC, V.*

¢ 🏨 **Quality Inn of the Rockies.** In keeping with downtown Kimberley's Bavarian theme, this outpost of the chain hotel has an exterior of exposed-wood beams and stucco. Dark-brown wood-veneer furniture fills the large rooms, which have small sitting areas. The restaurant serves good, reasonably priced Canadian cuisine including steak and seafood, and the pub hosts live entertainment on weekends. This is the only lodging next to the Platzl and the best of the mostly plain hotels in Kimberley. There's a small rate decrease during the off-season. ⊠ *300 Wallinger Ave., V1A 1Z4* ☎ *250/427–2266 or 800/661–7559* 🖶 *250/427–7621* ⊕ *www.qualityinn.kootenays.com* ➯ *45 rooms* ⌂ *Restaurant, hot tub, lounge, pub, Internet, business services, laundry facilities* ▤ *AE, D, DC, MC, V.*

Nightlife & the Arts

In summer, Bavarian bands in Kimberley strike up with oompah music on the Platzl, especially when an event such as the **Old Time Accordion Championships** (☎ 800/667–0871 ⊕ www.kimberleyvacations.bc.ca) is in full swing (early July).

Sports & the Outdoors

Kimberley Alpine Resort (⊠ Kimberly Ski Area Rd. ☎ 250/427–4881 or 877/754–5462 ⊕ www.skikimberley.com) has a vertical drop of 2,465 feet, 75 runs (plus tree runs), and 10 lifts, as well as mountain-top accommodations, restaurants, a lounge, and a rental shop. You can go night skiing Thursday to Saturday from late December to mid-March. Lift tickets for the day cost C$50. When the snow melts, you may want to duff your way through **Trickle Creek Golf Course** (888/874–2553), one of Canada's top courses.

THE CARIBOO-CHILCOTIN

This is British Columbia's wild west: a vast, thinly populated region stretching from the dense forests of the north to the rolling ranchlands of the south. The Cariboo-Chilcotin covers an area roughly bordered by Bella Coola in the west, Lillooet in the south, Wells Gray Park in the east, and Prince George in the north, though the part most visitors see is along Highway 97, which winds 640 km (397 mi) from Kamloops to Prince George.

In the 19th century thousands followed this route, called the Cariboo Wagon Road or the Gold Rush Trail, looking for—and finding—gold. Those times are remembered throughout the region, most vividly at the re-created gold-rush town of Barkerville. You can still pan for gold here, but these days most folks come for ranch and spa getaways, horseback riding, fly-fishing, mountain biking, and cross-country skiing.

The Cariboo Ranching Country

34 *73 km (44 mi) west of Kamloops.*

The Cariboo is home to some of the biggest working ranches in North America, bucking-bronco rodeos, and a number of guest ranches that provide everything from basic riding holidays (some alongside real-life cowboys) to luxurious full-service spa resorts.

You can tour an 1863 roadhouse, visit a First Nations pit house, and take a stagecoach ride on the old Cariboo Wagon Road at **Historic Hat Creek Ranch** (⊠ Hwy. 97, 11 km [7 mi] north of Cache Creek at junction with Hwy. 99 ☎ 250/457–9722 or 80/782–0922 ⊕ www.hatcreekranch.com), once a major stagecoach stop on the Gold Rush Trail. There's also a restaurant, gift shop, and campsite. The ranch is open mid-May to mid-October, daily 9 to 5; admission is C$8.

Where to Stay

★ **$$$$** ☒ **Echo Valley Ranch & Spa.** A palacelike Baan Thai ("Thai house") presides over a view-blessed hillside at this remote luxury resort, 48 km (30 mi) west of Clinton. The Baan Thai houses yoga classes and a lavish Thai-style guest suite. The spruce-log construction and vaulted ceilings of the resort's main lodge, guest lodge, and cabins are equally beautiful. You can enjoy a Thai massage in the full-service spa; ride horses; hike, bike, fish, or take an all-terrain vehicle safari of the Fraser Canyon; or simply enjoy the fresh mountain air. Meals, taken family-style in the main lodge, make use of the ranch's own organic produce. A three-night stay is required. ⌂ *Box 16, Jesmond V0K 1K0* ☎ *250/459–2386 or 800/253–8831* ⊟ *250/459–0086* ⊕ *www.evranch.com* ⇆ *15 rooms, 1 suite, 3 cabins* ⚲ *Dining room, fans, some refrigerators, indoor pool, gym, 2 outdoor hot tubs, sauna, spa, fishing, mountain bikes, billiards, hiking, horseback riding, shuffleboard, sleigh rides, recreation room, shop, laundry service, Internet, meeting room, airstrip, helipad; no room phones, no room TVs, no kids under 13, no smoking* ⊟ *MC, V* ⊗ *FAP.*

$$$$ ⛺ **Siwash Lake Ranch.** Getting to this small, wilderness ranch is half the fun and well worth the effort. A 45-minute back-road route, from 70 Mile House, takes you there, but you'll need to ask for directions. Once you arrive, you'll find a charming home set beside a tranquil lake amid several thousand acres of government-owned forest and meadows. Rooms are beautifully appointed with country-style, color-coordinated linens. A huge stone fireplace dominates a spacious lounge, and a farmhouse-style kitchen makes dining a social pleasure. You can horseback ride on your own or with a wrangler, and you can choose to participate in horse round-ups and care. Winter activities include dog sledding, cross-country skiing, and ice-fishing. There's an excellent children's program for youngsters from the end of June through August, although Siwash is a kids-free, romantic getaway the rest of the year. There's a minimum three-night stay. ⌂ *Box 39, 70 Mile House V0K 2K0* ☎ *250/395–6541* ⊕ *www.siwashlakeranch.com* ⇱ *6 rooms* △ *Dining room, picnic area, fans, boating, fishing, hiking, horseback riding, lounge; no a/c, no room phones, no room TVs, no smoking* ⊟ *MC, V* ☽ *Mid-Oct.–mid-May* ❙❍❙ *FAP.*

$$–$$$ ⛺ **The Hills Health Ranch.** Hiking, horses, hay rides, and line dancing mix with spa treatments, wellness programs, and aerobics classes at this homey, affordable, and long-established health retreat. You can book structured wellness packages such as weight loss, anti-aging, healthy heart, and other medi-oriented programs, or just relax and enjoy the many activities at your own pace. Accommodations include woodsy three-bedroom A-frame chalets (ideal for families) and lodge rooms with standard hotel decor. The spa cuisine is excellent (and calorie counted), but heartier ranch meals and continental fare are also available. ⊠ *108 Mile Ranch at Hwy. 97, 60 km (36 mi) south of Williams Lake, 180 km (108 mi) northwest of Kamloops, Box 26, V0K 2Z0* ☎ *250/791–5225 or 800/668–2233* 📠 *250/791–6384* ⊕ *www.spabc.com* ⇱ *26 rooms, 19 chalets* △ *Restaurant, dining room, picnic area, fans, some kitchens, indoor pool, health club, 2 hot tubs, sauna, spa, boating, mountain bikes, billiards, hiking, horseback riding, Ping-Pong, cross-country skiing, downhill skiing, ice-skating, ski shop, sleigh rides, snowmobiling, pub, recreation room, shop, playground, laundry service, Internet, business services, meeting rooms, airstrip, some pets allowed; no phones in some rooms, no smoking* ⊟ *AE, MC, V.*

$$ ⛺ **The Flying U Ranch.** Founded in 1849, Canada's oldest guest ranch oozes Wild West charm, right down to the swinging doors at the Longhorn Saloon. Rustic log cabins with a shared bathhouse and hearty, basic meals served family style in the 1880s lodge recall ranch life of a century ago. You can ride all you want through the miles of surrounding ranchland; guides are optional—the horses know their way home. Hayrides and square dances round out the days. A two- to three-day minimum stay applies; rates include riding and most other activities from birding and fishing to canoeing and swimming. ⊠ *North Green Lake Rd., 33 km (20 mi) south of 100 Mile House* ⌂ *Box 69, 70 Mile House V0K 2K0* ☎ *250/456–7717* 📠 *250/456–7455* ⊕ *www.flyingu. com* ⇱ *27 cabins without bath, 2 tepees, 2 tents* △ *Dining room, fans, lake, massage, sauna, dock, boating, fishing, hiking, horseshoes, volleyball,* *sleigh rides, snowmobiling, pub, piano, shop, babysitting, playground, meeting rooms, airstrip; no a/c, no room phones, no room TVs ⊟ MC, V ⊘ Closed Mar. and Nov.–mid-Dec.; no riding in winter ⊖ AP.*

Barkerville & Wells

㉟ *80 km (50 mi) east of Quesnel on Hwy. 26.*

In 1862, when news of a rich gold strike at this out-of-the-way spot reached the outside world, this tiny settlement rapidly boomed into the biggest town west of Chicago and north of San Francisco.

Fodor'sChoice **Barkerville Historic Town,** with 125 original and re-created buildings, is
★ now the largest heritage attraction in western Canada. Actors in period costume, merchants vending 19th-century goods, stagecoach rides, and live musical revues capture the town's heyday. The site is open year-round, but most of the theatrical fun happens in summer. ⊠ *Hwy. 26, Barkerville* ☎ *250/994–3332* ⊕ *www.barkerville.ca* ⊠ *Mid-May–Sept. 30, C\$12.50 for 2-day pass; free in winter* ⊘ *Daily 8–8.*

Bowron Lake Provincial Park (⊠ End of Hwy. 26 ☎ 604/435–5622, 800/435–5622 canoe trip reservations ⊕ www.bcparks.ca or www.hellobc.com), 30 km (19 mi) east of Barkerville by gravel road, has a 116-km (72-mi) chain of rivers, lakes, and portages that make up a popular canoe route. Canoeists must reserve ahead and pay a fee of C\$60 per person, plus an C\$18 per-boat reservation fee. The west side of the circuit can be paddled in two to four days; the fee is C\$30. Note that advance reservations are required; no date changes are permitted within 14 days of arrival.

Eight kilometers (5 mi) west of Barkerville, tiny **Wells** is a fascinating stop. A thriving mining town until the 1940s, it's now an atmospheric mountain village of brightly painted false-front buildings. The village, home to a vibrant arts community, has several art galleries and cafés and a summer arts school. A big draw is the **Jack 'O Clubs Casino** (☎ 250/ 994–3222) on Highway 26, a 1930s-theme casino with musical revues three times a day between May and September. All ages are welcome at the shows; you must be 19 to enter the casino.

Where to Stay

★ \$–\$\$\$ ⊞ **Elysia Resort on Quesnel Lake.** Set on the south shore of Quesnel Lake, the deepest fjord lake in the world, this full-service resort offers stunning scenery, terrific fishing, and a location that's just west of three provincial parks: Bowron Lake, Cariboo Mountains, and Wells Gray. All rooms, which were refurbished for 2005, have lake views and private balconies, and are furnished with plush duvets and a decor of rich earth tones to match the cedar trim. The fully licensed dining room has an extensive, ever-changing menu featuring B.C. produce; you can eat beside the fireplace or dine under the stars on the patio. Rates include boat moorage and the resort offers several all-inclusive packages such as photo safaris and fly-fishing. There are 12 full-service RV sites. ⊠ *5657 Marshall Creek Rd., Quesnel Lake Junction* ⊕ *Box 4069, Williams Lake V2G 2V2* ☎ *250/243–2433* ⊕ *www.elysiaresort.com* ⇆ *8 rooms, 11* *cabins ✍ Restaurant, some kitchens, lake, recreation room, marina, hot tub, horseshoes, volleyball, badminton, canoes, airstrip, pets allowed; no room phones, no room TVs, no smoking ⊟ AE, MC, V ⫶⊙⫶ EP.*

¢–$$ 🏨 **Wells Hotel.** The faithfully refurbished 1934 Wells Hotel makes a good base for visiting nearby Barkerville and the Bowron Lake canoeing area and for accessing the 80 km (50 mi) of hiking, biking, and cross-country ski trails nearby. Comfortable rooms and suites are decorated in a 1930s style with hardwood floors, local art, and period photos. *⊠ 2341 Pooley St., Wells ☎ Box 39, Wells V0K 2R0 ☎ 250/994–3427 or 800/ 860–2299 📠 250/994–3494 ⊕ www.wellshotel.com ⇔ 15 rooms, 9 with bath ✍ Restaurant, fans, outdoor hot tub, pub; no a/c, no room phones, no room TVs, no smoking ⊟ AE, MC, V ⫶⊙⫶ CP.*

NORTHERN BRITISH COLUMBIA

It's a truism that even those well traveled in B.C. rarely use the top half of their maps. The area most British Columbians refer to as "The North" comprises a full half of the province, most of it a little-visited, thinly populated, stunningly beautiful, wildlife-rich wilderness. The north is home to several groups of First Nations peoples who have lived in the regions for thousands of years and compose most of the population in many areas. Insights into these ancient cultures, at 'Ksan, near Hazelton, Kitwanga and Kitwancool on the Stewart Cassiar Highway, and in other towns and villages throughout the north are, for many, the most rewarding part of a trip north.

Outdoor adventure increasingly draws those seeking out the north's un-traveled hiking paths, canoe routes, white-water rivers, freshwater lakes, and backwater channels where exclusive fishing lodges nestle in the wilderness. Traveling the region feels like going on an adventure, as towns are few and far between, and drivers need a good spare tire and a sharp eye on the gas gauge. The rewards, though, are many: snow peaks; hot springs; sightings of bear, moose, and bighorn sheep; long summer days; and occasional glimpses of the northern lights.

Three major highways cross the north. Highway 16, the Yellowhead Highway, runs from Jasper in Alberta via Prince George to Prince Rupert, a route that can also be traveled by train on VIA Rail's Skeena line. Highway 97 heads north from Prince George to Dawson Creek, where it becomes the Alaska Highway. Farther to the west, the little-traveled Stewart-Cassiar Highway links Highway 16 to the Alaska Highway, making it possible to take a multiday circle tour of the region.

Prince George

❸❻ *786 km (487 mi) north of Vancouver, 412 km (247 mi) south of Dawson Creek, 440 mi (273 mi) southeast of Hazelton, 721 km (447 mi) east of Prince Rupert.*

At the crossroads of two railways, two highways, and two rivers, Prince George is the province's third-largest city and the commercial center of northern British Columbia.

The Exploration Place Science Centre and Museum has lots of fun, science-related exhibits for kids, including two life-size dinosaur models and a virtual-reality theater. Other exhibits feature re-creations of historic local buildings, and First Nations' artifacts and oral histories. ⊠ *333 Becott Pl., in Fort George Park at east end of 20th Ave.* ☎ *250/562–1612 or 888/562–1612* ⊕ *www.theexplorationplace.com* ⊠ *C$8.95, C$10.95, including virtual-reality theater* ⊙ *Mid-May–mid-Oct., daily 10–5; mid-Oct.–mid-May, Wed.–Sun. 10–5.*

Century-old cabooses, locomotives, dining cars, and luxury sleeping cars are some of the dozens of restored railcars collected at the **Prince George Railway and Forestry Museum,** an outdoor museum that also displays historic logging and sawmill equipment. ⊠ *850 River Rd., next to Cottonwood Park* ☎ *250/563–7351* ⊕ *www.pgrfm.bc.ca* ⊠ *C$6* ⊙ *Mid-May–Oct., daily 10–6; reduced hrs in winter.*

Two Rivers Gallery (⊠ 725 Civic Plaza ☎ 250/614–7800) has a changing roster of shows by local, national, and international artists, though the focus is on Canadian works. The gift shop is a good place to pick up local crafts. It's open Tuesday, Wednesday, Friday, and Saturday 10 to 5; Thursday 10 to 9; and Sunday noon to 5. Admission to the gallery is C$5, free Thursday 3 to 9.

Where to Stay

$$–$$$ 🏨 **Ramada Hotel.** You can't beat this hotel's central location for shopping, business, and sightseeing. It has a swimming pool, sauna, hot tub, a popular sports bar (watch for karaoke on Saturday), and Prince George's only casino. Rooms are spacious with an upbeat, comfortable ambiance; they range from a standard room with two double beds (some have a hide-a-bed sofa) to king size and Jacuzzi suites that are packed with amenities that include warmed bathroom floors, bathrobes, iron, hair dryer, and in-room coffeemakers. ⊠ *444 George St., V2L 1R6* ☎ *250/563–0055 or 800/830–8830* ⊠ *250/563–6042* ⊕ *www.ramadaprincegeorge.com* ⮑ *200 rooms, 1 suite* ⚫ *Restaurant, pub, casino, room service, in-room Internet, minibars, cable TV with movies and video games, indoor pool, sauna, hot tub, dry cleaning, laundry service, business services, shops, meeting rooms, some pets allowed (fee), no-smoking floors* ⊟ *AE, DC, MC, V.*

$–$$ 🏨 **Coast Inn of the North.** This centrally located, full-service hotel has a striking rosewood lobby with a brass fireplace. All the services are here, including a gym, a pool, and a day spa in the attached retail concourse. Rooms are attractive, with rosewood furniture and such added amenities as desks and coffeemakers. The standard rooms have two double beds, the premium rooms are corner units with balconies, and the suites have jetted tubs and fireplaces. The two restaurants include a clubby room serving continental fare and a traditional Japanese steak house. ⊠ *770 Brunswick St., V2L 2C2* ☎ *250/563–0121* ⊠ *250/563–1948* ⊕ *www.coasthotels.com* ⮑ *155 rooms, 2 suites* ⚫ *2 restaurants, coffee shop, room service, in-room data ports, some minibars, cable TV with movies and video games, indoor pool, gym, hair salon, hot tub, sauna, spa, lounge, pub, shops, dry cleaning, laundry service, business* *services, meeting rooms, some pets allowed (fee), no-smoking floors* ☰ *AE, DC, MC, V.*

Sports & the Outdoors

Strider Adventures (✉ 17075 E. Perry Rd. ☎ 250/963–9542 or 800/665–7752 ⊕ www.pgweb.com/strider) can take you on a trek through the local wilds with the help of friendly llamas. Two- to seven-day pack trips cost C$360 to C$1,210. Guided hikes are also offered starting at C$34.

Shopping

The **Prince George Native Art Gallery and Gift Shop** (✉ 1600 3rd Ave. ☎ 250/614–7726) sells traditional and contemporary works, including carvings, sculpture, jewelry, and literature. A second location is at the Via Rail Building (✉ *1500 1st Ave.* ☎ *250/564–3556.*).

> **off the beaten path**

FORT ST. JAMES NATIONAL HISTORIC SITE – This parklike site, 52 km (31 mi) north of Vanderhoof on Highway 27, on the south shore of Stuart Lake, is a former Hudson's Bay Company fur-trading post and the oldest continually inhabited European settlement west of the Rockies. Careful restoration of the original buildings, costumed staff, and demonstrations of aboriginal arts and food preparation help you experience life as a fur trader in 1896. ☎ *250/996–7191* ⊕ *www.parkscanada.gc.ca* ⊠ *C$6* ☉ *Mid-May–Sept., daily 9–5; reduced hrs in winter.*

Smithers

🚲 *371 km (222 mi) northwest of Prince George, 353 km (211 mi) northeast of Prince Rupert, 1,149 km (689 mi) northwest of Vancouver.*

The main town of the Bulkley Valley, Smithers sits under the snow-capped backdrop of 8,700-foot Hudson's Bay Mountain. The Bavarian-themed town center has hotels, restaurants, and several outdoor-equipment outfitters to help visitors explore the surrounding peaks and rivers.

The Hazeltons

🚲 *293 km (182 mi) northeast of Prince Rupert, 439 km (272 mi) northwest of Prince George, 1,217 km (755 mi) northwest of Vancouver.*

Three villages—New, Old, and South Hazelton, each a couple of miles apart—combine to form the Hazeltons, an area rich in the culture of the Gitxsan and Wet'suwet'en peoples. New Hazelton is a modern service strip along Highway 16; South Hazelton is a hamlet just off Highway 16. Old Hazelton is a delightful village of old-fashioned false-front buildings where an old paddle wheeler houses a café and art gallery. It's 4 km (2½ mi) north of New Hazelton, across the Bulkley River by suspension bridge. There are motels in New Hazelton, B&Bs in Old Hazelton, and a campsite and RV park adjacent to 'Ksan Historical Village and Museum.

At **Kispiox**, 11 km (7 mi) north of Old Hazelton on Kispiox Valley Road, you can see 15 intricately carved totems, some more than 100 years old. Guided tours and local crafts are available at the **Kispiox Cultural and Information Centre** (☎ 877/842–5911 or 250/842–7057).

★ **'Ksan Historical Village and Museum,** is a re-created Gitxsan village. The community of seven longhouses was built in 1965 as a replica of the one that stood on the site, at the confluence of the Skeena and Bulkley rivers, for thousands of years before European contact. Gitxsan guides lead informative tours through three of the longhouses. At the Frog House, artifacts and an audio presentation tell of life in the distant past; at the Wolf House, audiovisual effects re-create the experience of being an honored guest at a feast. The Fireweed House exhibits the elaborate performing regalia of the 'Ksan Performing Arts Group, who reenact ancient songs and dances of the Gitxsan people, Friday evenings during the summer. A gift shop sells goods from First Nations groups across the province; a café serves traditional Gitxsan foods. ⊠ *High Level Rd., Hwy. 62, Old Hazelton* ☎ *250/842–5544 or 877/842–5518* ⊕ *www. ksan.org* 🖃 *C$2, C$10 with tour* ☺ *June–Sept., daily 9–5, tours on the ½ hr; call for winter hrs.*

Sports & the Outdoors
Skeena Eco-Expeditions (☎ 250/842–7057 or 877/842–5911 ⊕ www. kispioxadventures.com) operates hiking, fly-fishing, and rafting tours, and rents canoes.

Terrace

147 km (88 mi) east of Prince Rupert on Hwy. 16, 577 km (346 mi) northwest of Prince George, 1,355 km (813 mi) northwest of Vancouver.

Terrace is a logging town and the major commercial center for the Skeena Valley. The region is also home to the Tsimchian peoples. The **Terrace Visitor Info Centre** (⊠ 4511 Keith Rd., Hwy. 16 ☎ 250/635–2063 ⊕ www.terracetourism.bc.ca) has information about area attractions.

Ferry Island Municipal Park, in the Skeena River on the east side of town and accessed by bridges, has a campground, picnic sites, and hiking trails. **Heritage Park** (⊠ 4113 N. Sparks St. ☎ 250/635–4546) is a re-created turn-of-the-20th-century village, with costumed guides and many original buildings. It's open daily 10 to 6, from May to September, with reduced hours October through April. Call ahead to confirm. Admission is C$4. **Lakelse Lake Provincial Park** (☎ 250/798–2466, 800/689–9025 camping reservations ⊕ www.discovercamping.ca), 15-minutes south of Terrace on Highway 37, has camping, hiking trails, and a swimming beach. At **Mt. Layton Hot Springs Resort** (⊠ Hwy. 37 S ☎ 250/798–2214) are public pools, waterslides, and restaurants. About 80 km (48 mi) north of Terrace, partly on gravel road, is the **Nisga'a Memorial Lava Bed Park** (☎ 250/798–2277), a dramatic and eerily moonlike landscape that marks the site of Canada's last volcanic eruption, more than 250 years ago.

About 35 km (21 mi) northwest of Terrace, off Highway 16, is the ski resort at **Shames Mountain** (☎ 250/635–3773, 250/638–8754 snow report ⊕ www.shamesmountain.com). It has a vertical rise of 1,608 feet, a double chairlift, and 20 trails. Anglers flock to the **Skeena River** and its tributaries for some of the province's richest sport fishing (a 99-pound salmon, said to be a world-record catch, was caught in the Skeena).

en route Traveling west toward Prince Rupert (⊕ www.tourismprincerupert. com), both Highway 16 and the railway line follow the wide Skeena River. The route, which passes under snowcapped mountain peaks and past waterfalls, is one of the most scenic in the province. Prince Rupert is where the ferries depart for the Inside Passage as well as across to the **QueenCharlotte Islands.**

The Alaska Highway

406 km (243 mi) from Prince George to Dawson Creek, 985 km (591 mi) from Dawson Creek to Watson Lake, Yukon.

From Prince George, Highway 97, or the Hart Highway, continues northeast to Dawson Creek, where it becomes the Alaska Highway, the most popular route north for Alaska-bound travelers. It then winds through the foothills and pine forests of the northern Rocky Mountains, past the communities of Fort St. John and Fort Nelson, before crossing the B.C.–Yukon border at Watson Lake and continuing to Delta Junction, near Fairbanks, Alaska.

The Alaska Highway skirts the edges of the Muskwa-Kechika Management Area, a vast, roadless wilderness so rich in wildlife it's been called the Serengeti of the North. Even from the highway, sightings of deer, moose, elk, mountain sheep, and bear are commonplace.

The two-lane highway is paved and open year-round. Communities along the way are small, but basic services (gas, food, lodging) are available at least every few hours en route. Pine Pass, about 200 km (132 mi) north of Prince George, marks the boundary between the Pacific and Mountain time zones. Clocks go forward an hour here.

Dawson Creek, a town of about 11,000, is best known as Mile Zero of the Alaska Highway. The much-photographed signpost is at **Mile Zero Square** (⊠ 10th St. and 102nd Ave., Dawson Creek). Also at the square is **Alaska Highway House** (⊠ 10201 10th St., Dawson Creek ☎ 250/782–4714), which has a small exhibit about the history of the highway. It's open weekdays 8:30–4:30. The **Station Museum** (⊠ 900 Alaska Ave., Dawson Creek ☎ 250/782–9595), in the town's old railway station, has natural history and railway history displays and shows a film several times a day about the building of the Alaska Highway. The station is also home to the Dawson Creek Tourist Information Centre, open daily from May to September. ⊠ 900 Alaska Ave. ☎ 250/782–9595 ⊕ www. tourismdawsoncreek.com.

To the north, **Stone Mountain Provincial Park,** 140 km (87 mi) west of Fort Nelson, gets its name from the dramatic rock formations and treeless tundra found in the park. At **Muncho Lake Provincial Park,** 250 km (150 mi) northwest of Fort Nelson, two campgrounds sit on the edge of pretty, blue Muncho Lake. Sheep, caribou, moose, and deer are attracted to salt licks along the highway here.

At **Liard River Hotsprings Provincial Park** (✉ 320 km [192 mi] northwest of Fort Nelson ☎ 800/689–9025 camping reservations ⊕ www. discovercamping.ca) heat from the springs has generated an oasis of tropical plants, including orchids, in this remote northern spot. Two natural outdoor hot-springs-fed pools are a short walk from the campground; there's a C$5 fee to use the pools. The campsite is very popular, and reservations are recommended.

Where to Stay

$–$$ ⬚ **Northern Rockies Lodge.** This modern log lodge on Muncho Lake, 30 minutes from Liard River Hot Springs, provides comfortable lodge rooms, rustic log cabins, lakefront chalets, and a campground with RV hookups. Boating and outdoor activities are available at the lakeside, and the owner's own bush plane can take you on photo safaris, flight-seeing tours, or fishing on a remote mountain lake. You can also stay overnight at one of the lodge's rustic fly-in outpost cabins. ✉ *Mi 462, Alaska Hwy., Box 8, Muncho Lake V0C 1Z0 ☎ 250/776–3481 or 800/663–5269 ☒ 250/776–3482 ⊕ www.northern-rockies-lodge.com. ⌁ 21 rooms, 19 cabins, 3 outpost cabins ⟡ Restaurant, fans, some refrigerators, cable TV, sauna, boating, fishing, mountain bikes, hiking, laundry facilities, Internet, business services, meeting rooms, airstrip, helipad, some pets allowed (fee), no-smoking rooms; no a/c, no room phones, no TV in some rooms* ▤ MC, V.

The Stewart-Cassiar Highway

725 km (450 mi) from Kitwanga on Hwy. 16 to Upper Liard, Yukon, on the Alaska Hwy.

Linking Highway 16 to the Alaska Highway (the Yellowhead Highway), Highway 37, also called the Stewart-Cassiar Highway, is the road less traveled between B.C. and the Yukon. Though challenging to drive, it's arguably prettier than the Alaska Highway, with striking mountain views at every turn.

Although most of Highway 37 is paved, there are still some gravel sections. Watch for potholes, logging trucks, single-lane bridges, and low-flying aircraft (parts of the road double as a landing strip). As in all other active logging areas, it's best to drive with your lights on during the day to stay visible to logging trucks. Settlements are small, gas stations and mechanics are few, and snow can fly at any time of year (though it's rare in summer). The provincial **Ministry of Transportation and Highways** (⊕ www.drivebc.ca) has up-to-date road reports.

A couple of miles north of the Yellowhead junction, the village of **Kitwanga** is home to a stunning array of ancient totems. Nearby is the **Battle Hill National Historic Site,** the site of a decisive First Nations battle in about 1600. One of the largest and oldest collection of totem poles in North America stands at **Kitwancool** (also known as Gitanyow), just 15 km (9 mi) north of the Yellowhead junction.

The 1.6-million-acre **Spatsizi Plateau Wilderness Park** is one of Canada's largest and most remote parks, and one of its richest wildlife reserves.

Home to caribou, grizzly bears, black bears, mountain goats, and 140 species of birds, it's virtually untouched wilderness, accessible only by foot, horseback, canoe, or floatplane. **B.C. Parks** (☎ 250/847–7320) in Smithers has information about guides and outfitters.

off the beaten path

THE GLACIER HIGHWAY – The Glacier Highway (Highway 37A) leaves the Cassiar Highway at **Meziadin Junction,** about 170 km (112 mi) north of the Yellowhead Junction, and travels 65 glacier-lined km (39 mi) west to the oddly paired towns of Stewart, B.C., and Hyder, Alaska. The towns sit about 3 km (2 mi) apart on either side of the international border at the head of the Portland Canal, a 112-km-long (70-mi) fjord on the edge of Alaska's Misty Fjords National Monument. **Stewart,** with a population of about 1,000, has a bank, hotels, restaurants, and camping. Across the border, tiny **Hyder,** with a population of about 100, has no road links to the rest of the United States, except the highway through Canada. The few shops here accept Canadian money. It's a tradition for visitors to get "Hyderized": essentially by downing a shot of grain alcohol at the bar.

TELEGRAPH CREEK – From Dease Lake, a scenic 115-km (71-mi) gravel road, steep and winding in places, leads to this picturesque ghost town of gold-rush-era buildings on the Stikine River, said to be the oldest community in northern B.C. The folks at **Stikine Riversong** (☎ 250/235–3196 ⊕ www.stikineriversong.com), in the original Hudson's Bay Company store, have food, accommodations, guided hikes, and river tours.

Where to Stay

$–$$ 🏨 **Bell II Lodge.** Fly-fishing and heli-skiing are the specialties at this riverside resort, though travelers overnighting on the long drive north will also appreciate the comforts here. The guest rooms, in attractive modern log chalets, all have separate entrances, soapstone fireplaces, pine furniture, and down duvets. There are RV and tent sites here, too. ⊠ At Bell II, 250 km (150 mi) north of Hwy. 16 junction ⫏ Box 1118, Vernon, BC V1T 6N4 ☎ 604/639–8455 or 800/530–2167 ⊟ 604/639–8456 ⊕ www.bell2lodge.com ⊅ 20 rooms ⟐ Restaurant, coffee shop, exercise equipment, outdoor hot tub, sauna, fishing, billiards, Ping-Pong, lounge, recreation room, shop, laundry facilities, Internet, meeting room, some pets allowed (fee); no room TVs, no a/c, no smoking ⊟ AE, MC, V.

NORTH COAST

Gateway to Alaska and the Yukon, this vast, rugged region is marked by soaring snowcapped mountain ranges, scenic fjords, primordial islands, and towering rain forests. Once the center of a vast trading network, the mid- and north coasts are home to First Nations peoples who have lived here for 10,000 years and to immigrants drawn by the natural resources of fur, fish, and forest. The region is thin on roads, but you can travel by ferry, sailboat, cruise ship, plane, or kayak to explore the ancient villages of the coast and the Queen Charlotte Islands. The climate of this mist-shrouded region is one of the world's wettest. Winters see torrential rains, and summers are damp; rain gear is essential year-round.

Inside Passage

★ 40 *507 km (314 mi), or 274 nautical mi, between Port Hardy on northern Vancouver Island and Prince Rupert.*

The Inside Passage, a sheltered marine highway, follows a series of natural channels along the green-and-blue-shaded B.C. coast. The undisturbed landscape of rising mountains and humpbacked islands has a striking, prehistoric look. You can take a ferry cruise along the Inside Passage or see it on one of the luxury liners that sail from Vancouver to Alaska.

The comfortable ***Queen of the North*** ferry carries up to 800 passengers and 157 vehicles and has cabins, a cafeteria, buffet, gift shop, elevator, children's play areas, and licensed lounge on board. Between mid-May and late September, sailings from Port Hardy on Vancouver Island to Prince Rupert (or vice versa) are direct and take 15 hours, almost entirely in daylight. Sailings are less frequent and longer the rest of the year, as the ferry makes stops along the way. Reservations are required for vehicles and recommended for foot passengers. You can order meal packages (breakfast and dinner for C$35 per person) when you reserve space. It's also a good idea to make hotel reservations at Port Hardy and Prince Rupert. ✉ *BC Ferries, 1112 Fort St., Victoria V8V 4V2* ☎ *250/386–3431, 888/223–3779 in B.C., Alberta, and Washington state* 🖷 *250/381–5452* 🌐 *www.bcferries.com* 💵 *One-way summer passage for car C$263, campers C$436 and up, depending on length, each driver or adult passenger C$111, cabin C$55–C$65; fares lower Oct.–May* ⏲ *Mid-May–Sept., departing on alternate days from Port Hardy and Prince Rupert at 7:30 AM, arriving 10:30 PM.*

Discovery Coast Passage

★ 41 *258 km (160 mi), or 138 nautical mi, between Port Hardy on northern Vancouver Island and Bella Coola.*

This BC Ferries summer-only service travels up the Inside Passage to the First Nations community of Bella Bella and then turns up Dean Channel to the mainland town of Bella Coola. The scenery is stunning, and the route allows passengers to visit communities along the way, including Shearwater, Klemtu, and Ocean Falls. It also provides an alternative route into the Cariboo region, via the steep and winding Highway 20 from Bella Coola to Williams Lake. Lodging at ports of call varies from luxury fishing lodges to rough camping, but it's limited and must be booked in advance.

The ***Queen of Chilliwack,*** carrying up to 389 passengers and 115 vehicles, takes from 13 to 30 hours (depending on the number of stops) to travel from Port Hardy on Vancouver Island to Bella Coola. Reservations are required for vehicles and advised for foot passengers. There aren't any cabins. ✉ *BC Ferries, 1112 Fort St., Victoria V8V 4V2*

☎ 250/386–3431, 888/223–3779 in B.C. only 🖶 250/381–5452 ⊕ www. bcferries.com ✉ One-way fares between Port Hardy and Bella Coola for each driver or adult traveler C$115, cars C$231, campers C$295 and up ⊙ Mid-June–early Sept., departs Port Hardy Tues., Thurs., and Sat.; leaves Bella Coola Mon., Wed., and Fri.

Prince Rupert

42 1,502 km (931 mi) by road and 750 km (465 mi) by air northwest of Vancouver, 15 hrs by ferry northwest of Port Hardy on Vancouver Island.

The port of Prince Rupert is the largest community on British Columbia's north coast. Set on Kaien Island at the mouth of the Skeena River and surrounded by deep green fjords and coastal rain forest, Prince Rupert is rich in the culture of the Tsimshian, people who have been in the area for thousands of years.

As the western terminus of Canada's second transcontinental railroad and blessed with a deep natural harbor, Prince Rupert was, at the time of its incorporation in 1910, poised to rival Vancouver as a center for trans-Pacific trade. This didn't happen, partly because the main visionary behind the scheme, Grand Trunk Pacific Railroad president Charles Hays, went down with the *Titanic* on his way back from a financing trip to England. Prince Rupert turned instead to fishing and forestry. New to tourism, this community of 15,000 retains a laid-back, small-town air.

Prince Rupert is the final stop on the BC Ferries route through the Inside Passage, as well as the base for ferries to the Queen Charlotte Islands and a port of call for Alaska ferries. The terminals for both BC and Alaska ferries and the VIA Rail Station are side by side, about 2 km (1 mi) from town; Farwest Bus Lines (☎ 250/624–3343) has service between the ferry terminals and the city center.

Prince Rupert is also a port of call for a growing number of Alaska-bound cruise ships; the city's two cruise-ship terminals are both near downtown, in the Cow Bay district.

Cow Bay, a 10-minute walk from downtown, is a historic waterfront area of shops, galleries, seafood restaurants, and fishing boats. Cow Bay takes its name seriously: lamp posts, benches, and anything else stationary is painted Holstein-style. Prince Rupert's **Visitor Information Centre** (☎ 250/624–5637 or 800/667–1994 ⊙ May–Aug., daily 9–8; Sept., Mon.–Sat. 10–4) is at the Atlin cruise ship terminal in Cow Bay.

★ The **Museum of Northern British Columbia,** in a longhouse-style facility overlooking the waterfront, has one of the province's finest collections of coastal First Nations art, with artifacts portraying 10,000 years of Northwest Coast history. Artisans work on totem poles in the carving shed nearby and, at the museum's longhouse, you can catch performances of Tsimshian storytelling, song, and dance twice daily between mid-May and mid-October. In summer, museum staff also offer a variety of museum and city tours and operate the **Kwinista Railway Museum,** a five-minute walk away on the waterfront. ⊠ *100 1st Ave. W* ☎ *250/624–3207* ⊕ *www.museumofnorthernbc.com.* ⊠ *C$5; additional fees for performances* ☉ *Oct.–mid-May, Mon.–Sat. 9–5; mid-May–Aug., Mon.–Sat. 9–6, Sun. 9–5; Sept., daily 9–5.*

In the late 19th century, hundreds of cannery villages, built on pilings on the edge of the wilderness, lined the coast between California and Alaska. Most are gone now, but B.C.'s oldest (it dates to 1889) and most ★ ☾ complete is the **North Pacific Historic Fishing Village** in Port Edward, 20 km (12 mi) south of Prince Rupert at the mouth of the Skeena River. Once home to more than 700 people during each canning season, the town, of 28 buildings including managers' houses, the company store, and cannery works, is now a national historic site. Staff lead tours and demonstrations about the canning process and the unique culture of cannery villages. Live performances, including a one-person play about the area's history and a reenactment of a First Nations legend, run daily in peak season. The site also has a seafood restaurant and overnight accommodation. Farwest Bus Lines (☎ 250/624–3343) buses travel here from Cow Bay, though service is infrequent. ⊠ *Off Hwy. 16, Port Edward,* ☎ *250/628–3538* ⊕ *www.cannery.ca.* ⊠ *C$12* ☉ *Mid-May–mid-Sept., daily 9:30–5.*

Where to Stay & Eat

★ **$$** ✕ **Cow Bay Café.** Fresh, local seafood and creative vegetarian dishes shine at this tiny waterfront café, where the friendly chef-owner makes almost everything (including breads and desserts) from scratch. What's on the chalkboard menu depends on what's fresh that day but could include curries, Mexican dishes, or the popular crab cakes. The bright solariumlike room with floor-to-ceiling ocean-view windows only seats 35, so book ahead. ⊠ *25 Cow Bay Rd.* ☎ *250/627–1395* ▭ *AE, MC, V* ☉ *Closed Mon. No dinner Tues. or Sun.*

$$ ✕ **OPA: A Japanese Sushi Story.** Owner Yoshinari Nakamura scoured the Pacific Coast for the freshest possible fish before setting up shop in Prince Rupert's Cow Bay. Locals and visitors flock here for *nigiri* and *maki* made with B.C. salmon, prawns, octopus, and other treats from the sea; this spot is for purists though, as sushi and miso soup are the only things on the menu. The loft space in a former fish net factory has the appropriate nautical roots. ⊠ *34 Cow Bay Rd.* ☎ *250/627–4560* ▭ *MC, V* ☉ *Closed Sun. and Mon.*

¢ ✕ **Cowpuccino's Coffee House.** When Rupertites need a place to while away a wet afternoon, they flock to this cozy meeting place in Cow Bay. You can curl up on the sofa with an espresso and a magazine, strum on the café's guitar, or pull up a chair for homemade soup, sandwiches, crêpes, and luscious house made desserts (try the cow patty: a chocolate macaroon concoction). Hearty breakfasts are served here, too. Tables on the patio are a great place to watch eagles gathering across the street. ⊠ *25 Cow Bay Rd.* ☎ *250/627–1395* ▭ *MC.*

$$–$$$ ✕▥ **Crest Hotel.** On a bluff overlooking the ocean, this full-service hotel has Prince Rupert's best views. The restaurant, lounge, most of the guest rooms, and the outdoor hot tub all command expansive vistas of the harbor and outlying forested islands. The rooms are large, comfortable, and modern; the pricier rooms have double Jacuzzi tubs set before ocean-view windows. The restaurant ($$$–$$$$), decorated with brass rails and beam ceilings, specializes in seafood, particularly salmon. You can also book cruises and fishing charters from here. ⊠ *222 1st Ave. W, V8J 1A8* ☎ *250/624–6771 or 800/663–8150* 🖷 *250/627–7666* ⊕ *www.cresthotel.bc.ca* ⤴ *102 total rooms, 2 suites* ♻ *Restaurant, coffee shop, room service, IDD phones, fans, some in-room safes, some minibars, cable TV, some in-room VCRs, Wi-Fi, gym, outdoor hot tub, steam room, fishing, lounge, shop, babysitting, dry cleaning, laundry facilities, laundry service, meeting rooms, some pets allowed (fee), no-smoking floor; no a/c* ▭ *AE, D, DC, MC, V.*

Shopping

Prince Rupert has a great selection of locally made crafts and First Nations artwork which, thanks to a favorable exchange rate, are often better value than in Alaska. The **Blue Heron Gallery** (⊠ 123 Cow Bay Rd. ☎ 250/624–5700) has Northwest Coast First Nations art and work by other local artists. The **Cow Bay Gift Galley** (⊠ 24 Cow Bay Rd. ☎ 250/627—1808) has gifts, souvenirs, and local art.

Queen Charlotte Islands (Haida Gwaii)

★ ㊽ *93 nautical mi southwest of Prince Rupert, 367 nautical mi northwest of Port Hardy.*

The Queen Charlotte Islands, or Haida Gwaii (Islands of the People), have been called the Canadian Galápagos. Their long isolation off the province's North Coast has given rise to subspecies of wildlife found nowhere else in the world. The islands are also the preserve of the Haida people, who make up about half the population. Their vibrant culture is undergoing a renaissance, evident throughout the islands.

Most of the islands' 5,400 permanent residents live on Graham Island—the northernmost and largest of the group of 150 islands—where 108 km (65 mi) of paved road connects the town of Queen Charlotte in the south to Masset in the north. Moresby Island, to the south, is the second-largest of the islands and is largely taken up by the Gwaii Haanas National Park Reserve and Haida Heritage Site, a roadless ecological reserve with restricted access. The wildlife (including bears, eagles, and otters), old-growth forest, and stunning scenery are like nothing else on earth, and kayaking enthusiasts from around the world are drawn to its waterways. Towns on Graham Island have the most services, including banking, grocery stores, and a range of accommodation and campsites; accommodation is also available in Sandspit, on Moresby Island. In summer it's a good idea to make hotel reservations before arriving.

The **visitor-information center** on Wharf Street in Queen Charlotte has information about area activities, including visits to Gwaii Haanas.

Eagle Transit (☎ 250/559–4461 or 877/747–4461 ⊕ www.qcislands. net/eagle) buses meet each ferry from Prince Rupert and run about once a day between the airport in Sandspit, Queen Charlotte, and Masset. **Eagle Cabs,** at the same phone number, also provides transportation on the islands.

Fodor'sChoice
★ The 1,470-square-km (570-square-mi) **Gwaii Haanas National Park Reserve and Haida Heritage Site,** managed jointly by the Canadian government and the Council of the Haida Nation, protects a vast tract of wilderness, unique flora and fauna, and many historic and cultural sites. These include the island of SGang Gwaay (Anthony Island) a UNESCO World Heritage Site, where SGang Gwaay llnagaay is an excellent example of a traditional Northwest Coast First Nations village site, with 21 standing mortuary and memorial poles and the remains of massive cedar longhouses. The reserve is on Moresby Island and 137 smaller islands at the archipelago's southern end. The protected area, accessible only by air or sea, is both ecologically and culturally sensitive. One way to visit—and highly recommended for those unfamiliar with wilderness travel—is with a licensed operator. Parks Canada and the Queen Charlotte Visitor Information Centre have information about operators. To visit on your own (without a licensed operator), you must make a reservation, register for each trip, and attend a mandatory orientation session. Park-use fees start at C$10 per person per day, plus a C$15 per-person reservation fee. ⌂ *Parks Canada, Box 37, Queen Charlotte V0T 1S0* ☎ *250/559–8818, 800/435–5622 information pack and reservations* 🖷 *250/559–8366* ⊕ *www.pc.gc.ca/gwaiihaanas.*

Fodor'sChoice
★ Just 1 km (½ mile) north of the Skidegate ferry terminal, the **Haida Gwaii Museum at Qay'llnagaay** is set in a striking longhouse-style facility on a bluff overlooking the water. Six totem poles, erected in 2001, stand outside. The museum's collection of Haida masks, totem poles, works by contemporary Haida artists, carvings of silver and argillite (soft black slate), and other artifacts is expanding with the addition of works repatriated from other museums. A gift shop sells Haida art, and a natural-history exhibit gives interesting background on island wildlife. By the summer of 2006, an expanded museum will be part of the **Qay'llnagaay Heritage Centre,** a multifaceted cultural center, which was, at this writing, under construction next to the existing museum. Built in the style of a traditional Haida village on a site once occupied by the old village of Qay'llnagaay, or Sea Lion Town, the center will include a theater, an art school, and a canoe-house sheltering *The Lootaas,* a 50-foot canoe created by renowned Haida artist Bill Reid. ⊠ *2nd Beach Rd. off Hwy. 16, Skidegate* ☎ *250/559–4643* ⊕ 🖾 *C$5; higher charges once the heritage center opens* ⊗ *June–Aug., weekdays 10–5, weekends 1–5; May and Sept., weekdays 10–noon and 1–5, Sat. 1–5; Oct.–Apr., Tues.–Sat., 10–noon and 1–5.*

East Beach, an 80-km (50-mi) stretch of sand, runs the length of **Naikoon Provincial Park** (☎ 250/557–4390), in the northeast corner of Graham Island. Untouched forests, bogs, and wildlife, including some of North America's largest black bears, fill the interior of this vast wilderness preserve. At the south end of the park, in Tlell, are the Park Headquarters and Misty Meadows Campground, which has nonreservable drive-in camping. From the Tlell day-use area nearby, a 10-km (6-mi), three-hour round-trip hike leads onto East Beach and to the wreck of a 1928 logging vessel, the *Pesuta.* At the park's north end, near the town of Masset, Agate Beach has nonreservable drive-in beachfront camping. A one-hour round-trip climb up 400-foot Tow Hill gives stunning views of the wide beach at McIntyre Bay. It's possible to walk along East Beach for days, though hikers planning extended trips in the park are advised to register with B.C. Parks or the Royal Canadian Mounted Police in Masset before setting out, as the area is very remote.

Where to Stay & Eat

¢–$ ✕ **Queen B's.** This little café offers made-from-scratch soups, quiches, wraps, pastas, and baked goods. It also doubles as a gallery space for a movable feast of local art, most of it for sale; watch for live music, poetry readings, and other cultural events. Seafood dinners may be available on summer evenings. ⊠ *3208 Wharf St.* ☎ *250/559–4463* ⌂ *Reservations not accepted* ▭ *MC* ⊘ *No dinner.*

$ ⌂ **Alaska View Lodge.** On a clear day you can see the mountains of Alaska from the large front deck of this B&B, 13 km (8 mi) east of Masset. A 10-km-long (6-mi-long) sandy beach borders the lodge on one side, and there are woods on the other. Eagles are a familiar sight, and in winter you can often catch glimpses of the northern lights. Common areas are attractively decorated with European antiques. Two rooms in the main lodge share a bathroom; rooms in the guesthouse each have a private deck overlooking the wide beach. ⊠ *12291 Tow Hill Rd., Box 227, Masset V0T 1M0* ☎ *250/626–3333 or 800/661–0019* ☒ *250/626–3303* ⊕ *www.alaskaviewlodge.ca* ⌂ *4 rooms, 2 with bath* ⌂ *Beach, hiking; no a/c, no room TVs, no kids, no smoking* ▭ *MC, V* ⌐◯⌐ *BP.*

¢–$ ⌂ **Dorothy and Mike's Guest House.** Folk art, batiks, and other treasures from Dorothy and Mike's travels decorate the pretty rooms at this view-blessed B&B on a hill overlooking the village. Hand-built of hand-milled cedar, the house feels spacious and comfortable, with high ceilings and hardwood floors. You can kick back in the book-lined common room, on either of the two water-view decks, or in the whimsical driftwood gazebo in the garden. ⊠ *3127 2nd Ave., Queen Charlotte V0T 1S0* ☎☎ *250/559—8439* ⊕ *www.qcislands.net/doromike* ⌂ *6 rooms, 3 with bath; 3 suites with bath* ⌂ *Cable TV, some kitchens, some pets allowed; no phones in some rooms, no a/c, no smoking* ▭ *No credit cards* ⌐◯⌐ *BP.*

¢–$ ⌂ **Spruce Point Lodge.** This cedar-sided building, encircled by a balcony, is right on the water's edge at the west end of Queen Charlotte, about 5½ km (3½ mi) from the ferry terminal at Skidegate. Rooms are bright and simple, with modern pine furniture; the suite has a full kitchen. All rooms open onto the veranda, providing views of the water and passing eagles. An on-site tour company, Queen Charlotte Adventures, rents kayaks and offers a range of tours. ⊠ *609 6th St., Box 735, Queen Charlotte V0T 1S0* ☎☎ *250/559–8234* ⊕ *www.qcislands.net/sprpoint* ⌂ *6 rooms, 1 suite* ⌂ *Kitchen, some kitchenettes, refrigerators, cable TV, boating; no a/c, no smoking* ▭ *MC, V* ⌐◯⌐ *CP.*

Sports & the Outdoors

Parks Canada, Gwaii Haanas (☎ 250/559–8818 ⊕ www.pc.gc.ca/gwaiihaanas) has a list of tour companies licensed to operate in Gwaii Haanas. On Moresby Island, **Moresby Explorers** (⊠ 469 Alliford Bay Rd., Sandspit ☎ 250/637–2215 or 800/806–7633 ⊕ www.moresbyexplorers.com) is a source for kayak rentals, kayak transport, and kayak and Zodiac tours in Gwaii Haanas National Park Reserve. **Queen Charlotte Adventures Eco-Tours** (☎ 250/559–8990 or 800/668–4288 ⊕ www.queencharlotteadventures.com), in Queen Charlotte, rents kayaks and leads a variety of kayak, and boat tours around the islands.

Shopping

The Haida carve valuable figurines from argillite, a variety of soft, black slate. Other island specialties are silk-screen prints and silver jewelry. In Queen Charlotte, the wacky-looking **Rainbows Gallery** (✉ 3201 3rd Ave. ☎ 250/559–8420) is hard to miss, with its Tree of Lost Soles (old shoes) and tangle of fishing floats outside. Inside is an excellent selection of original Haida Art, including paintings and argillite carvings. **Northwest Coast Books** (✉ 720 Hwy. 33 ☎ 250/559–4681) has an excellent collection of Northwest Coast First Nations books.

BRITISH COLUMBIA A TO Z

To research prices, get advice from other travelers, and book travel arrangements, visit www.fodors.com.

AIR TRAVEL

Air Canada subsidiaries connect most major towns in the province.

Central Mountain Air flies from Vancouver to Campbell River, Comox, Dawson Creek, Fort Nelson, Fort St. John, Kamloops, Kelowna, Prince George, Quesnel, Smithers, Terrace, and Williams Lake. Regional 1 Airlines serves Kelowna from Victoria and the Vancouver Airport South Terminal.

Kenmore Air Harbor has summer floatplane service from Seattle to Pender Harbour, Pender Island, and Salt Spring Island. Northwest Seaplanes offers summer floatplane service between Seattle and fishing lodges in the Inside Passage.

Harbour Air Seaplanes provides regular service from downtown Vancouver and Vancouver Airport to the southern Gulf Islands. North Pacific Seaplanes runs scheduled floatplane service from Prince Rupert to Sandspit, Masset, and Queen Charlotte City.

Pacific Coastal Airline has scheduled and charter service from Vancouver International Airport South Terminal to the Sunshine Coast, Inside Passage, Kootenays, Cariboo, Queen Charlotte Islands, and Vancouver Island. Pacific Spirit–Tofino Air has scheduled floatplane service from Vancouver International Airport to Sechelt. Seair Seaplanes flies from Vancouver Airport to all the Southern Gulf Islands. Westjet connects Vancouver, Abbotsford, Comox, and Victoria to Kelowna and Prince George.

🛫 Airlines & Contacts Air Canada Jazz ☎ 888/247–2262 ⊕ www.aircanada.ca. **Central Mountain Air** ☎ 888/865–8585 ⊕ www.centralmountainair.com. **Harbour Air Seaplanes** ☎ 604/274–1277 or 800/665–0212 ⊕ www.harbour-air.com. **Kenmore Air Harbor** ☎ 425/486–1257 or 800/543–9595 ⊕ www.kenmoreair.com. **North Pacific Seaplanes** ☎ 250/627–1341, 800/689–4234 in B.C. ⊕ www.northpacificseaplanes.com. **Northwest Seaplanes** ☎ 800/690–0086 ⊕ www.nwseaplanes.com. **Pacific Coastal Air-**

lines ☎604/273-8666 or 800/663-2872 ⊕www.pacific-coastal.com. **Pacific Spirit/Tofino Air** ☎250/247-9992 or 800/665-2359 ⊕ www.tofinoair.ca. **Regional 1 Airlines** ☎888/802-1010 ⊕ www.regional1.ca. **Seair Seaplanes** ☎ 604/273-8900 or 800/447-3247 ⊕ www.seairseaplanes.com. **WestJet Airlines** ☎ 800/538-5696 ⊕ www.westjet.com.

AIRPORTS

British Columbia is served by Vancouver International Airport. An alternative is Abbotsford International Airport, about an hour drive from Vancouver. There are domestic airports in most cities.

🛈 Airport Information **Abbotsford International Airport** ☎ 604/855-1135 ⊕ www.abbotsfordairport.ca. **Vancouver International Airport** ☎ 604/207-7077 ⊕ www.yvr.ca.

AIRPORT TRANSFERS LimoJet Gold runs a limousine service from Vancouver International Airport to Whistler for C$295 per trip. Perimeter Whistler Express has daily service from Vancouver International Airport to Whistler (11 times a day in ski season, 7 times a day in summer). Perimeter has a ticket booth at domestic arrivals Level 2 and one at the airport's international receiving lounge. The fare is C$65 one-way; reservations are highly recommended.

🛈 Taxis & Shuttles **LimoJet Gold** ☎ 604/273-1331 or 800/278-8742 ⊕www.limojetgold.com. **Perimeter Whistler Express** ☎ 604/266-5386 or 877/317-7788 ⊕ www.perimeterbus.com.

BOAT & FERRY TRAVEL

THE GULF ISLANDS BC Ferries provides service to the Southern Gulf Islands (Galiano, Mayne, Pender, Saturna, and Salt Spring) from Tsawwassen, about an hour south of Vancouver. Vehicle reservations, at no extra charge, are recommended and are required on some sailings. You can also sail to the Southern Gulf Islands from Swartz Bay, on Vancouver Island (reservations are not accepted). Salt Spring Island can also be reached from Crofton on Vancouver Island. The northern Gulf Islands, including Gabriola, Denman, Hornby, Quadra, and Cortes, can be reached from ports on Vancouver Island. The schedules do not always lend themselves to island hopping, but if you're planning several sailings, you may save some money with BC Ferries SailPass, which offers multiple crossings for a set fare.

On Salt Spring Island the *Queen of de Nile* runs from Ganges Marina to Ganges town center. Gulf Islands Water Taxi runs passengers and bicycles between Salt Spring, Mayne, and Galiano islands. The boats run Wednesday and Saturday in summer and on weekdays the rest of the year. Reservations are recommended.

THE KOOTENAYS The Ministry of Highways operates several lake and river ferries in the interior, including the world's longest free ferry ride, a 45-minute crossing of Kootenay Lake between Balfour, north of Nelson and Crawford Bay.

THE NORTH COAST BC Ferries sails along the Inside Passage from Port Hardy to Prince Rupert (year-round) and from Port Hardy to Bella Coola (summer only). Reservations are required for vehicles and recommended for foot passengers.

QUEEN
CHARLOTTE
ISLANDS (HAIDA
GWAII)

The *Queen of Prince Rupert,* a BC Ferries ship, sails six times a week in July and August, reducing to three times per week in winter. The crossing from Prince Rupert to Skidegate, near Queen Charlotte on Graham Island, takes about seven hours. High-season fares are C$26.25 per adult passenger, C$97.50 per car and C$159.50 and up for campers (depending on length). Some sailings are overnight; cabins are available for an additional C$45 to C$50. Reservations are required for vehicles and recommended for foot passengers; it's a good idea to book as early as possible, as summer sailings fill quickly. BC Ferries also connects Skidegate Landing to Alliford Bay on Moresby Island (near the airport at Sandspit). Access to smaller islands is by boat or air; make plans in advance through a travel agent.

SUNSHINE COAST

BC Ferries has passenger and vehicle service between Horseshoe Bay north of Vancouver and Langdale on the Sunshine Coast; Earls Cove to Saltery Bay (these places are about halfway up the coast); and Powell River on the coast to Comox on Vancouver Island. The company also has service to Texada Island off the coast of Powell River. These routes cannot be reserved. If you're planning to combine travel to the Sunshine Coast and Vancouver Island, ask BC Ferries about discount packages.

🛈 Boat & Ferry Information **BC Ferries** ☎ 250/386-3431, 888/223-3779 in B.C., Alberta, and Washington state ⊕ www.bcferries.com. **Gulf Islands Water Taxi** ☎ 250/537-2510 ⊕ www.saltspring.com/watertaxi. **Kootenay Lake Ferry** ☎ 250/229-4215 ⊕ www.th.gov.bc.ca/bchighways/inlandferryschedule/ferryschedule.htm. *Queen of de Nile* ☎ 250/537-5252 Salt Spring Island Visitor Centre for details.

BUS TRAVEL

Greyhound Canada connects destinations throughout British Columbia with cities and towns across Canada and along the Pacific Northwest coast. The company has service to Whistler from the downtown Vancouver depot every few hours; service is also available from Vancouver Airport to Whistler. West Vancouver Blue Buses provides direct service from downtown Vancouver to Horseshoe Bay.

The Whistler and Valley Express (WAVE) transit system operates a free public transit system within Whistler village, and paid public transit throughout the Valley and north to Pemberton. Malaspina Coach Lines has routes from Vancouver to towns on the Sunshine Coast. Sunshine Coast Transit serves towns between Langdale and Halfmoon Bay on the Sunshine Coast. BC Transit's Web site has information about local transit in most BC communities, including Whistler, the Sunshine Coast, West Vancouver, and Prince Rupert.

🛈 Bus Information **BC Transit** ⊕ www.busonline.ca. **Downtown Vancouver Depot** ✉ 1150 Station St. ☎ No phone. **Greyhound Canada** ☎ 604/482-8747 or 800/661-8747 ⊕ www.greyhound.ca. **Malaspina Coach Lines** ☎ 604/885-2217 or 877/227-8287 ⊕ www.malaspinacoach.com. **Sunshine Coast Transit** ☎ 604/885-3234. **West Vancouver Blue Buses** ☎ 604/985-7777. **Whistler and Valley Express** ☎ 604/932-4020.

CAR RENTAL

Most major agencies, including Avis, Budget, Enterprise, National Tilden, Thrifty, and Hertz, serve cities in the province. With Vancouver All-Terrain Adventures you can charter a four-wheel-drive Suburban from the Vancouver airport or downtown Vancouver to Whistler. The vehicles travel regardless of the weather and can stop for sightseeing along the way. The cost ranges from C$300 to C$350 one-way for up to seven passengers.

🚹 Local Agency **Salt Spring Marine Rentals** ☎ 250/537–5464 ⊕ www.saltspring.com/rentals rents cars on Salt Spring Island. **Vancouver All-Terrain Adventures** ☎ 604/984–2374 or 888/754–5601 ⊕ www.all-terrain.com.

CAR TRAVEL

Driving time from Seattle to Vancouver is about three hours by Interstate 5 and Highway 99. From other Canadian regions, three main routes lead into British Columbia: through Sparwood, in the south, Highway 3; from Jasper and Banff, in the central region, highways 1 and 5; and through Dawson Creek, in the north, highways 2 and 97.

Highway 99, also known as the Sea to Sky Highway, connects Vancouver to Whistler and continues to Lillooet in the interior. The Trans-Canada Highway (Highway 1) connects Vancouver with Kamloops and points east via the Fraser Canyon. Highway 3 winds along the province's southern edge, from Hope to the Rockies. The Coquihalla Highway (Highway 5), a toll road (C$10 for cars and vans) linking Hope and Merritt, is the fastest route to the interior. Highway 101, the Pan-American Highway, serves the Sunshine Coast from Langdale to Lund. Highway 97, the Cariboo Highway, links Kamloops to Dawson Creek, where it becomes the Alaska Highway. Highway 16 cuts east–west across the north, linking Jasper to Prince Rupert. Highway 37, the Stewart Cassiar Highway, travels through the northwest, linking Highway 16 to the Alaska Highway. Highway 20, the Freedom Highway, is a steep, winding, partially paved route linking Williams Lake to Bella Coola on the coast.

ROAD CONDITIONS Major roads, and most secondary roads, are paved and well engineered, although snow tires and chains are needed for winter travel. Many wilderness and park-access roads are unpaved, and there are no roads on the mainland coast between Powell River and Bella Coola. Before using logging or forestry-service roads, check with the forest-service office in the area where you plan to travel (Enquiry BC can refer you to the relevant office) about logging activity. You can also check the Ministry of Forests Web site. The Ministry of Transportation's Web site has up-to-date road reports.

🚹 **Enquiry BC** ☎ 800/663–7867 in B.C., 604/660–2421 in Vancouver and outside B.C. ⊕ www.mser.gov.bc.ca/prgs/enquiry_bc.htm. **Ministry of Forests** ⊕ www.gov.bc.ca/for/cont. **Ministry of Transportation** ⊕ www.th.gov.bc.ca/bchighways/roadreports.

EMERGENCIES

A few areas do not have 911 service, so if you don't get immediate response, dial "0." British Columbia has many hospitals, including Kelowna General Hospital, Lady Minto Hospital in Ganges on Salt Spring Island, Prince George Regional Hospital, and Royal Inland Hospital in Kamloops. The Ministry of Forests operates an emergency call service to report forest fires.

🚹 **Ambulance, fire, police, poison control** ☎ 911 or 0. **Forest fires** ☎ 800/663–5555, *5555 on a cellular.

🚩 Hospitals **Kelowna General Hospital** ✉ 2268 Pandosy St., Kelowna ☎ 250/862–4000. **Lady Minto Hospital** ✉ 135 Crofton Rd., Ganges, Salt Spring Island ☎ 250/538–4800. **Prince George Regional Hospital** ✉ 1475 Edmonton St. ☎ 250/565–2000. **Royal Inland Hospital** ✉ 311 Columbia St., Kamloops ☎ 250/374–5111.

SPORTS & THE OUTDOORS

BIKING Most of B.C.'s ski resorts run their ski-lifts through the summer for lift-accessed mountain biking. Contact the resorts directly for details. One of B.C.'s most spectacular long distance bike routes follows the abandoned 600-km-long (370-mi) Kettle Valley Railway through the mountains of the B.C. interior. Although parts of the trail are no longer passable after a fire destroyed several trestles in 2003, large sections are still open. Tourism Kelowna has details.

🚩 **Tourism Kelowna** ☎ 250/861–1515 or 800/663–4345 ⊕ tourismkelowna.com.

FISHING Separate licenses are required for saltwater and freshwater fishing. Both are available at sporting-goods stores, government-agency offices, and most fishing lodges and charter-boat companies. A one-day license for nonresidents costs C$20 for freshwater fishing and C$7.50 for saltwater fishing. Additional fees apply for salmon fishing. For information about saltwater-fishing regulations, contact Fisheries and Oceans Canada, visit ⊕ www.sportfishing.bc.ca, or pick up a free *Sport Fishing Guide*, available at most tourist-information centers or from Hello BC.

🚩 **Fisheries and Oceans Canada** ☎ 604/666–2828 ⊕ www-comm.pac.dfo-mpo.gc.ca. **Hello BC** ☎ 800/435–5622 ⊕ www.hellobc.com.

GOLF There are courses throughout the region, though Whistler and the Okanagan are the most popular golf destinations. Most courses are open April to mid-October, with greens fees ranging from about C$80 to C$115, including a cart. Whistler courses, usually open May to late September, are pricier, with greens fees of C$125–C$205.

You can arrange advance tee-time bookings at courses in Whistler, the Rockies, and the Okanagan Valley by calling Last Minute Golf. The company matches golfers and courses, sometimes at substantial greens-fee discounts.

🚩 **Last Minute Golf** ☎ 604/878–1833 or 800/684–6344 ⊕ www.lastminutegolfbc.com.

SKIING B.C. has more than 30 full-service downhill ski resorts and countless miles of groomed cross-country tracks. The Canada West Ski Areas Association has details and can also provide information about helicopter- and Snow-Cat-skiing operators in the province.

🚩 **Canada West Ski Areas Association** ☎ 250/542–9020 ⊕ www.cwsaa.org.

HIKING 🚩 **B.C. Parks** ⬧ Box 9398, Station Provincial Government, Victoria V8W 9M9 ☎ No phone ⊕ www.bcparks.ca.

TAXIS

For a cab in Whistler call Sea to Sky Taxi. Advance reservations are recommended for taxi service on the Gulf Islands. Sunshine Coast Taxi operates along the coast. Call Kami Cabs in Kamloops, Checkmate Cabs in Kelowna, and Skeena Taxi in Prince Rupert.

🚩 Taxi Companies **Checkmate Cabs** ☎ 250/861–1111. **Go Galiano** ☎ 250/539–0202. **Kami Cabs** ☎ 250/554–1377. **Mayne Island Taxi Company** ☎ 250/539–3132. **Pender**

Island Taxi ☎ 250/629-3555. **Salt Spring Silver Shadow Taxi** ☎ 250/537-3030. **Sea to Sky Taxi** ☎ 604/932-3333. **Skeena Taxi** ☎ 250/624-2185. **Sunshine Coast Taxi** ☎ 604/886-7337.

TOURS

ADVENTURE
TRIPS
Bluewater Adventures has 8- to 10-day sailing and natural history tours of the Central Coast, Johnstone Strait, and the Queen Charlotte Islands. Canadian River Expeditions specializes in multiday wilderness rafting expeditions on the Chilcotin, Fraser, Babine, Skeena, and Tatshenshini. Ecosummer Expeditions has guided multiday sea-kayaking and sailing trips to the Gulf Islands, the Inside Passage, Johnstone Strait, and the Queen Charlotte Islands, including an inn-to-inn kayaking trip in the Gulf Islands. Some trips involve both sailing and kayaking.

Fraser River Raft Expeditions, with bases in Yale and Lytton in the Fraser Canyon, offers a range of day trips and longer expeditions on several rivers. Fresh Tracks Canada has dozens of outdoor-adventure trips around the province, including hiking, kayaking, river-rafting, rail journeys, and sailing adventures. Gabriola Cycle and Kayak runs multiday paddles to the Queen Charlottes. Hyak Wilderness Adventures, with bases in Lytton and Chilliwack, picks up at Vancouver hotels for rafting on the Chilliwack and Thompson rivers.

Kanata Adventure Specialists, based in Clearwater, operates multiday guided hiking, riding, and canoeing trips in Wells Gray Provincial Park and canoeing and riding trips in the Bowron Lakes. Dogsledding, snowmobiling, snowshoeing, and skiing trips are run in winter.

Ocean West Expeditions conducts multiday camping and lodge-based kayaking tours to the Gulf Islands, Johnstone Strait, and Desolation Sound. Mothership Adventures runs sea kayak expeditions into Desolation Sound and the mid-coast using the *Columbia III*, a vintage 68-foot vessel as a floating base camp.

🚩 **Fees & Schedules Bluewater Adventures** ☎ 604/980-3800 or 888/877-1770 ⊕ www.bluewateradventures.ca. **Canadian River Expeditions** ☎ 604/270-7238 or 800/898-7238 ⊕ www.canriver.com. **Ecosummer Expeditions** ☎ 250/674-0102 or 800/465-8884 ⊕ www.ecosummer.com. **Fraser River Raft Expeditions Ltd** ☎ 604/863-2336 or 800/363-7238 ⊕ www.fraserraft.com. **Fresh Tracks Canada** ☎ 604/737-8743 or 800/667-4744 ⊕ www.freshtracks.ca. **Gabriola Cycle and Kayak** ☎ 250/247-8277 ⊕ www.gck.ca. **Hyak Wilderness Adventures** ☎ 604/734-8622 or 800/663-7238 ⊕ www.hyak.com. **Kanata Adventure Specialists** ☎ 250/674-2774 or 866/452-6282 ⊕ www.canadian-adventures.com. **Mothership Adventures** ☎ 250/202-3229 or 888/833-8887 ⊕ www.mothershipadventures.com. **Ocean West Expeditions** ☎ 250/362-7599 or 604/688-5770 ⊕ www.ocean-west.com.

CRUISES
Celebrity Cruises offers 3- to 5-day cruises along B.C.'s coast. The Seattle-based ships sail in September and October and include port calls at Victoria, Vancouver, Nanaimo, and Prince Rupert.

🚩 **Fees & Schedules Celebrity Cruises** ☎ 305/539-6000 or 800/437-3111 ⊕ www.celebrity.com

HELICOPTER TOURS
Blackcomb Helicopters has year-round flightseeing tours over Whistler's stunning mountains and glaciers. In summer, it offers heli-hiking, -biking, -fishing, -picnics, and even heli-weddings.

🛂 Fees & Schedules **Blackcomb Helicopters** ☎ 604/938-1700 or 800/330-4354 ⊕ www.blackcombhelicopters.com.

SIGHTSEEING TOURS
In winter, Glacier Transportation and Tours runs day trips from Whistler to Vancouver for guided city tours and also offers outings to see NHL ice-hockey games in Vancouver. At press time, they planned to offer guided trolley tours around the Whistler area in summer 2006.

With Okanagan Limousine you can tour the wine area in chauffeur-driven style. Okanagan Wine Country Tours offer narrated wine-country tours using Ford Expeditions. West Coast Sightseeing offers a sightseeing tour to Whistler that allows you to stay over and return on your date of choice to Vancouver. The tours run year-round; the cost is about C$78 round-trip.

🛂 Fees & Schedules **Glacier Transportation and Tours** ☎ 604/932-2705 or 866/905-7779 ⊕ www.glaciercoachlines.com. **Okanagan Limousine** ☎ 250/717-5466 or 866/366-3133 ⊕ www.ok-limo.com. **Okanagan Wine Country Tours** ☎ 250/868-9463 or 866/689-9463 ⊕ www.okwinetours.com. **West Coast Sightseeing** ☎ 877/451-1777, 604/451-1600 in Vancouver ⊕ www.vancouversightseeing.com.

TRAIN TOURS
Rocky Mountaineer Vacations is a luxury, catered train tour that travels across British Columbia from Vancouver to Jasper (in Alberta) and from Vancouver to Calgary via Banff. The train runs April through October.

🛂 Fees & Schedules **Rocky Mountaineer Vacations** ☎ 604/606-7200 or 800/665-7245 ⊕ www.rockymountaineer.com.

TRAIN TRAVEL
VIA Rail offers service between Vancouver and Jasper (in Alberta) and from Prince Rupert to Jasper with an overnight stop in Prince George.

🛂 **VIA Rail** ☎ 888/842-7245 ⊕ www.viarail.ca.

VISITOR INFORMATION
Hello BC, run by the provincial ministry of tourism, has information about the province. The principal regional tourist offices are as follows: Cariboo, Chilcotin, Coast Tourism Association; Kootenay Rockies Tourism Association; Northern British Columbia Tourism Association for information on the Queen Charlotte Islands and northern British Columbia; Thompson Okanagan Tourism Association; Vancouver, Coast & Mountains Tourism Region for information about the Coast Mountain Circle and the Sunshine Coast. Many towns in the region also have visitor-information centers, though not all are open year-round.

🛂 Regional Tourist Information **Cariboo, Chilcotin, Coast Tourism Association** ✉ 118A N. 1st Ave., Williams Lake ☎ 250/392-2226 or 800/663-5885 ⊕ www.landwithoutlimits.com. **Hello BC** ☎ 888/435-5622 ⊕ www.hellobc.com. **Kootenay Rockies Tourism Association** ✉ 1905 Warren Ave., Box 10, Kimberley V1A 2Y5 ☎ 250/427-4838 or 800/661-6603 ⊕ www.kootenayrockies.com. **Northern British Columbia Tourism Association** 🖃 Box 2373, Prince George V2N 2S6 ☎ 250/561-0432 or 800/

663-8843 ⊕ www.northernbctourism.com. **Thompson Okanagan Tourism Association** ✉ 1332 Water St., Kelowna V1Y 9P4 ☎ 250/860-5999 or 800/567-2275 ⊕ www.thompsonokanagan.com. **Vancouver, Coast & Mountains Tourism Region** ✉ 250-1508 W. 2nd Ave., Vancouver V6J 1H2 ☎ 604/739-9011 or 800/667-3306 ⊕ www.vcmbc.com. ✈ Local Tourist Information **Dawson Creek Visitor Info Centre** ✉ 900 Alaska Ave., off Alaska Hwy. ☎ 250/782-9595 or 866/645-3022. **Galiano Island Travel InfoCentre** ☎ 250/539-2233 or 866/539-2233 ⊕ www.galianoisland.com. **Gibsons & District Visitor Info Centre** ✉ 417 Marine Dr. ☎ 604/886-2374. **Harrison Hot Springs Visitor Info Centre** ✉ 499 Hot Springs Rd. ☎ 604/796-5581. **Hope Visitor Info Centre** ✉ 919 Water Ave., off Hwy. 1 ☎ 604/869-2021 or 866/467-3842. **Kamloops Visitor Info Centre** ✉ 1290 W. Trans-Canada Hwy. ☎ 250/374-3377 or 800/662-1994. **Nelson Visitor Info Centre** ✉ 225 Hall St. ☎ 250/352-3433 or 877/663-5706. **South Cariboo Visitor Info Centre** ✉ 422 Hwy. 97, 100 Mile House ☎ 250/395-5353 or 877/511-5353. **Penticton Visitors Information Centre** ✉ 553 Railway St. ☎ 250/493-4055 or 800/663-5052. **Powell River Visitors Bureau** ✉ 4690 Marine Ave. ☎ 604/485-4701 or 877/817-8669. **Prince Rupert Visitor Info Centre** ✉ 100-215 Cow Bay Rd. ☎ 250/624-5637 or 800/667-1994. **Queen Charlotte Island Visitor Information Centre** ✉ 3220 Wharf St., Queen Charlotte ☎ 250/559-8316 ✉ 1 Airport Rd., in the airport terminal, Sandspit ☎ 250/637-5362. **Salt Spring Island Visitor Information Centre** ✉ 121 Lower Ganges Rd. ☎ 250/537-5252 or 866/216-2936 ⊕ www.saltspringtoday.com. **Sechelt Visitor Information Centre** ✉ 5790 Teredo St. ☎ 604/885-1036 or 877/885-1036 ⊕ www.secheltvisitorinfo.com. **Terrace Visitor Information Centre** ✉ 4511 Keith Ave., Hwy. 16 ☎ 250/635-2063 ⊕ www.terracetourism.bc.ca. **Tourism Kelowna** ✉ 544 Harvey Ave. ☎ 250/861-1515 or 800/663-4345 ⊕ www.tourismkelowna.com. **Tourism Prince George** ✉ 1300 1st Ave. ☎ 250/562-3700 or 800/668-7646 ⊕ www.tourismpg.bc.ca. **Tourism Whistler** ✉ 4010 Whistler Way ☎ 800/944-7853, 604/664-5625 in Vancouver ⊕ www.mywhistler.com. **Whistler Activity and Information Center** ✉ 4010 Whistler Way ☎ 604/932-2394.

UNDERSTANDING VANCOUVER & BRITISH COLUMBIA

THE BEAUTY & THE BUZZ

THE BEAUTY & THE BUZZ

T'S FAIR TO SAY that British Columbia, from the fjord-cut coast to the forests, lakes, and mountains inland to the wilderness of the north, is one of the most beautiful places on earth. Even the metropolis of Vancouver, with 2 million people and counting, enjoys a dramatic natural setting, with the sea at its toes and the mountains as a backdrop.

The scenery, of course, has always been here (and much of the environmentally conscious population is working hard to keep it that way), but what's new is the buzz. Every time you turn around, a fashionable new restaurant opens in Yaletown, another Rodeo Drive transplant pops up on Robson Street, a music festival is launched, and even a new downtown neighborhood springs up from behind the construction cranes, which, like the mountains, are now a fixture of Vancouver's growing skyline. The growth shows no signs of slowing down, either. Residents are getting ready for another flurry of construction (and some handy new infrastructure) as Vancouver and Whistler prepare to host the 2010 Winter Olympics. Vancouver isn't getting bigger exactly (there's not much room left on the downtown peninsula), but it is getting interesting, more populated, and more vibrant by the day.

It wasn't always like this. In 1886, when a small town site on Burrard Inlet was incorporated as the City of Vancouver, it amounted to little more than a sawmill, a few saloons, and enough shacks for about 400 frontier types. Vancouver was a rough town in those days. Saloons outnumbered churches, and city fathers, unwilling to tax one another, filled their coffers by fining the local prostitutes. It was a good place to make money, though, especially if you turned your hand to lumber, whiskey sales, or land speculation.

The next 100 years or so were a bit, well, dull. For most of the 20th century Vancouver was a staid, provincial little place,

its multiculturalism buried under a cloak of British colonial propriety. Vancouverites looked to the old country (be that England or Ontario) for new fashions and ideas; turned some of their best waterfront property over to warehouses, industry, and rail yards; and had so little regard for their early history that at one point there were plans (happily scuttled) to build a freeway through the oldest part of the city.

Things lightened up a bit in the 1960s, when thousands of young Canadians—and Americans—flocked to the West Coast under the misguided notion that it was an easygoing place. It wasn't, but by sheer weight of numbers they made it so. Vancouver's hippie legacy is manifest in funky shops along 4th Avenue and Commercial Drive, a popular nude beach, the Vancouver Folk Music Festival and other long-running events, and a deep-seated reputation for flakiness.

The biggest change happened in the mid-1980s, when the city cleaned up a section of its old industrial waterfront and invited the planet to Expo '86, the World's Fair. The event was uncommonly profitable and entertaining, but few envisioned the watershed in Vancouver's history that it would become. To this day people define Vancouver as two different cities: pre- and post-'86. "Expo changed everything," they'll say, often with mixed emotions.

What happened? The fair opened up a good stretch of waterfront to public use and left the city a number of other people-friendly legacies, including the cruise-ship terminal and convention center at Canada Place, and the SkyTrain, a rapid-transit link. It also showed millions of visitors something that they, and many locals, had overlooked: that Vancouver is one of the most beautifully situated cities anywhere.

As growing numbers of tourists were discovering Vancouver during the 1980s and

'90s, so were thousands of newcomers from Asia. The wave of immigration, led by relatively well-off people from Hong Kong and Taiwan, boosted property values, dramatically improved the culinary scene, and added an element of urban sophistication that was new to Canada's west coast. The Vancouver of 2006 is a modern metropolis, with one foot in Asia, the other in the Pacific Northwest, and better access than ever before to the surrounding wilderness—nothing like the sleepy backwater it used to be.

Of course, you can pine for the pre-1986 days, when traffic was lighter and that famous laid-back West Coast attitude more evident. For that, though, there's Victoria, British Columbia's capital, at the tip of Vancouver Island. Worth the trip for the ferry or seaplane ride alone, Victoria, a virtually industry-free government town, has always been a looker. Its Inner Harbour, bobbing with sailboats, lined with hanging flower baskets and stately Victorian brick edifices, has impressed visitors from the early days.

When James Douglas, British Columbia's first governor, arrived in 1842, he wrote: "The place appears a perfect Eden in the midst of the dreary wilderness of the Northwest Coast, and so different is its general aspect . . . that one might be pardoned for supposing it had dropped from the clouds." Yes, Victoria is a pretty town; however, the surrounding wilds have been occupied for at least 10,000 years by native peoples who, thanks in part to the wealth of forest and sea, were able to create one of the richest cultures in North America. Their legacy is in evidence in British Columbia's two leading museums—the Royal British Columbia Museum in Victoria and the Museum of Anthropology in Vancouver—as well as in villages and museums throughout the province.

Fortunately, much of British Columbia's hinterland is intact, in provincial and national parks and in such thinly populated areas as the roadless fjords of the northern coast and the forests of the far north. You'll find some of the last remaining true wilderness in North America here, and, despite the pleasures of the cities, a chance to experience this wild, from a kayak, sailboat, floatplane, or hiking path—while lodging at a luxury resort or a simple campsite—is the main attraction for many visitors to the province.

The sheer size of British Columbia means that even long-term residents find they have to pick and choose their experiences: the old-growth rain forest and Pacific surf of Vancouver Island, the hiking trails and ski resorts of the interior mountains, the Okanagan wine country and Cariboo guest ranches, or the pure wilderness of the northern coast. Chances are no one has ever seen it all.

—Sue Kernaghan

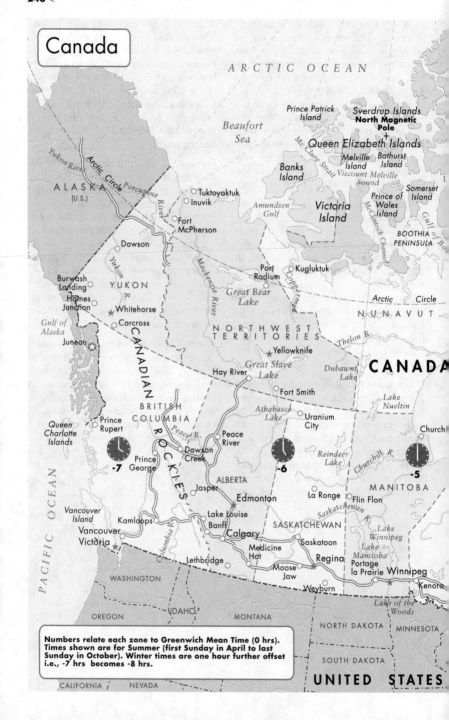

Canada

ARCTIC OCEAN

Beaufort Sea

Prince Patrick Island

Sverdrup Islands
North Magnetic Pole
+

Queen Elizabeth Islands

Melville Island

Bathurst Island

Viscount Melville Sound

Banks Island

ALASKA (U.S.)

Yukon River

Arctic Circle

Porcupine River

Tuktoyaktuk
Inuvik

Amundsen Gulf

Victoria Island

Prince of Wales Island

Somerset Island

BOOTHIA PENINSULA

Fort McPherson

Dawson

Yukon R.

Mackenzie River

Port Radium

Kugluktuk

Coppermine

Arctic Circle

Burwash Landing

Haines Junction

YUKON

Whitehorse

Carcross

Great Bear Lake

NUNAVUT

Gulf of Alaska

Juneau

NORTHWEST TERRITORIES

Thelon R.

CANADA

Yellowknife

Great Slave Lake

Dubawnt Lake

Hay River

Lake Nueltin

Fort Smith

BRITISH COLUMBIA

Athabasca Lake

Uranium City

CANADIAN ROCKIES

Prince Rupert

Peace R.

Peace River

Dawson Creek

Reindeer Lake

Churchill R.

Church

Queen Charlotte Islands

Prince George

-7

-6

-5

Jasper

ALBERTA

La Ronge

Flin Flon

Vancouver Island

Edmonton

Saskatchewan R.

MANITOBA

Kamloops

Lake Louise

Banff

Columbia R.

Vancouver

Victoria

Calgary

SASKATCHEWAN

Saskatoon

Lake Winnipeg

Lake Manitoba

PACIFIC OCEAN

Medicine Hat

Lethbridge

Moose Jaw

Regina

Portage la Prairie

Winnipeg

WASHINGTON

Weyburn

Kenora

OREGON

IDAHO

MONTANA

NORTH DAKOTA

Lake of the Woods

MINNESOTA

Numbers relate each zone to Greenwich Mean Time (0 hrs). Times shown are for Summer (first Sunday in April to last Sunday in October). Winter times are one hour further offset i.e., -7 hrs becomes -8 hrs.

CALIFORNIA

NEVADA

SOUTH DAKOTA

UNITED STATES

INDEX

ABOUT OUR WRITERS

Carolyn B. Heller, who updated the Dining and Shopping sections of Vancouver, has been enthusiastically exploring—and eating—her way across her adopted city of Vancouver since she relocated here in 2003. Her travel and food articles have appeared in publications ranging from the *Boston Globe* and the *Los Angeles Times,* to *FamilyFun* magazine and *Travelers' Tales Paris,* and she's contributed to more than 25 Fodor's guides for destinations from New England to New Zealand.

Vancouver-born freelance writer **Sue Kernaghan** has written about British Columbia for dozens of publications throughout North America and the United Kingdom. A fourth generation British Columbian, she has contributed to several editions of *Fodor's Guide to Vancouver & British Columbia,* as well as to *Fodor's Alaska, Great Canadian Vacations, Healthy Escapes,* and *Escape to Nature Without Roughing It.* She lives on Salt Spring Island with her partner and small son.

An award-winning, freelance travel writer, **Chris McBeath**'s more than 25 years in tourism have given her an insider's eye as to what makes a great vacation experience. Whether routing through backcountry, or discovering a hidden-away inn, Chris has combined history, insight, and anecdotes into her research for this book, and of her home, British Columbia. Many of her articles can be found at www. greatestgetaways.com.